Toronto:
Tributes + Tributaries, 1971–1989

AF587979

Toronto:
Tributes + Tributaries, 1971–1989

Edited by Wanda Nanibush

Gchi-oodenaang:
Ezhi-mina-waajimong Eni-naabiischigeng

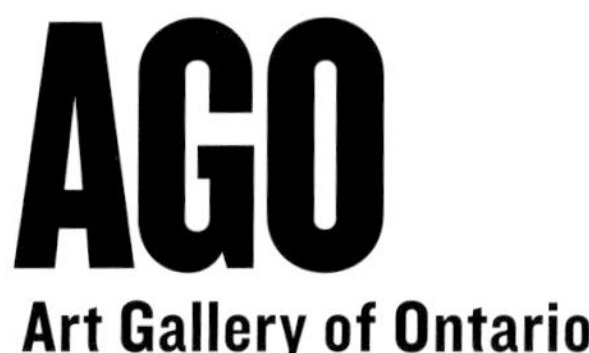

Art Gallery of Ontario

Works

Essays

Land Acknowledgement

Ki nsadwaamdaming

The Art Gallery of Ontario operates on land that has been a site of human activity for over 15,000 years. This land is the territory of the Anishinaabe nation and was also the territory of the Huron-Wendat, Neutral, and Seneca nations. The Dish with One Spoon Wampum Belt Covenant is an agreement between the Haudenosaunee Confederacy and the Anishinaabe Three Fires Confederacy to peaceably share and care for the resources around the Great Lakes. Toronto is also governed by a treaty between the federal government of Canada and the Mississaugas of the New Credit (Anishinaabe nation). Toronto has always been a trading centre for First Nations.

Maanda Gchi-Mzinbiige-gamig Ontario, nji-nokiimgad akiing gaa-shkwangaadeg minik eko-nsa-biboon ooshime Mdaaswi-shi-naaning mdaaswaak biboon. Maanda aki awan Anishinaabek debendimoowaad ezhi-ngo-doodenaawziwaad miiniwaa dash go bekish giw Huron-Wendat, Neutral, Seneca gewii gii-dibendaagoziwag. Maanda bezhig naagan geye emkwaan Wampum Gchi-pizowin nendimoowin aawan maamowi giizhendamowwaadjin Haudenosanunee e-zhi-maamowiziwaad miiniwaa dash Anishinaabe Nswi Ishkoden, bzandamowaad ji maamowi nakazwaad miiniwaa ji-maamowi gnowenjigaadeg kina gegoo eteg gaataaying Gchi-gimiing. Gewii maanda gchi-oodeno (Toronto ezhinikaadeg) pane gii-zhi-gimaakidaajigaade gchi-kwiinwin nji-sa gchi-gimaanaang mompii Canada miiniwaa giiw Mississaugas odi New Credit Ntam Anishinaabeg. Toronto pane gii-ni-aawan gii-meshtoonmaaged-enji maawnijiding nji sa giw Ntam Anishinaabeg.

Toronto: Tributes + Tributaries, 1971–1989

Director's Foreword

On behalf of the Art Gallery of Ontario, I am pleased to present this catalogue for *Toronto: Tributes + Tributaries, 1971–1989*. The exhibition highlighted the AGO's collection of work by Toronto-based artists, focusing on a key time period for the development of the city's art scene, the 1970s and 1980s.

This ambitious project was an important celebration of the many local artists who have helped to establish Toronto's reputation as a vibrant and cutting-edge art centre. My appreciation is extended to everyone who contributed to the success of *Tributes + Tributaries*. My foremost thanks to Wanda Nanibush for curating a challenging and well-articulated exhibition that was warmly received by our audiences. Together, Wanda and I offer enormous gratitude to the more than 120 artists whose work was exhibited, screened, or performed. A special thank-you is owed to the artists who not only lent their artwork but also assisted in the visioning of the project.

The exhibition and related programs were made possible in part by support from Ontario150 and the Canada Council for the Arts. This project has been an occasion to recognize and honour the many collectors, gallery dealers, past curators, and artists who have built the AGO's collection of Toronto art.

Finally, much appreciation is due to the staff of the AGO, each of whom has brought a vast amount of expertise and creativity to bear on the exhibition, through shipping, conservation, installation, and public programming. This publication has been over a year in the making, and I wish to thank the publishing department for the expertise and dedication that it has brought to this project. *Tributes + Tributaries* was an ambitious undertaking with ongoing installation and conservation demands, and our team produced a beautiful exhibition.

Stephan Jost
Michael and Sonja Koerner Director, and CEO
Art Gallery of Ontario

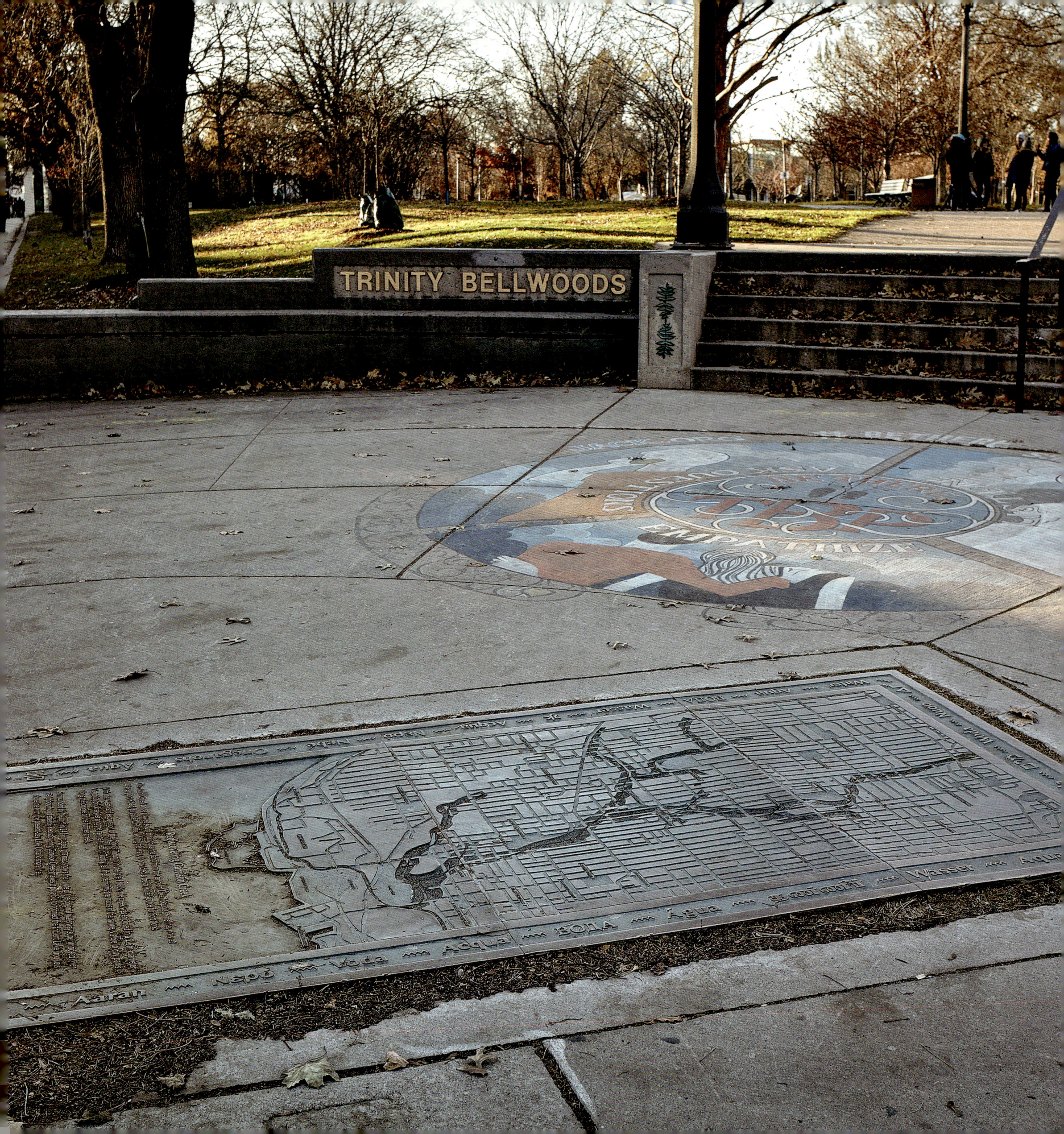
TRINITY BELLWOODS
EMPATHIZE
Wasser

A Curator's Process, by Way of Introduction

Wanda Nanibush

"Toronto's one of my favourite places. If I were to move anywhere out of California, it would be Toronto. Definitely."
—Kendrick Lamar[1]

"There were Italian neighbourhoods and Vietnamese neighbourhoods in this city; there are Chinese ones and Ukrainian ones and Pakistani ones and Korean ones and African ones. Name a region on the planet and there's someone from there, here. All of them sit on Ojibway land, but hardly any of them know it or care because that genealogy is wilfully untraceable except in the name of the city itself. They'd only have to look, though, but it could be that what they know hurts them already, and what if they found out something even more damaging? These are people who are used to the earth beneath them shifting, and they all want it to stop—and if that means they must pretend to know nothing, well, that's the sacrifice they make."
—Dionne Brand[2]

"If you can get with the freaks, then we want you here."
—Sarah Liss[3]

"It seemed to me that everybody ended up in Toronto at least for a little while."
—Alice Munro[4]

"We all speak from a particular place, out of a particular history, out of a particular experience, a particular culture, without being contained by that position as 'ethnic artists' or film-makers. We are all, in that sense, ethnically located and our ethnic identities are crucial to our subjective sense of who we are. But this is also a recognition that this is not an ethnicity which is doomed to survive, as Englishness was, only by marginalizing, dispossessing, displacing, and forgetting other ethnicities. This precisely is the politics of ethnicity predicated on difference and diversity."
—Stuart Hall[5]

Toronto: Tributes + Tributaries, 1971–1989 is a collection-based exhibition that tells a vast and always-changing story about the artists who made Toronto what it is today, to arrive at alternative stories of both Toronto and Toronto art. Constructed from the position of now, the exhibition invokes questions about where artists wanted us to go and where we are. Working thematically to prompt a revision of the present, *Toronto: Tributes + Tributaries* presents so much more than a history of Toronto art in the 1970s and 1980s.

The AGO's collection of art from the 1970s and 1980s was built largely through donations from the artists, and through collecting by former AGO curators Barbara Fischer, Philip Monk, Jessica Bradley, Michelle Jacques, and others. Over the past decade, several AGO curators had pitched ideas for a Toronto exhibition based on the collection, but none were realized. The exhibition that became *Tributes + Tributaries* was my response to this history.

My mission, as I saw it, was to create an exhibition that wasn't historical but sought out histories. That wasn't affiliated politically but showed the politics. That wasn't exhaustive but pointed in new directions. That didn't give only information but offered visitors a series of experiences that would flesh out the question of how far we had come. How would I select works to help me accomplish this, and how would I begin? My answer came from a personal experience with a public artwork in Toronto.

Tributaries: Bringing What Was Buried to the Surface

A couple of years ago, I was feeling the weight of being in the city—the fast pace, the lack of waterfront access, the scheduled life that requires appointments with friends, the constant hustle to afford living in one of the most expensive cities in the world. As an Anishinaabe (Chippewa) woman who grew up partly on an island in Georgian Bay, my body is oriented to wide expanses of sky and water. In Toronto, it is hard to look out at the world with so many buildings in the way. The sky is carved up by streetcar power lines and hydro wires and hidden by the desire to build higher and higher, denser and denser. Here, my perspective shifts towards architecture and the ground.

Opposite: Robert Houle, map of Garrison Creek, Trinity Bellwoods Park, Toronto. © Robert Houle.

—

1. Interview with *HipHopCanada*, December 23, 2011, available online.

2. Dionne Brand, *What We All Long For* (New York: St. Martin's Press), 2008.

3. Sarah Liss, *Army of Lovers: A Community History of Will Munro* (Toronto: Coach House Books, 2013).

4. Alice Munro, *Dear Life* (Toronto: McClelland & Stewart, 2012).

5. Stuart Hall, "Race, Articulation, and Societies Structured in Dominance," in *Black British Cultural Studies: A Reader*, eds. Houston A. Baker Jr., Manthia Diawara, and Ruth H. Lindeborg (Chicago: University of Chicago Press, 1996), 170.

Like many Torontonians feeling the stress, I went to a park—Trinity Bellwoods. Looking at the ground, I noticed a bronze map on the sidewalk at the edge of the park[6] that marks the buried Garrison Creek and bears the word for water in many languages, including my own, *nibi.* I thought of the beauty of a city where you can hear ten different languages while walking down a couple of blocks. I slowly strolled down Walnut Avenue towards Stanley Park. Suddenly, bronze figures embedded into the sidewalk came into view: little frogs and fish. My mood began to shift as my sadness was released by the surprises of a stroll. I looked up and saw the sign for Meegwetch Lane and felt even more at home. *Meegwetch,* "thank you" in my language, externalized my feelings for the artist who made these bronze relatives and knew to place them in the ground. I followed the figures to Stanley Park, where I found more along the short wall surrounding the children's sandy play area. The figures were at child-height, made to touch. The artist's sensitivity anticipated the way we move through the space. I found myself sitting in the sand with the kids playing, no longer feeling the weight of the city but instead engaging its possibilities.

Later, I found out that the artist is my friend and fellow Anishinaabe (Saulteaux), Robert Houle. He brought what was buried to the surface: Garrison Creek is composed of ice-age waters, pure and old, which early colonialists built over. The life of the creek became part of the new city's sewage system, and all the life that thrived from it was lost. Houle honoured that life. This experience led me to develop the notion of "tributaries" as one of my approaches to the exhibition. I wanted to make sure I brought out buried histories of the art scenes in Toronto in the 1970s and 1980s, paying special attention to Indigenous artists, artists of colour, and parts of the city not normally included in exhibitions on Toronto art and artists in this time period.

I found that the AGO's collection wasn't representative of the whole city, only a slice of it—largely Queen St. West and commercial galleries—and overwhelmingly contained works by white artists. I sought out other scenes, like Regent Park and North Toronto, because they were integral at the time but remain unrepresented in most histories. I sought out artists like June Clark and Jayce Salloum, who were not in the collection despite being major figures in Toronto's photography scene in the 1980s and part of the Toronto Photographers Workshop. Because of time, space, knowledge, and available works in the collection, I could not possibly include every artist relevant to this history. I prioritized telling alternative stories and bringing to the surface work that is acknowledged less often than it should be.[7]

The notion of tributaries also encompasses my hope for the visitor experience: for each visitor to follow their own path of interest based in desire and connection, rather than information and conclusions. I wanted a visit to the exhibition to mimic the experience of wandering the streets of a city, where images and experiences collide without obvious connections.

The first thing visitors encountered upon entering the exhibition was a paragraph acknowledging the erased Indigenous history of Toronto, in both English and Anishinaabemowin (the Indigenous language of Toronto).[8] This particular buried history allows us to see Toronto as Indigenous territory and greatly informs the curation of the exhibition. I used the Anishinaabe language in the introduction as a visual way of showing this. Indigenous artists Rebecca Belmore, Robert Houle, Rita Letendre, Robert Markle, Norval Morrisseau, Shelley Niro, Duke Redbird, Arthur Shilling, and Jeff Thomas were exhibited, but not singled out as such. Instead, I allowed their work to intervene naturally within the exhibition's themes. For example, Duke Redbird's poem can be found under the theme of "The Body," where it serves to remind us of an older way of thinking of the earth as a body, specifically a mother's body. I was interested in the way a thematic trajectory changes when an artist is introduced; without Redbird here, the earth would not have been included, as the topic of "The Body" is generally dominated by white feminist perspectives. I made sure no artist was singled out for their cultural background for this reason: I let the work speak for itself and perform its natural intervention, which it does because it comes from a different set of concerns and starting places.

Opposite: Robert Houle, creatures that once lived in Garrison Creek, Walnut Ave., Toronto. © Robert Houle.

—

6. At the corner of Queen Street W. and Gore Vale Avenue.

7. Still, there are some glaring omissions. I regret not being able to include some of the large sculptures in the AGO's collection by Kim Adams, Robin Collyer, and many more, or the performance work of David Buchan, Elizabeth Chitty, Margaret Dragu, and Tanya Mars. I borrowed work mainly from artists of colour not included in the collection, and from white artists whose work in the collection is not the best representation of their approach. There are many white artists who are not in the exhibition as they were never collected by the AGO.

8. See page 7 in this book.

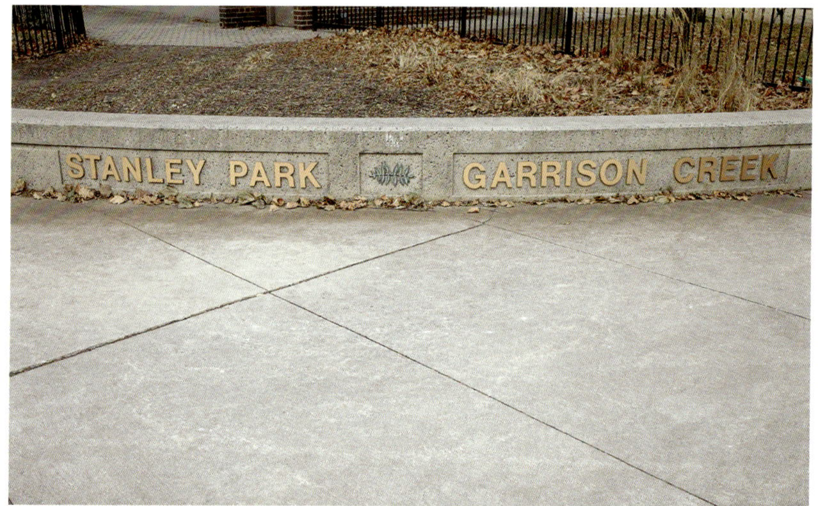
STANLEY PARK
GARRISON CREEK
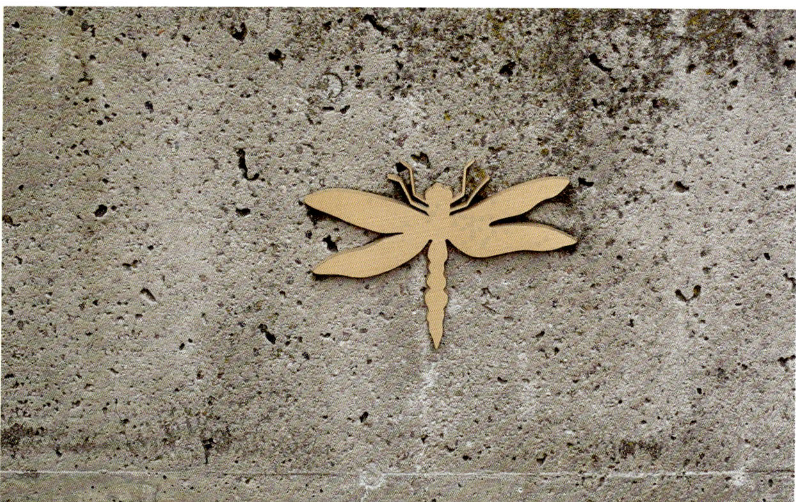
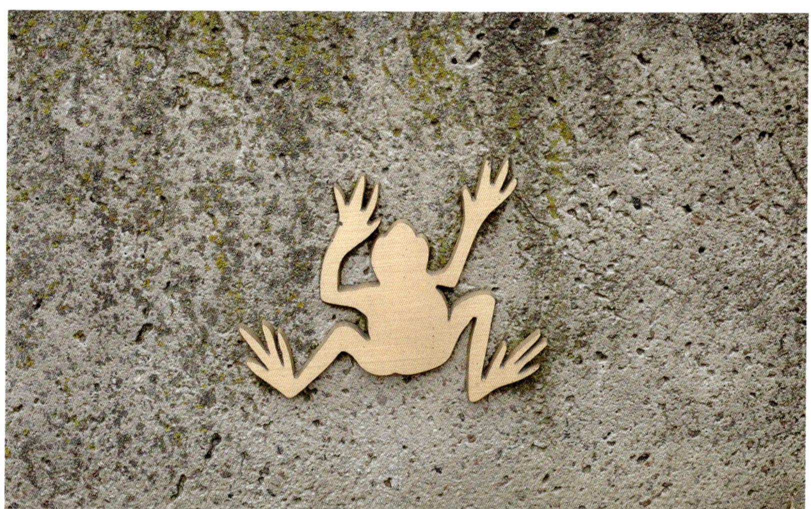
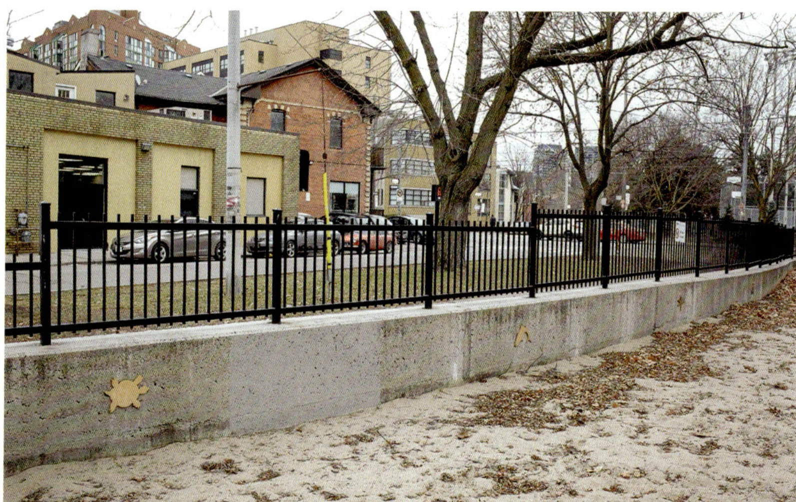
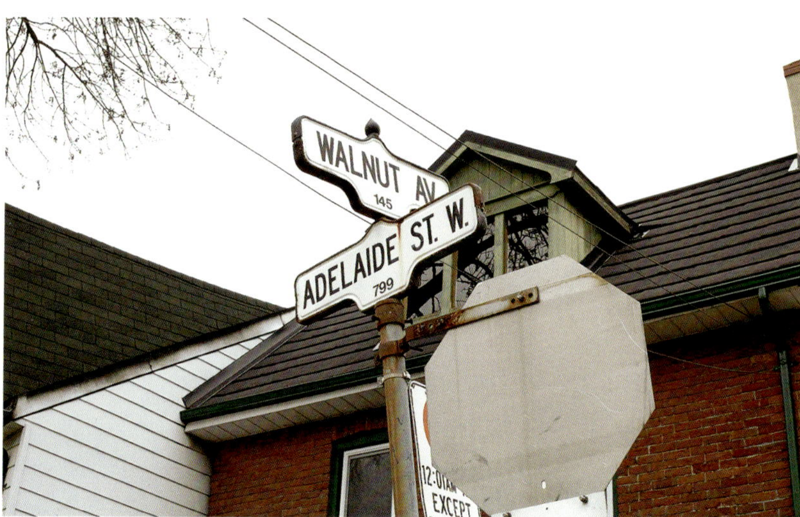
WALNUT AV
145
ADELAIDE ST. W.
799
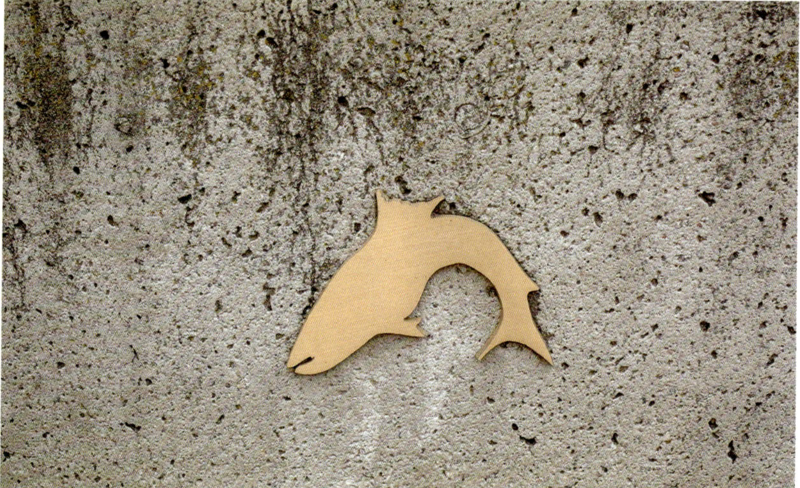

The first image visitors saw after the land acknowledgement was *Bear Portrait, No. 1, Culture Revolution* (1984) by Onondaga artist Jeff Thomas, who moved from Buffalo to Toronto in the same year he made the work. The photograph was shot on Queen Street West, the heart of Toronto's art scene. Thomas's son, Bear, is standing in an alley next to the spray-painted words "culture revolution." He wears a baseball cap adorned with a photograph of Chief Two Moons (taken by Edward S. Curtis). With this artwork as an introduction, I position Queen Street—and Toronto art—as part of a broad cultural revolution against modernism, starting here in the 1970s. Thomas's work contextualizes the revolution in art alongside the cultural revolution taking place across Turtle Island (North America) in its Indigenous communities. Art by Indigenous artists flourished as part of a response to the cultural genocide of the previous century. Toronto was (and continues to be) a site for this cultural renaissance, where artists like Thomas, Robert Houle, Alex Janvier, Norval Morrisseau, Daphne Odjig, Bill Reid, and Arthur Shilling show work in commercial galleries. In *Bear Portrait, No. 1, Culture Revolution,* Thomas introduced the artistic concern for signs of Indigenous presence in urban spaces.

The first thing visitors heard in the exhibition was Lillian Allen's Juno Award-winning dub reggae album *Revolutionary Tea Party* (1986). Allen has been a leader in the development of dub poetry and a major figure in the Toronto art scene since the 1970s. She now teaches at OCAD University. Her work brings a Black aesthetic to the question of revolution. She invites us to a kitchen table revolution, joining domestic space, art, community, and revolution—so much of what takes place in an art scene happens in this very space. The following lyrics to "Revolutionary Tea Party" also point to the working definition of a contemporary artist that I used for this exhibition: someone able to look back, from the vantage point of the present, in order to divine the future.

You who know what the past has been
You who work in the present tense
You who see through to the future
Come mek wi work together
Come sit here with me
An mek we drink tea
A mek wi talk
A mek wi analyse
You who've been burned by vanguardism
Come mek wi give you little nurturing
Come sit awile
A mek wi drink tea
A mek wi talk
A mek wi stategise

The final introductory work that fed into *Tributes + Tributaries* was *Art Is Political* (1975), by Carole Condé and Karl Beveridge. It comprises nine prints created from 35mm negatives, with Condé and Beveridge using steel minimalist sculptural forms to form the letters in the statement "Art Is Political." In a sequence of images, the work shows a movement from minimalism into collective action that informed many artists' shifts at the time. The work was originally exhibited at the AGO in 1976 to some controversy: in *Tributes + Tributaries,* it locates the AGO and artists' relationships to it as part of Toronto art history, and captures the way the 1970s art scene challenged the separation of art and society, and art and politics. The 1976 AGO exhibition, titled *It's Still Privileged Art*, was spurred by the duo asking why Beveridge's minimalist sculpture was doing better in the art world than Condé's. Their feminist response to that question became the basis of the show. Consisting of text-based works wrapping around the walls in multiple directions, alongside narrative photoseries, *It's Still*

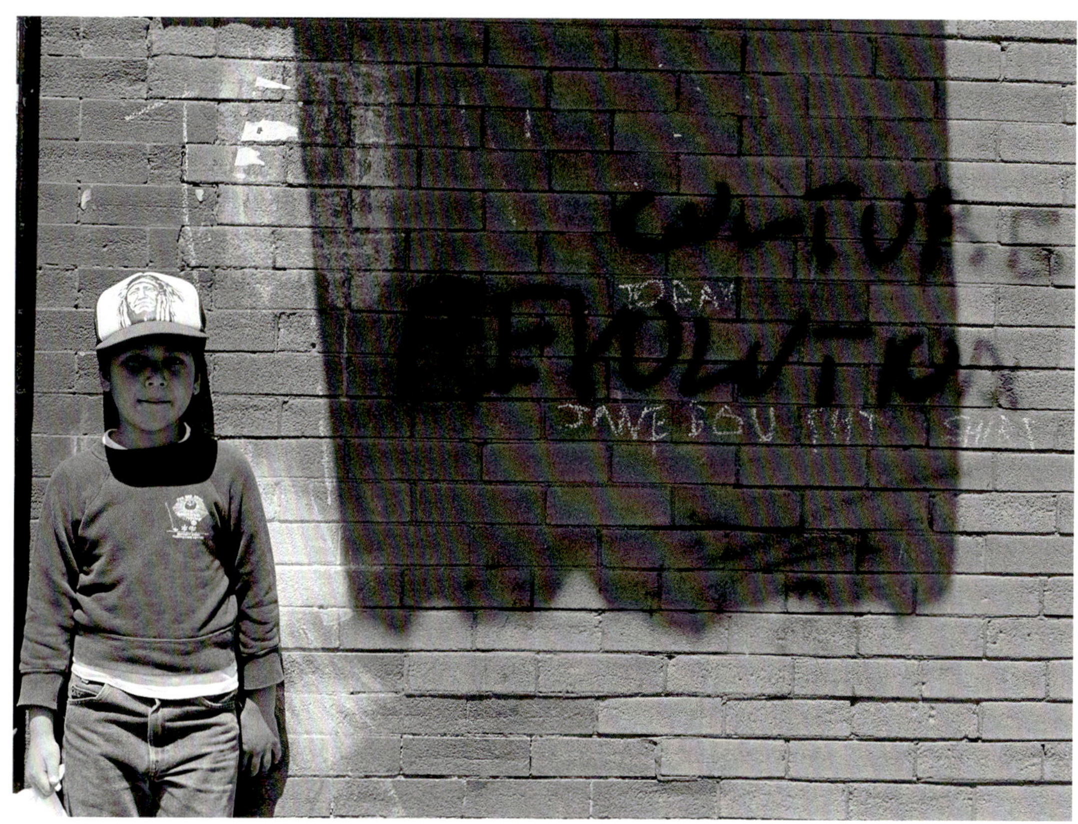

Top: Jeff Thomas, *Bear Portrait, No. 1, Culture Revolution,* 1984, from the *Bear Portrait* series. Art Gallery of Ontario, purchase with assistance from an anonymous donor and James Lahey, 2016. 2016/44.1-.14. © Jeff Thomas.

Bottom: Album cover of Lillian Allen's *Revolutionary Tea Party* (1986). Artwork by Sunday Harrison.

Privileged Art was a shock for the art world, and really challenged artists to think of themselves as part of systems of oppression and power, with art as a space to confront those structures.

Tributes: Honouring Minor Histories

"Tributes" is the second concept guiding my curatorial approach, and it comes directly from looking through works in the collection. Tributes refers to the way artists cite each other's work and respond to what others have done before them—common features of many of the contemporary works in the AGO's collection. Of course, "tributes" also names the exhibition itself, as a way of paying tribute to the artists in Toronto in the 1970s and 1980s. Following from the notion of tributaries, I wanted to make sure that the artists I selected are not only the most commonly acknowledged but also those who are frequently left out of histories. These selection criteria allow the themes to be developed out of the works (rather than coming up with themes first and then choosing works accordingly).[9] It also results in an exhibition of artists who all still have a major stake in the city of Toronto—many are professors, run arts institutions, and continue to be activists. The majority of the artists are still practising today and the city owes them a great debt—we would be in an entirely different city without them.

The act of paying tribute was central to the development of a live performance series that was part of the exhibition. With my colleagues in public programming, Sean O'Neill and Bojana Stancic, we asked artists from the 1970s and 1980s to create new works, while also inviting a younger generation of artists to respond to their elders, or pay tribute to performance art of the 1970s and 1980s. The results were durational, humorous, dance- and theatre-based, queer, shocking, participatory, conceptual, and certainly broke boundaries...[10] Similarly, the film and video festival I developed in conversation with my colleague Kathleen McLean illustrated the volume of influential moving image work produced by artists in the 1970s and 1980s. The festival was a combination of a program I put together and curated programs by two artist-run production distribution centres, Vtape and CFMDC. Both were started within the time frame of the exhibition and are still central to Toronto today.[11]

The exhibition also pays tribute to the artist-run centres (ARCs) that have had a huge influence on the development of Toronto art. The development of artist-run culture marked a shift in Toronto artmaking towards experimentation and anti-capitalism; collective creation and organization was the desired state for an artist-centred culture. Artist-run centres' exhibitions and activities engaged the most cultural diversity. The Canada Council for the Arts and provincial arts councils started funding ARCs in the 1960s, and by the 1980s they functioned as a parallel system to large public and small commercial galleries.[12] An installation of posters and a timeline was included in *Tributes + Tributaries*, with a crucial difference from other histories: the Association of Native Development in the Performing and Visual Arts and Immi-Can were acknowledged as important to the history of ARCs.

ANDPVA was the first ARC devoted to Indigenous arts in Canada and was founded by James Buller (Cree, Sweetgrass band, Saskatchewan). Buller was a true innovator in the Toronto Indigenous theatre scene, who also started the Native Theatre School (now the Centre for Indigenous Theatre). The Indigenous theatre scene in the 1970 and 1980s was very international and held annual conferences in Toronto and Peterborough. ANDPVA was incorporated in 1972. Along with James Buller, artists Graham Greene, Tomson Highway, René Highway, and Makka Kleist all had roles in founding it. Plagued by a necessarily large mandate, ANDPVA, as Canada's oldest Indigenous arts service organization, continues to support Indigenous artists working in all visual and performing arts media.

Immi-Can began in 1976 as a space for Caribbean youth arts education and training in Regent Park. It included a storefront, located at 234 Parliament Street, where community members could sell their art and learn the fundamentals of running a business. Dub poet Lillian Allen and visual artist Ato Seitu were both community workers at Immi-Can. Seitu was the organizational force behind Truths & Rights, a reggae band made up of the influential

9. The named sections of this book correspond to the thematic sections I developed.

10. See essay by Bojana Stancic on page 181 in this book.

11. See full program on page 148 in this book.

12. Many artists felt even the ARCs were closed to them, so they started collectives to create and exhibit on their own terms—these include ChromaZone, Fringe Artists Inc., and General Idea. Today, largely due to funders' pressure to professionalize, ARC have boards, curators, and directors, and are no longer so collectively artist-run in their structure. They still focus on emerging artists and practices, though, and show the most cultural diversity in their programming. The history and role of ARCs has been documented elsewhere by Philip Monk and AA Bronson.

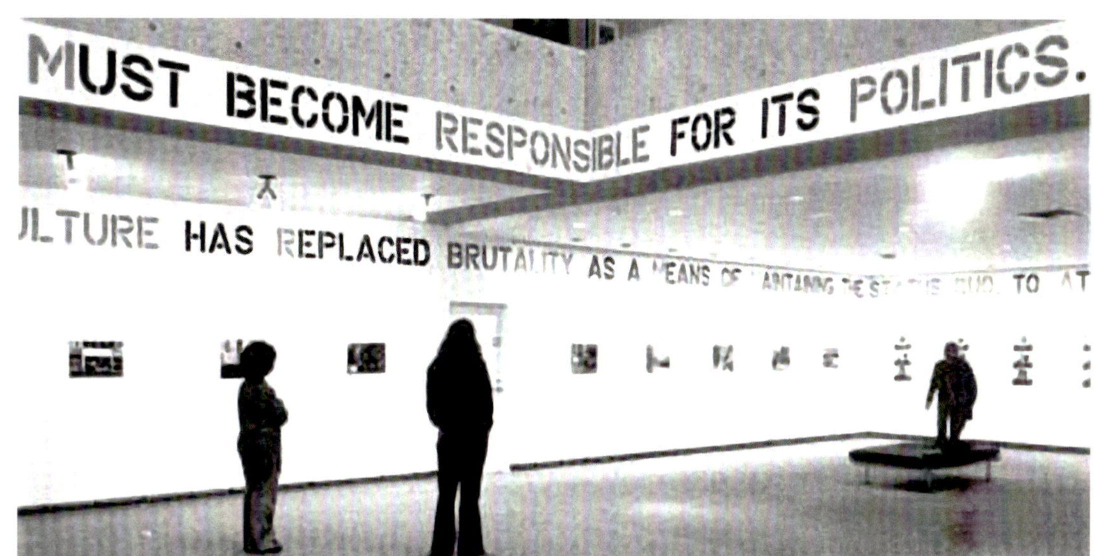

Left: Carole Condé and Karl Beveridge, installation view from *It's Still Privileged Art,* 1976. Exhibition at the Art Gallery of Ontario. © Carole Condé and Karl Beveridge.

Bottom left: Elizabeth Chitty, *History, Colour T.V. & You,* 1982. Performance. © Elizabeth Chitty.

Bottom right: Tanya Mars performing *Pure Sin* with Angelo Pedari, Kevin McGugan, Colin Campbell, Andrew J. Paterson, and John Greyson, A Space, Toronto, 1986. Photo by Isaac Applebaum. © Tanya Mars.

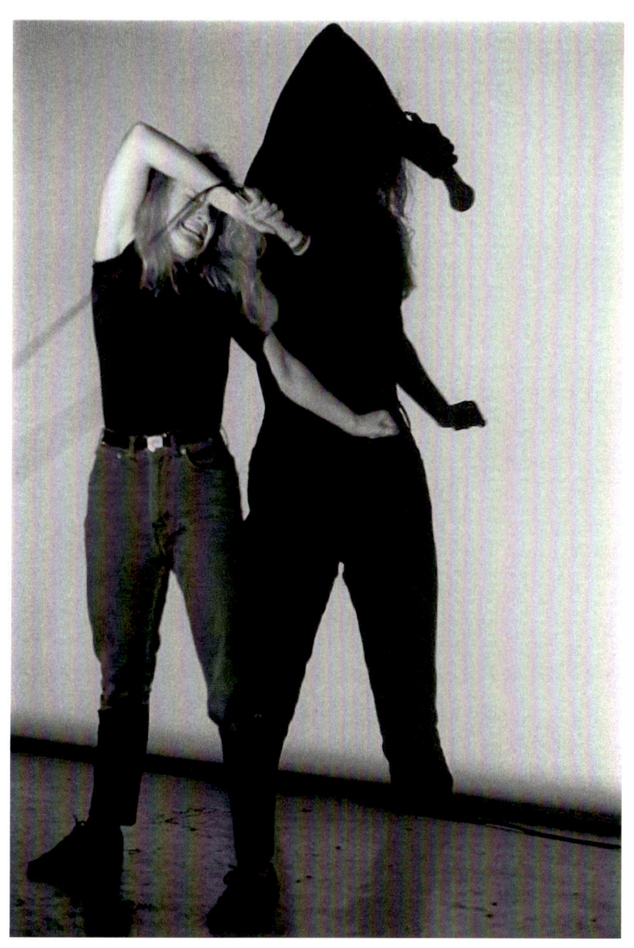

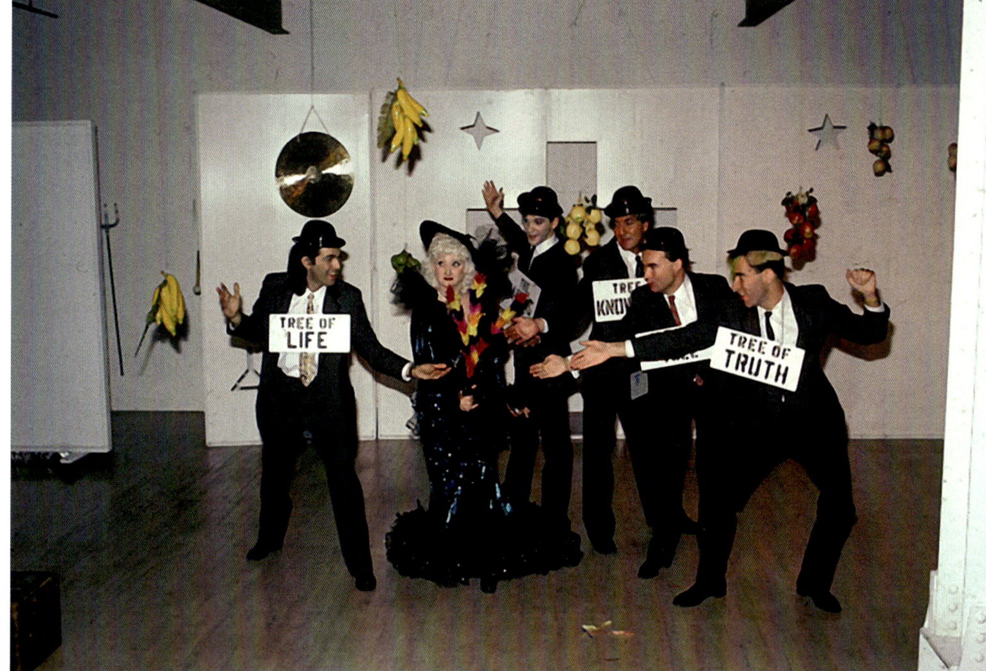

artists Mohjah, Rudi Quammie Williams, Iauwata, Abna Dengal, Xola, Ahmid, Vance Tynes, Ovid Reid, and Chico Paul. The band formed at Immi-Can, going on to become a popular and politically conscious Canadian presence. They influenced other 1980s bands, like Parachute Club. The inclusion of Allen, Seitu, and the photo-documentation of Regent Park by David Zapparoli in *Tributes + Tributaries* expands both the history of Toronto and its art.

These minor histories show the reality of an art scene that is not separated from social justice, service agencies, bars, politics, music, theatre, and writing. In *Tributes + Tributaries*, ARC event posters illustrate how programming was often linked to socio-political events and included other art forms like music and theatre; artists in the 1970s and 1980s were active in or collaborating across all these areas. It was only in the 1990s, with the backlash against demands for racial equality and equity in the arts, that the division instated by the modernist mantra "Art for art's sake" was racialized—to the point where, today, many art historians, curators, and writers speak dismissively of "identity politics" in art.

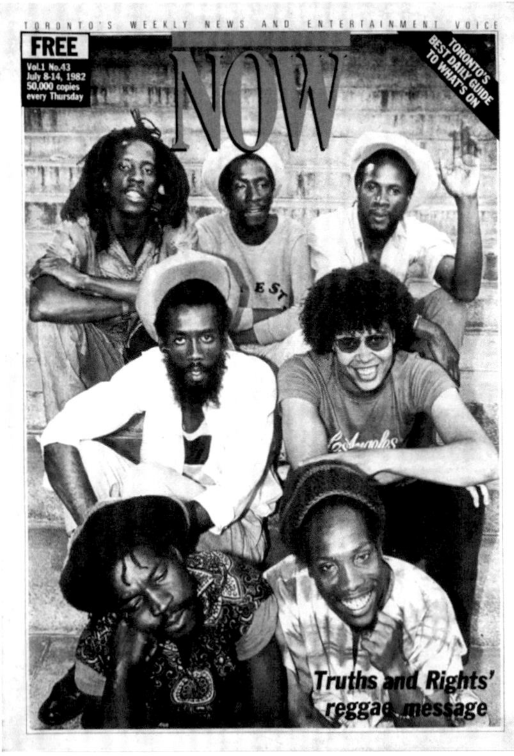

Above: Truths & Rights featured on the cover of *NOW Magazine*, July 8–14, 1982, 1, no. 43. © Ben Mark Holzberg.

1971–1989: A Tale of Two Dresses

The years between 1971 and 1989 saw profound challenges to the status quo—all the things that we take for granted as right, true, real, and unchanging. They brought to light many invisible aspects of life (much like how Robert Houle brings the buried life of the city to the surface of its sidewalks at Garrison Creek). The time frame of *Tributes + Tributaries* comes from two important works in the collection that deploy performance and challenge the status quo: the *Miss General Idea Pageant* (1971), by General Idea, and *Rising to the Occasion* (1987–1991), by Rebecca Belmore. The dates of the works mark the edges of the exhibition's time frame—in 1989, the dress Belmore wore in her performance *Twelve Angry Crinolines* (1987) became the artwork *Rising to the Occasion.*

The *Miss General Idea Pageant* was part performance, part mail art, and was deeply embedded in the mainstream art scene to which the AGO belongs while also lobbing critique at it. In other words, it is a perfect example of conceptual art of the era. General Idea mailed out a simple blue dress to artists they knew across Canada, asking them to take a photograph of themselves wearing it and mail it into a competition promising "fame, fun, and fortune." In grand beauty pageant style, the awards ceremony was held at the AGO, in Walker Court. The judges were well-known artists in their own right, like Dorothy Cameron, Daniel Freedman, and David Silcox. Vancouver artist Marcel Dot (a.k.a. Michael Morris) was crowned the winner for "glamour without falling into it," encapsulating General Idea's longstanding critique of the developing art star system.

Two decades later, another dress—half beaver dam and half Victorian gown—was created by Anishinaabe artist Rebecca Belmore far from Toronto, in Thunder Bay. It was created to be worn in a street protest—outside of any institution—against a visit from the British royal family, who enacted stereotypical First Nations activities during their visit with no real understanding of Indigenous life or colonialism on the ground in Canada. Belmore had moved to Thunder Bay from Toronto after quitting Ontario College of Art (the epicentre of arts training in Toronto at the time) when a professor asked her "if her Indianness was going to interfere with her artwork."[13] Her move out of Toronto shows the exclusions that came to define art in this period, and her work opens the 1990s, when the Toronto art scene contended most openly with race and indigeneity. *Tributes + Tributaries* engages with the way in which every history is marked by exclusions, and how those exclusions—when they form the centre of new histories—can open up new futures.

Exclusion was also challenged by artists through participation in larger political protests. In order to show this relation between art and protest, I selected three historical events to be represented as interpretive wall panels.[14] Each moment had a profound effect on individual artists in the exhibition and gave birth to a number of artistic responses.

The first moment was the Pierre Trudeau government's introduction of the 1969 White Paper, which called for the end of the reserve system, the elimination of "special" status for First

13. Wanda Nanibush, "An Interview with Rebecca Belmore," *Decolonization: Indigeneity, Education & Society* 3, no. 1 (2014): 214, available online.

14. Thanks to AGO interpretive planner Laura Robb for her research and writing on these protests.

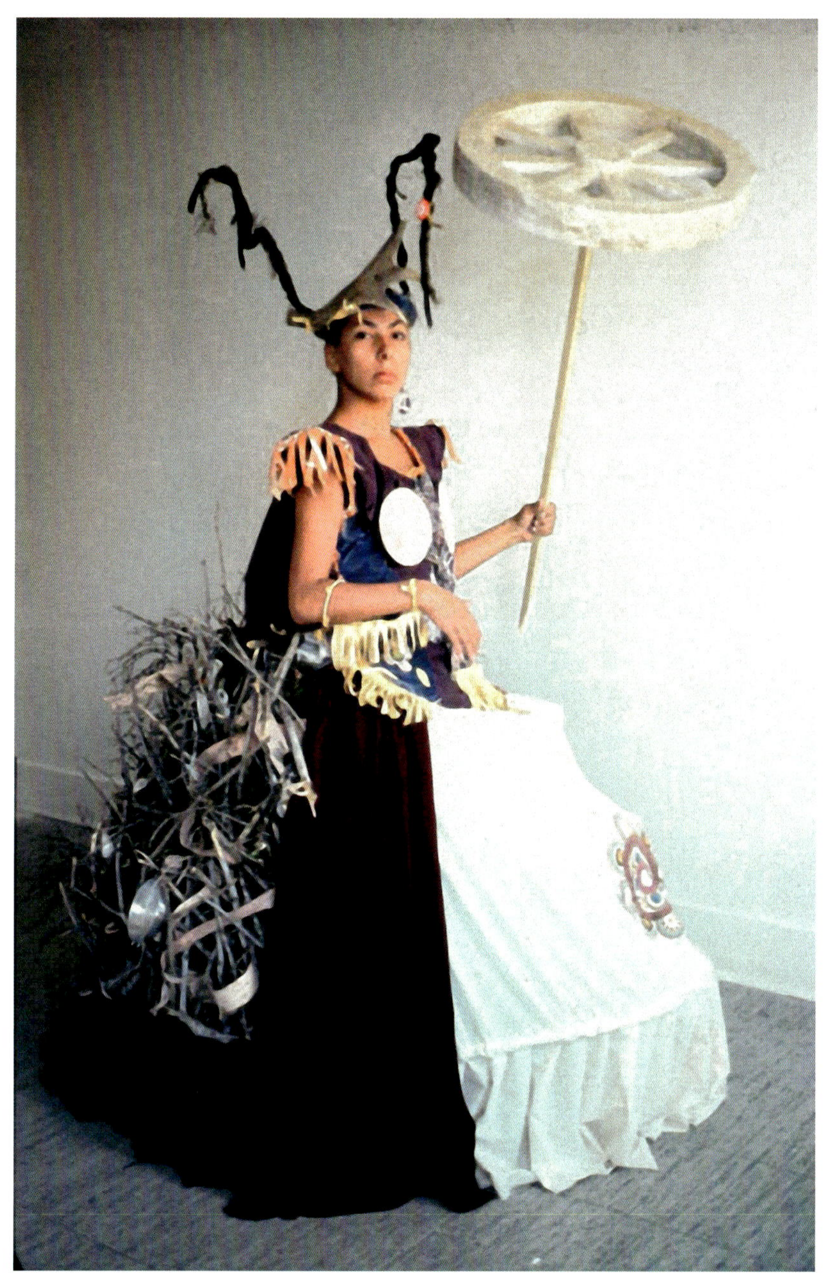

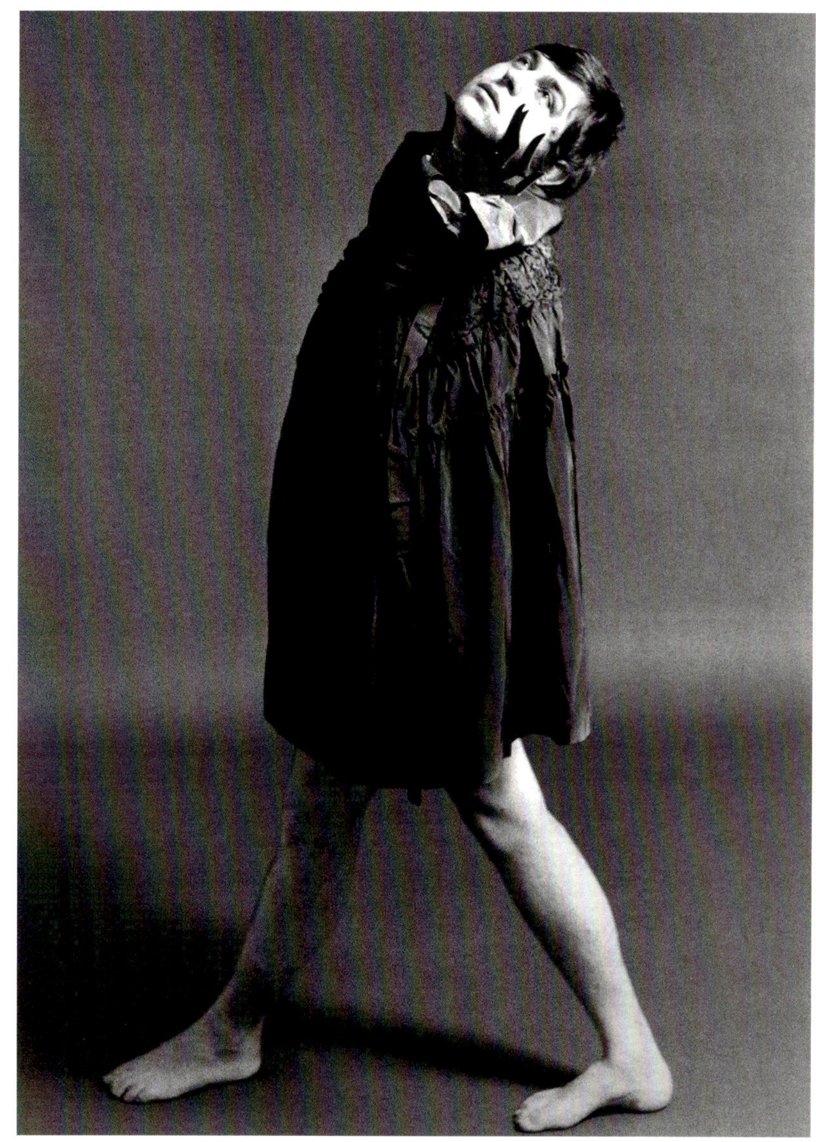

Left: Rebecca Belmore, *Rising to the Occasion,* 1987. © Rebecca Belmore.

Right: Marcel Dot (a.k.a. Michael Morris), Miss General Idea 1971–1983. Photo © Vincent Trasov.

Peoples, and the rejection of the government's treaty obligations. The policy has come to be referred to as the "termination policy" because it outlined the end of First Peoples as a distinct rights-holding group. The policy ignored decades of systemic, institutional racism and absolved Canada of its colonial history.

A decade later, on February 5, 1981, Toronto Police stormed the city's gay bathhouses, arresting more than 300 men. Dubbed "Operation Soap," the raids were Canada's largest and most violent police-led attack on a gay community. *The Body Politic*, the city's biggest gay publication, quickly responded with a protest and rally on February 6, and scores of people came out in a collective demonstration against the police. The police publicly apologized for this event during Pride Toronto 2016, two months before *Tributes + Tributaries* opened.

The third moment comprises the protests launched during the Royal Ontario Museum's exhibition *Into the Heart of Africa* (1989), an exhibition that was planned as a critical examination of European colonialism. Instead, it made colonialism look inevitable, and enforced the discourse of primitivism. A group of activists, initiated by Afua Cooper, and led by Cooper and Ras Rico—dubbed the Coalition for the Truth about Africa—offered to consult with the exhibition team to reform the offensive presentation, but the message was short and clear: no—you're not curators. The lives of artists like Winsom Winsom were greatly altered—Winsom was assaulted and arrested by the police, who didn't know (or care) she was working with the ROM as a consultant. Eleven protesters in total were arrested and named the ROM11. The Coalition demonstrated every week, and, in the end, every partner museum pulled the exhibition from their calendars. The ROM also apologized for this exhibition in November 2016, during the run of *Tributes + Tributaries*.

Toronto: All These Things Exist Today

Toronto is a Wendat (Huron) word that refers to fishing weirs constructed of standing sticks in the water, placed in the rivers and creeks of Toronto. The word means "sticks standing in the waters." Historian Rodney Bobiwash writes, "While some have narrowly assumed that the name Toronto as the 'gathering place' is an inaccurate 'mistranslation,' the multilayered understanding of a single item such as a fishing weir in terms of its natural, sacred, political, and social meanings is in keeping with the Indigenous knowledge frameworks of the peoples of this area."[15] He is referring to the fact that Toronto was the gathering place of many nations—even before colonization—as First Nations came to trade, do ceremony, and marry on the shores of Lake Ontario. The weirs gathered together many different types of fish from all the rivers and lands in which they flowed, to be shared amongst the many nations.

The Wendat (Huron), as one of the oldest occupiers of Toronto, are evidenced in archeology and oral history. The Anishinaabe (Chippewa, Mississaugas, Odawa, and Ojibway) also occupied Toronto annually for the purposes of ceremony, governance, fishing, and trading. The Wendat had alliances with the Anishinaabe, which came into effect when one of the Six Nations of the Haudenosaunee, the Seneca,[16] from the southern part of Lake Ontario, decided to make Toronto their home. The first Seneca village, Teiaiagon, was erected south of High Park on the Humber River in approximately 1665. The Neutrals were an Iroquoian nation who also occupied and traded in Toronto, after having been dispersed by the Seneca from their lands in western New York and the Niagara region. Two other Iroquoian peoples also traded in Toronto in great numbers: the Petun, from Collingwood, and the Erie. The wars between the Haudenosaunee and the Anishinaabe came after all of the other Iroquoian-speaking nations (Petun, Erie, Neutral, and Wendat) had been dispersed. By 1701, the Anishinaabe had pushed the Haudenosaunee back to New York. The land in Toronto has always been governed by the Dish with One Spoon Wampum Belt Covenant, which allows both the Haudenosaunee and the Anishinaabe to continue to hunt in Toronto as long as either party doesn't deplete the shared resources.

During this pre-colonial era, Toronto was home to over 400 plants that were used for medicine and sustenance. The forest here was cultivated by First Nations for maximum attractiveness

15. Rodney Bobiwash and Heather Howard, "Toronto's Native History," *FNH Magazine* 1, no. 1: 7. Rodney Bobiwash and Heather Howard have documented the Indigenous history of Toronto, and that legacy continues today with the organization First Story Toronto.

16. The Haudenosaunee confederacy comprises six Iroquois nations today: Mohawk, Oneida, Onondaga, Cayuga, Seneca, and Tuscarora.

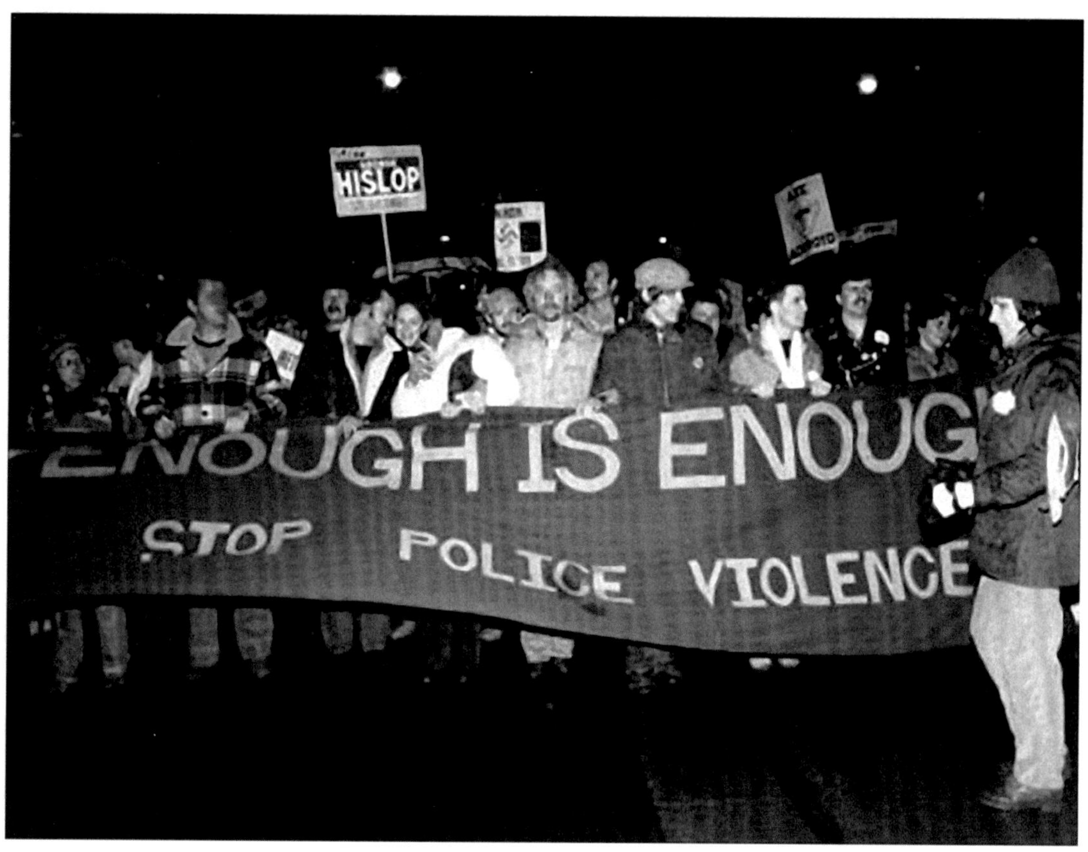

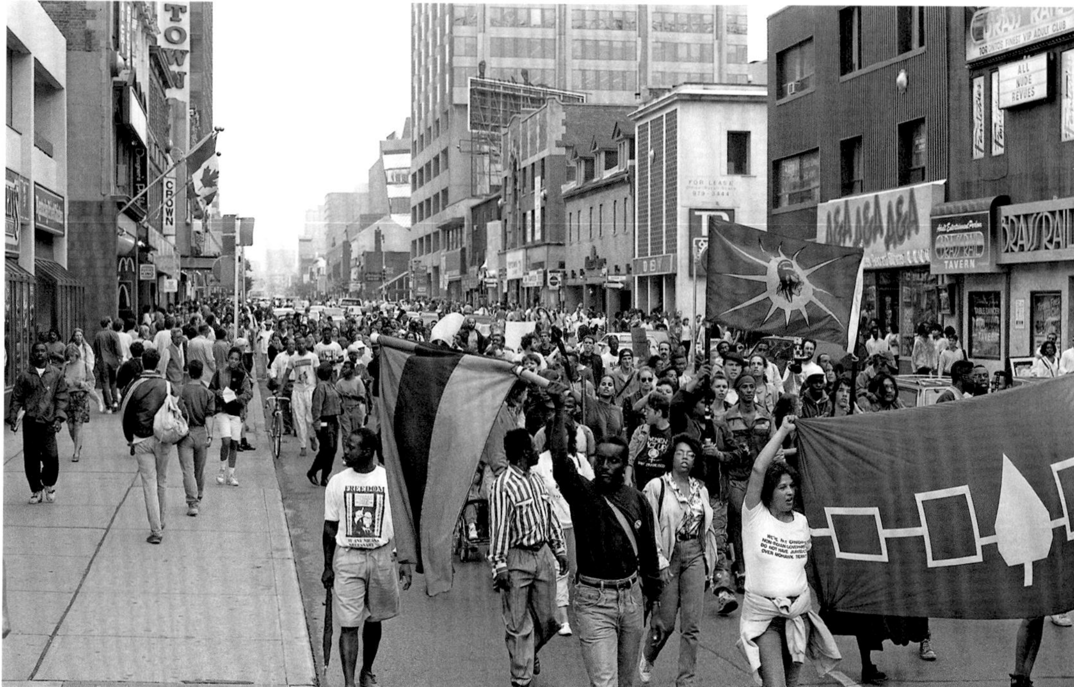

Top: Protesters denouncing the 1981 bathhouse raids, Toronto. Photo © Gerald Hannon, courtesy of Pride Toronto and Torontoist.

Bottom: Protesters marching on Yonge Street in response to the ROM's *Into the Heart of Africa* exhibition, 1989. Photo © Lana Lovell.

to small and large game animals. Farming took place with corn, beans, squash, tobacco, wild rice, and more. The buried creeks of Toronto, where I first began envisioning *Tributes + Tributaries*, are connected to the ways the original caretakers of this land are often erased from the history of the city and its physical landscape.

Toronto was incorporated as a city in 1834, well before the first constitution of Canada in 1867. Incorporation legally required a treaty between the Mississauga Anishinaabe and the British Crown. Most Canadians will learn that the Treaty of Paris (1783) ended the Seven Years' War between the British and the French, and about the Battle of the Plains of Abraham and the death of General Wolfe. Rarely do they learn about the Royal Proclamation of 1763, which was signed in order to appease First Nations allies to the British, without whom they could not have won the war against the French. Many First Nations banded together under Tecumseh, a chief who was pushing for First Nations to control their own lands. Many leaders were resisting the encroachment onto and theft of their territories by colonial settlers, religious orders, businessmen, and the military. The Royal Proclamation declared all land west of the original colonies as Indigenous territory, which could only be transferred to the Crown through fairly negotiated treaties. Treaties acknowledged the sovereignty of First Nations and our inherent right to the land, and placed the Crown in a protective role in regard to First Nations. No longer could anyone acquire land (except for the Crown). This implementation of the treaty system did not correct past wrongdoings, nor was it meant to prevent future broken promises. Treaties guaranteed peace for colonialists at a time when the First Nations could easily have won a war, and Toronto prospered under this peace. But its roots in the willingness of the First Nations to share the land with newcomers is lost like the creeks and rivers that connected the North, East, and West to Lake Ontario.[17]

The Mississauga Anishinaabe signed the Toronto Purchase in 1787, which was contested and revisited in 1805. The 1787 Purchase, according to British records, consisted of the Mississaugas of New Credit surrendering lands along Lake Ontario, totalling 250,808 acres. The land was "bounded by Lake Ontario to the south; and approximately Etobicoke Creek/ Highway 27 to the west; Ashbridge's Bay/Woodbine Avenue-Highway 404 to the east; and south of Sideroad 15–Bloomington Road to the north."[18] The exchange value was paid in money and goods. As is usual with treaties, the First Nations had no understanding of land as something they could sell; the Mississaugas believed that the agreement allowed the British to use the land in exchange for gifts and presents in perpetuity.[19] The Mississaugas were frustrated by the failure of the British to live up to the promises of the treaty. To add fuel to the fire, their Chief Wabakinine and his wife were murdered in 1796 at what is currently St. Lawrence Market.

As described by First Story Toronto, "The St. Lawrence Market area has been a place where Aboriginal people have traded with Europeans for many years, before the official market block. The first permanent structure was established in 1803 by Lieutenant Governor Peter Hunter; it was constructed of wood and was built at the north end of the market block, between King and Front Streets."[20] Wabakinine and his family had travelled to the market to trade salmon, which was one of the plentiful resources in the local rivers now destroyed by colonial pollution, overfishing, and dams. (The salmon is also the fish immortalized and remembered in Robert Houle's homage to Garrison Creek.) Charles McCuen, a soldier in the Queen's Rangers at Fort York, murdered Wabakinine and his wife in August 1776, following an altercation caused by the soldiers who had abducted Wabakinine's sister. The colony tried to stop a counterattack by putting McCuen on trial for murder, but he was acquitted due to a supposed lack of evidence. The Mississaugas approached their allies for support in an attack on the fort, but one of the leaders of the Haudenosaunee, Joseph Brant, advised them not to attack. These events are part of a long history of unpunished murders of Indigenous people and violence against Indigenous women that continues today.

17. The Great Lakes are huge basins created by retreating ice sheets about 12,500 years ago, when the last ice age ended. The basins deepened significantly as the ice melted, the lakes becoming much larger than they are today. "Lake Ontario at this stage is known as 'glacial Lake Iroquois'" (First Story Toronto, "Lake Ontario," *First Story* blog, April 29, 2014).
During the 18th century, Lake Ontario became a site of European military conflict. In order to maintain control of Lake Ontario, Lieutenant Governor Simcoe ordered the construction of Fort York, a naval base, at the site of present-day Toronto in 1793. Toronto took the status of capital city from Niagara and was renamed "York," an unpopular change with the locals. Since the 1850s, the waterfront has been filled in to the point where Fort York is no longer on the north shore of the harbour entrance, but inland.

18. Wikipedia, "Toronto Purchase," last edited September 17, 2017, available online.

19. Donald B. Smith, *Sacred Feathers* (Toronto: University of Toronto Press, 1987), 26.

20. First Story Toronto, "St. Laurence Market and the Story of Chief Wabakinine," *First Story* blog, February 21, 2013.

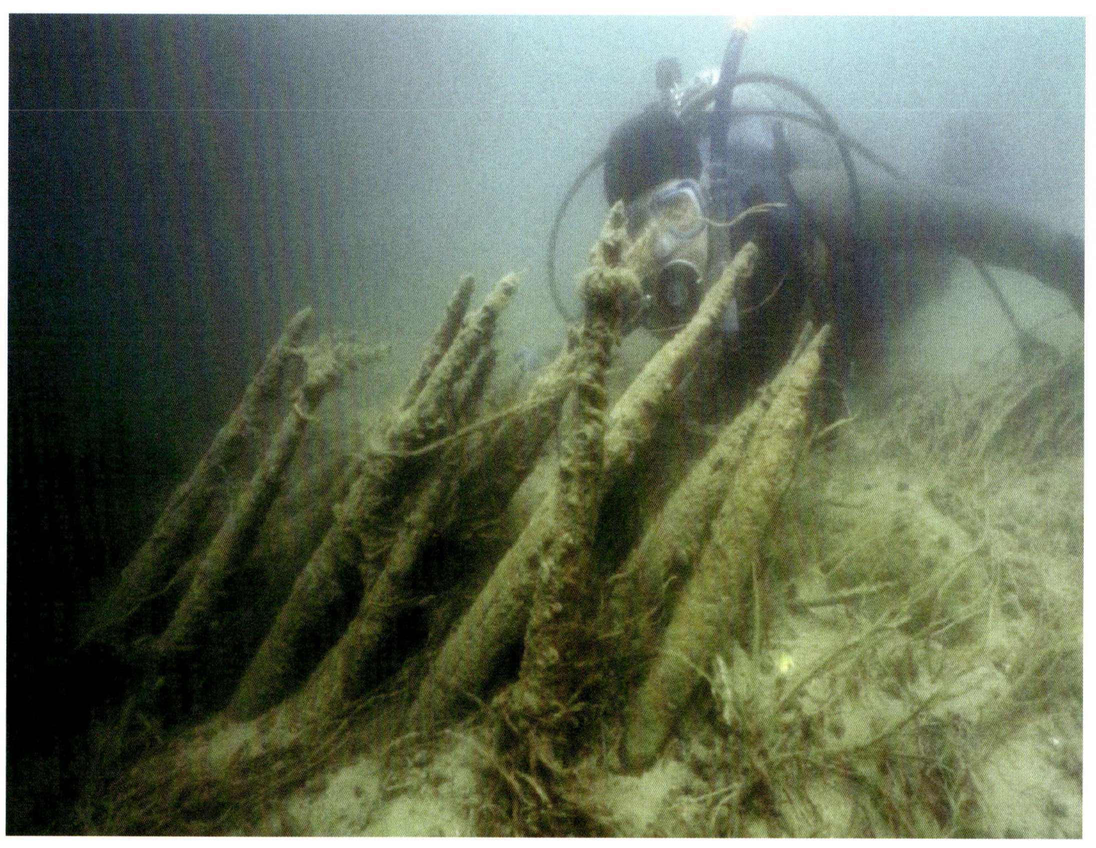

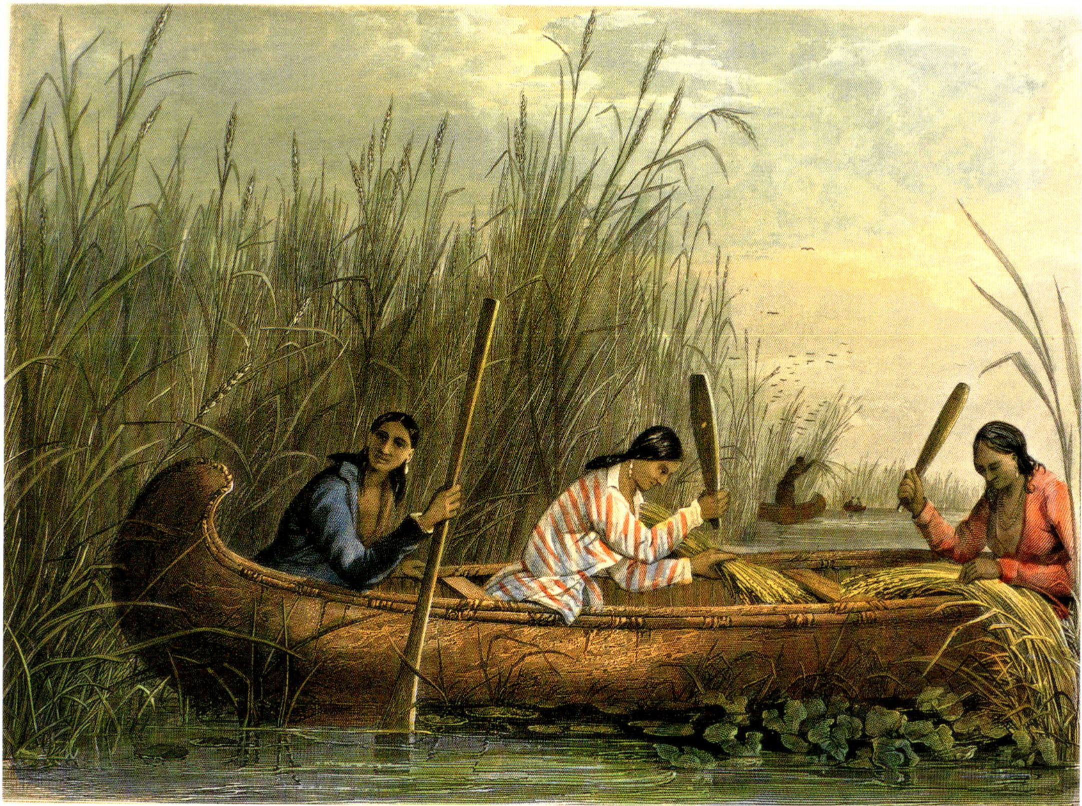

Top: View of Huron-Wendat-era underwater weir stakes, 2006. Agence Parcs Canada/Parks Canada Agency, 2006.

Bottom: Seth Eastman, "Gathering Wild Rice," 1853. From *The American Aboriginal Portfolio* by Mary H. Eastman, ca. 1953. Newberry Call Number: Ayer 250.45 E2 1853a. Newberry Digital Collections for the Classroom.

Despite these kinds of violent and unequal encounters, the British needed Indigenous allies to win the War of 1812. More than 10,000 First Nations warriors fought alongside the British, preventing Canada from falling to the Americans. They were honouring their side of the peace and friendship treaties. They still await the British and Canadians to honour their obligations within those treaties.

These stories, and many others, point out the blind spots in histories of Toronto that fail to include Indigenous perspectives and presence, and reveal parallel blind spots in Toronto's art histories that fail to take into account the diversity of people, places, and practices. There can be no definitive linear history of Toronto art in the 1970s and 1980s, so I opted to use many tributes and tributaries to tell many stories. A city is a complex of many neighbourhoods, cultures, and histories that diverge, overlap, emerge, or get buried, depending on the forces of power and prejudice in any given time.

The AGO collection and loaned artworks assembled in *Tributes + Tributaries* helped me understand art as a refuge—the other side of hospitality, when the invitation is accepted.[21] Institutions, like cities, can be places with no barriers to entry. While this may seem impossible, the act of experimenting means that exhibitions and cities can be dreams of a future—ones that could still come to pass. By expanding our criteria of art in Toronto between 1971 and 1989, and envisioning art as an area that breaks rather than builds boundaries, we can start to see Toronto from an Indigenous perspective—as a site of economic and cultural trade between nations, a space of asylum for those seeking new spaces of refuge, a site of treaty making, and a space of experimentation. All these things exist today, even if largely buried under the mass of capital accumulation and commodity culture.
In the following pages you can trace the many tributaries that the themes and works in *Toronto: Tributes + Tributaries, 1971–1989* reveal.

21. In the same way that Jacques Derrida believes cities should be refuges, or spaces of open hospitality. Jacques Derrida, *On Cosmopolitanism and Forgiveness* (Oxford: Taylor & Francis, 2003).

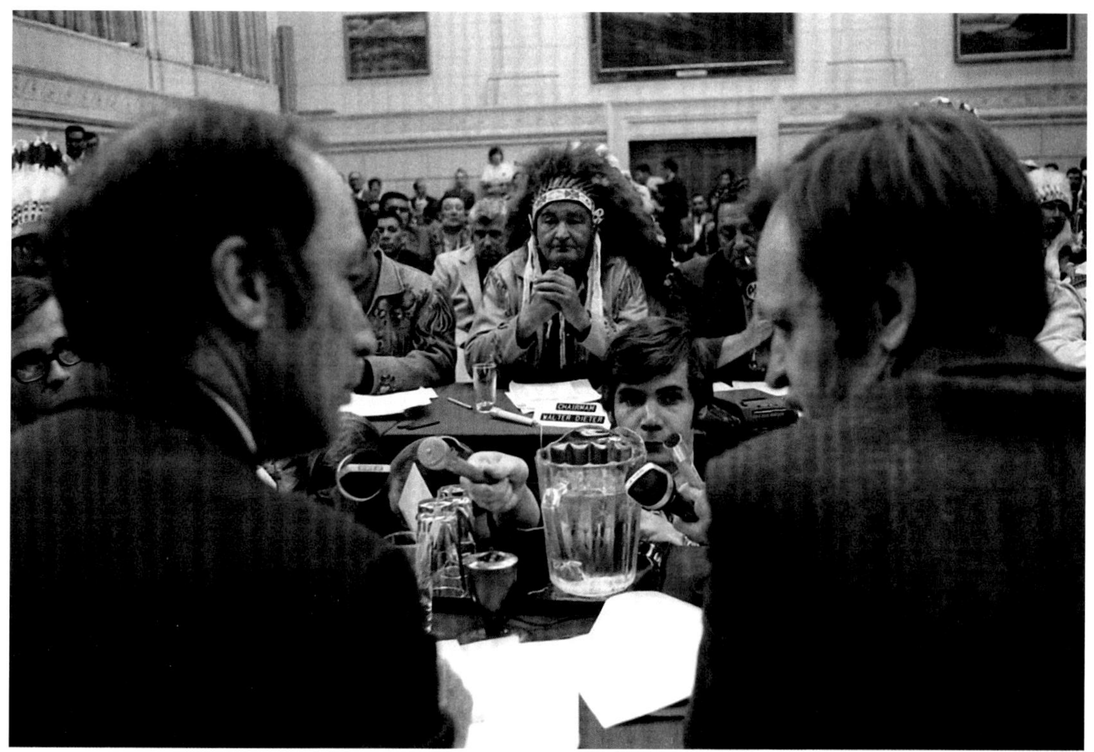

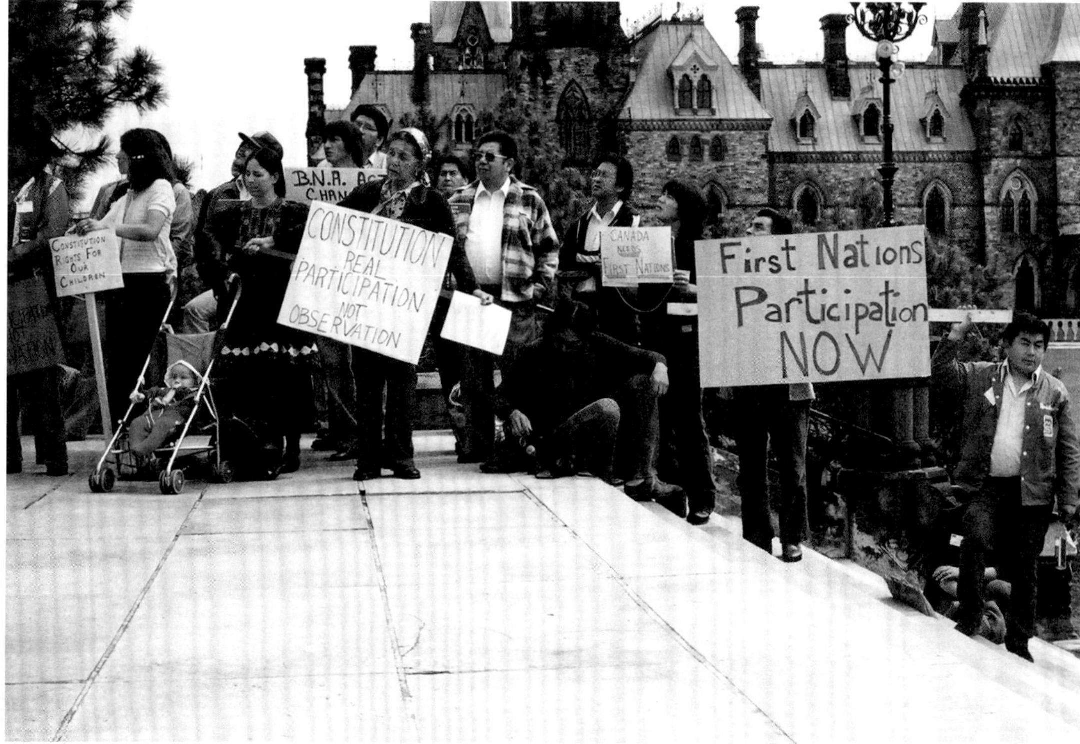

Top: Red Paper Brief to Government, 1970. In response to the 1969 White Paper, the Chiefs of the Indian Association of Alberta presented a counter-document titled Citizens Plus: the Red Paper, in resistance to the policies of assimilation. Library and Archives Canada/ Credit: Duncan Cameron/Duncan Cameron fonds/ e011065966. © Library and Archives Canada. Reproduced with the permission of Library and Archives Canada.

Bottom: Constitution Express, Ottawa, 1980. The Constitution Express was a successful, national protest movement to ensure that the Constitution Act of 1982 included Indigenous rights. Photo courtesy of the Union of British Columbia Indian Chiefs, B.CE104.

TORONTO
TRIBUTES+TRIBUTARIES
1971–1989

Gchi-oodenaang pii gii-yaawong 1970 miiniwaa 1980: memoonji-minawendaagok, memoonji-nigaa-naagok, ooshime gchi-gimaakidaagewin. Nindan enji-giziibiigezheng-gamigoong gii-gbaakoogaad-enoon, gii-bkinaagaadeg maanda sa Spadina(Spidinaang) Ge-zhiibiideg miikan, gewii kwewag ezhi-mindizowaad nokiiwinan, gewii maanda AIDS (gchi-aakoziwin) gii-maajiishkaamgwak, ooshime gi-niwaawaad gonda Caribbean miiniwaa Africa ngodwenaawziwinan, miiniwaa dash go gewii Anishinaabeg ezhi-nigaakimiiwaad. Kina go maanda – miiniwaa dash gwa ooshime – gii-ni-naabiisin nongo maanda gchi-oodenoo ezhi-kendimong nongo.

Nindan dash gaa-zhiwebkin bkaan zhichiganan gii-bgomshkaanoon naakonigewinan e-mina-dibaa-biishkoojigemgok, e-yaawing, dino'oonh, wiinziwin miiniwaa waabshkiye-nendimoowin kina nongo ezhi-ntaa-nokii-chigaadeg wenjishing. Enji-mina-waabiischigaadeg kidwenan, enji-ntaa-nokiichigaa-deg-gamigoong, ezhi-maanjiining miiniwaa mzinaateschige ntaa-nokiichigewin kina gii-bgomshkaa e-zhi-shkiiwong zhichiganan ji-gnowaabnjigaadeg miiniwaa ji-bigidnind maabaa bezhig wiin ji-dibaatang ezhi-mindizod.

Maanda oodenoo kenjigaaded ji-bzwaamjigaadeg gegoo – mewzha, bebesha endaadaajig, nbiing mibsong. Maanda zhinoomaagewin aawan gbeying eko-baabiichigaadeg zhindibesewin gonda sa nji aanand e-ntaa-nokii-chige-jig miiniwaa ezhi-ngodoodenaawzing gaa-zhitoojig maanda oodeoo non-go ezhi-kendimong, booj dash go aabji-kijgaade dibishkoo tkibiinsan miiniwaa ziibiin negaaj emijoong naamkamig oodenaa-miikanaang. Maamowi dash, gonda ezhi-ntaa-nokii-chigejig dooshtoonaawaa shki'ii zhichigan: Maanda e-ntaa-nokiichigaadeg ni-naaknaan maanda ngodoodenaawin miiniwaa ni-aanjtoon ezhi-nsastamong monpii Akiing endaaying.

Toronto in the 1970s and 1980s: exciting, tragic, overtly political. The bathhouse raids, the defeat of the Spadina Expressway, the feminist movement, the AIDS crisis, the flourishing of the Black community, and the Indigenous cultural renaissance. All of this – and more – shaped the city we know today.

These movements against the status quo brought issues of democracy, race, gender, sexuality and colonialism into art in exciting ways. Dub poetry, artist-run centres, performance and video art all surfaced as new media to explore and express one's own experience.

This city tends to bury things – histories, neighbourhoods, waterways. This exhibition is a long-overdue nod to some of the artists and communities who formed the city we know today, yet remain hidden like the creeks and rivers trickling beneath our streets. Together, these artists offer a revolutionary provocation: that art builds communities and changes our understanding of the world we live in.

@AGOToronto
#TOtributes
Personal photography encouraged

Organized by the Art Gallery of Ontario

Supported by
Canada Council for the Arts / Conseil des arts du Canada

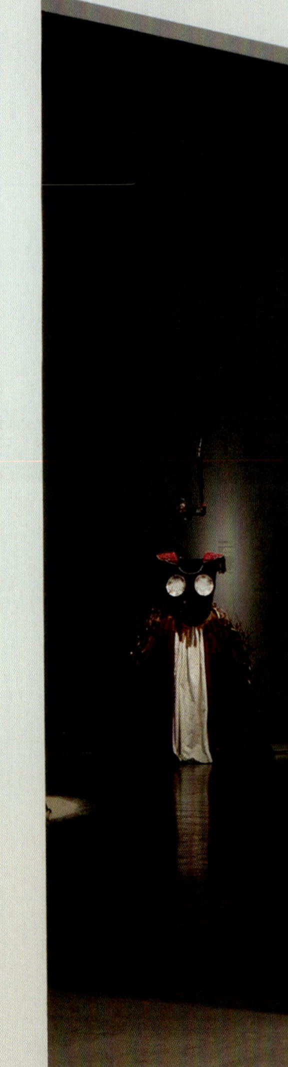

Beginnings

Maajtang

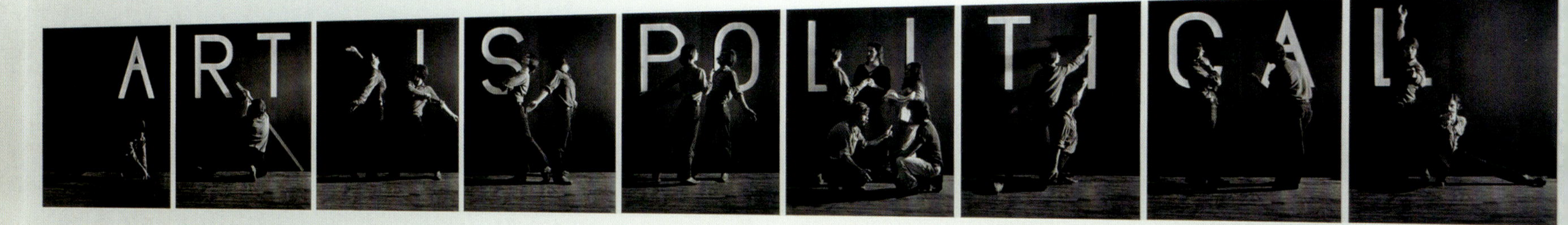

Jeff Thomas

Bear Portrait, No. 1, Culture Revolution, 1984
14 photographic prints
From *Bear Portrait*
Dimensions variable
Art Gallery of Ontario, purchase with assistance from an anonymous donor and James Lahey, 2016, 2016/44.1-.14

"When I saw Bear in front of the brick wall, not only was I looking at my son through the viewfinder, but I was looking at myself, my father, and my grandfather. I was seeing what I didn't see in the photographic archives—images of First Nations people in the urban landscape." —Jeff Thomas

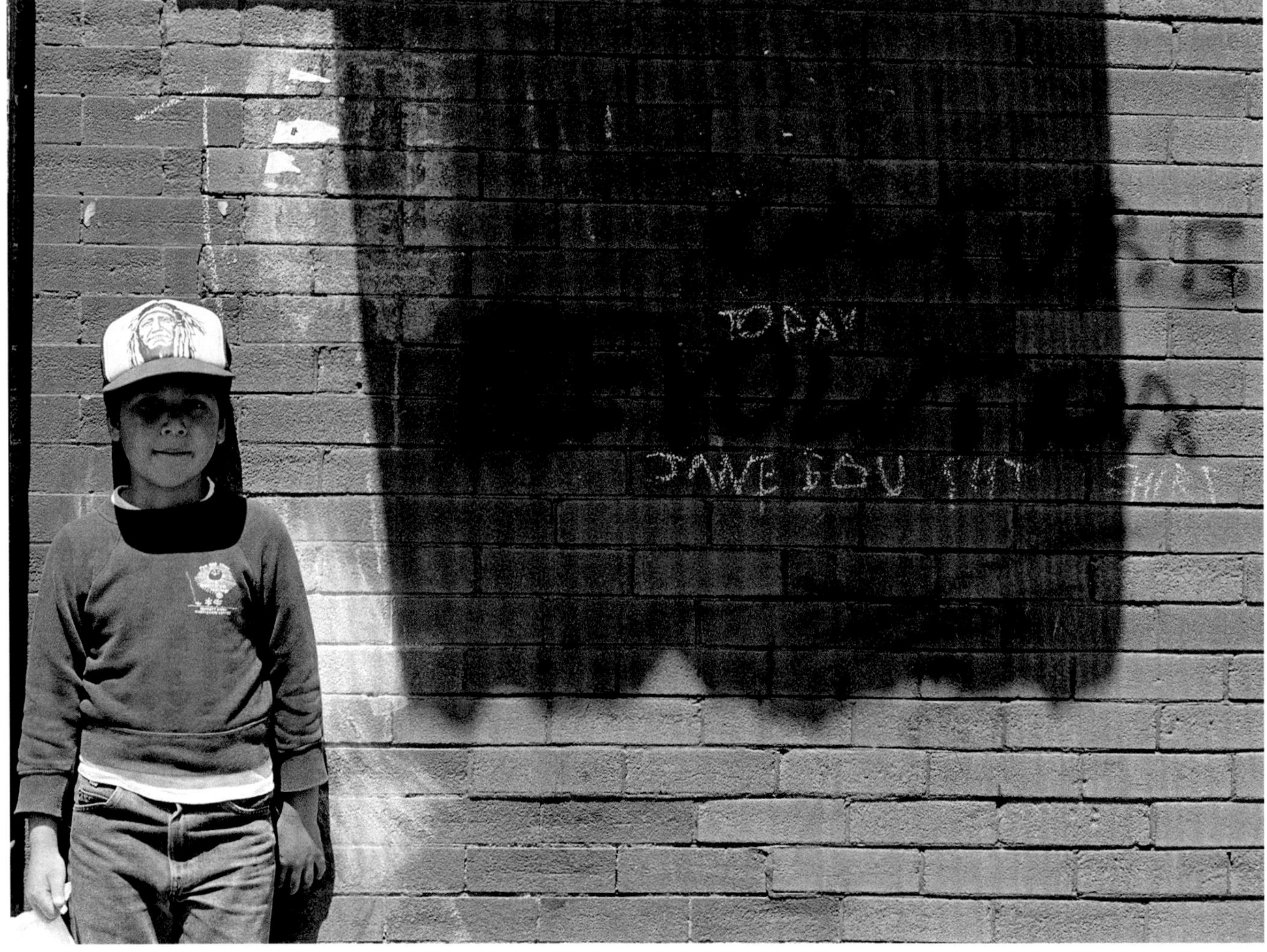

Lillian Allen

Lyrics from "Revolutionary Tea Party"
From *Revolutionary Tea Party*, 1986
Audio recording, 7:07 min.

"Dub poetry—part of its intention is to disrupt traditional discourse. To call attention to a whole life that's being ignored, that's happening, and that actually feeds the other life: the middle class and colonial life, through its labour, its style, its energy." —Lillian Allen

You who know what the past has been
You who work in the present tense
You who see through to the future
Come mek wi work together
Come sit here with me
An mek we drink tea
A mek wi talk
A mek wi analyse
You who've been burned by vanguardism
Come mek wi give you little nurturing
Come sit awile
A mek wi drink tea
A mek wi talk
A mek wi stategise
You who believe in the future
And in transforming by your labour
Let the future be in good favour
We who create the wealth of the world
and only get scrapings from them in control
When wi siddown and look at the system
Check out the way that things been
Wi haffi say, wi haffi say
It rank how the system stay
Wi haffi say, wi haffi say
The system in a really bad way
A way it a defend
You who see for peace a future
You who understand the past
You who create with yu sweat from the heart
Let's talk. Let's make art. Let's love. Dance
Rebel in the streets if that's the beat
Rebel in the streets if that's the beat
Demonstrate protest. Chant
You who see for us a future
Come sit here with we
Mek we drink tea
Let's talk
Mek wi analyse
Mek wi strategise
Mek we work together

Carole Condé and Karl Beveridge

Art Is Political, 1975
9 prints on vinyl
79.4 × 62.2 cm each
Collection of the artists

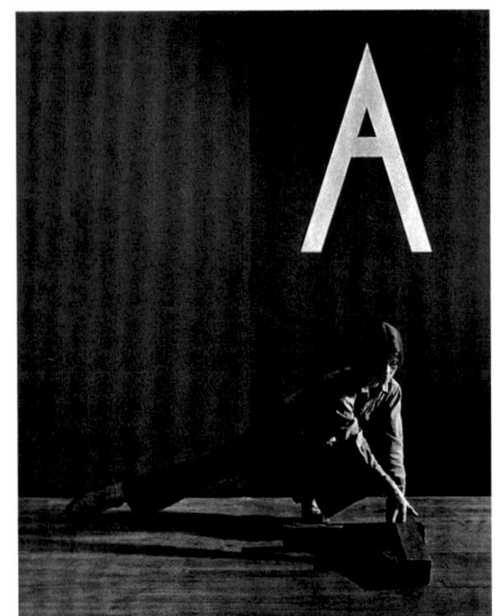

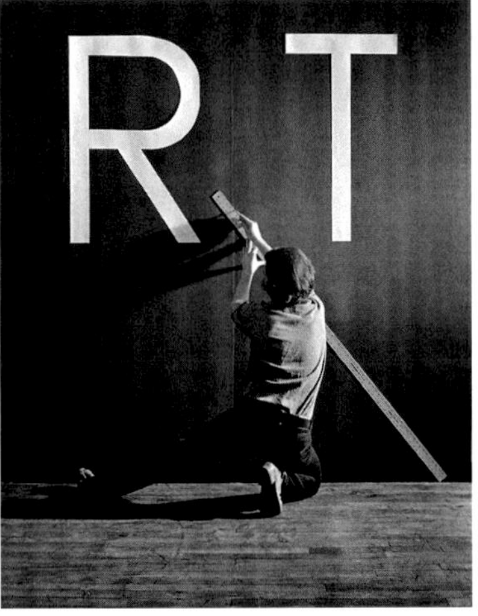

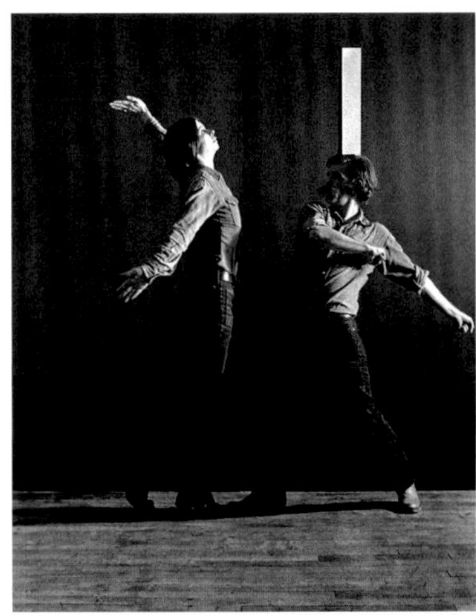

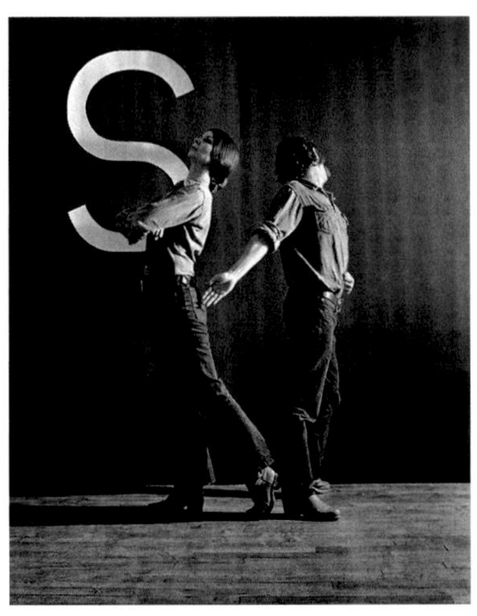

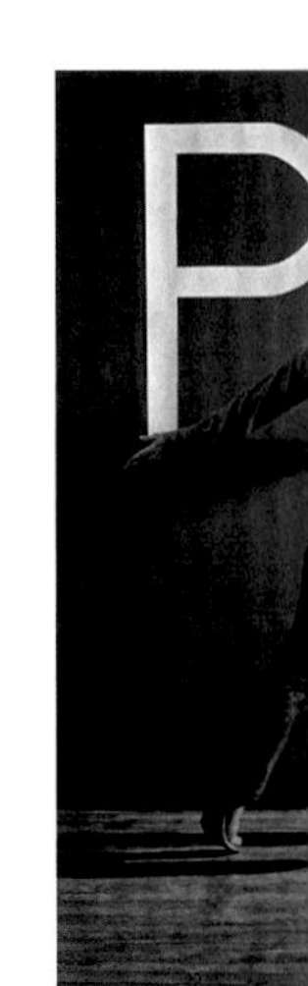

...*It's Still Privileged Art* (not shown here)
Artist book and exhibition catalogue
Toronto: Art Gallery of Ontario, 1976
E.P. Taylor Library & Archives, Art Gallery of Ontario

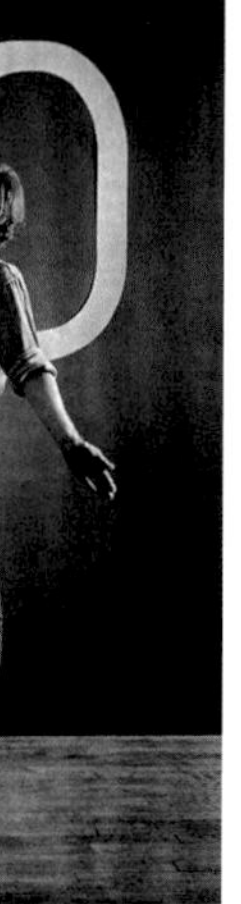
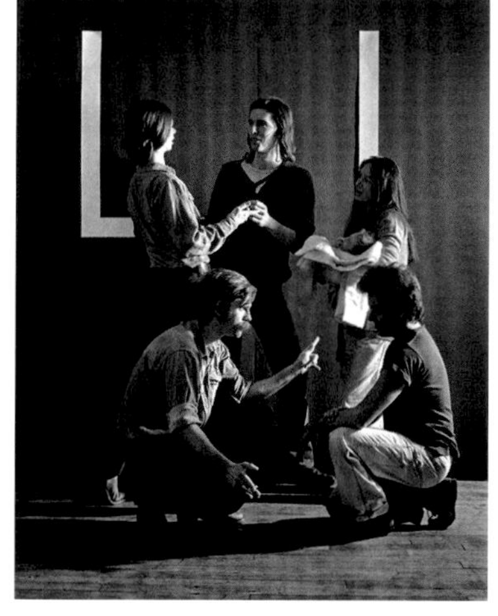

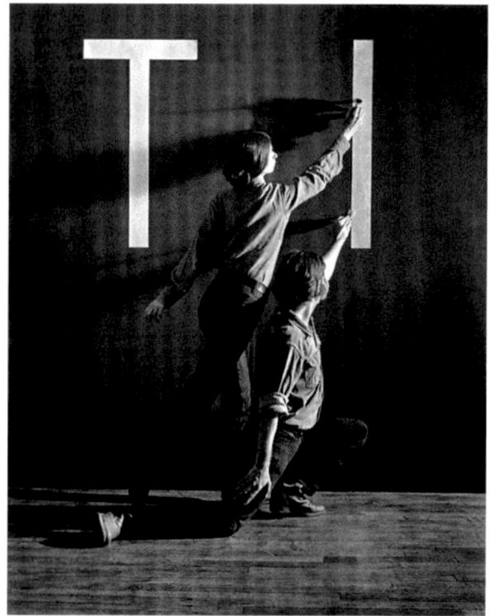

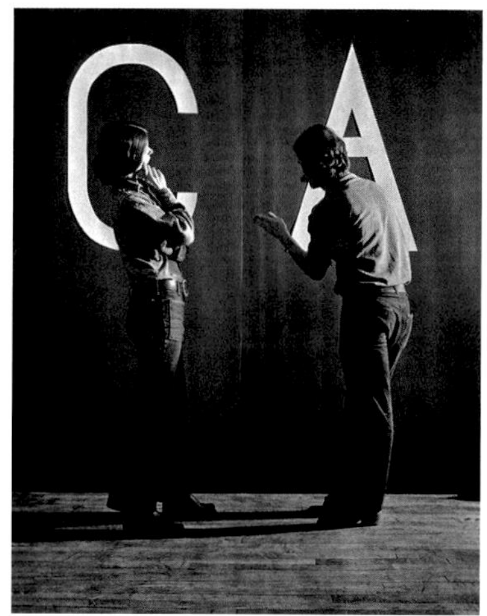

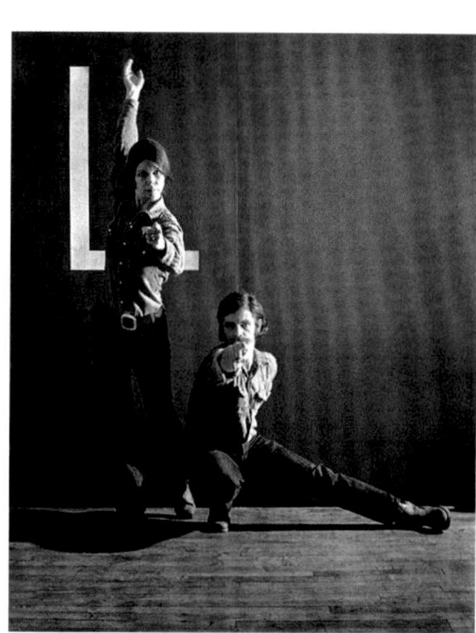

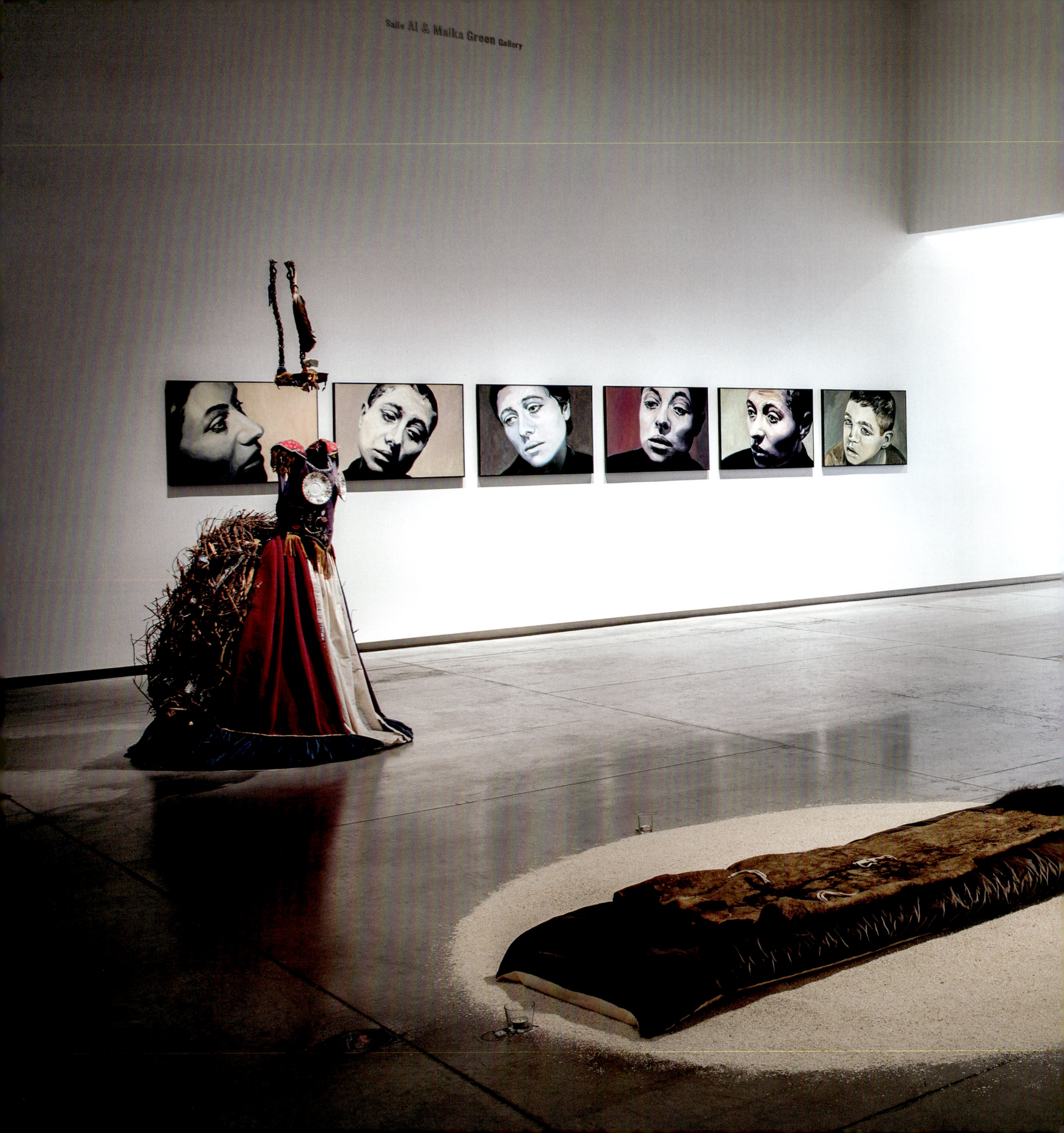

Salle Al & Malka Green Gallery

Performance

Maanjiindowin e-zhintaa-nokiichigaadeg

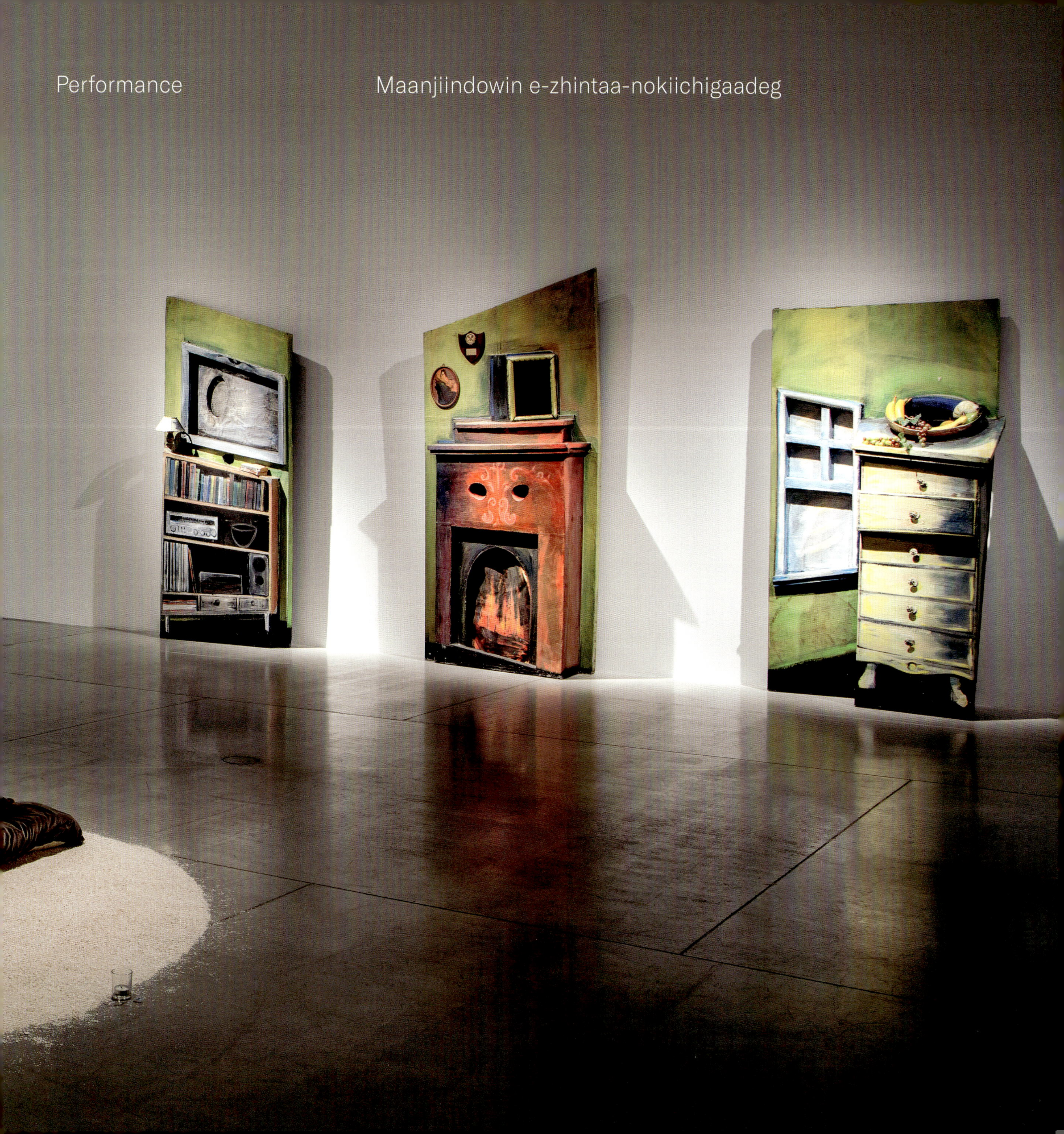

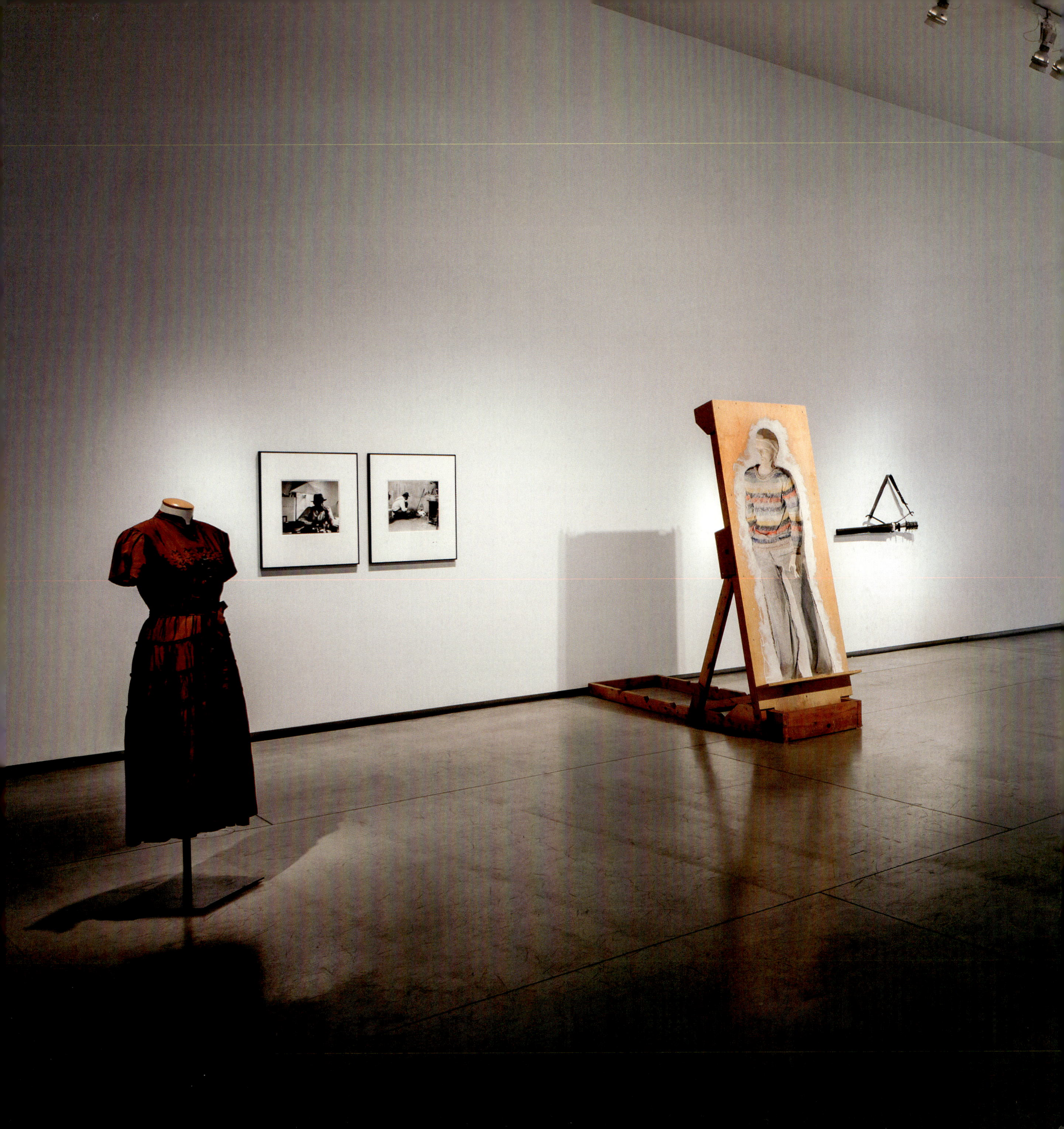

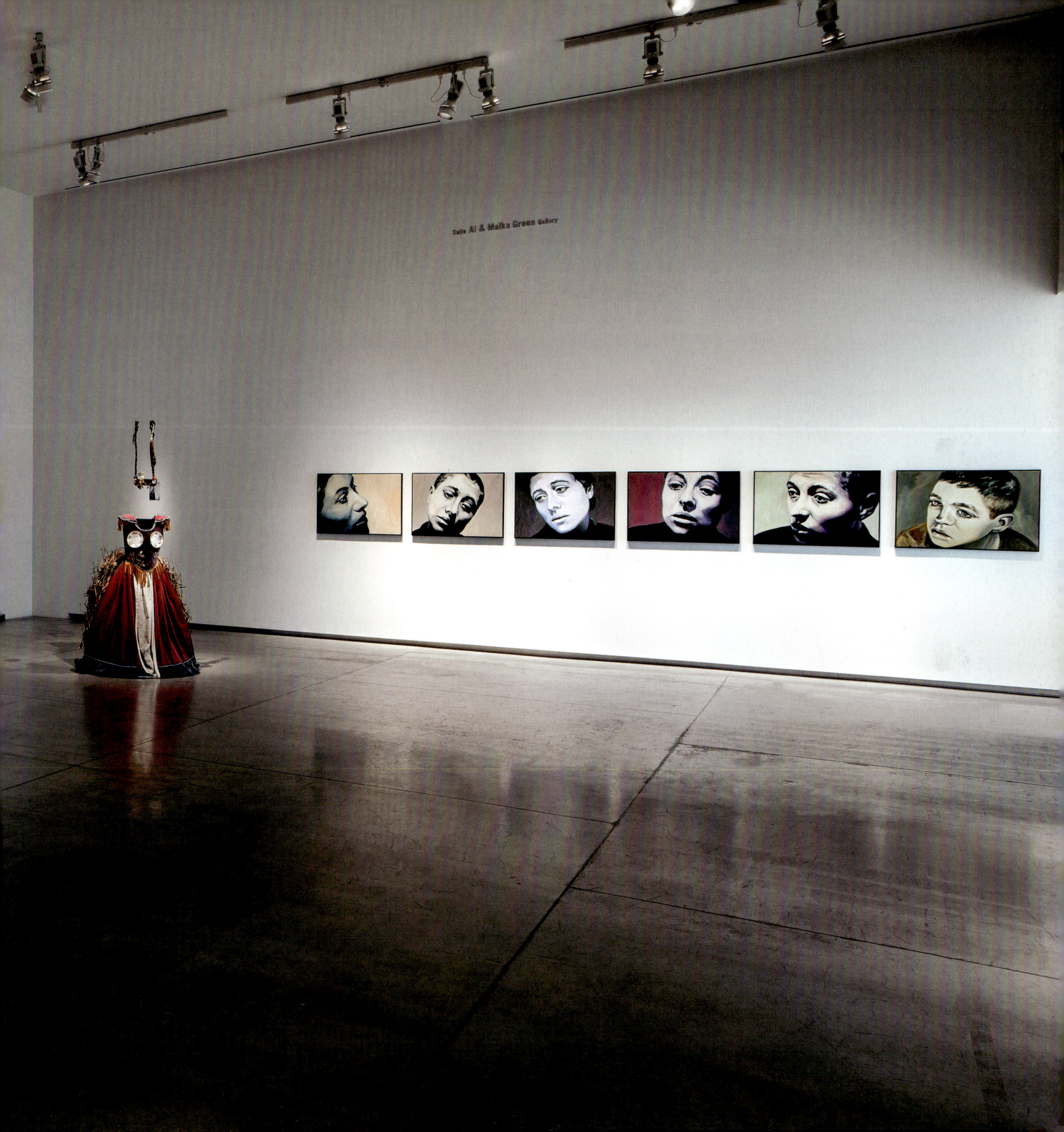
Salle Al & Malka Green Gallery

General Idea

Artist's Conception: Miss General Idea, 1971
Screenprint on paper
101.7 × 66.2 cm
Art Gallery of Ontario, gift of AA Bronson, 1998, 98/316

The 1971 Miss General Idea Pageant poster, 1971
Offset lithograph on paper
101.6 × 66 cm
Art Gallery of Ontario, gift of AA Bronson, 1998, 98/310

"Right from the beginning, we saw the beauty pageants as a critique. It was our examination of the existing art world. There was all the parody aspect—but it was quite obvious that it operated like that. It was a questioning of the process by which masterpieces are created, or validated, or selected, and worshipped." —Felix Partz, General Idea

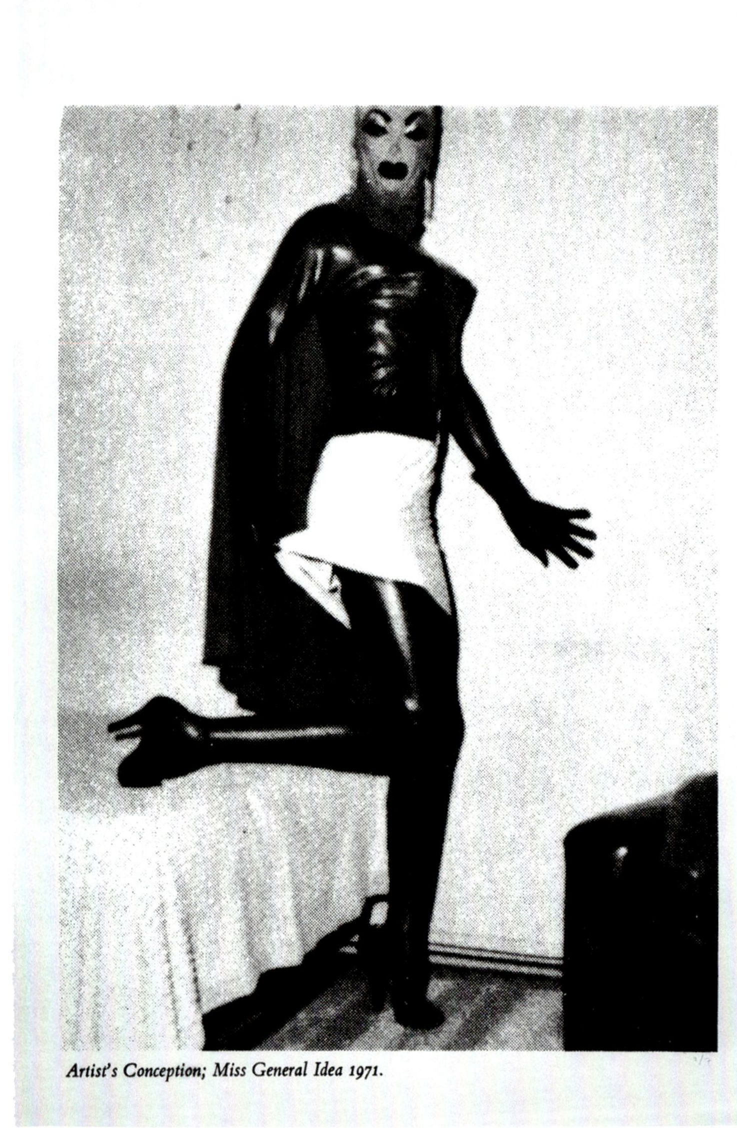

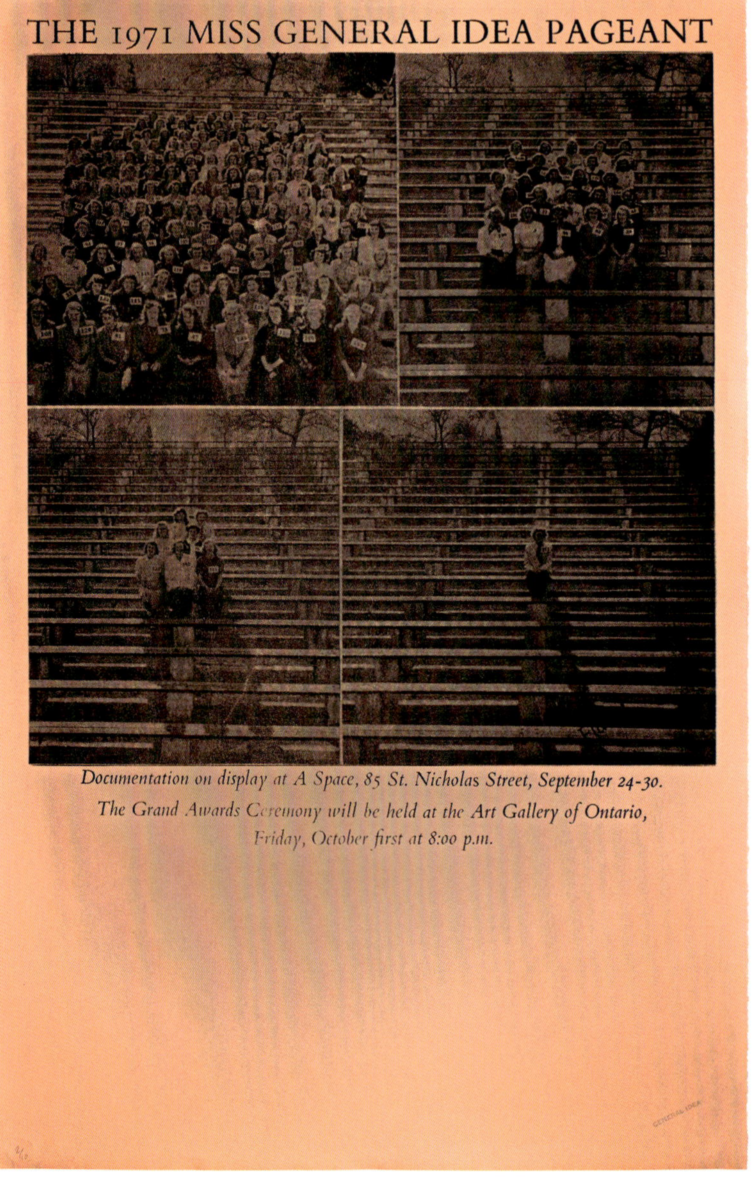

The Miss General Idea Gown, 1971
Cellulose acetate "taffeta" dress with a paper tag (with black and orange letterpress)
123 × 135 cm
Art Gallery of Ontario, gift of AA Bronson, 1998, 98/315

Invitation to the Miss General Idea Pageant event, October 1, 1971, 1971
Two colour letterpress on embossed card
11.2 × 14 cm
Art Gallery of Ontario, gift of AA Bronson, 1998, 98/314

Beauty Without Cruelty, 1971
Offset print on paper
6.1 × 11.7 cm
Art Gallery of Ontario, gift of AA Bronson, 1998, 98/312

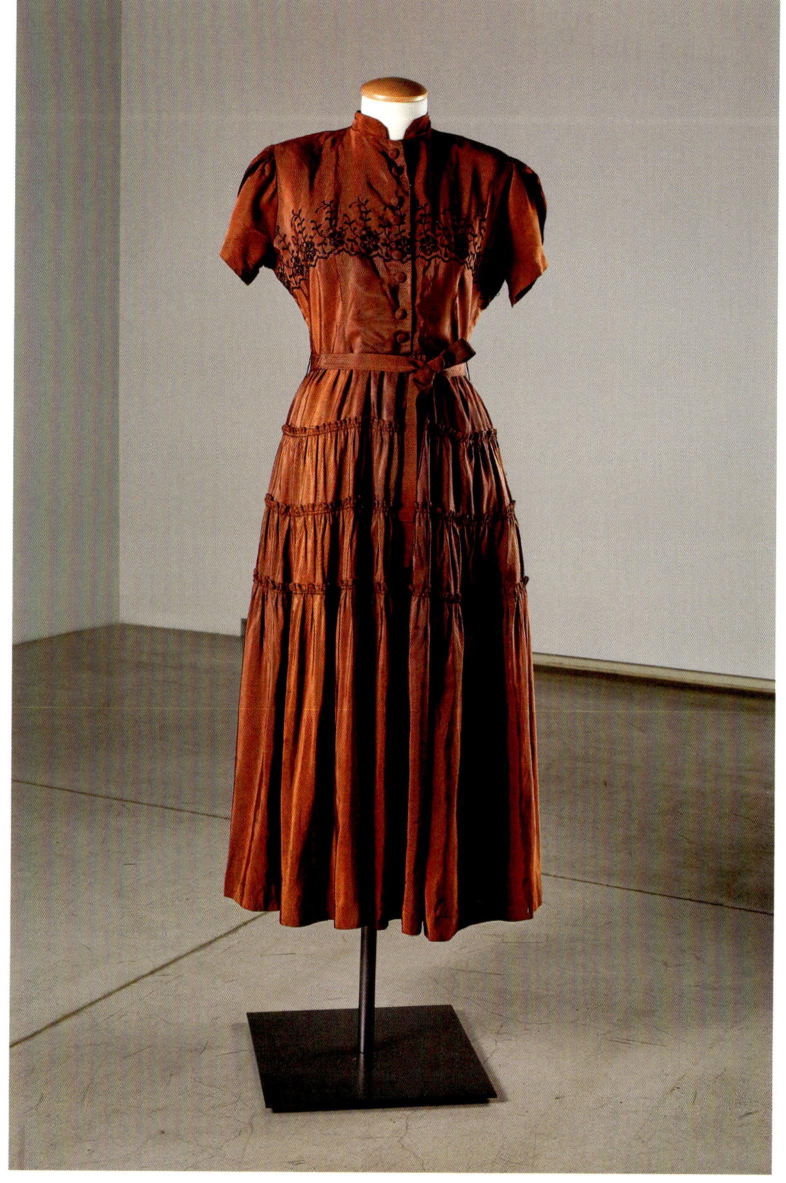

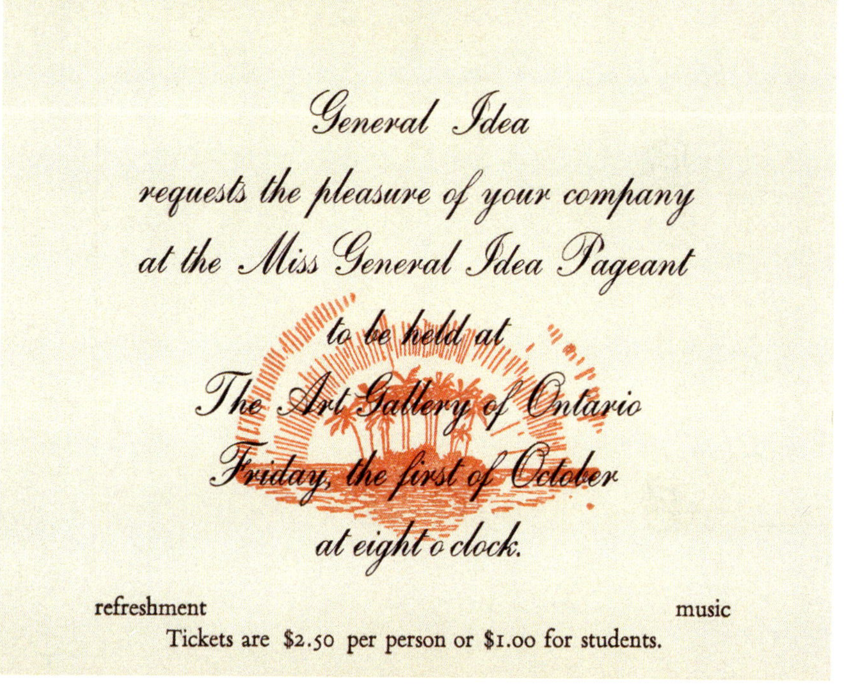

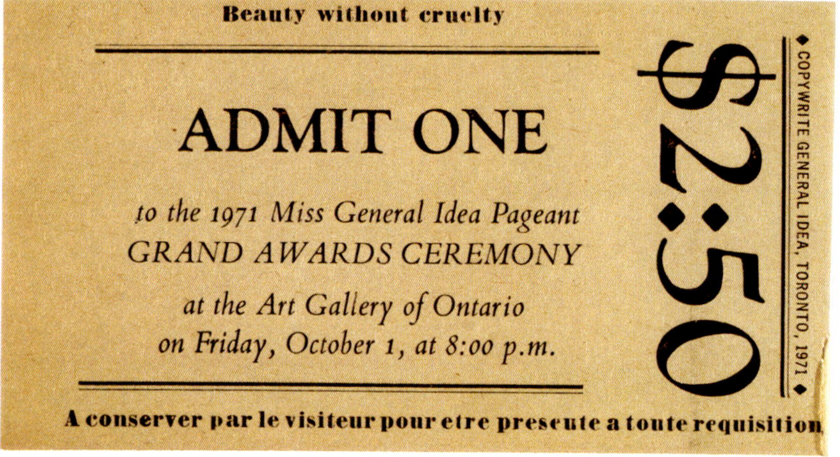

Rebecca Belmore

Rising to the Occasion, 1987–1991
Mixed media
200 × 120 × 100 cm
Art Gallery of Ontario, gift from the Junior Volunteer Committee, 1995, 95/173

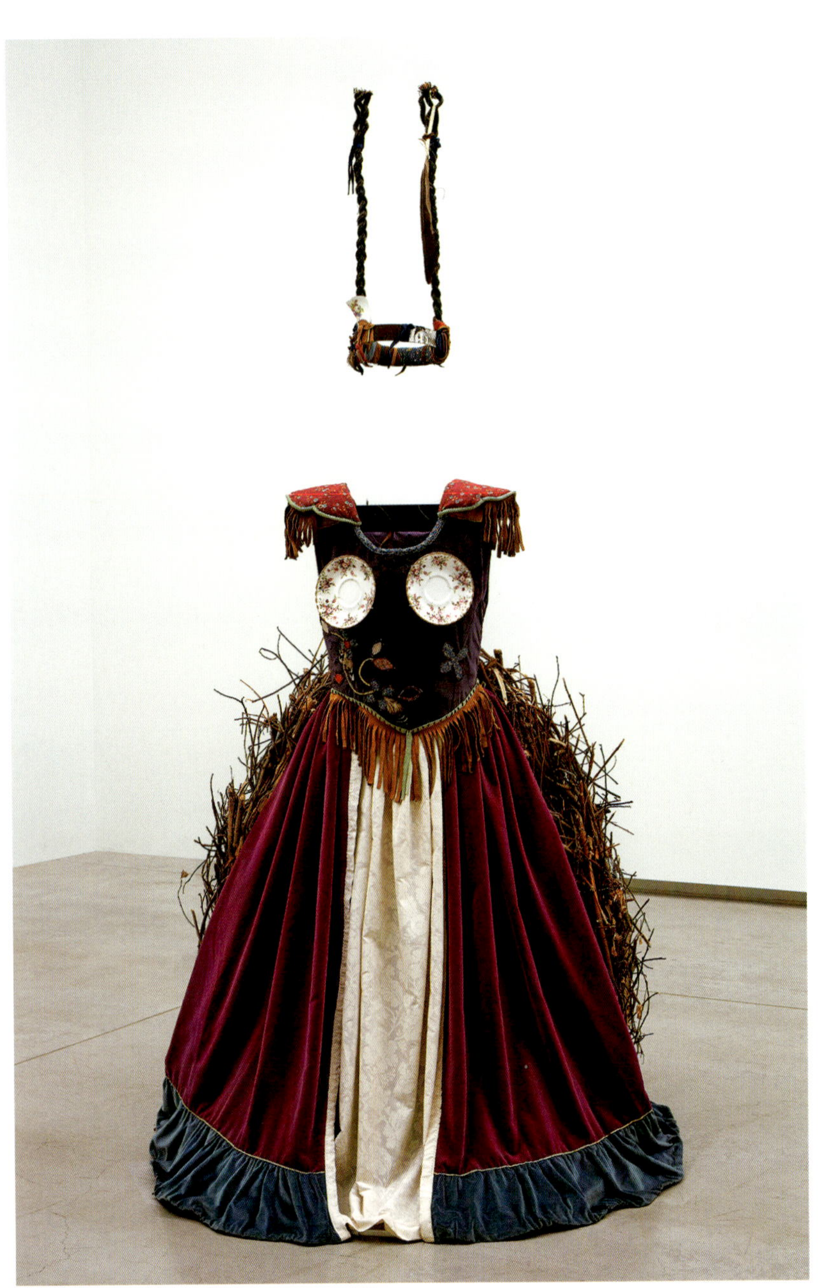

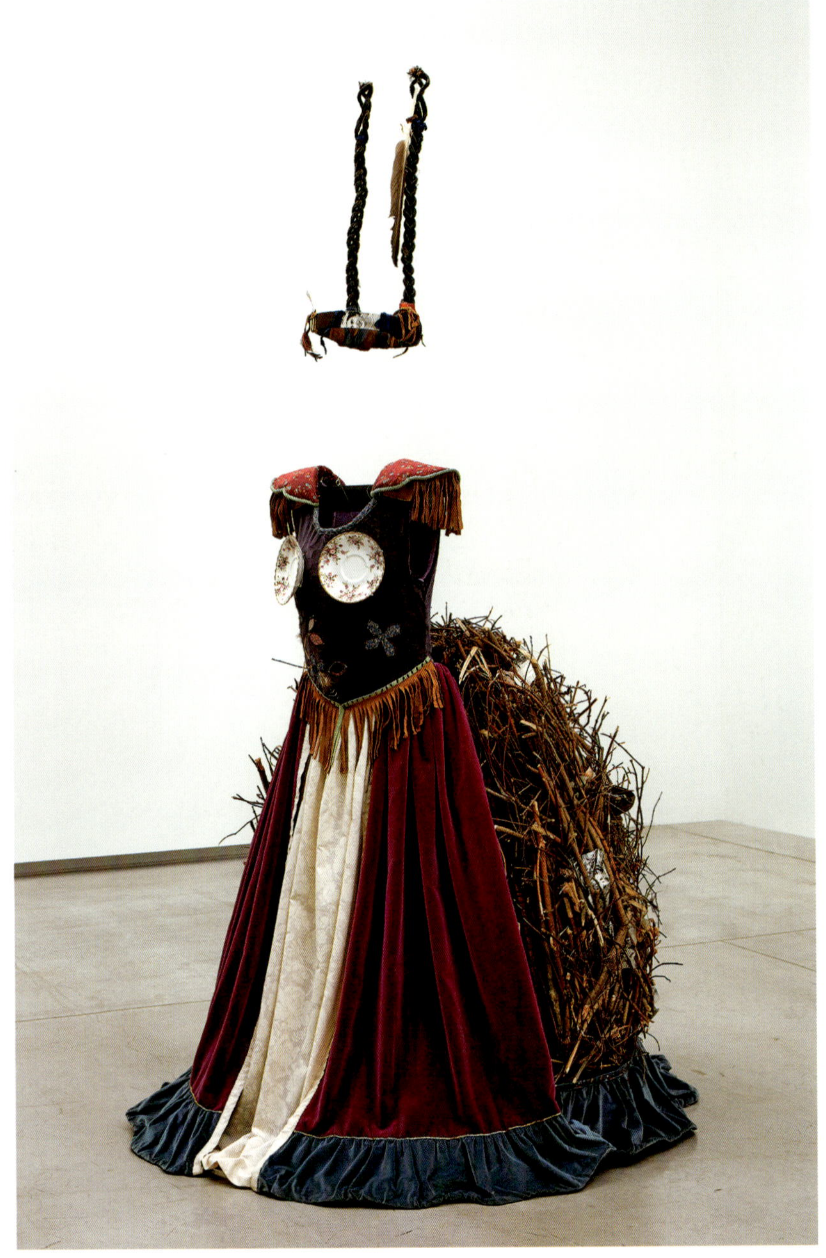

"That summer the royal newlyweds, Prince Andrew and Sarah Ferguson, paid a royal visit to a reconstructed fur-trading fort, Old Fort William…My contribution to the procession was *Rising to the Occasion*, a dress that was part 'Victorian' ball gown and part beaver dam. The royals came to our city for a handful of hours as performers, replaying colonial history complete with birch bark canoes and a fake fort. This was incredibly absurd to me. What to wear for such an absurd occasion?" —Rebecca Belmore

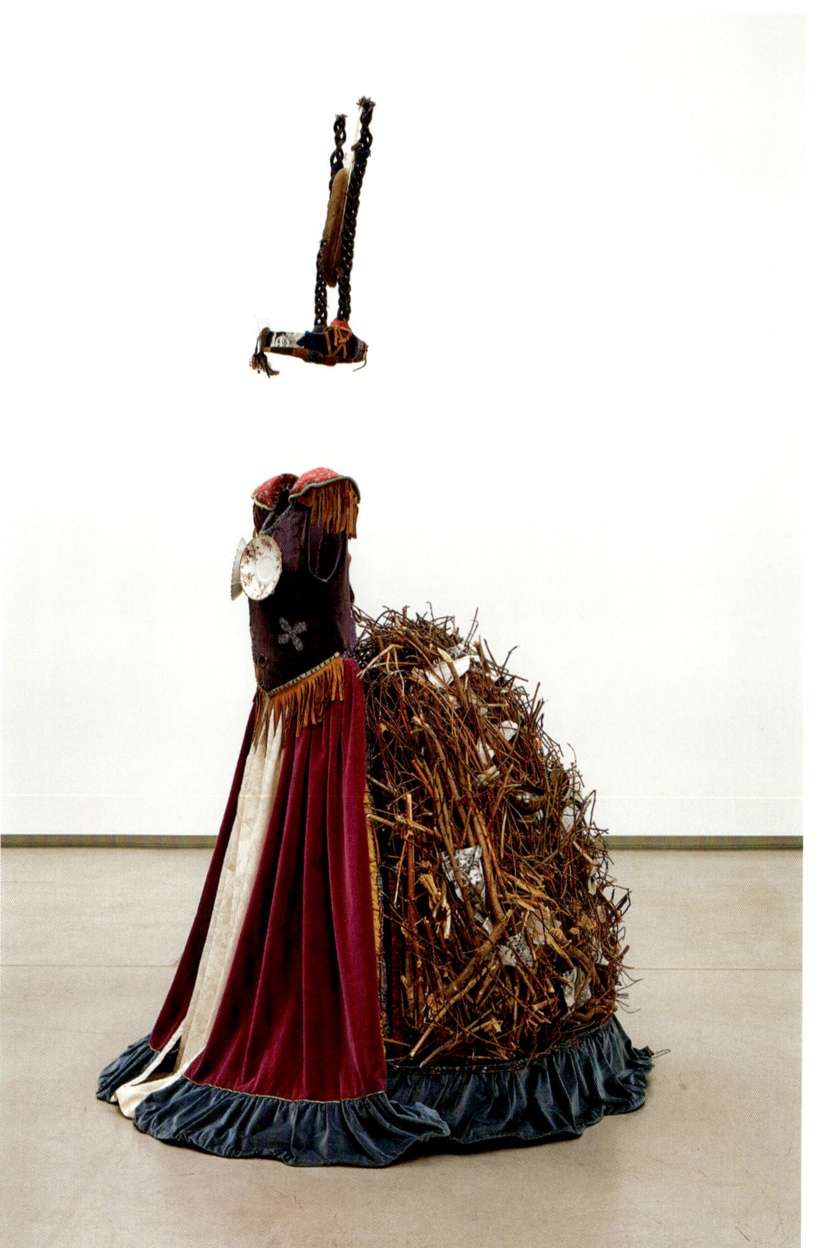

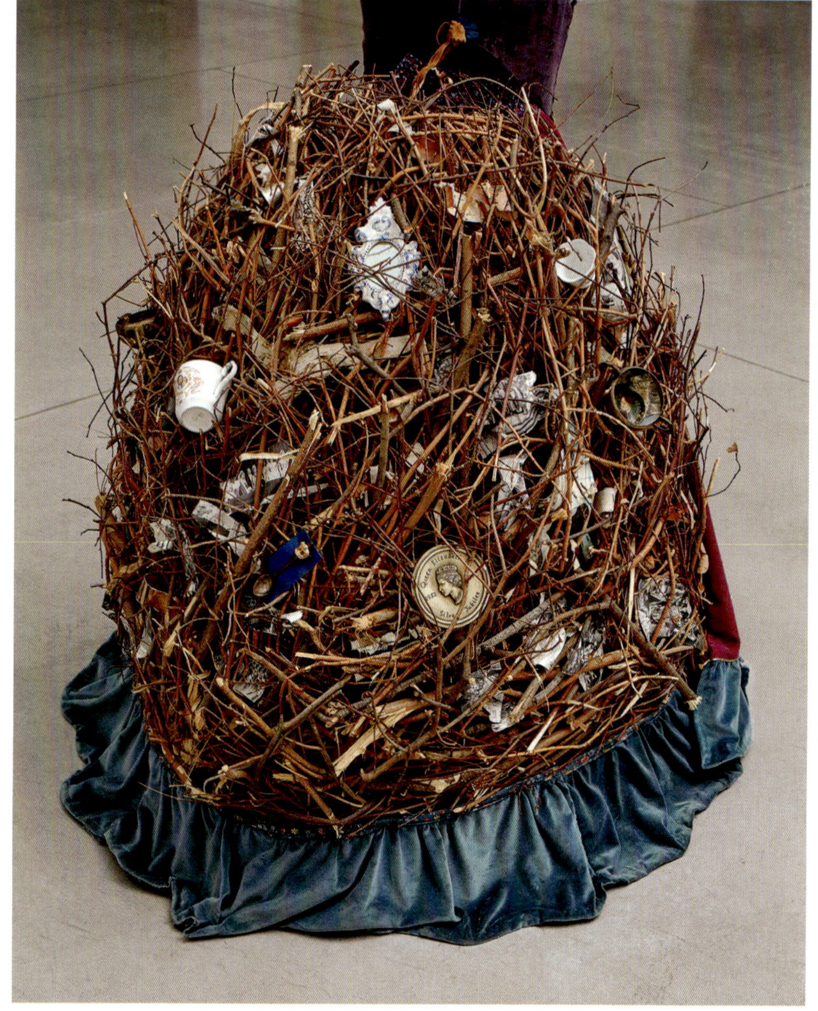

Will Gorlitz

Genre XVI, 1984
Oil on canvas
61 × 89 cm
Art Gallery of Ontario, gift of Price Waterhouse, Toronto, 1994, 94/328

Genre XIII, 1984
Oil on canvas
61 × 89 cm
Art Gallery of Ontario, gift of Price Waterhouse, Toronto, 1994, 94/327

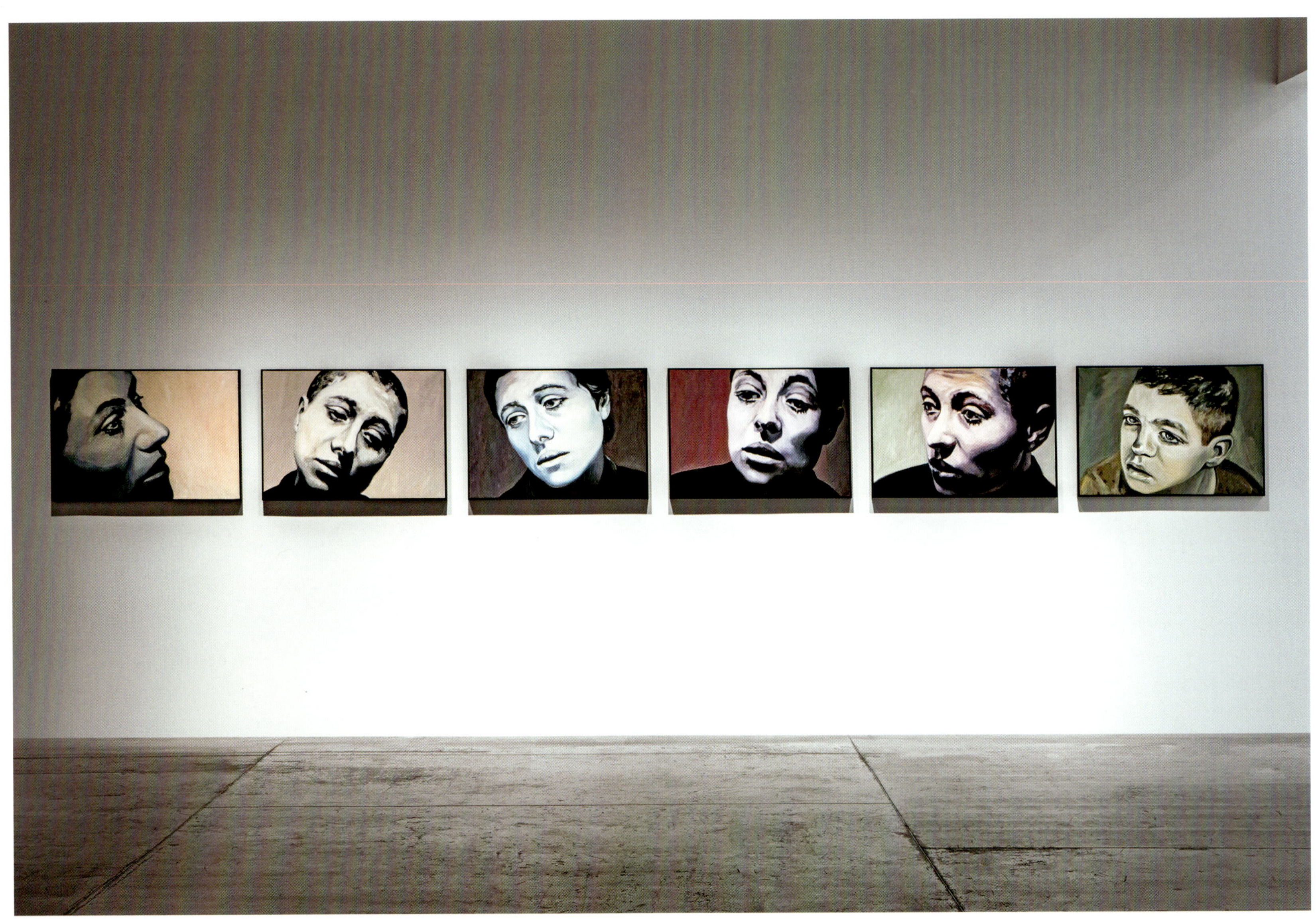

Genre II, 1984
Oil on canvas
61 × 89 cm
Art Gallery of Ontario, gift of Alison and Alan Schwartz, 1997, 97/165

Genre IV, 1984
Oil on canvas
61 × 89 cm
Art Gallery of Ontario, gift of Alison and Alan Schwartz, 1997, 97/164

Genre VII, 1984
Oil on canvas
60.5 × 88.8 cm
Art Gallery of Ontario, gift of Price Waterhouse, Toronto, 1994, 94/325

Genre VIII, 1984
Oil on canvas
60.5 × 88.8 cm
Art Gallery of Ontario, gift of Price Waterhouse, Toronto, 1994, 94/326

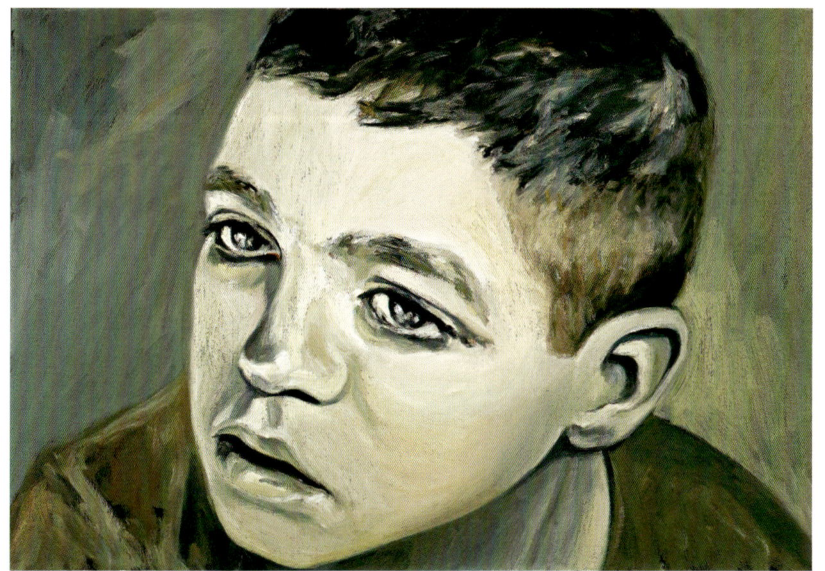

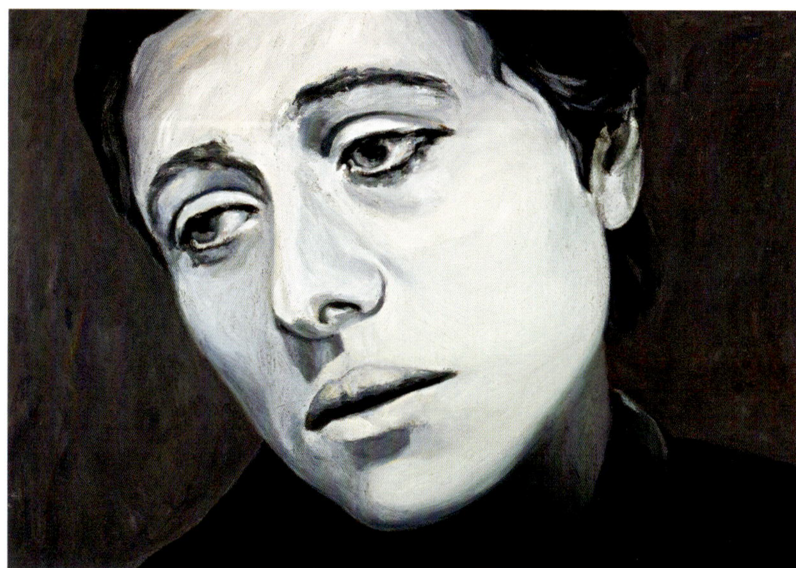

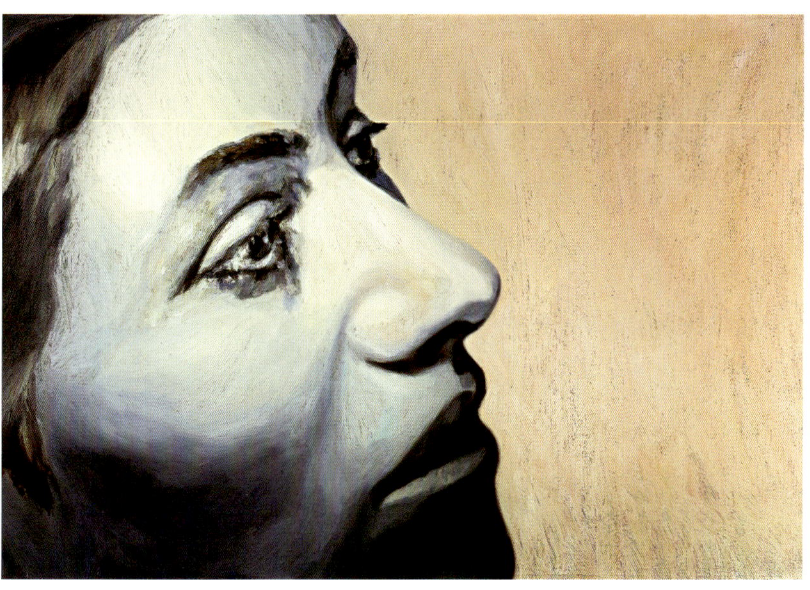

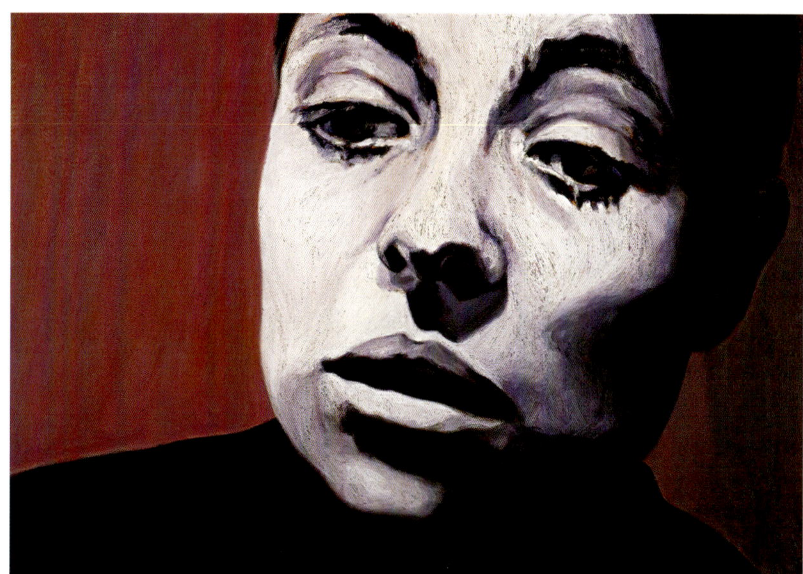

Colette Whiten

Colette, 1978
Plaster, burlap, plywood, pine, mixed fibres, and mixed hardware
254 × 74.8 × 34 cm
Art Gallery of Ontario, gift of the artist, 1999, 99/720

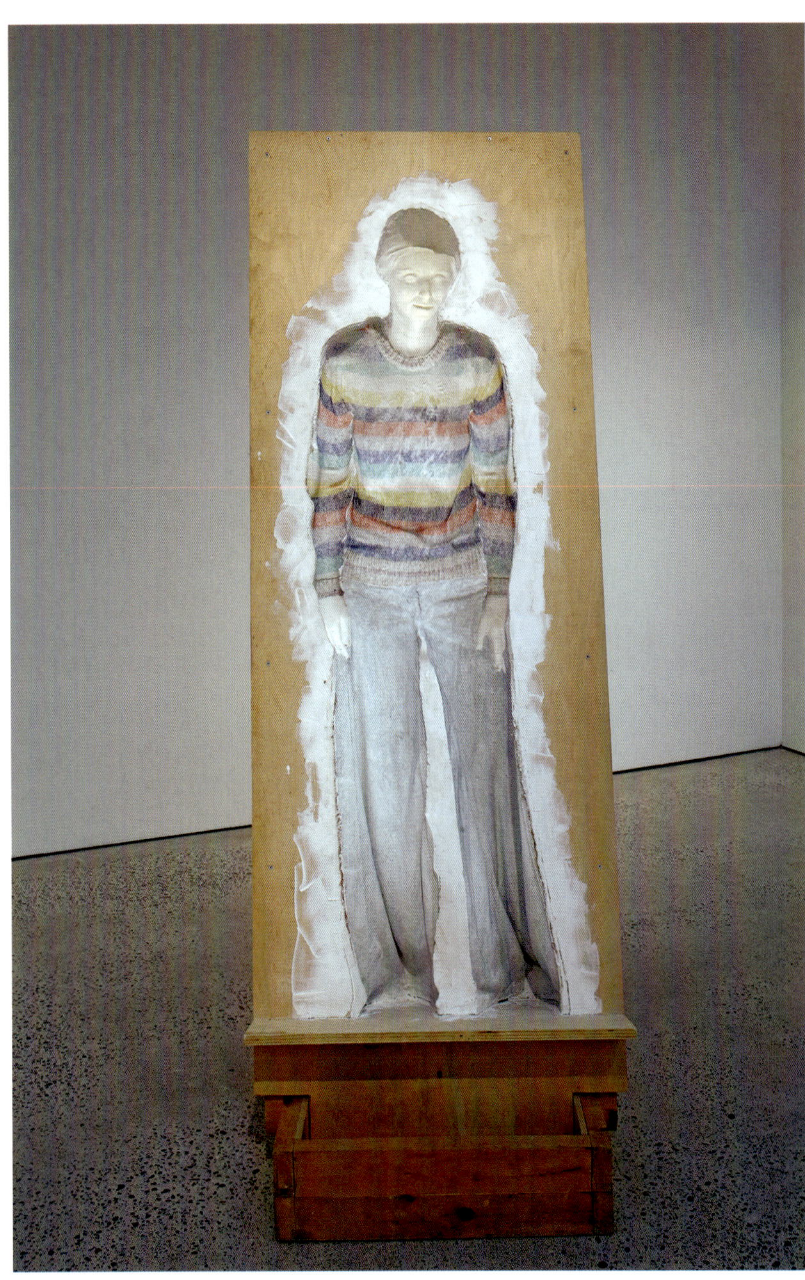

Ron Giii

Untitled (Dictator's Opera), 1986
75 × 55.5 cm
Art Gallery of Ontario, gift of Robert MacIntyre, 1991, 91/170

Untitled (Dictator's Opera), 1986
75 × 55.8 cm
Art Gallery of Ontario, gift of Robert MacIntyre, 1991, 91/171

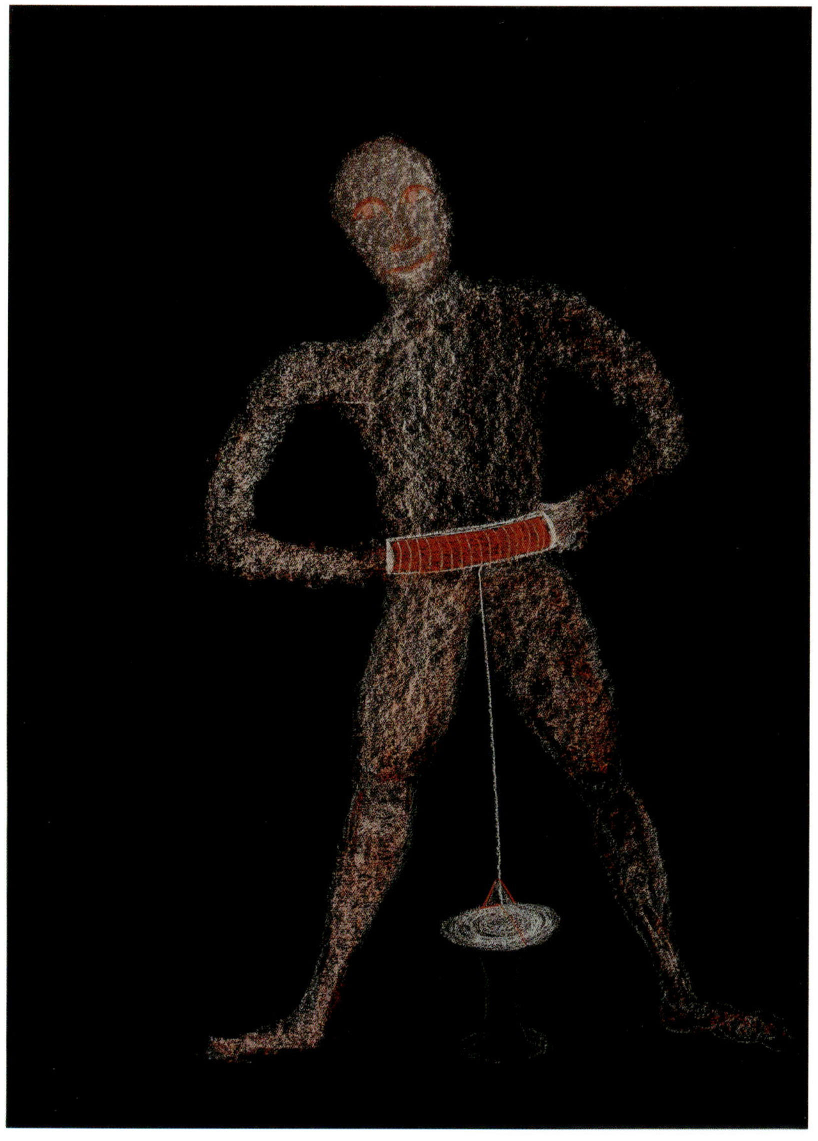

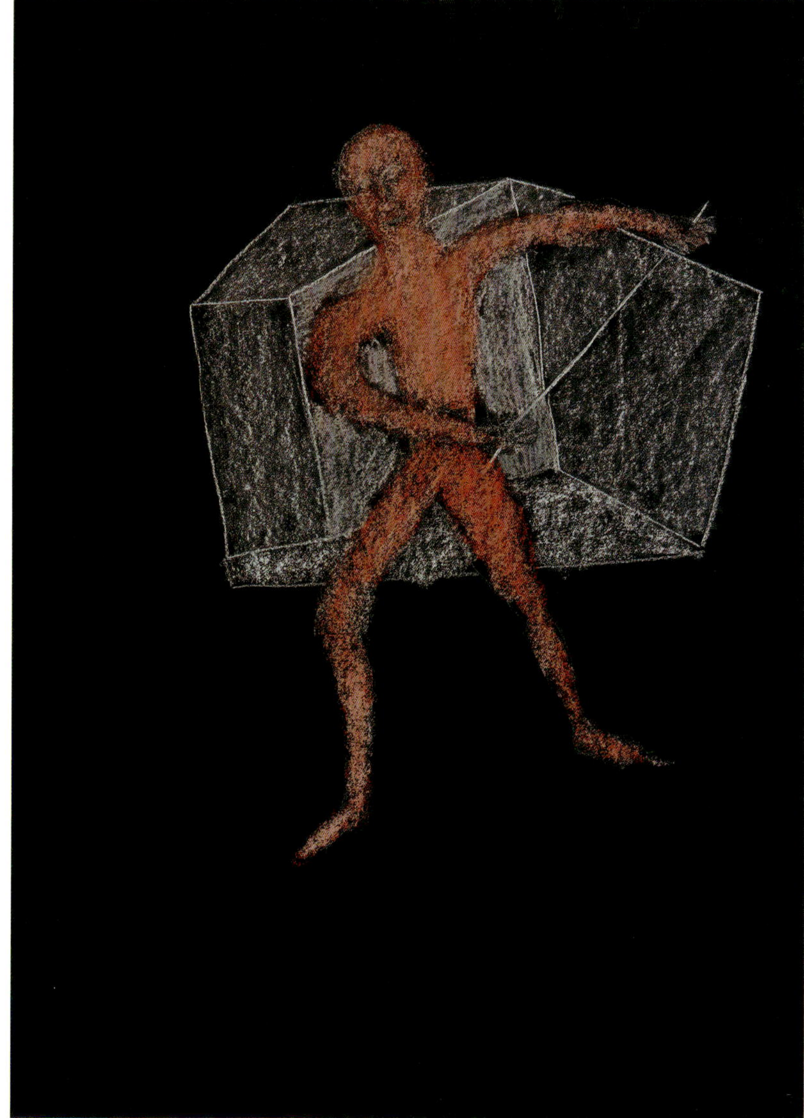

Tim Whiten

Metamorphosis, 1978–1989
Ritual vessel (completely tanned bearskin, brass bells, cotton ties), grey pillow (cotton with synthetic foam), crushed eggshells, 4 glass votive containers and candles, and 4 incense tiles
254 × 254 cm
Art Gallery of Ontario, purchase with assistance from the Estate of P.J. Glasser, 2016, 2016/42

Documentation of the Ritual Process, Stages 1.2, 1.8, 1.24, and *3*, 1978
Ink-jet prints on paper
61 × 45.7 cm
Courtesy of the artist

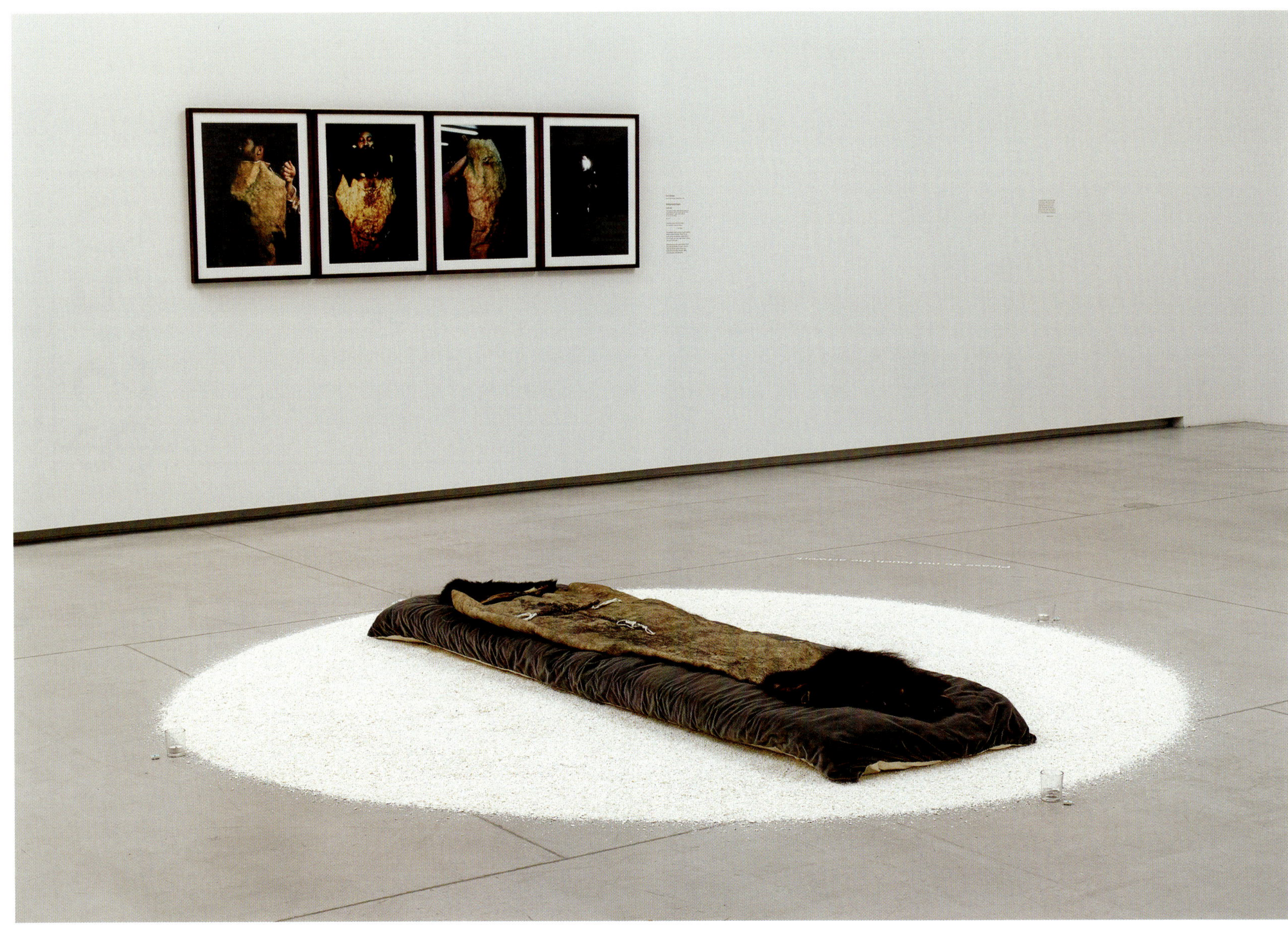

"The piece is about birth and rebirth. It's a remnant, a memory device." —Tim Whiten

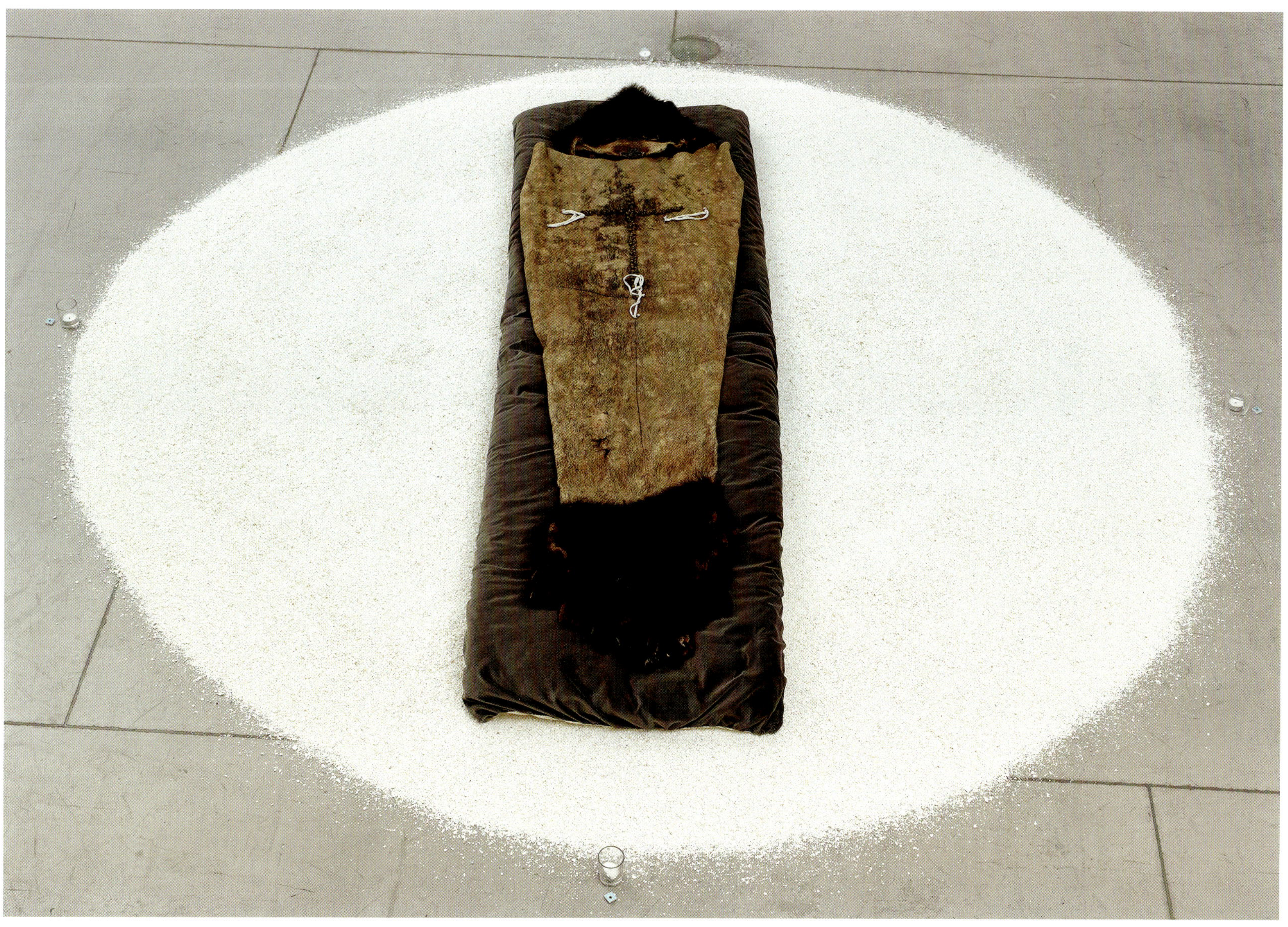

Ian Carr-Harris

Fred, 1972
Painted wood, glass, Letraset, and paper
144.5 × 61.5 × 57.3 cm
Art Gallery of Ontario, purchase, 1985, 85/31

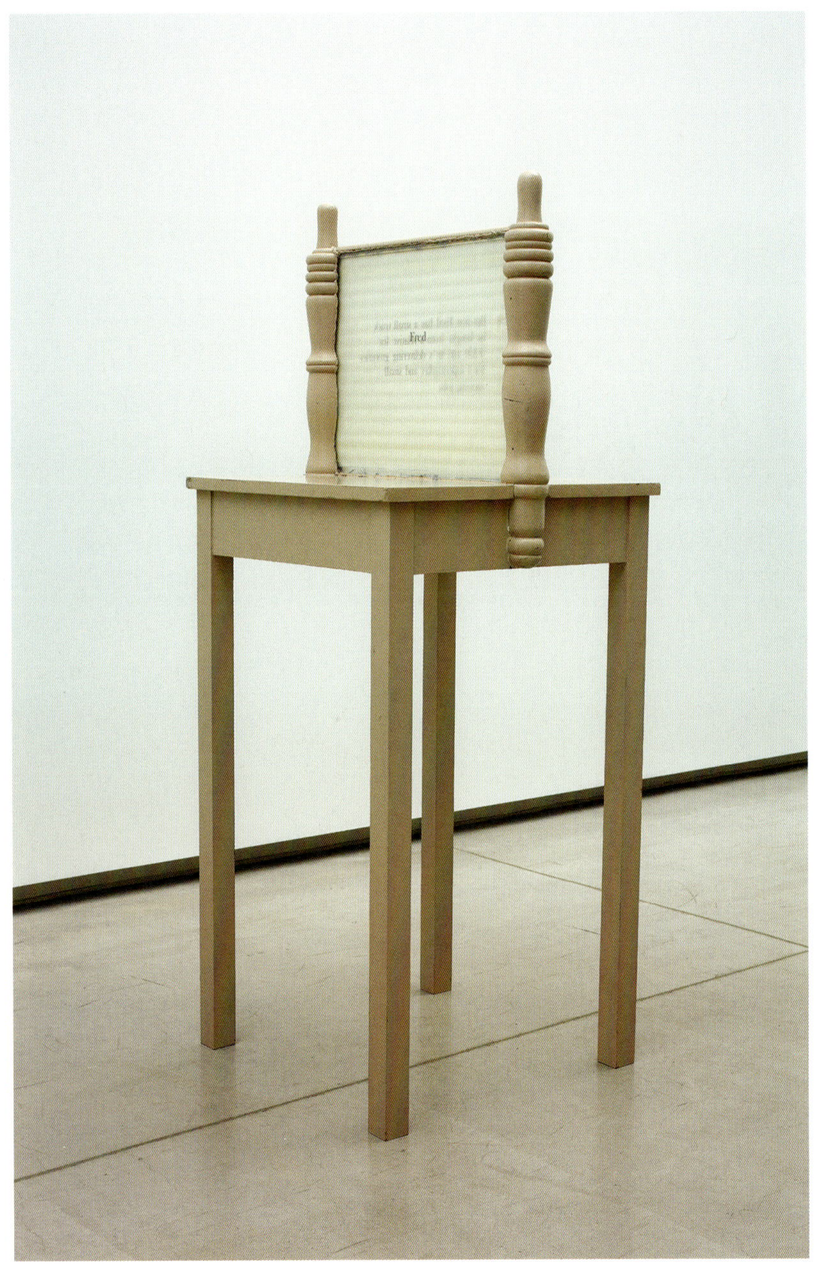

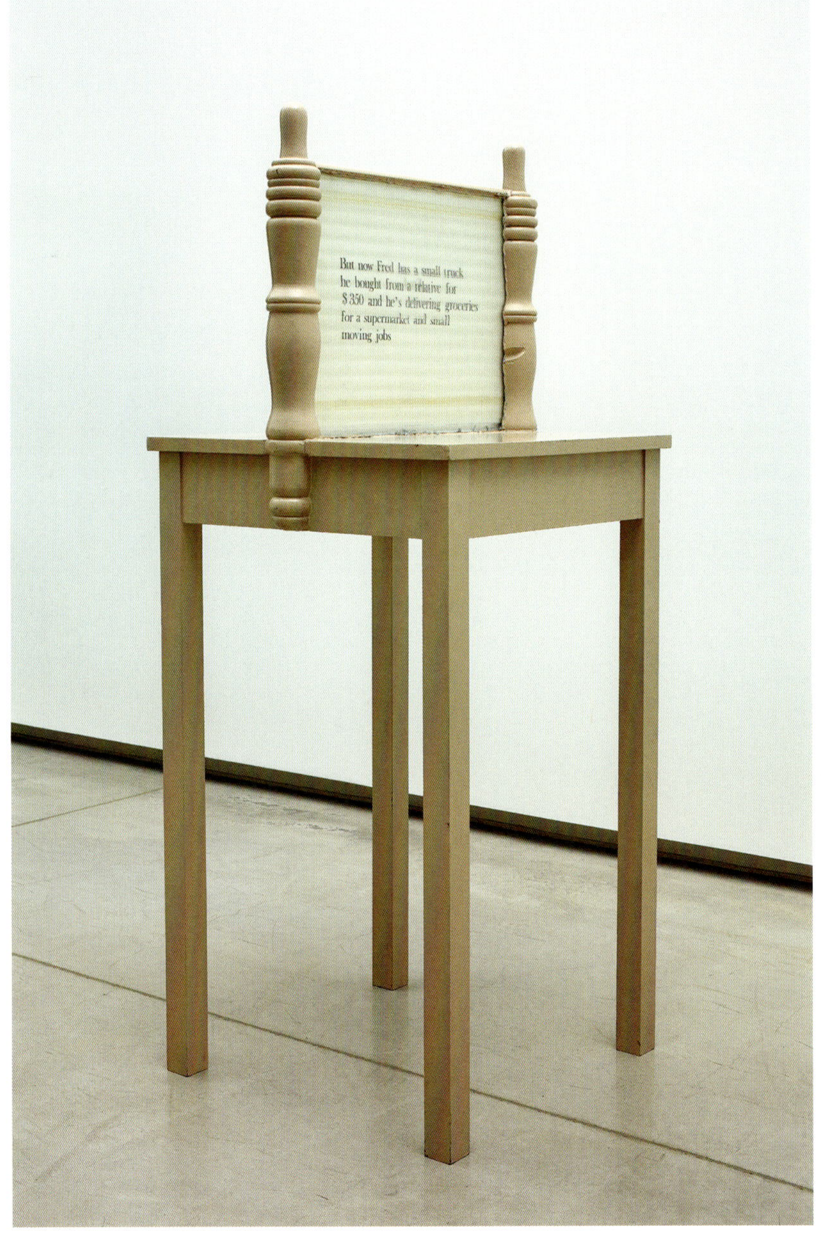

Murray Favro

Welded Steel Guitar, 1979
Steel, leather, and electric guitar hardware
51 × 97.5 × 6.3 cm
Estate of the late Marie LeSueur Fleming, 1998

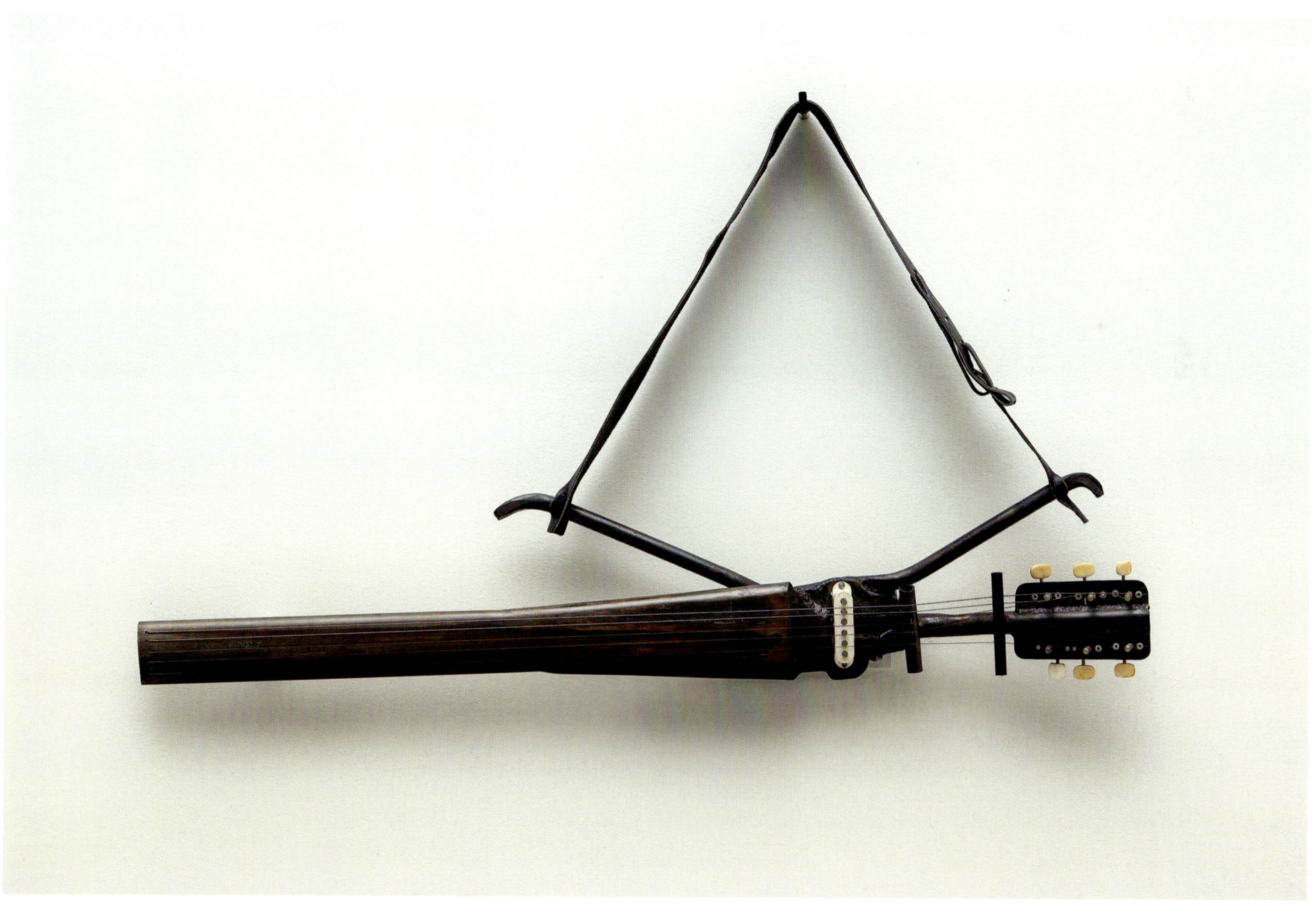

The Clichettes (Louise Garfield, Janice Hladki, and Johanna Householder)

Up Against the Wallpaper, 1988–1989
Performance set pieces and costumes by Renée Van Halm and The Clichettes
Video documentation by Michael Balser
Collection of the artists

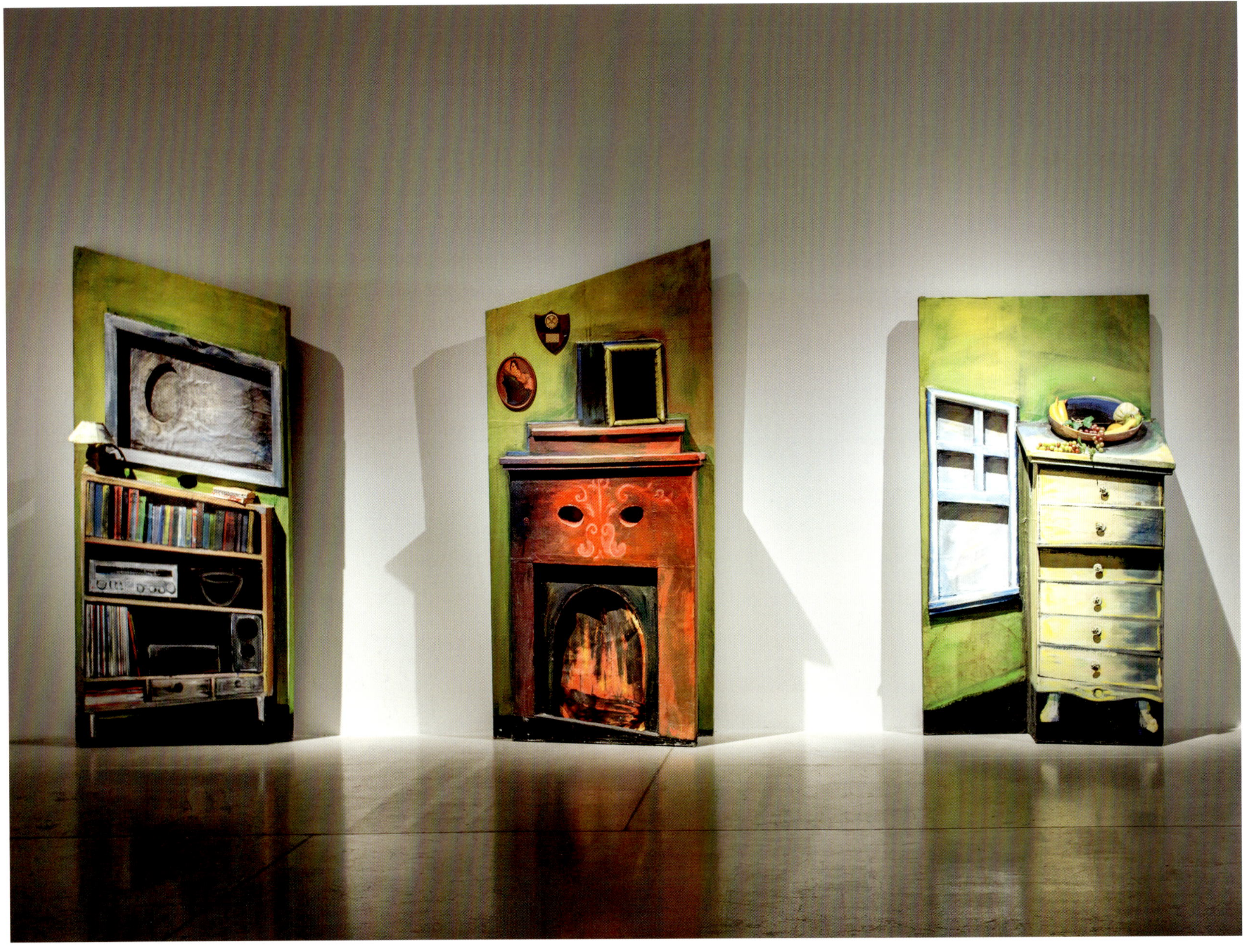

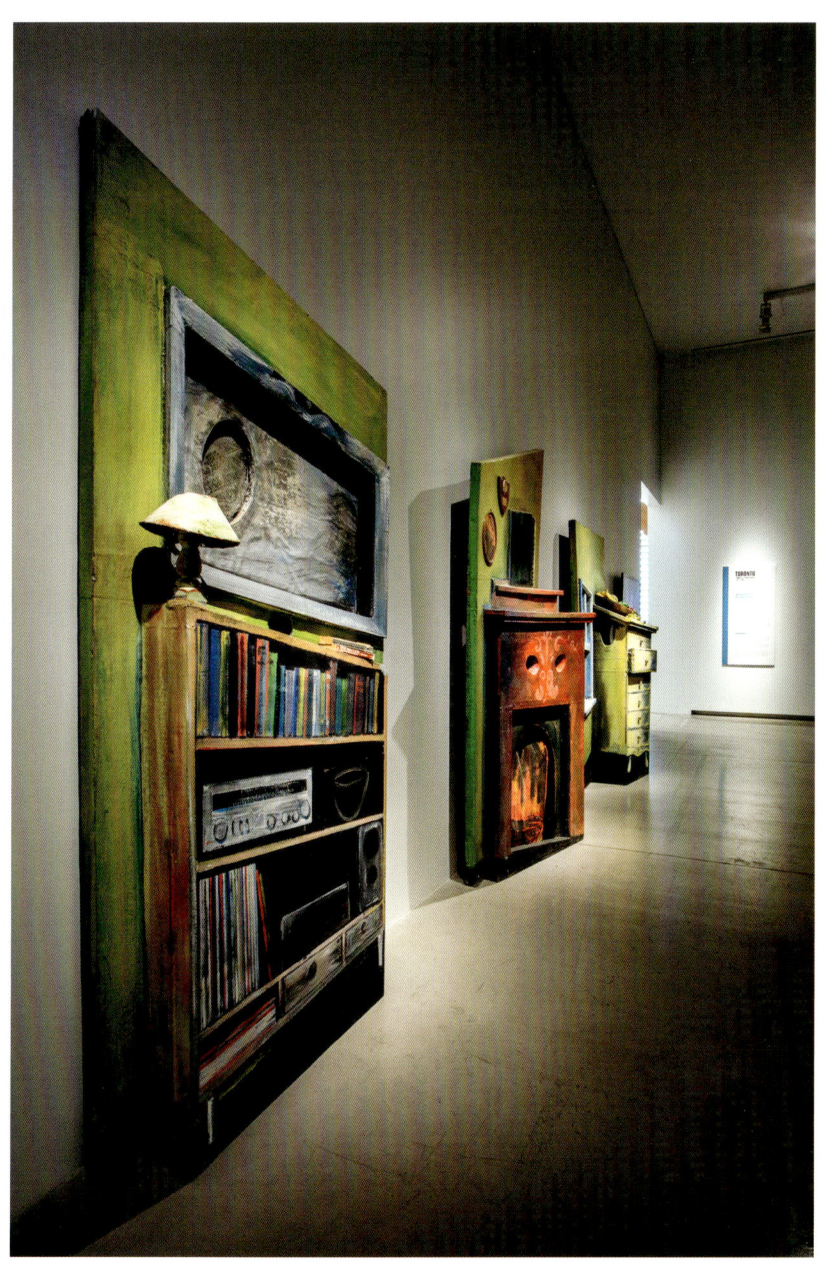

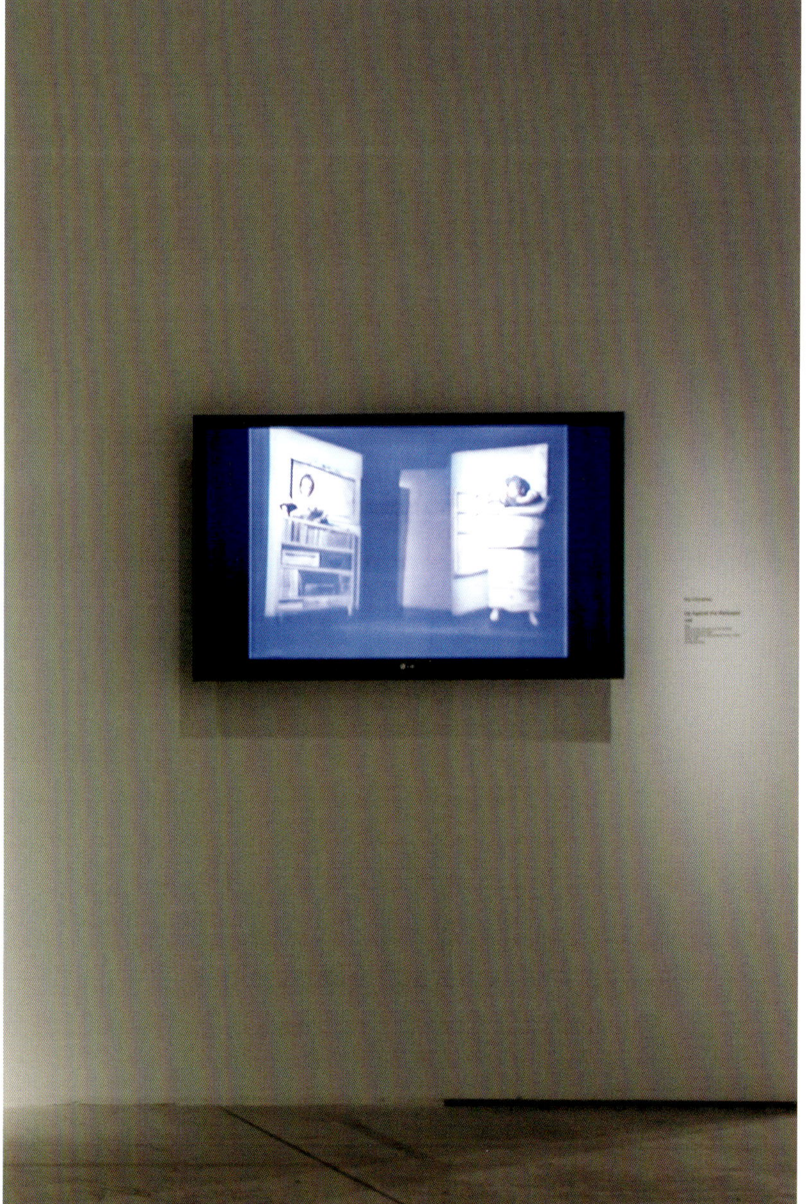

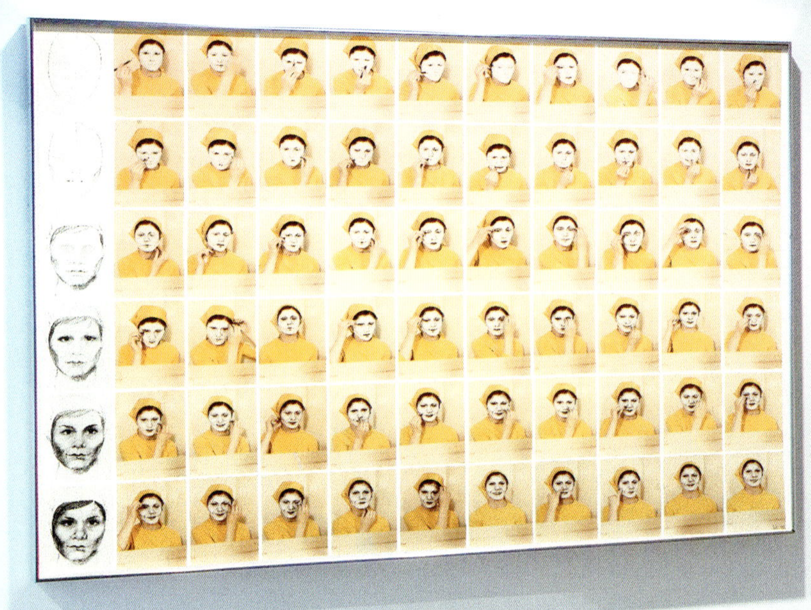

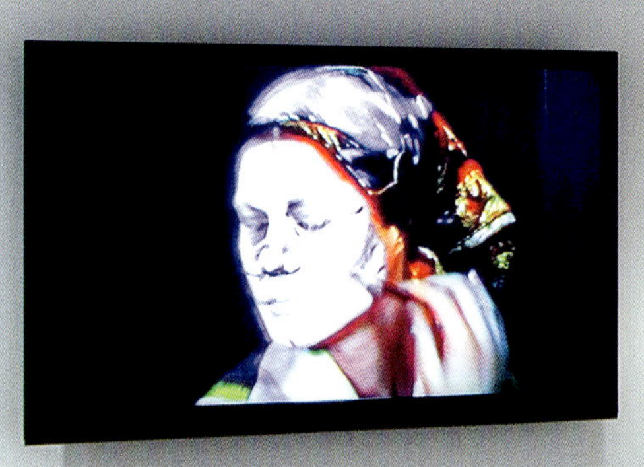

Ndoo-mzinchigan

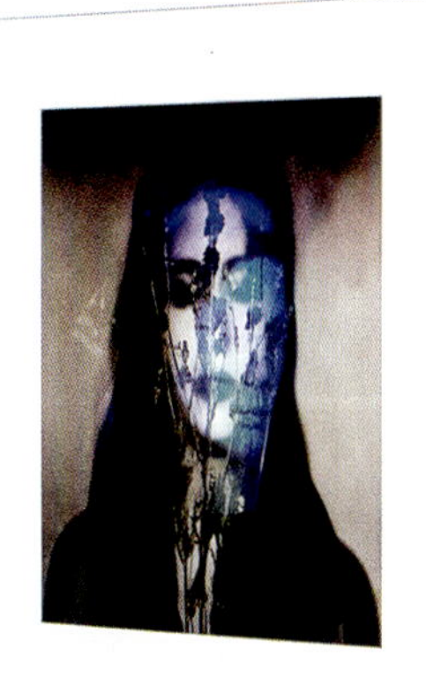
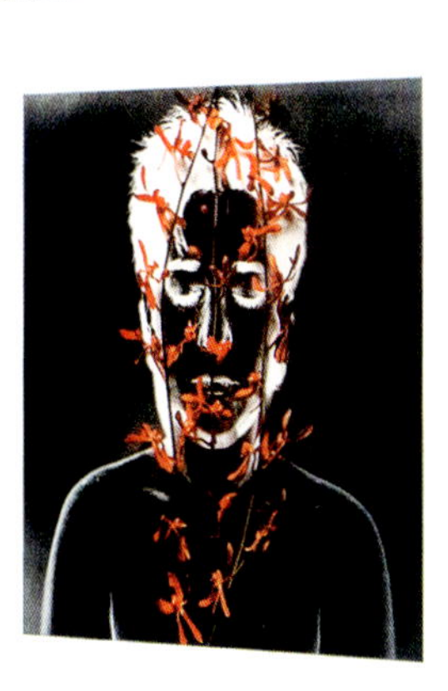
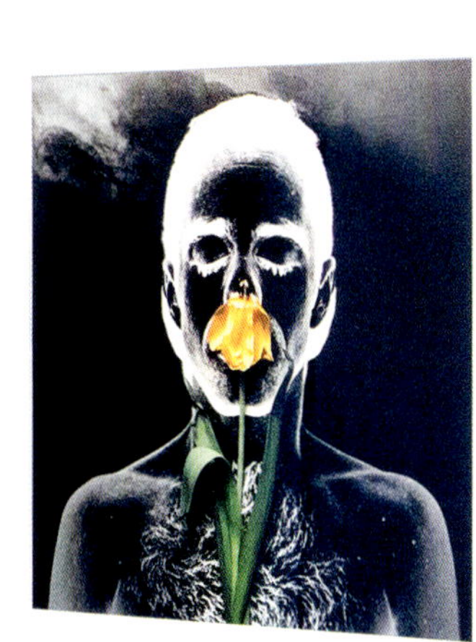
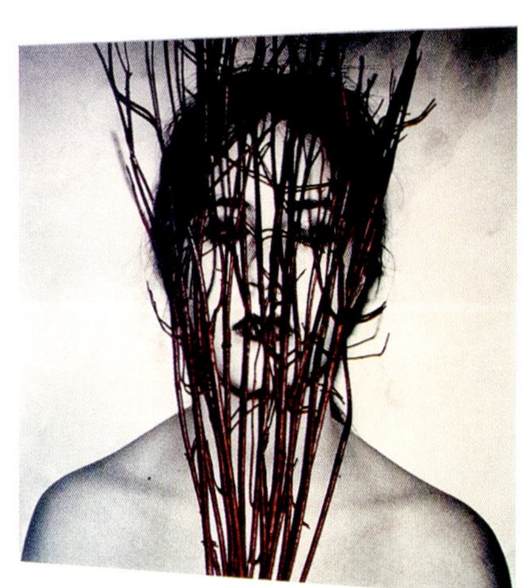

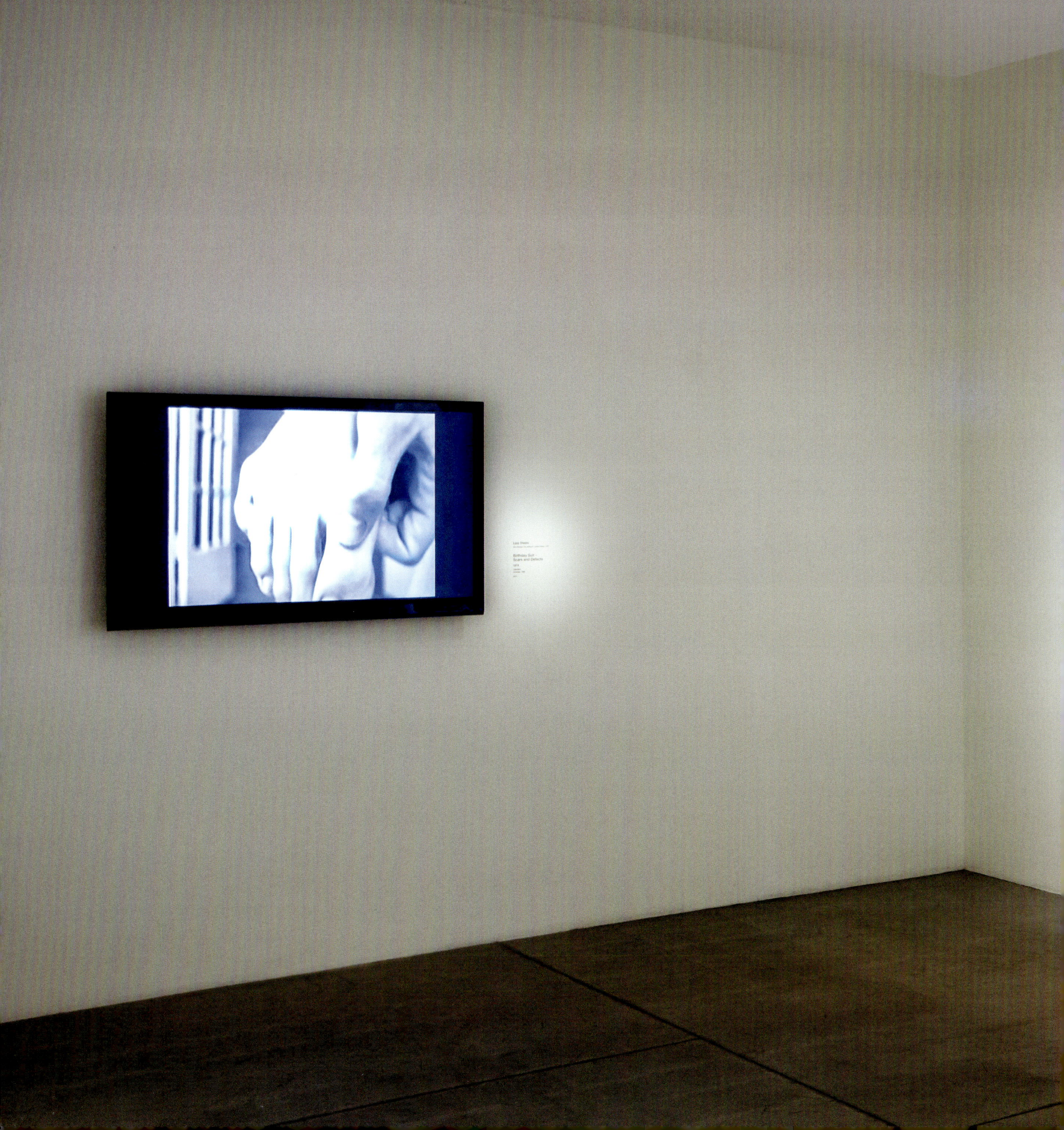

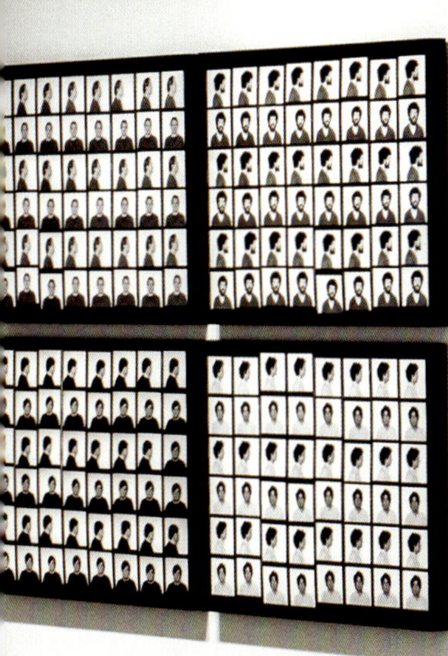
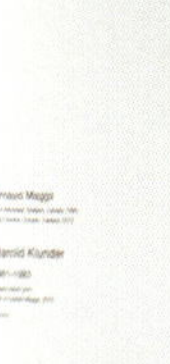
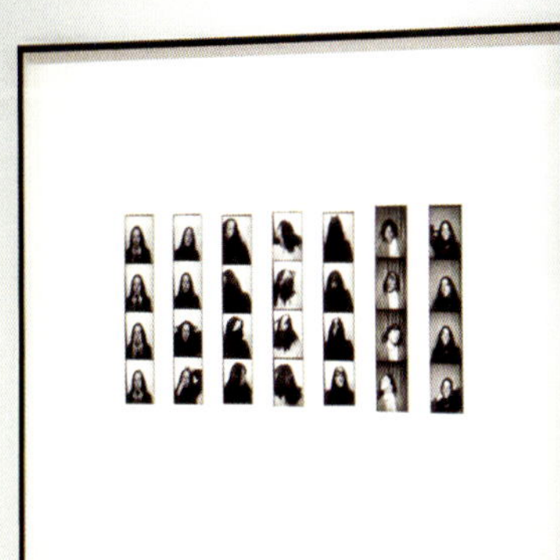
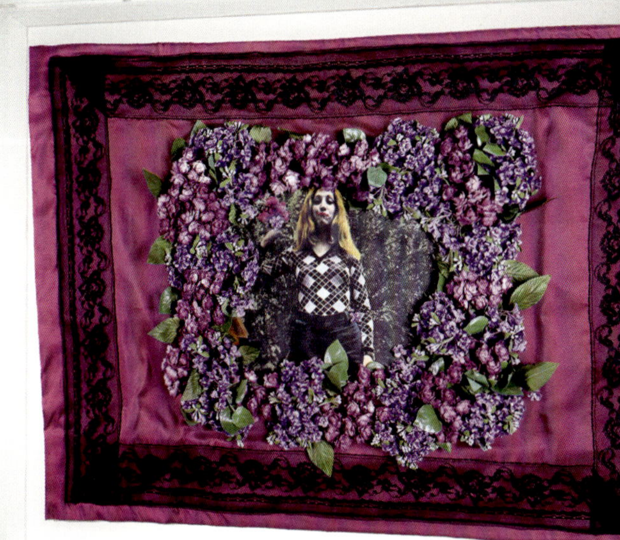

Barbara Astman

Carol Performing Lilac Tricks, 1974
Photograph on fabric mounted on
satin border of lace and cloth flowers
64.8 × 87.6 cm
Art Gallery of Ontario, purchase, 1975, 74/369

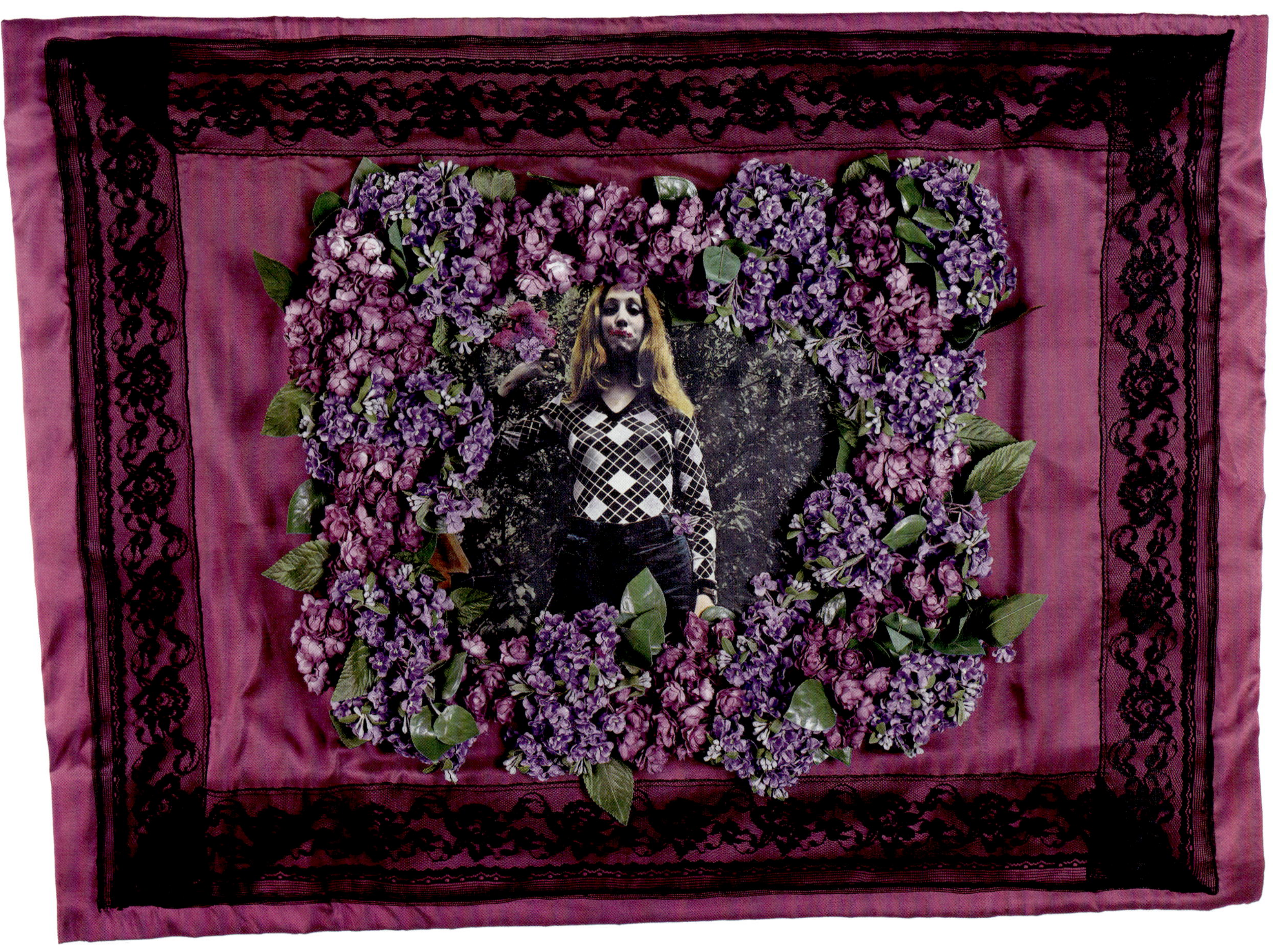

Photobooth Portraits, 1970s
Gelatin silver prints
20.5 × 4 cm each
Collection of the artist

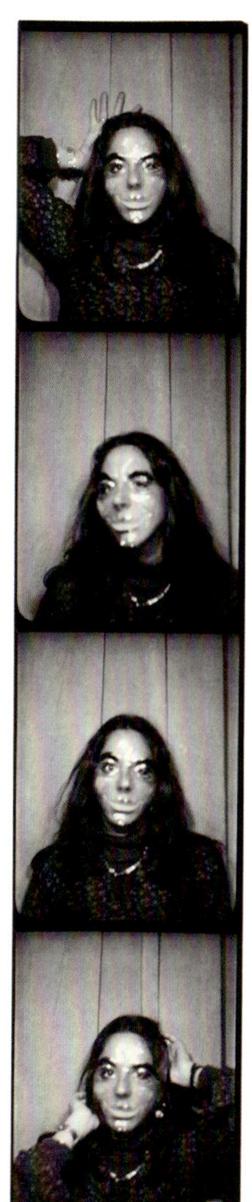
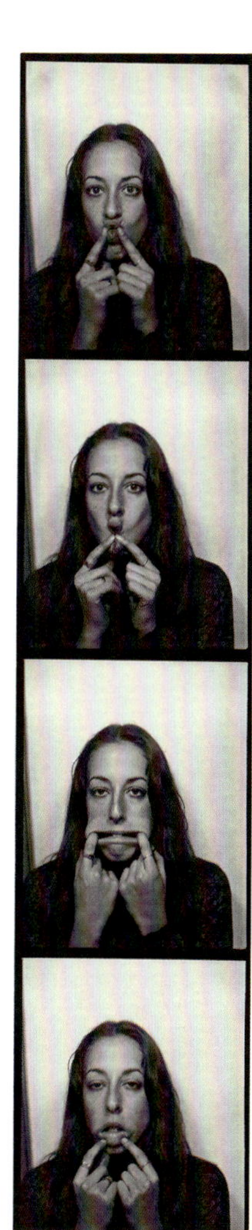
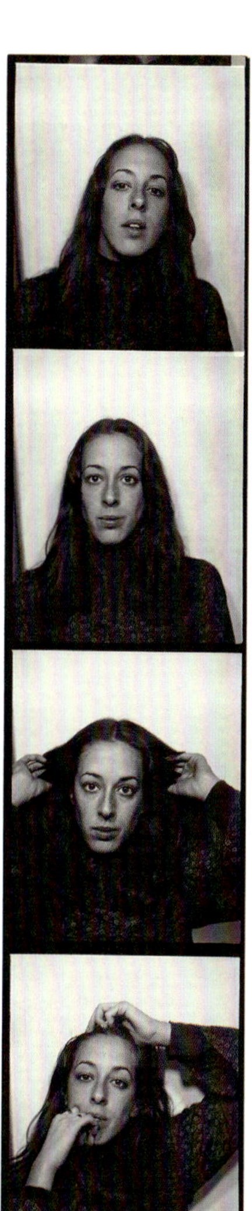
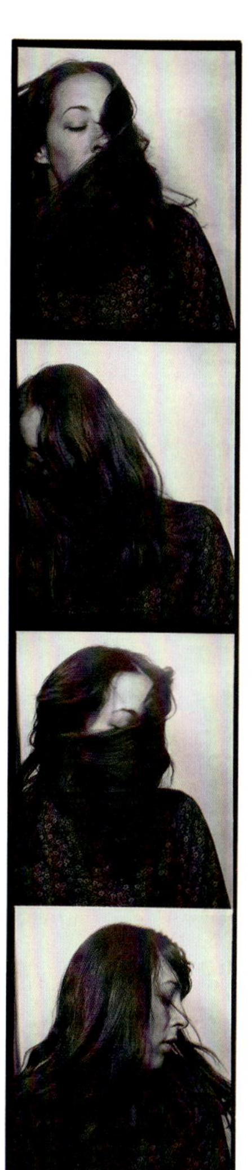
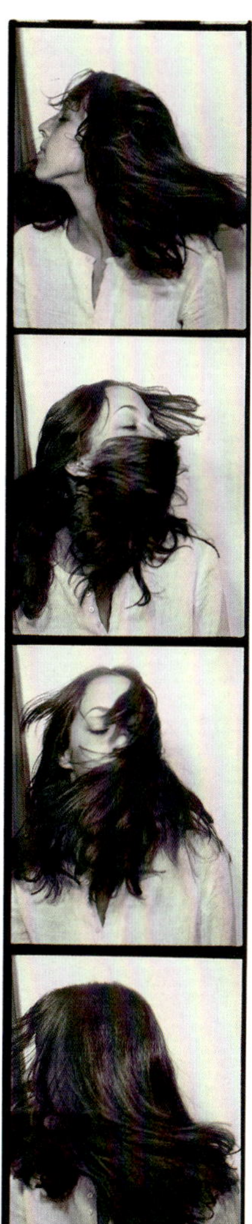
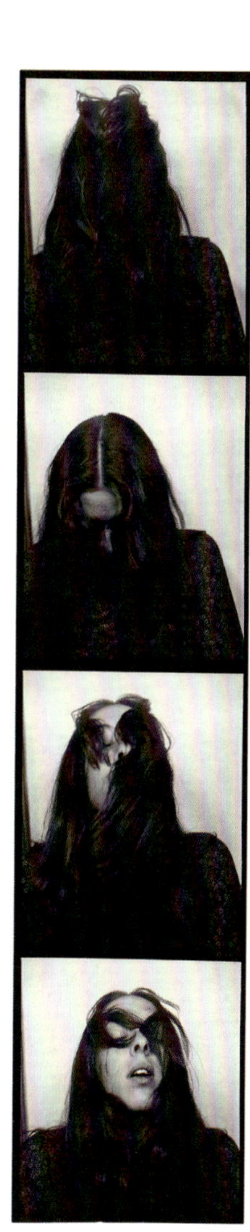
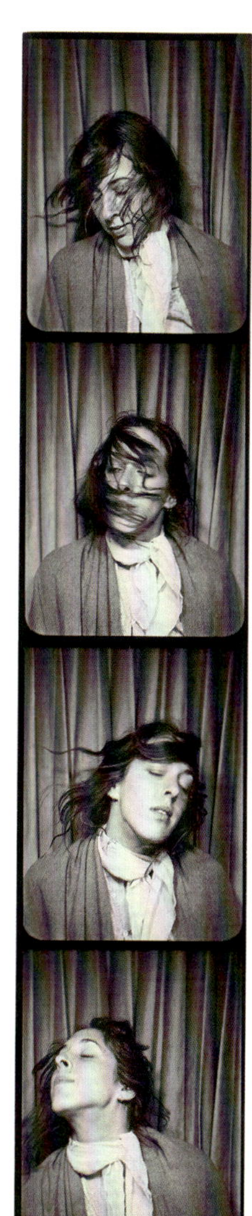

Suzy Lake

The Natural Way to Draw, 1975
Colour emulsion transfer on uncoated canvas
102.5 × 134 cm
Art Gallery of Ontario, gift of Nancy Hushion, 2009, 2009/107

The Natural Way to Draw, 1975
Colour video with sound, 15:00 min.
Art Gallery of Ontario, purchased with funds donated by AGO members, 2009, 2009/26

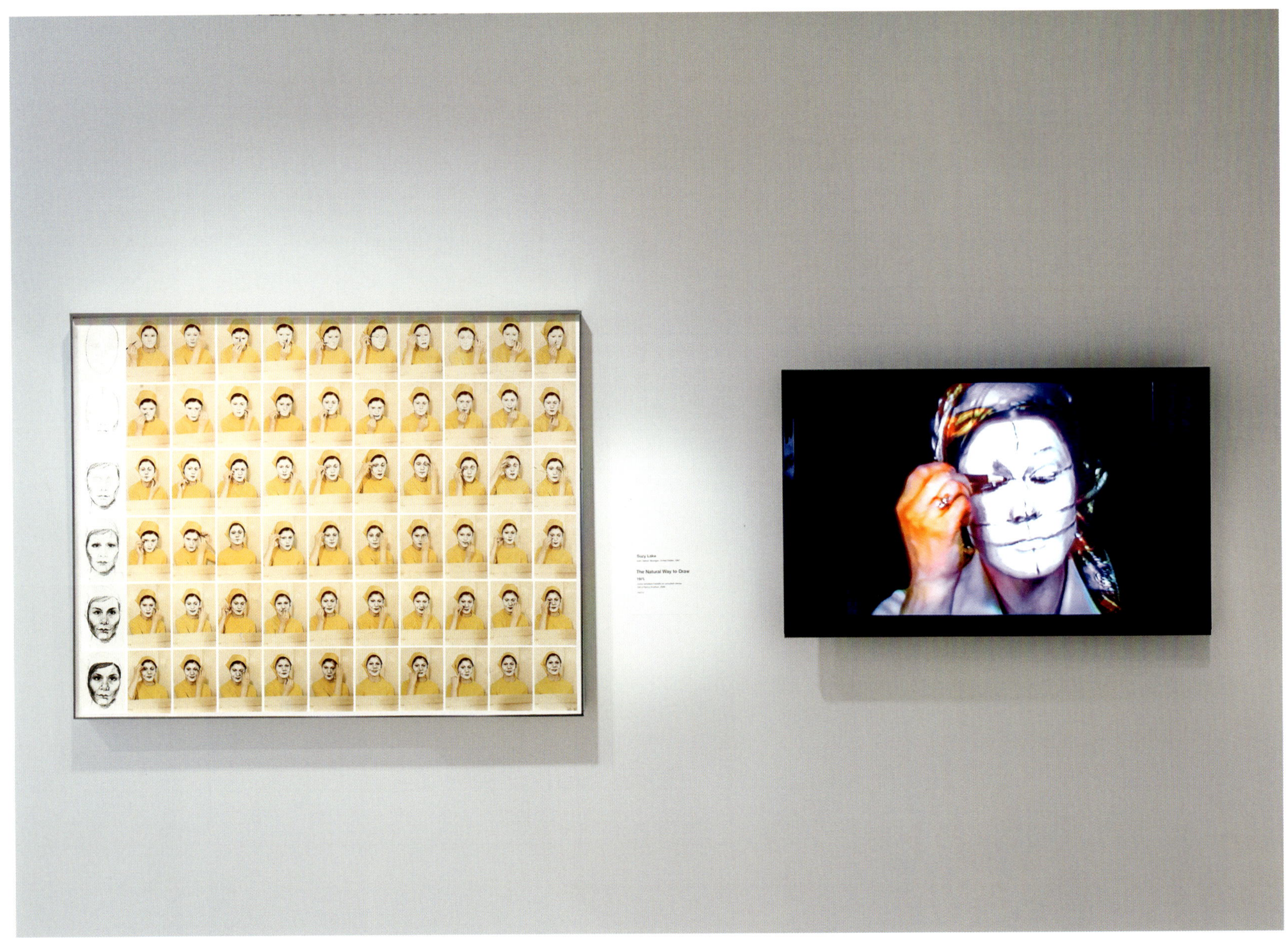

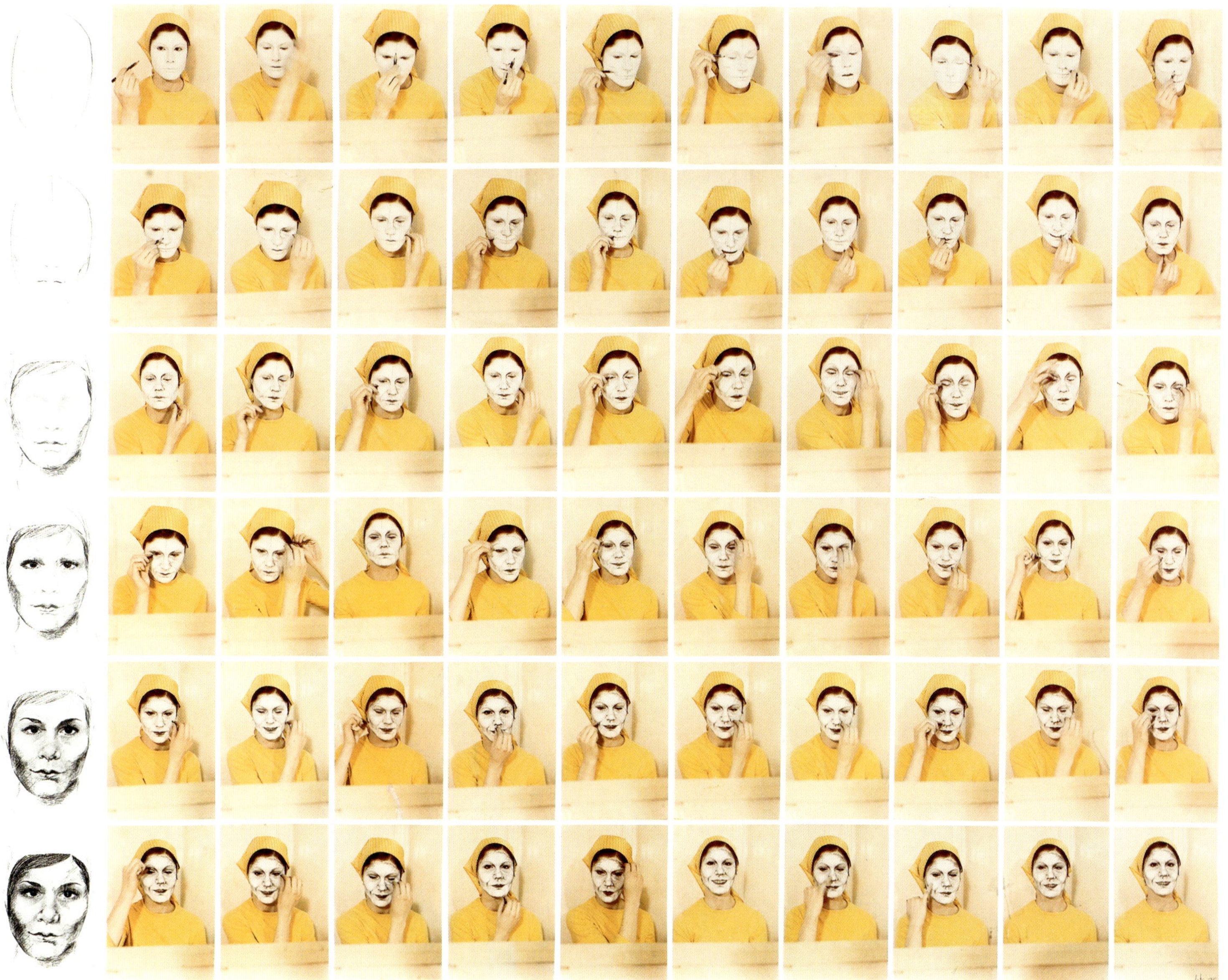

Arnaud Maggs

Colin Campbell, 1981–1984
Gelatin silver print
40.6 × 50.8 cm
Art Gallery of Ontario, gift of Caitlan Maggs, 2013, 2013/291

Jaan Poldaas, 1981–1983
Gelatin silver print
40.6 × 50.8 cm
Art Gallery of Ontario, gift of Caitlan Maggs, 2013, 2013/296

Geoffrey James, 1981–1983
Gelatin silver print
40.6 × 50.8 cm
Art Gallery of Ontario, gift of Caitlan Maggs, 2013, 2013/293

Harold Klunder, 1981–1983
Gelatin silver print
40.6 × 50.8 cm
Art Gallery of Ontario, gift of Caitlan Maggs, 2013, 2013/294

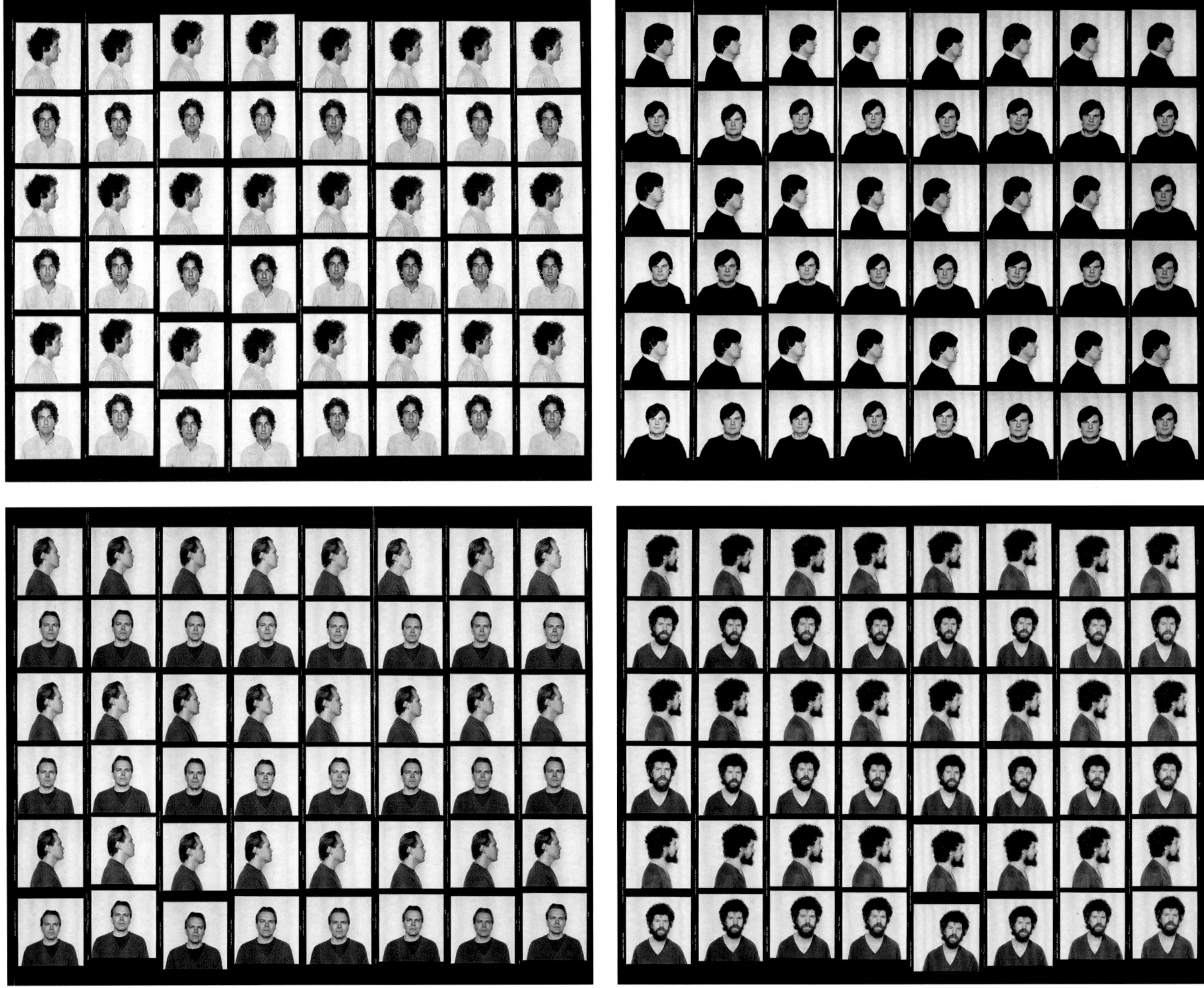

Lisa Steele

Birthday Suit—Scars and Defects, 1974
Videotape, 13:20 min.
Art Gallery of Ontario, purchase, 1988, 88/101

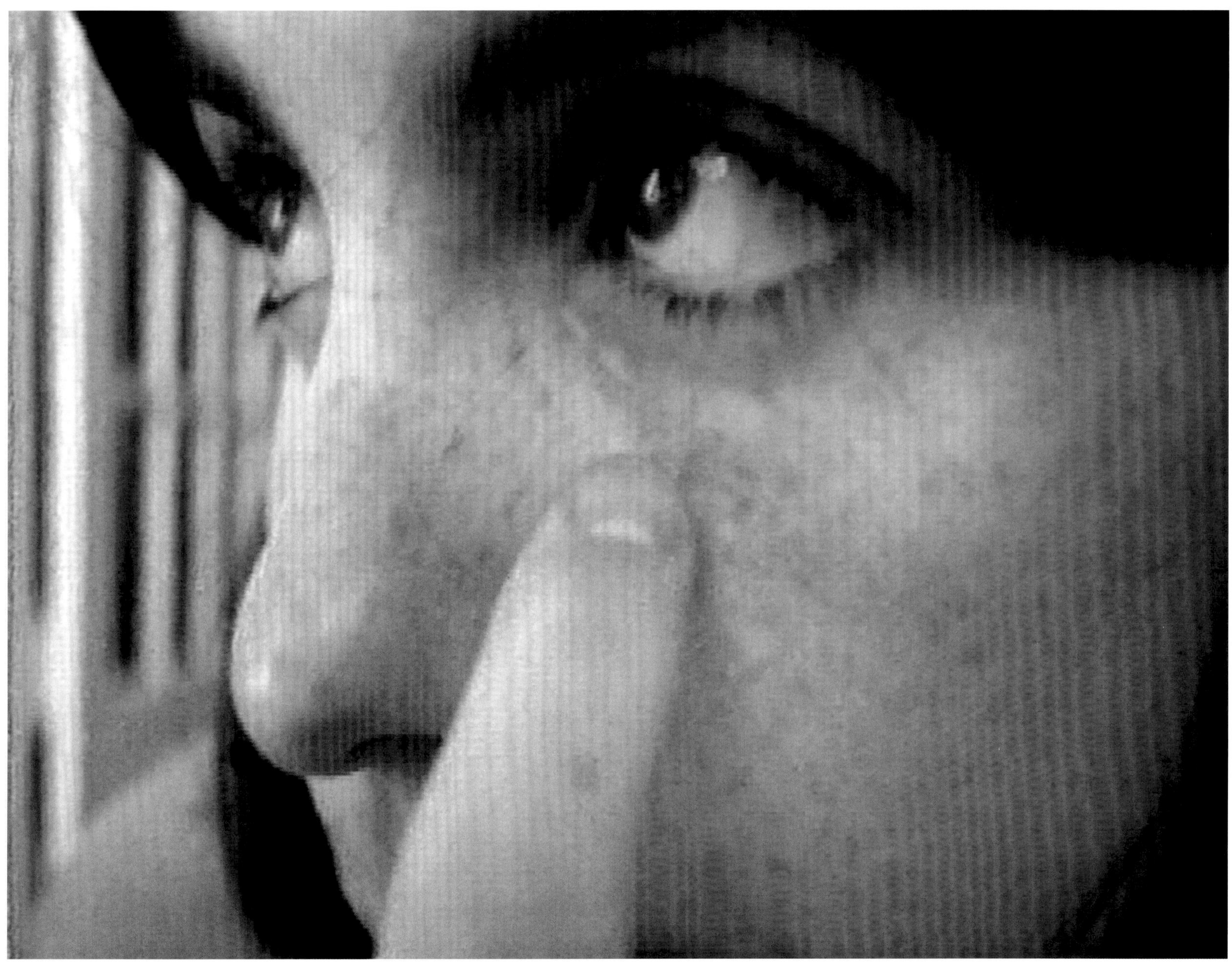

David Rasmus

Untitled (Lisan), 1989
Chromogenic print
68.6 × 68.6 cm
Collection of the artist, courtesy Paul Petro Contemporary Art, Toronto

Untitled (Nina), 1989
Chromogenic print
68.6 × 68.6 cm
Collection of the artist, courtesy Paul Petro Contemporary Art, Toronto

Untitled (Rob), 1989
Chromogenic print
68.6 × 68.6 cm
Collection of the artist, courtesy Paul Petro Contemporary Art, Toronto

Untitled (Lisan), 1989
Chromogenic print
68.6 × 68.6 cm
Collection of the artist, courtesy Paul Petro Contemporary Art, Toronto

Untitled (Tim), 1988
Chromogenic print
68.6 × 68.6 cm
Collection of the artist, courtesy Paul Petro Contemporary Art, Toronto

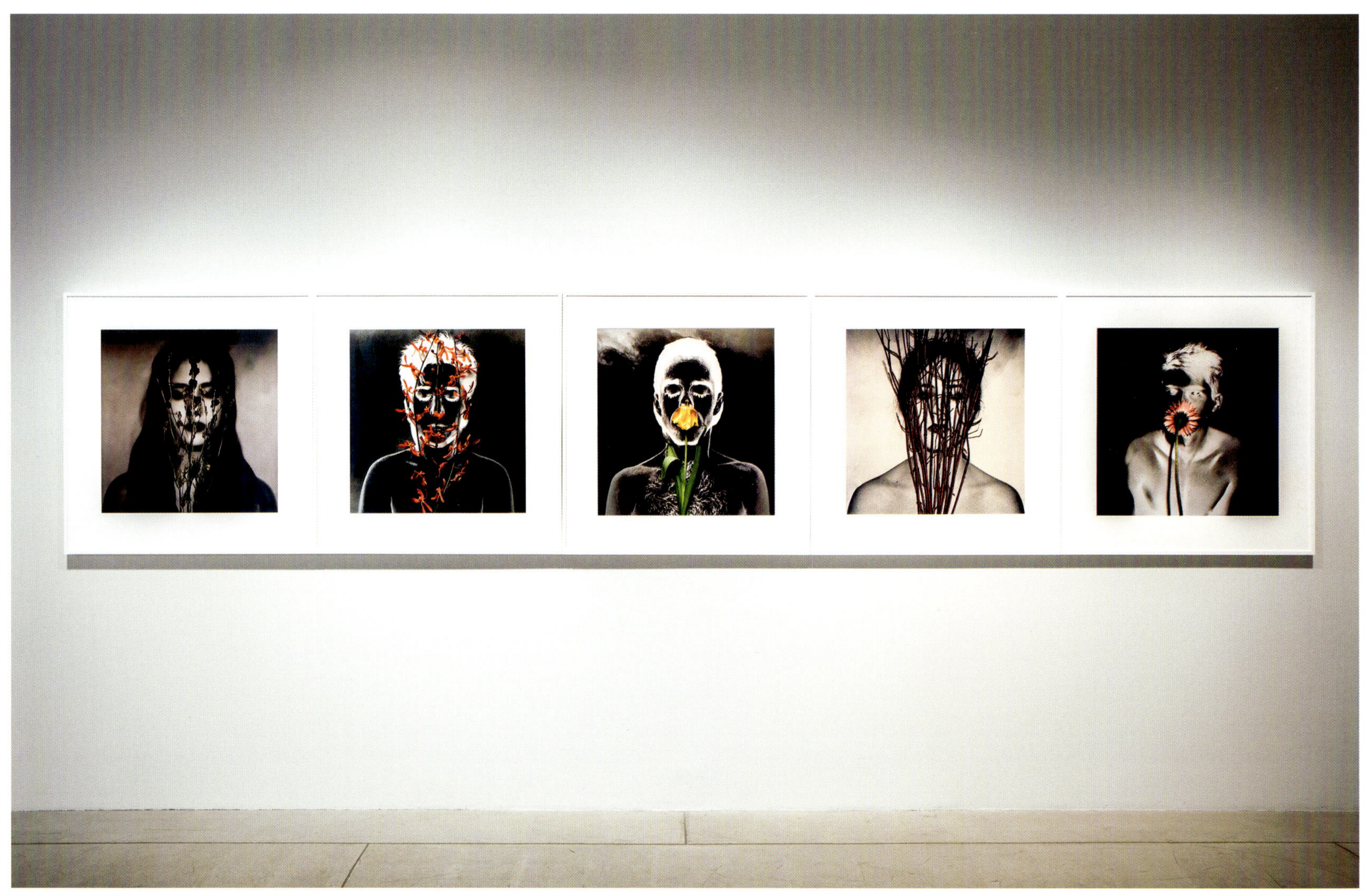

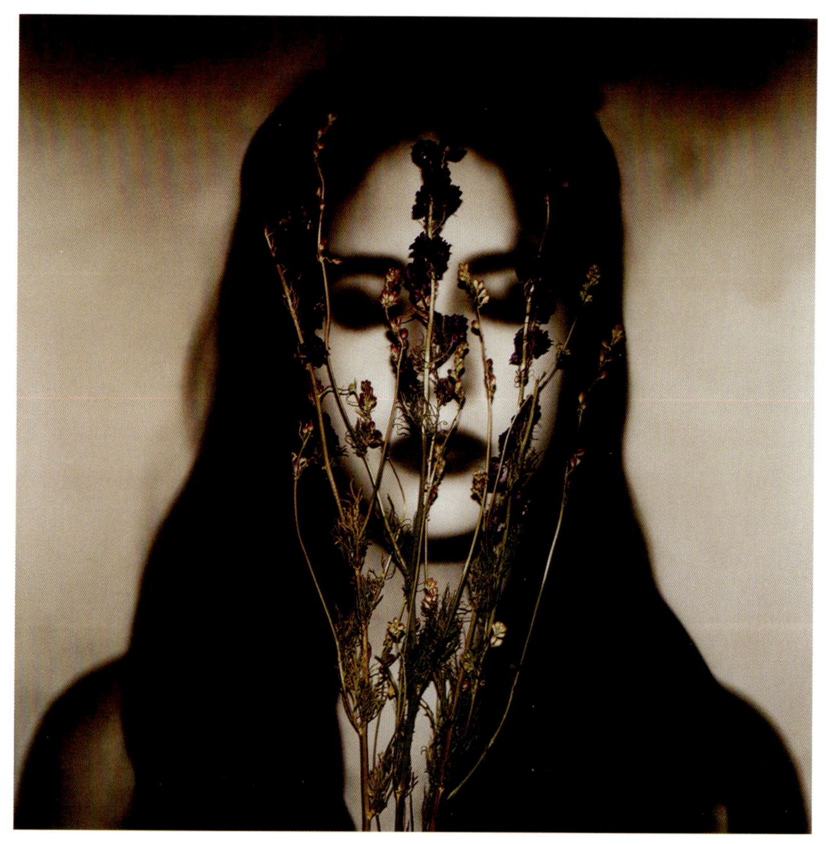
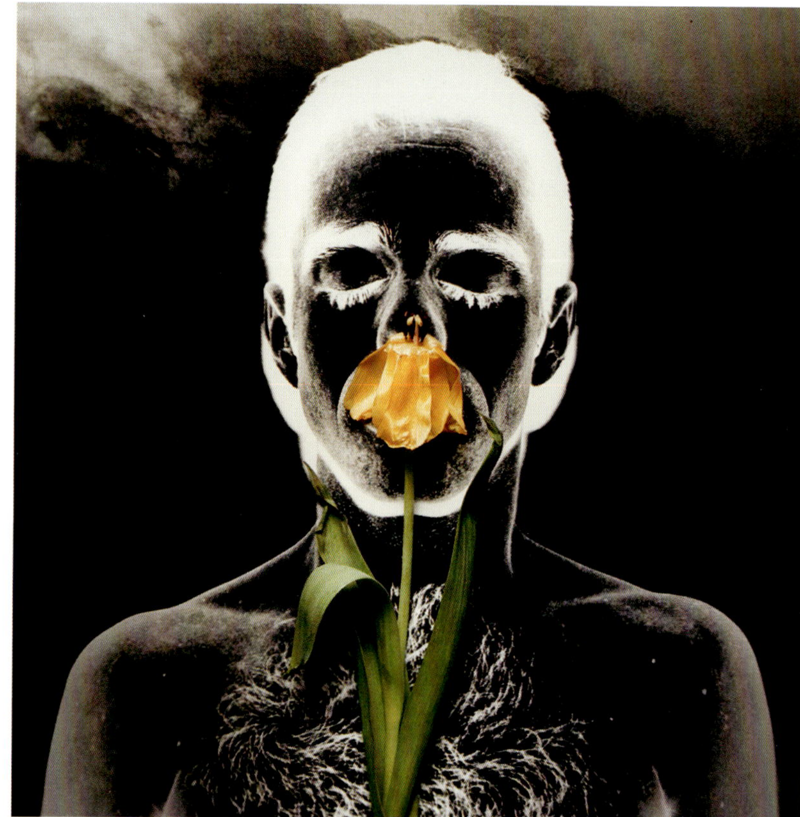
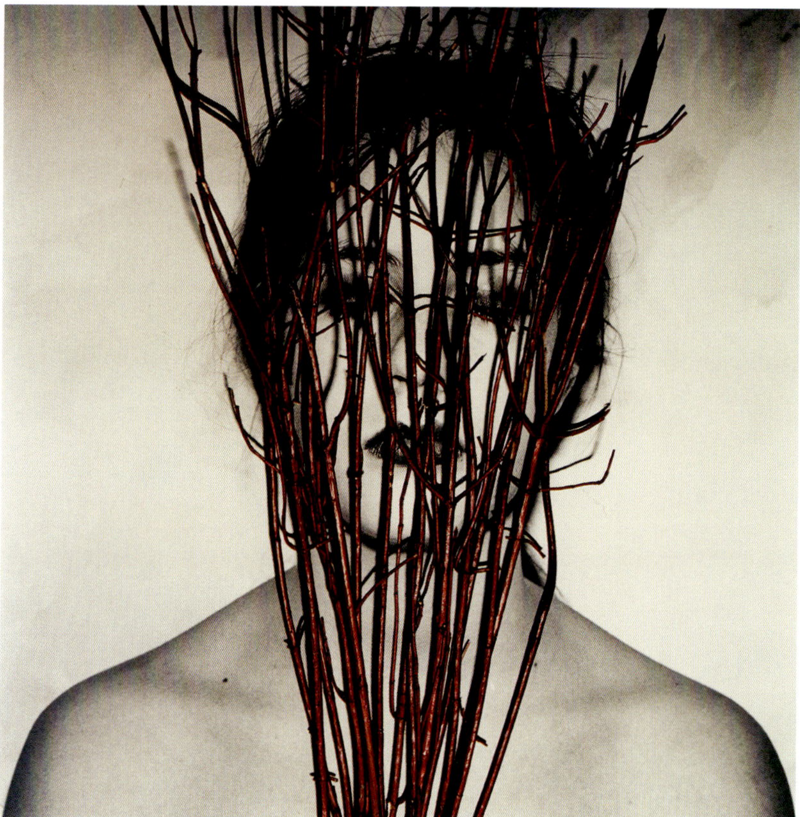
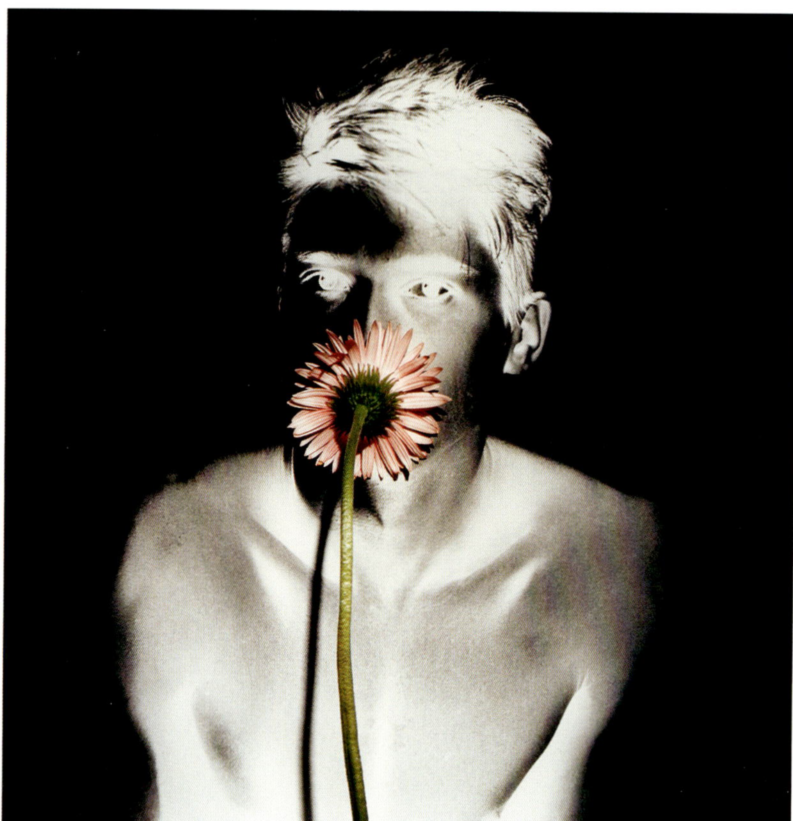

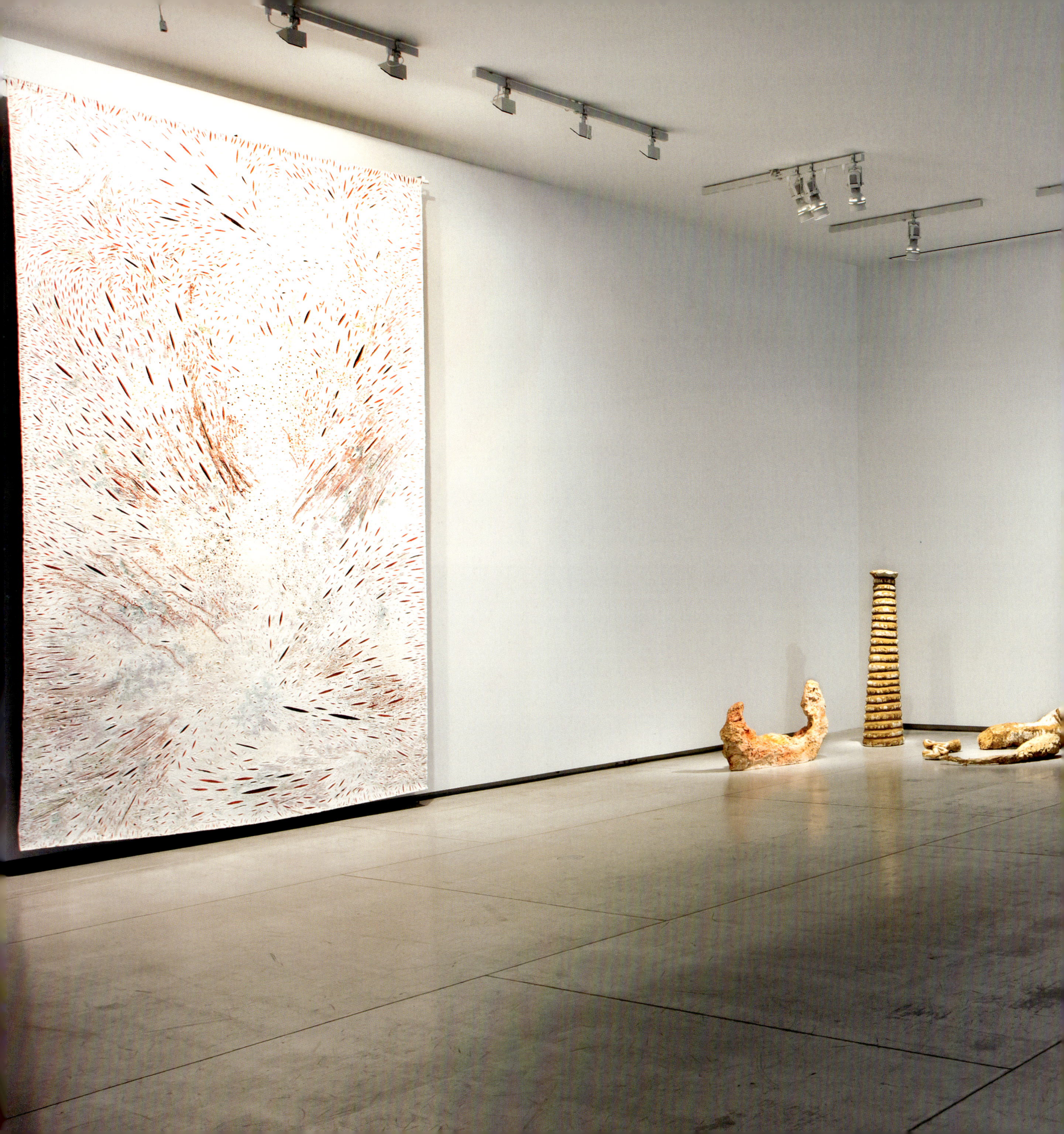

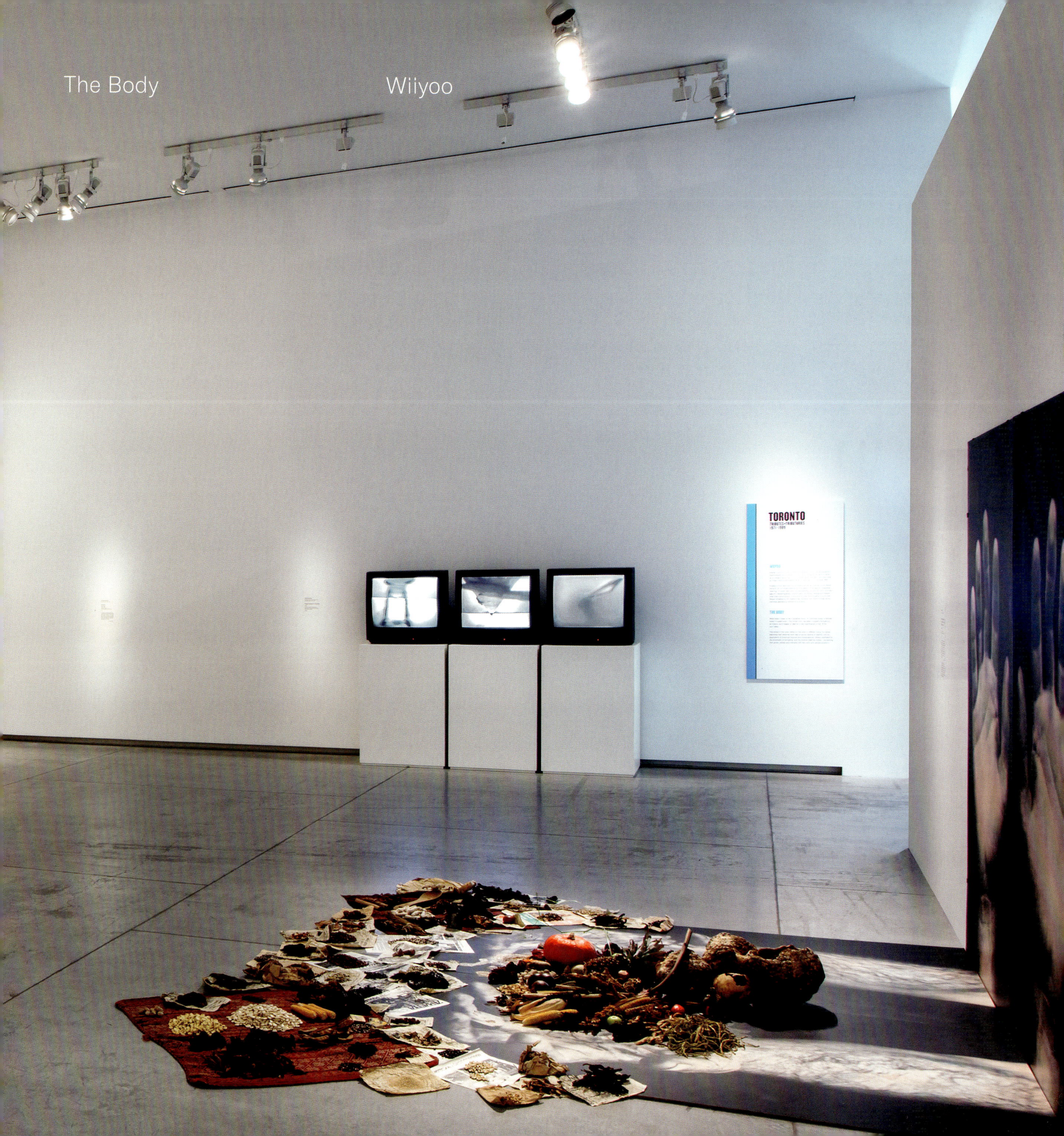

The Body

Wiiyoo

Jamelie Hassan

Vitrine 448, 1988
Mixed media installation
309.9 × 950 × 27.9 cm
Art Gallery of Ontario, gift of Jamelie Hassan, 2016, 2016/441

Vitrine 448 (artist book), 1987 (not shown here)
Xerox printing and gelatin silver prints
21.5 × 30.2 cm each sheet
Art Gallery of Ontario, gift from The Peggy Lownsbrough Fund, 1988, 88/8.1-.19

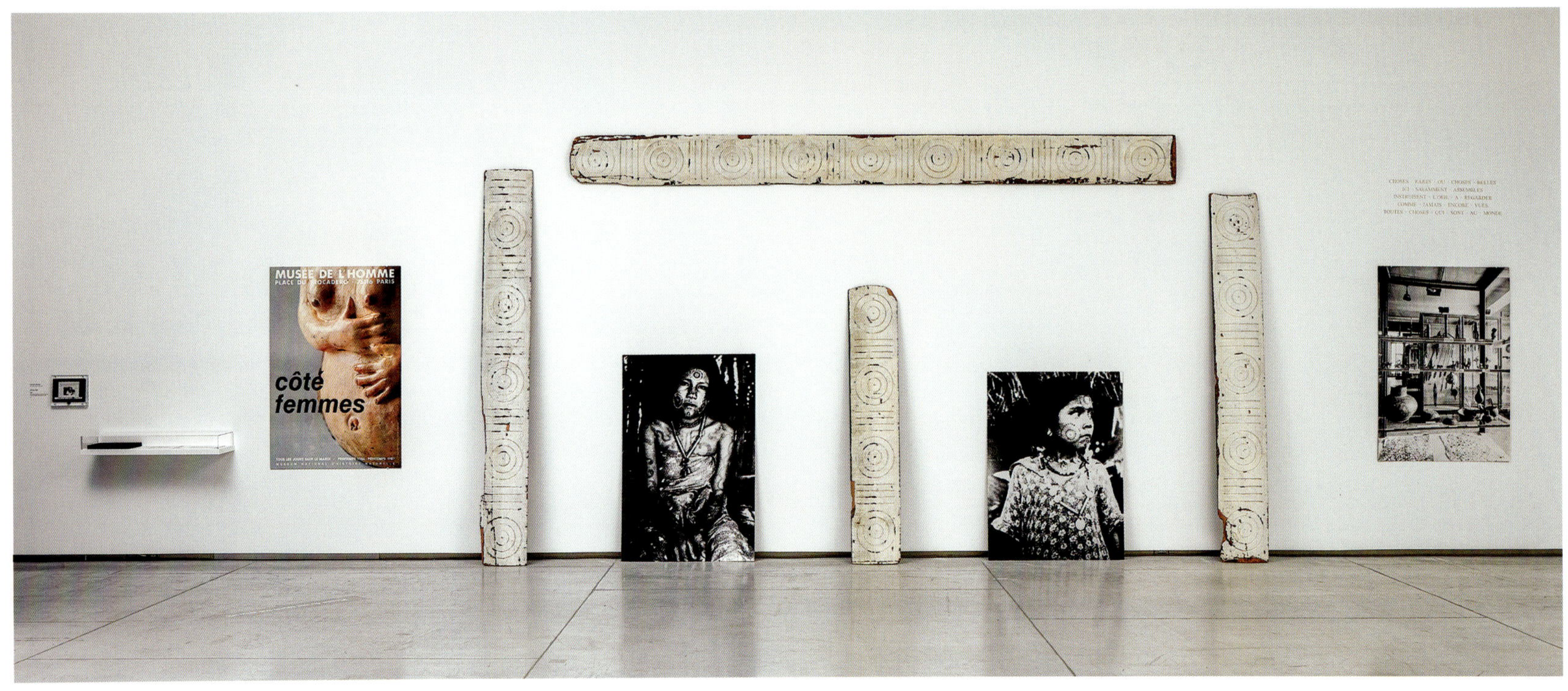

Catharine MacTavish

Arms Race, 1984
Acrylic, glass and plastic beads, and metal grommets
471 × 293 cm
Art Gallery of Ontario, gift of Gerald and Hyla Prenick, 2008, 2009/153

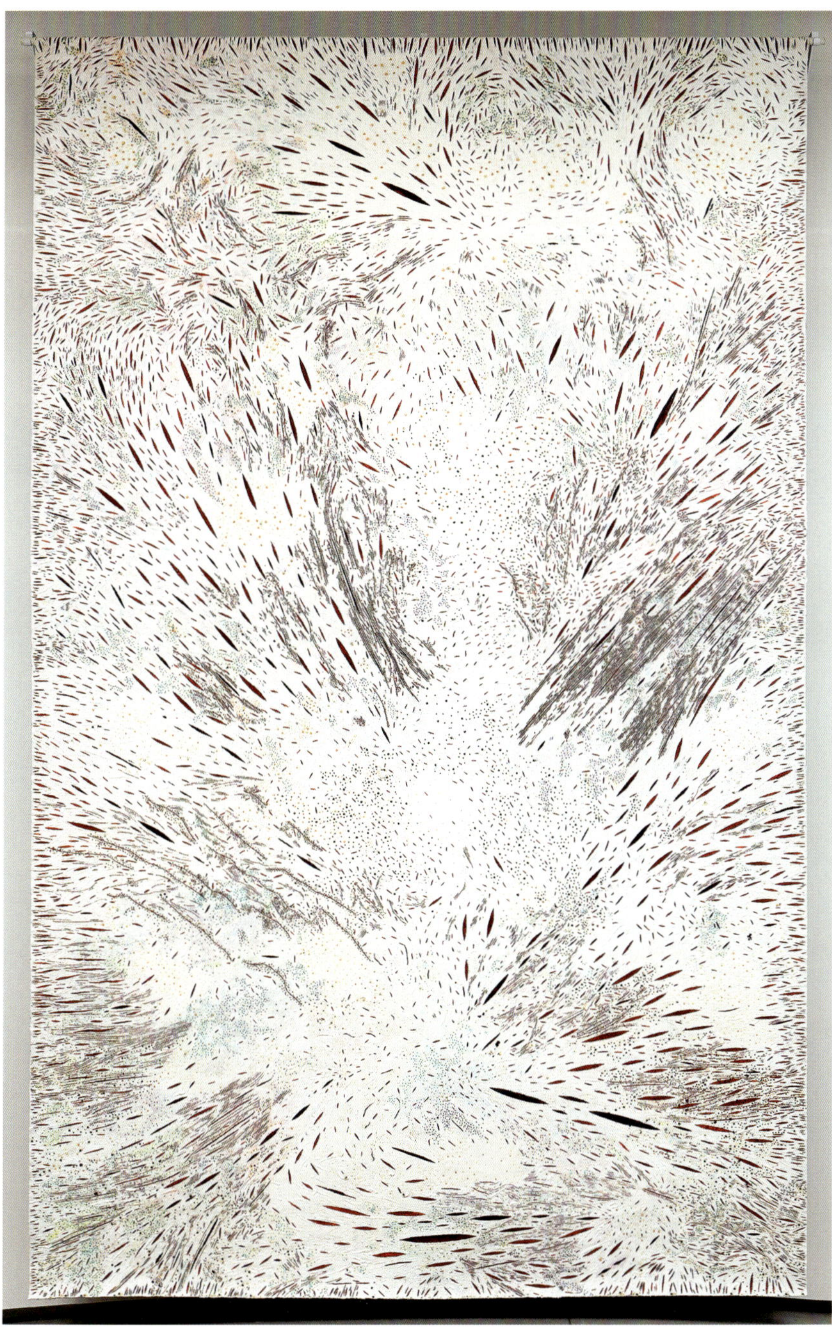

Ron Benner

Anthro-Apologies (And the trees grew inwards—for Manuel Scorza), 1979–1980
Gelatin silver prints and photo-oil colours
Art Gallery of Ontario, gift from
The Peggy Lownsbrough Fund, 1994, 94/299

"I guess the first work that specifically deals with food crops, and the politics of food crops, was *And the trees grew inwards—for Manuel Scorza*...It came out of visiting the market in Lima... I realized later, as soon as I got back home, that I had all this information, and that there were very few other people who knew about this diversity and that it came from all Native people." —Ron Benner

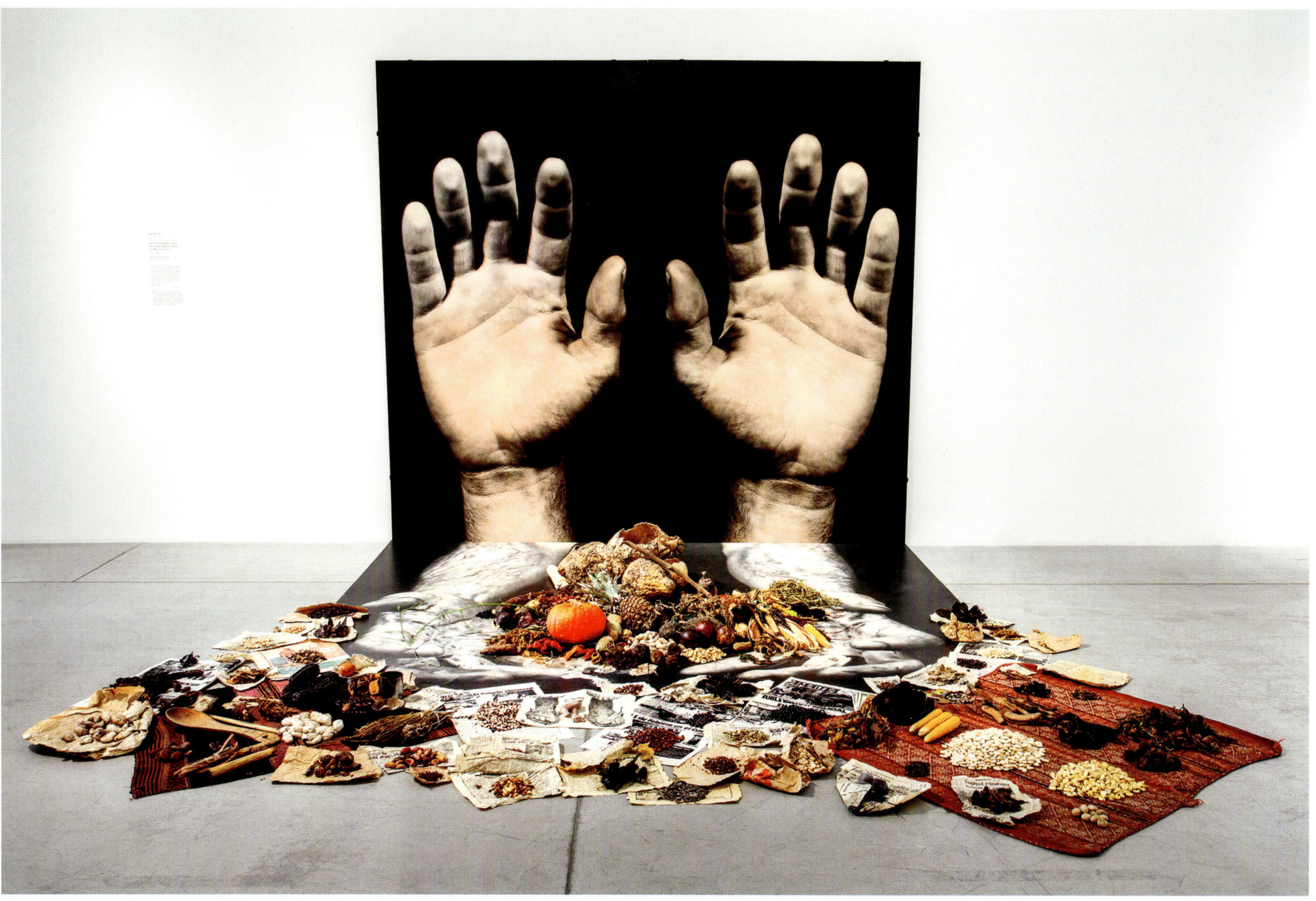

Louise Noguchi

Corpus, 1983–1984
Clay, pigment, plaster, and oil
172.5 × 342.5 × 191 cm
Art Gallery of Ontario, gift of the Canada Council Art Bank, 2004, 2004/811

"My earliest work revolved around dreams I had had and how these dreams connected with the reality of the world…In all, I hope that my work looks at the structures behind reality and art to address the questions of what we hold as belief, at the present, and the power that this gives us." —Louise Noguchi

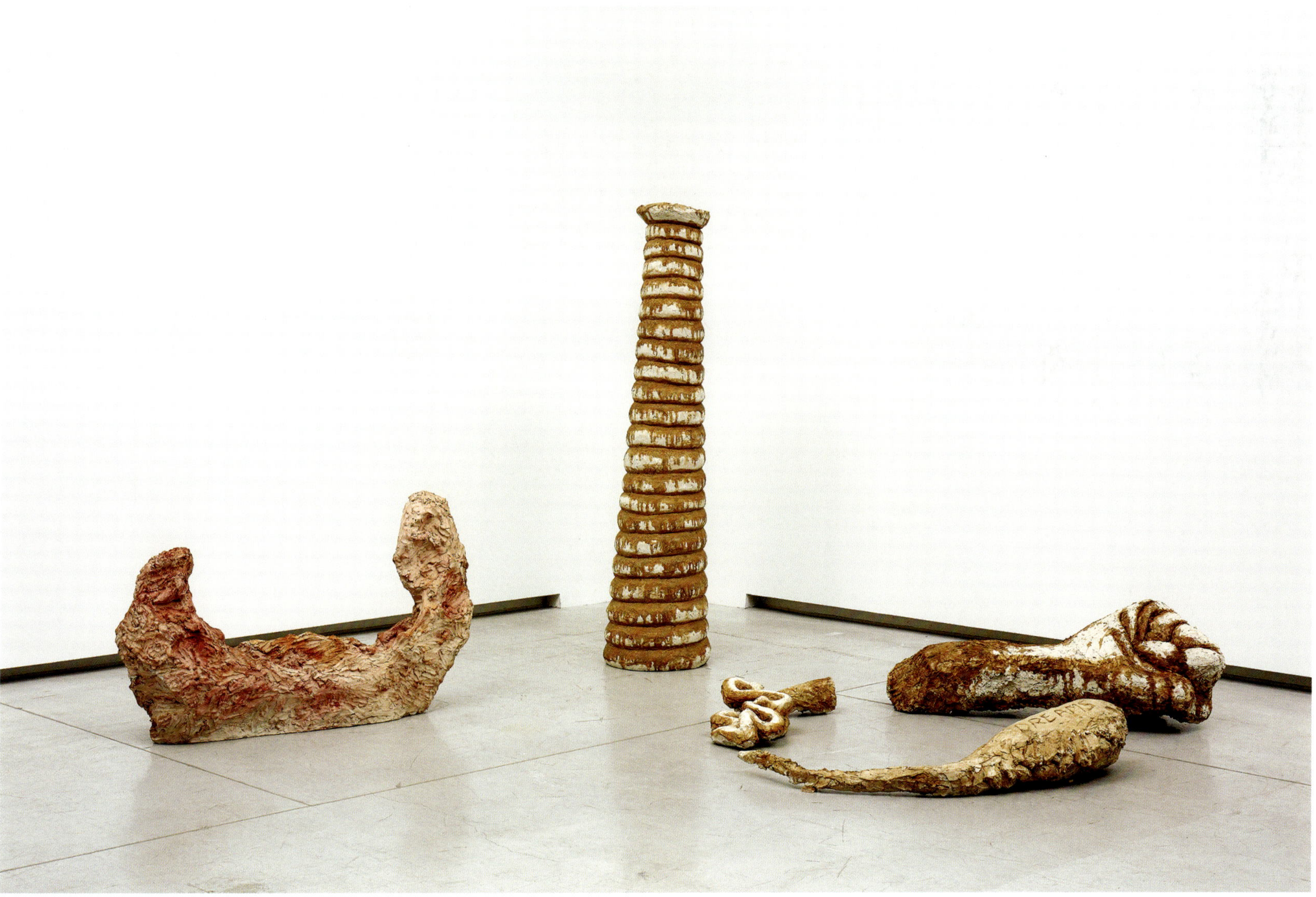

Noel Harding

Three Pieces for Circuits, 1975
Black and white videotape, three channels,
three-minute loops on three-quarter videocassette
Art Gallery of Ontario, gift of Noel Harding, 2002,
2002/10840

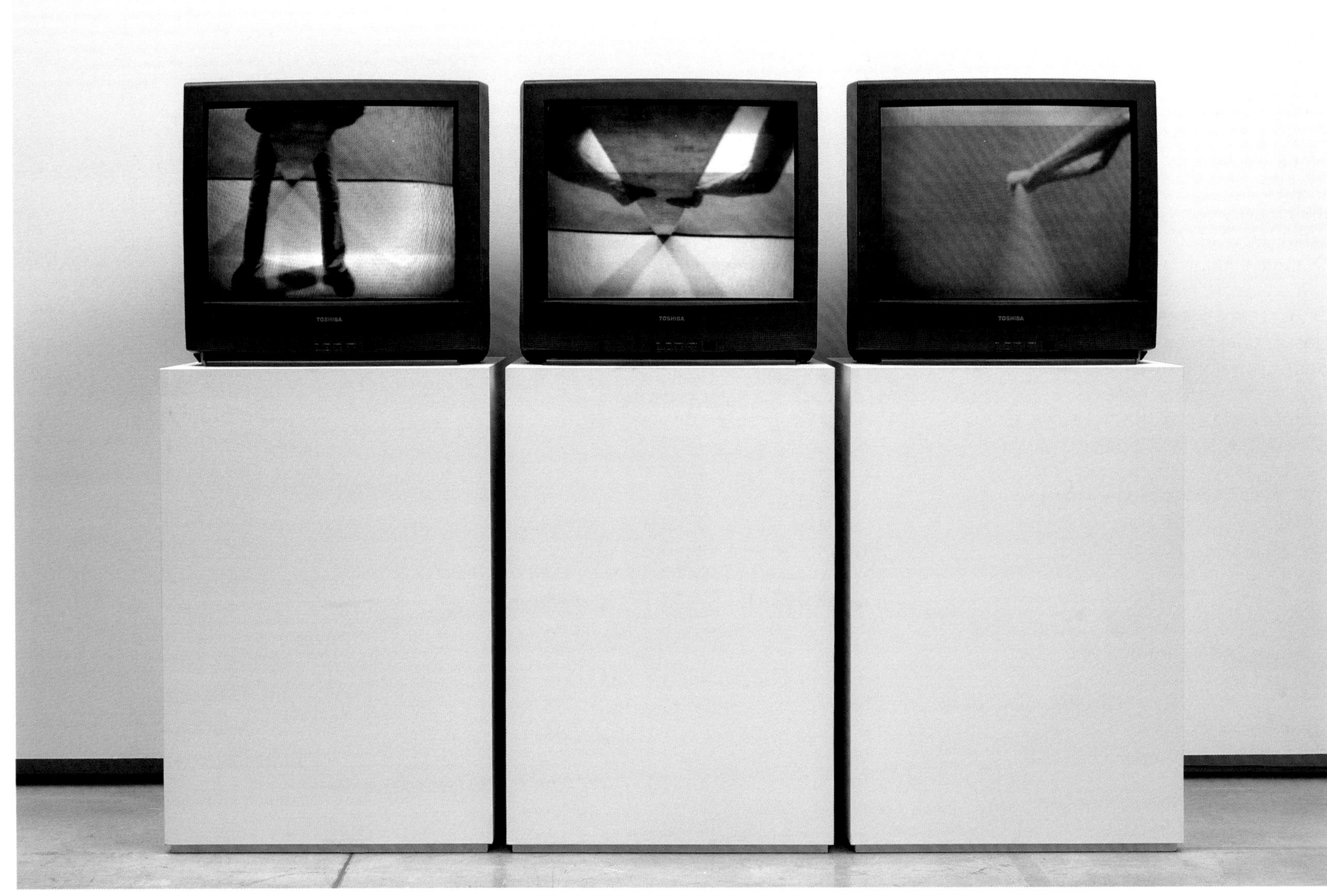

Duke Redbird

Old Woman, 1981
Poem (audio recording), 3:55 min.

Old woman in the field
Bent low, immobile and still
What thoughts tumble about
Behind those sad black eyes
That have not felt the moist
Edges and wet bodies of heartbroken tears
Since the hunger pangs of transgression
And broken promises
melted away with the passing years
What language does the stream
Of consciousness employ?
Is it sound, or words, or mists
Of past reflections
Hastily snatched, before the precious
Breath of life forsakes you entirely.
No time now old woman for
Multiplication tables and essays
No time now for politics and religion
No time now for polite conversation;
How close you are to the earth
How low you've bent;
In the lengthening shadows
You appear to be another stone
On the bare horizon
And the bright sun of your youth
Has faded softly behind you
So that now the rays only
Reflect your image across the naked desert.
And what of you
Will you sink below the surface
Of my perception
And slip away from my understanding
And stand in the darkness.
Old woman I know who you are
I know this barren waste land
Upon which I stand
Was once a forest.
And you old woman
Had life and beauty
Energy and passion
Love and abundance
Freedom and chatter with the gods
Birch trees cried, 'here take my bark
That you might sleep in my arms'
And the great creatures of the forests
Dropped their fur clothing and said
'Let my warmth be your warmth
Make a pillow for your head.'
And birds swooped down
And laid their finest plumage at your feet
And bade you wear them
For you were their child
Their brown golden child
Who sang their praises
And danced their dance
No, your eyes have not harboured tears
But your body carried the burden
Of sorrow and the weight of treachery
For others came, pale helpless souls
And your golden arms encircled them
And your golden heart embraced them
And your golden mouth kissed them
This was your youth old woman
Bent so low.
Where are they now
After they cut down your beloved forest
And slaughtered your animals brothers
And tore wings from your bright birds
And ground your mountains to dust
Did they leave you anything at all
Except pain and misery and hunger
What thoughts have you
What last word, before you give up
Your spirit to eternity
Did they leave you even that
One word,
one thought
To take with you to
the last hunting ground
Love?

FASTWÜRMS

Wall of Fatigue, 1983
Industrial galvanized metal panels, four pulleys, and four burlap sacks full of potatoes
Dimensions variable
Courtesy of the artists and Paul Petro Contemporary Art, Toronto

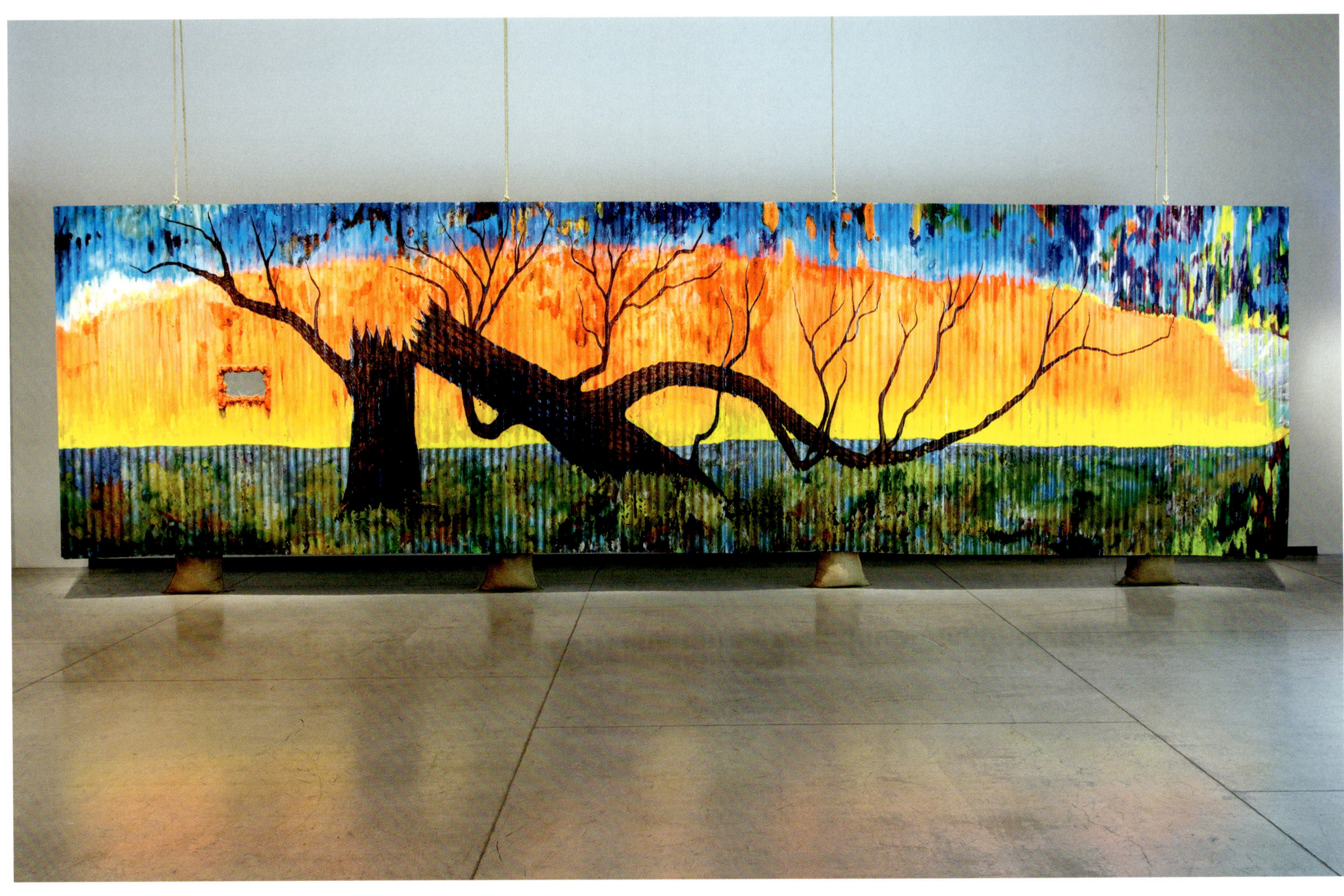

Robert Flack

Bullets, 1987
Chromogenic print
101.6 × 76.2 cm
Collection of Robert Edmund Flack Sr., courtesy
Paul Petro Contemporary Art, Toronto

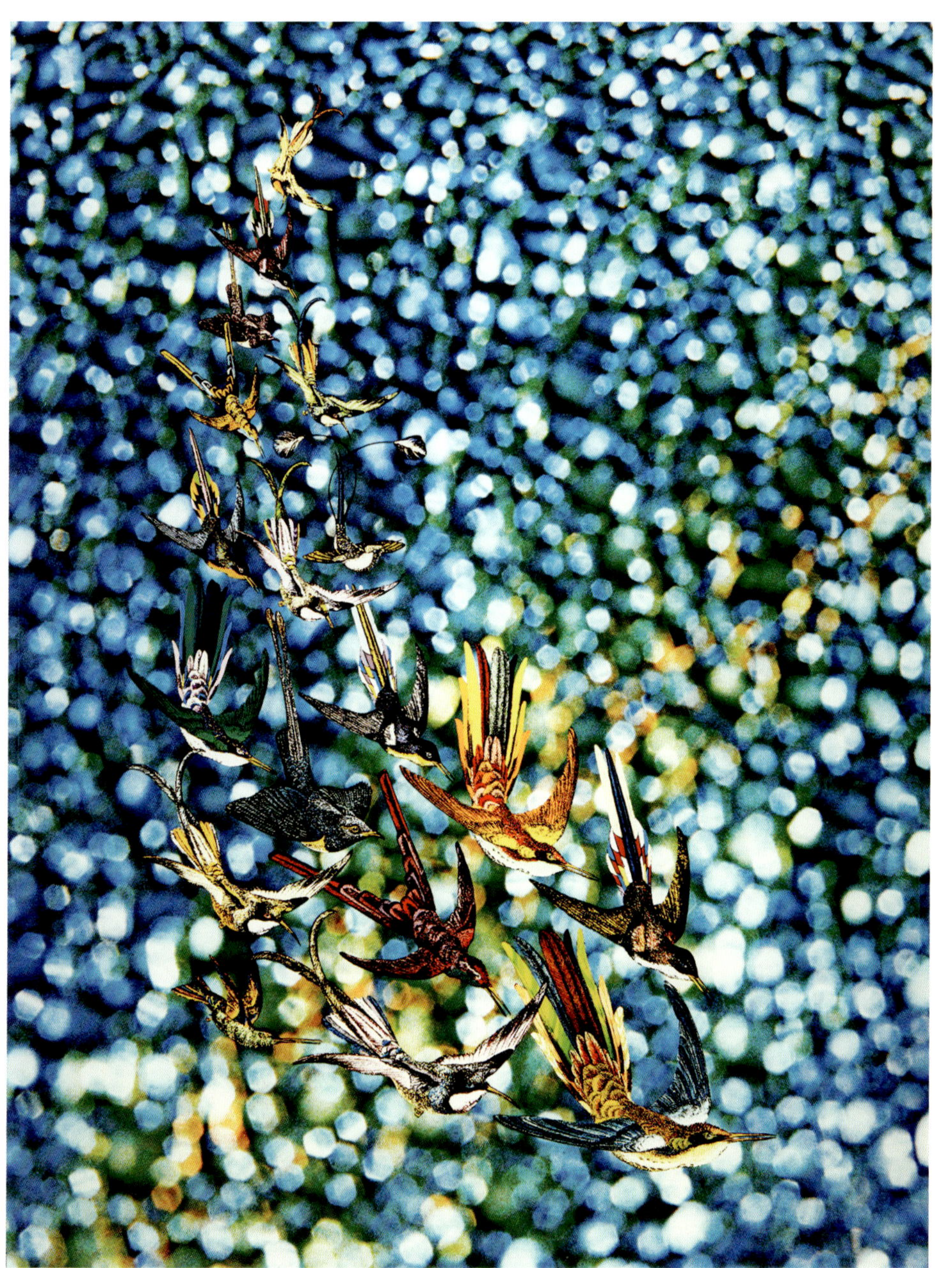

Shelagh Alexander

In the City of the Faithful, 1986
Diptych—compilation photographs
133.5 × 211 cm
Collection of the artist

The Gate from The Voices of the Unclean, 1983
Gelatin silver prints
133.5 × 211 cm
Collection of the artist

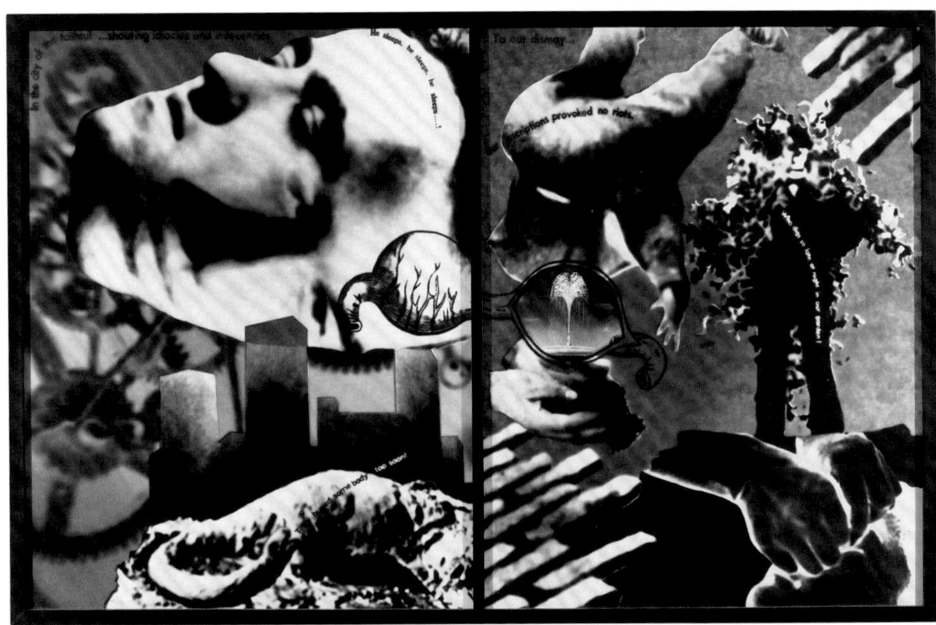

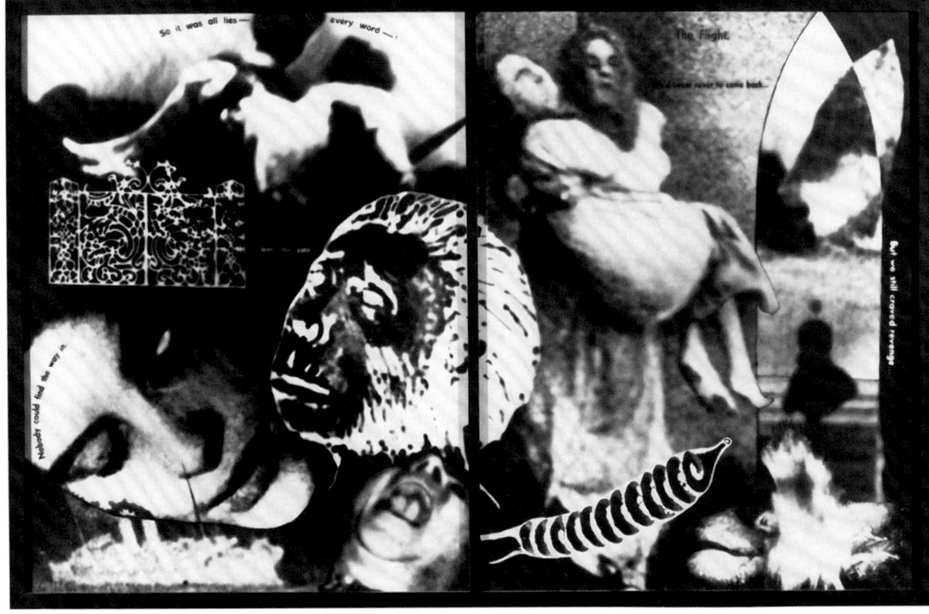

John Massey

Versailles, 1985
Black screenprint and colour photomechanical on paper
127.2 × 96.9 cm
Art Gallery of Ontario, gift of Harry and Ann Malcolmson, 2001, 2001/255

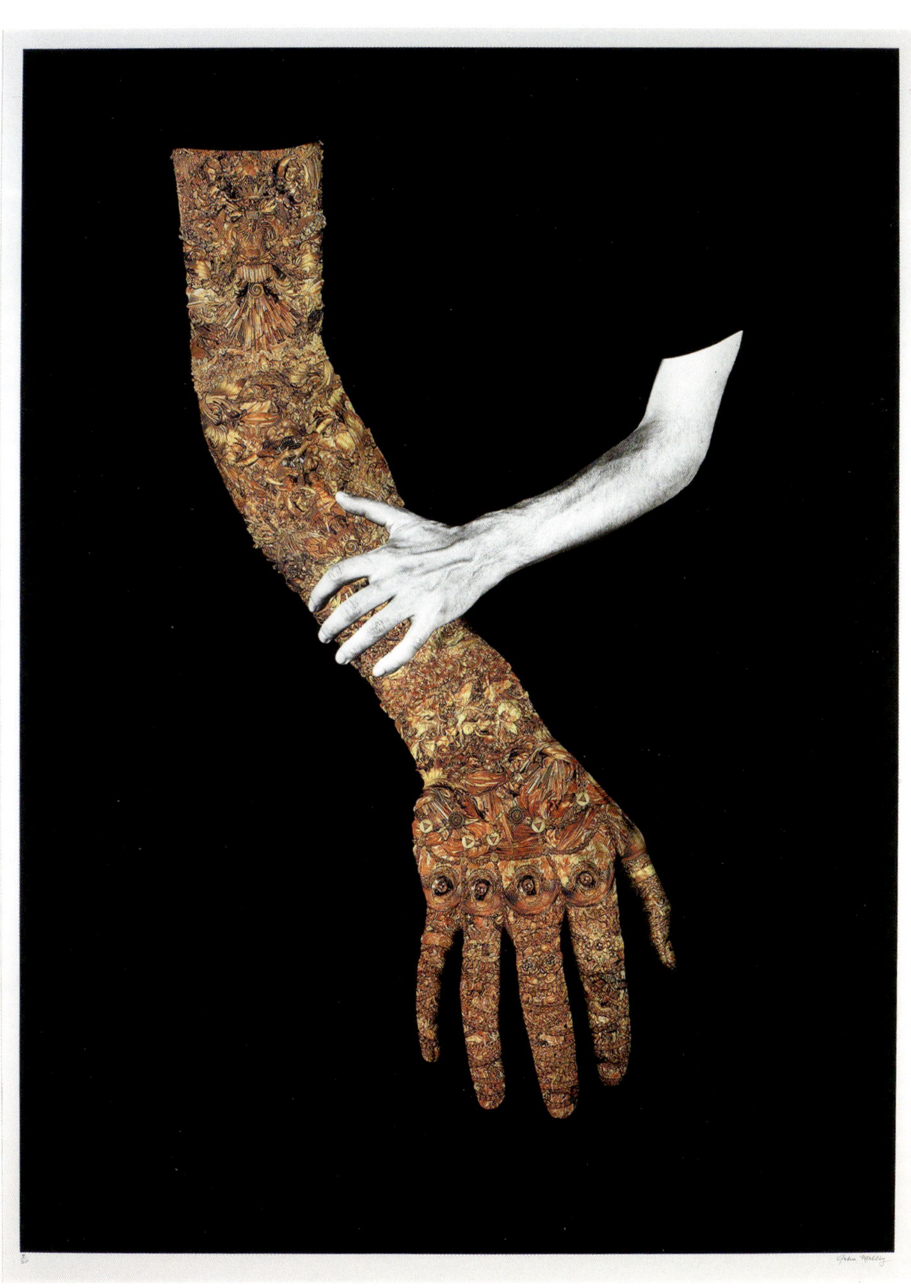

Joyce Wieland

Squid Jiggin' Grounds, 1973
Colour lithograph on paper
52.5 × 75 cm
Art Gallery of Ontario, purchase, 1987, 86/284

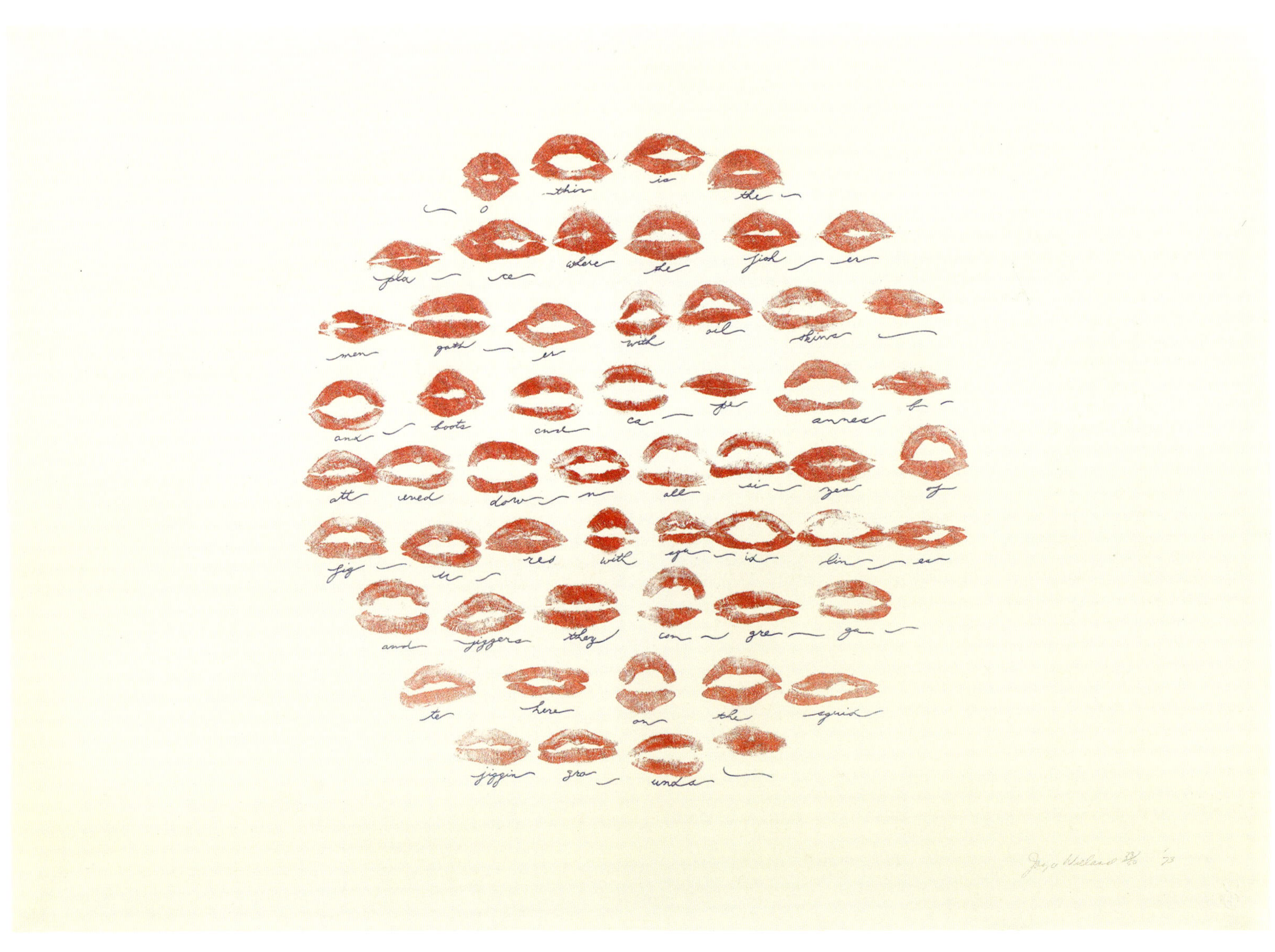

Stephen Andrews

Four Inhabitants of North America, 1987
Graphite, oil stick, and wash on pieced tracing paper
43.1 × 63 cm
Art Gallery of Ontario, gift from the Collection of
Dr. Michael Braudo, 2000, 2000/149

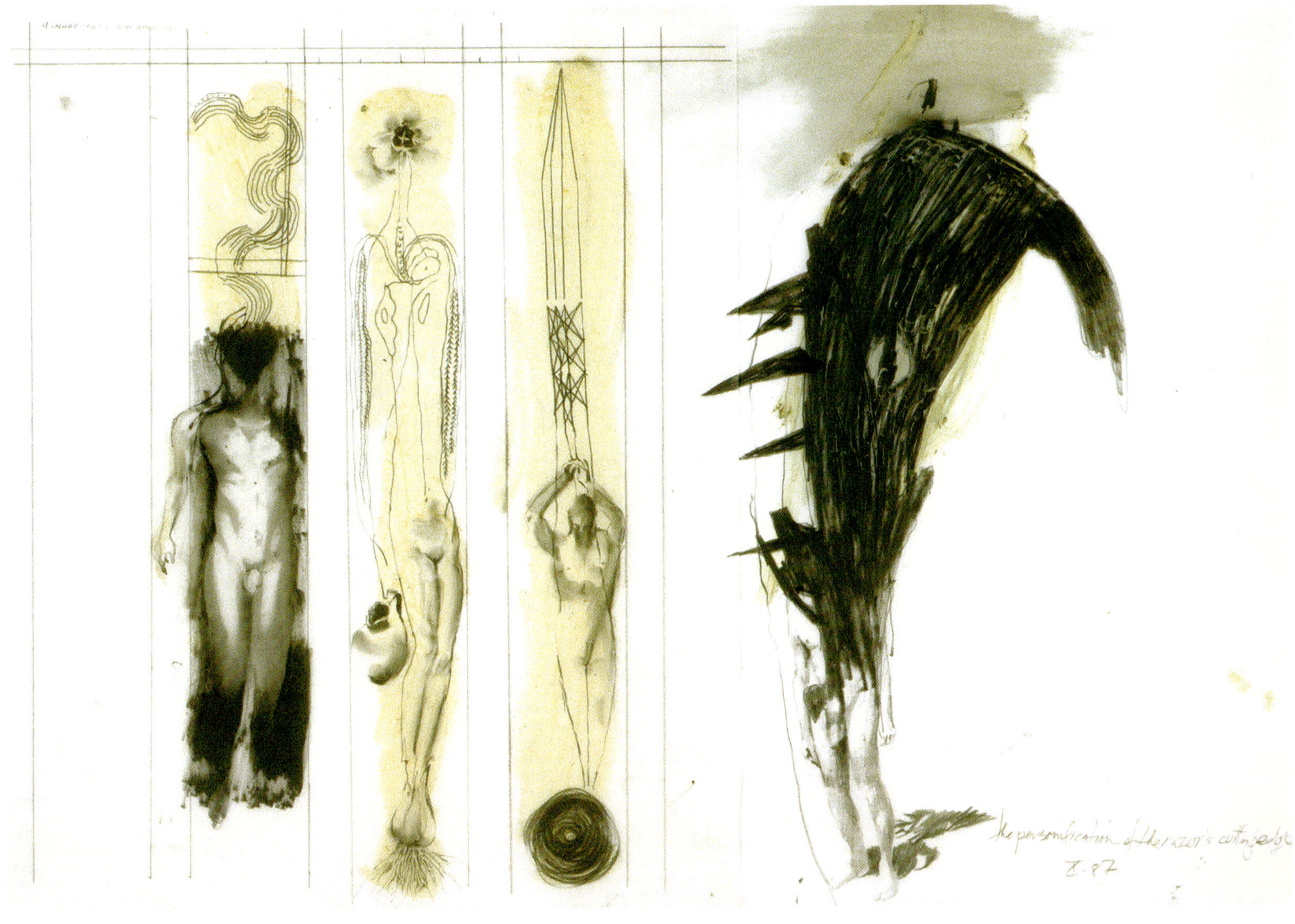

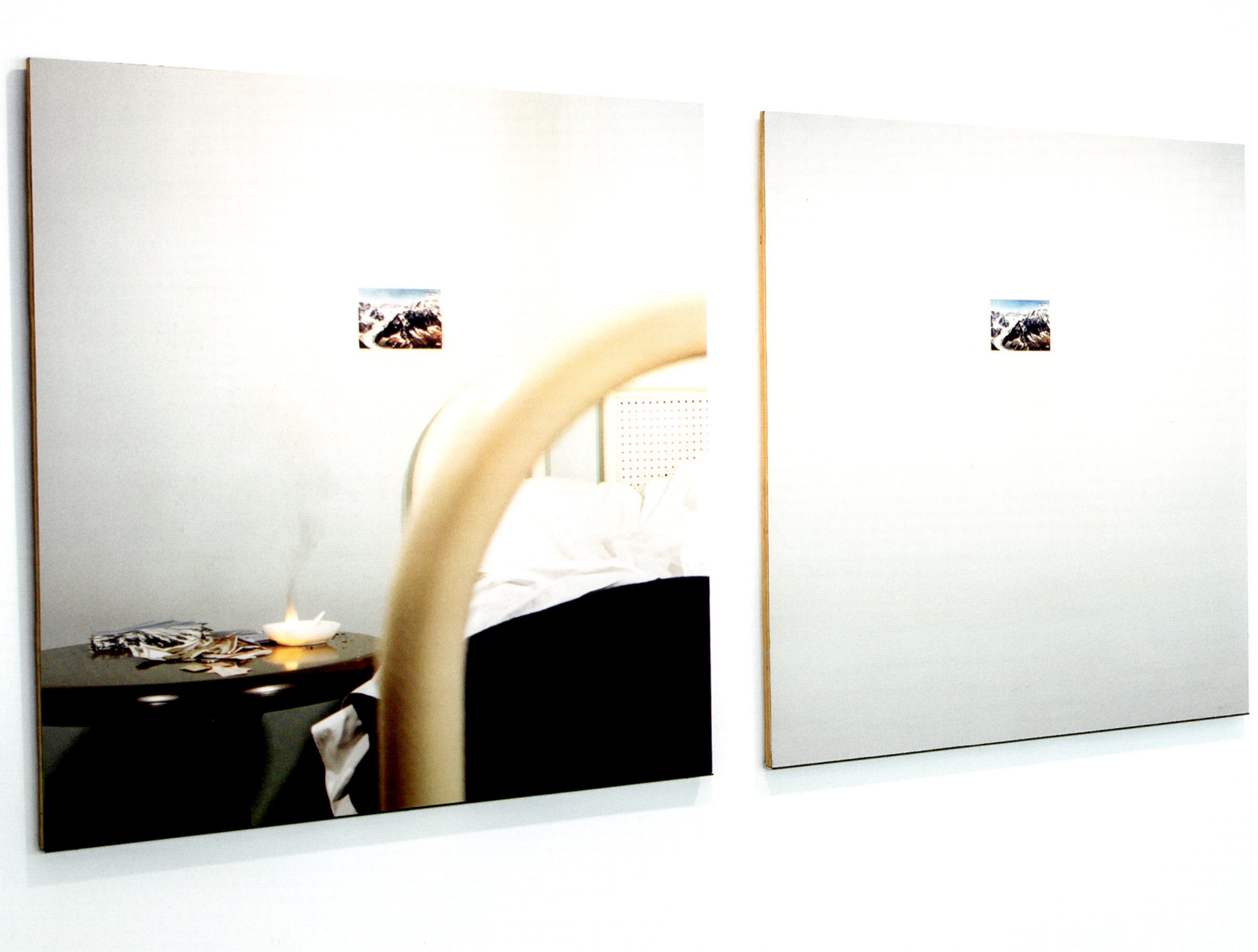

The Image

E-waabndaman

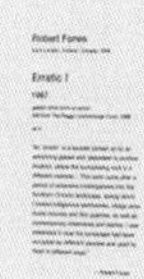

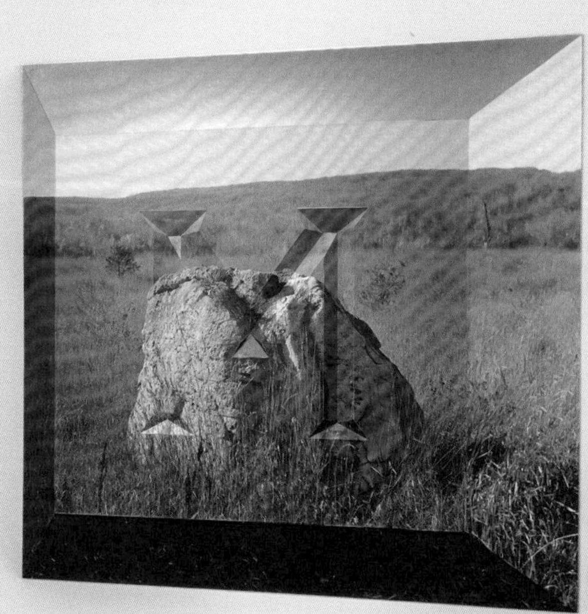

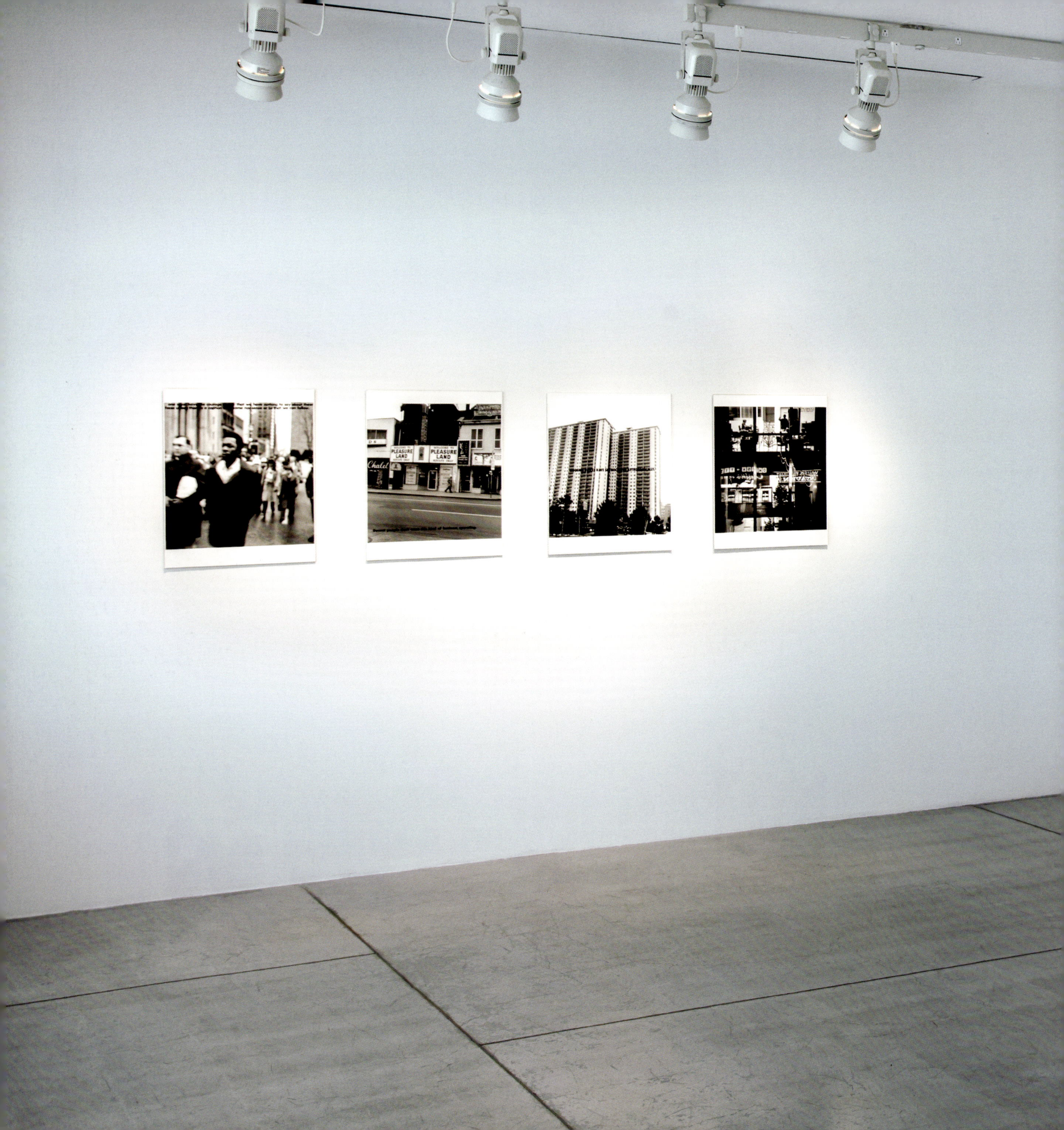
PLEASURE LAND
PLEASURE LAND
Chalet

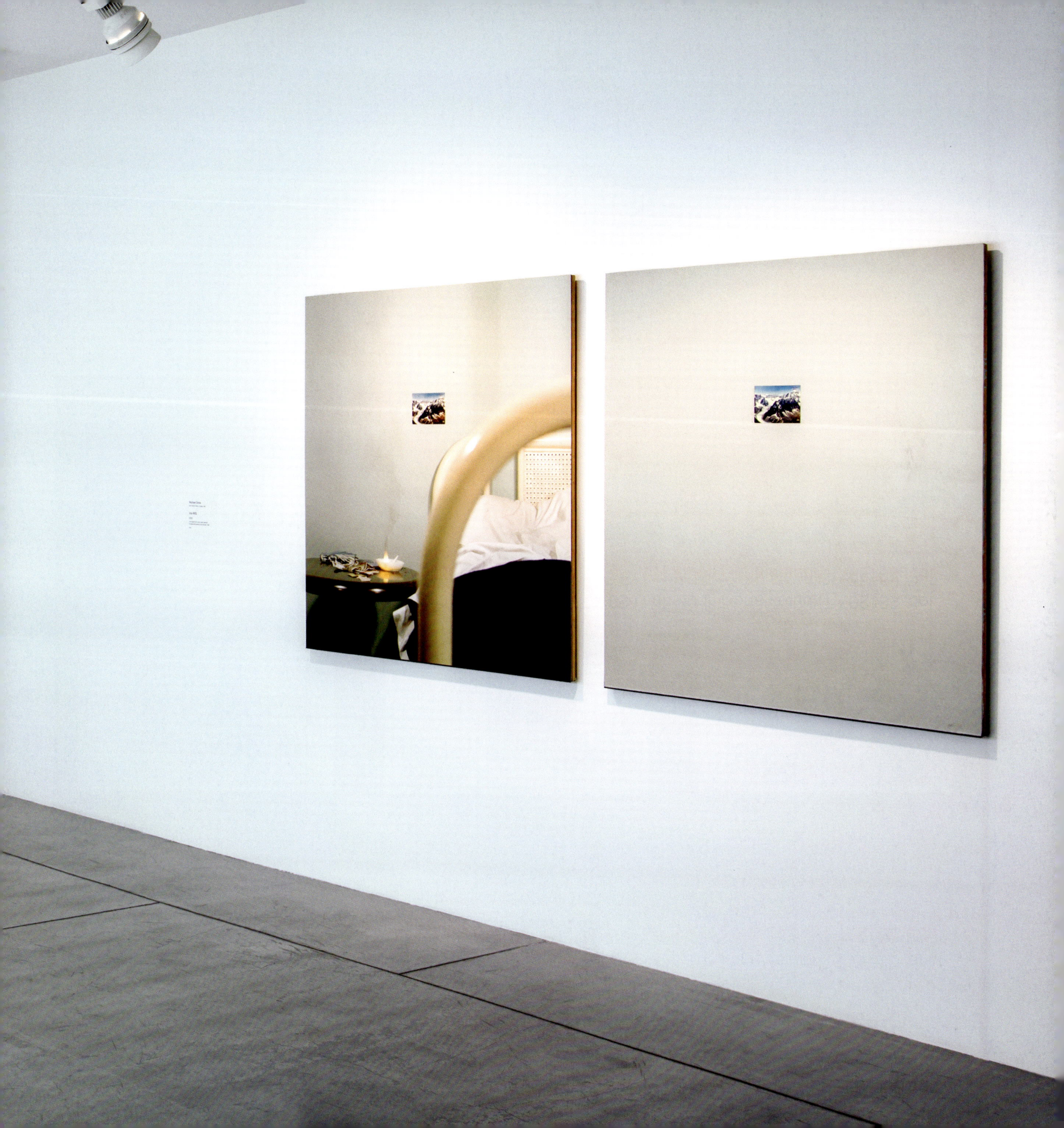

June Clark

Formative Triptych, 1989
Three duratrans in lightboxes
111.5 × 152.2 cm each
Art Gallery of Ontario, purchase with assistance from the Estate of P.J. Glasser, 2016, 2016/43

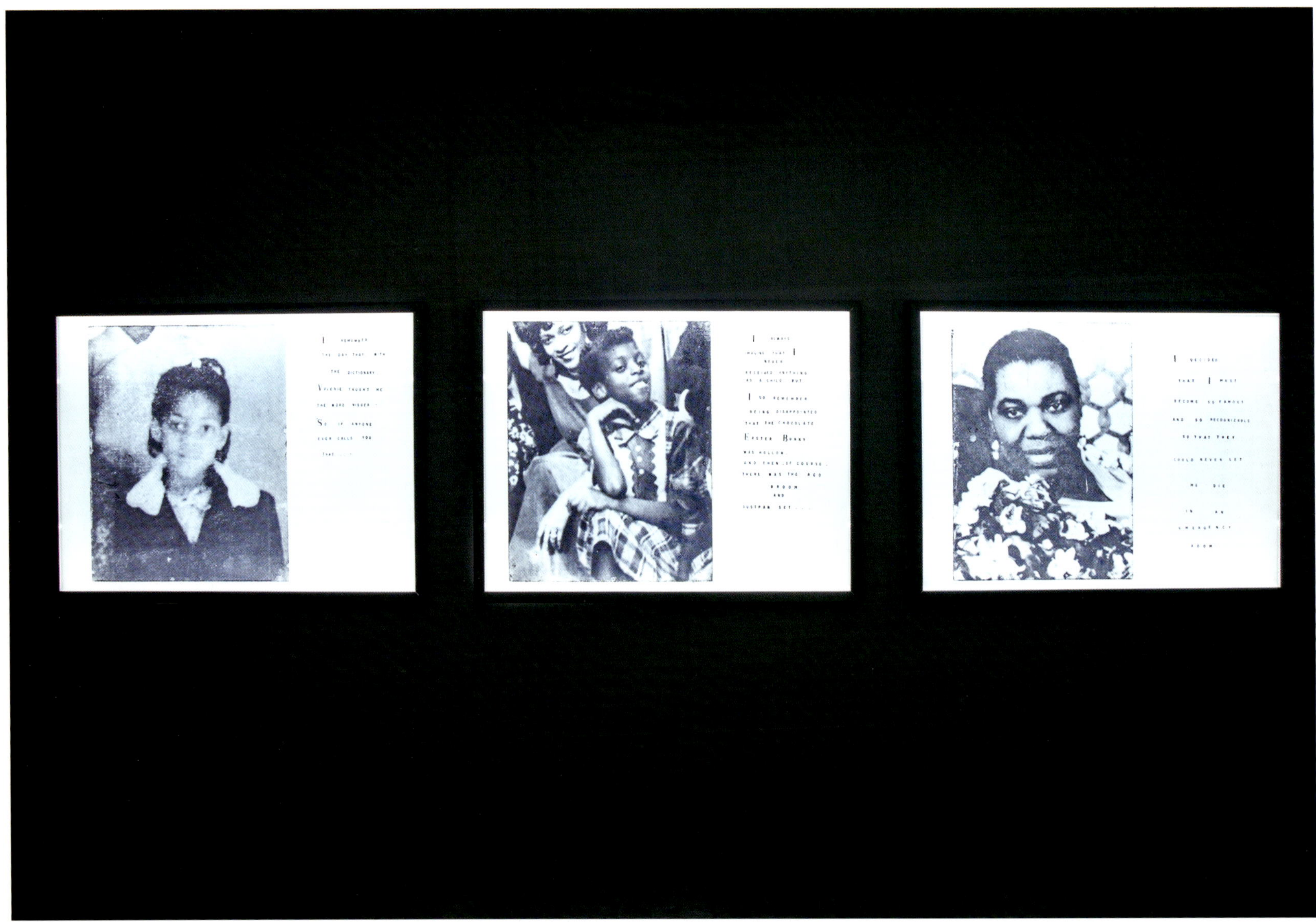

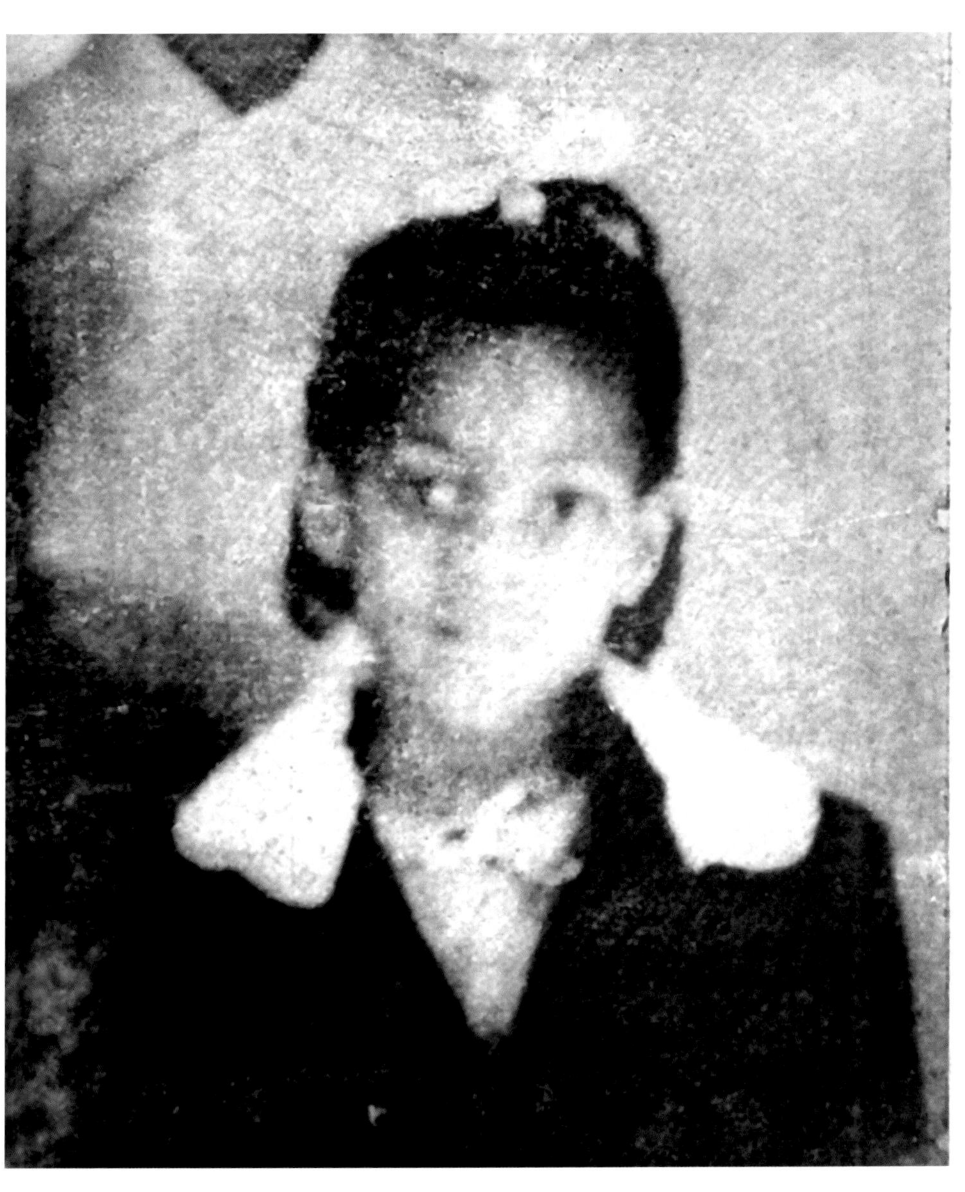

I . REMEMBER

THE DAY THAT., WITH

THE DICTIONARY,

VALERIE TAUGHT ME

THE WORD NIGGER

SO, IF ANYONE

EVER CALLS YOU

THAT . . .

Robin John Collyer

Untitled #1, 1975
Gelatin silver print
60.5 × 49.8 cm
Art Gallery of Ontario, gift from
The Peggy Lownsbrough Fund, 1987, 87/26

Untitled #2, 1975
Gelatin silver print
60 × 49.8 cm
Art Gallery of Ontario, gift from
The Peggy Lownsbrough Fund, 1987, 87/27

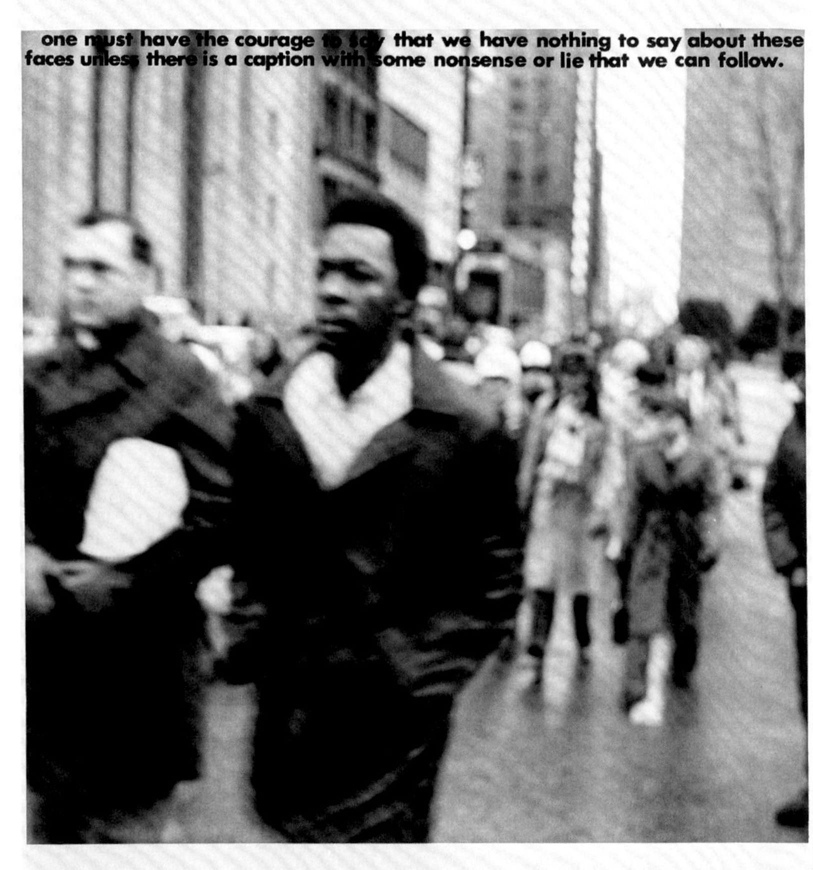

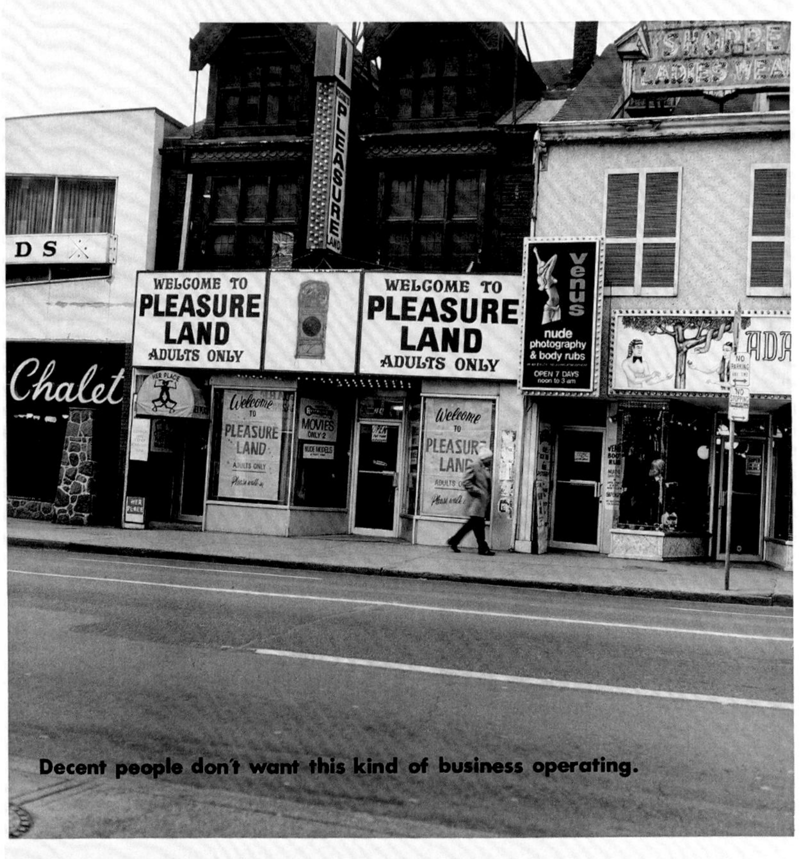

Untitled #3, 1975
Gelatin silver print
60.3 × 49.7 cm
Art Gallery of Ontario, gift from
The Peggy Lownsbrough Fund, 1987, 87/28

Untitled #4, 1975
Gelatin silver print
60.5 × 49.8 cm
Art Gallery of Ontario, gift from
The Peggy Lownsbrough Fund, 1987, 87/29

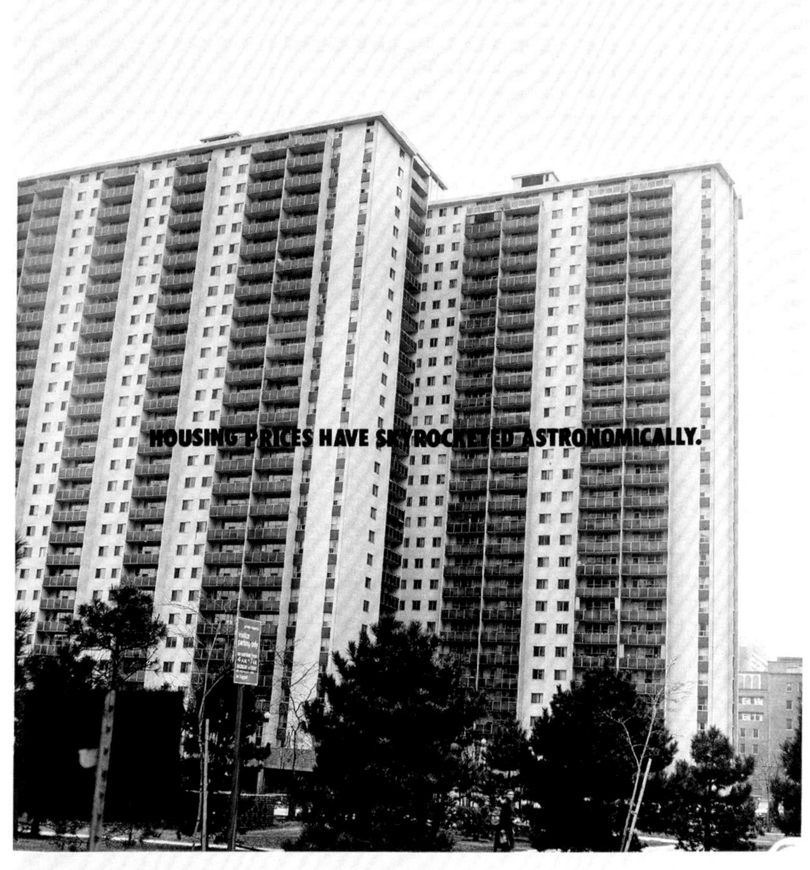

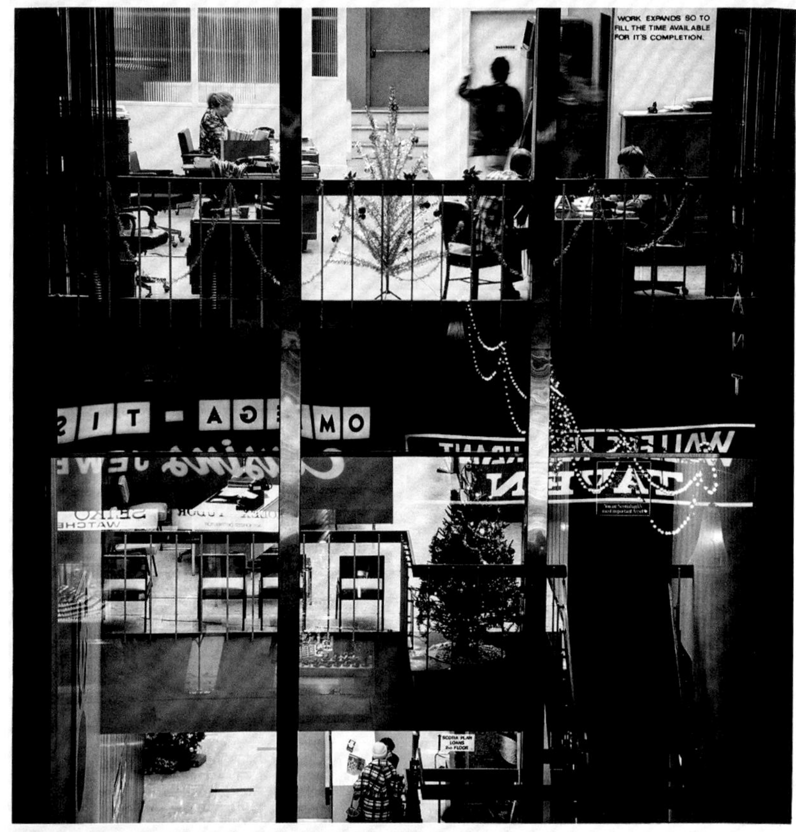

Michael Snow

iris-IRIS, 1979
Chromogenic print, acrylic paint, and postcard
121.9 × 119.4 cm each
Art Gallery of Ontario, purchase with assistance from Wintario, 1980, 79/325

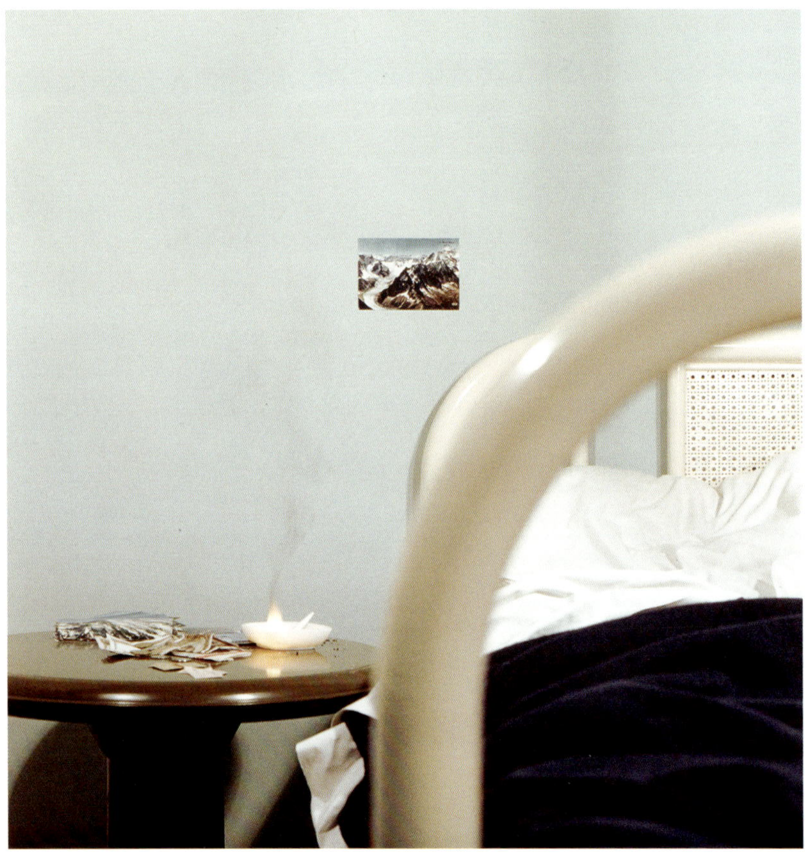

Robert Fones

Erratic I, 1987
Gelatin silver print on wood
100 × 107.5 cm
Art Gallery of Ontario, gift from
The Peggy Lownsbrough Fund, 1988, 88/14

"An 'erratic' is a boulder picked up by an advancing glacier and deposited to another location, where the surrounding rock is a different material…This work came after a period of extensive investigations into the Southern Ontario landscape, during which I visited Indigenous earthworks, village sites, burial mounds, and flint quarries, as well as contemporary creameries and dairies. I was interested in how the landscape had been occupied by different peoples and used by them in different ways." —Robert Fones

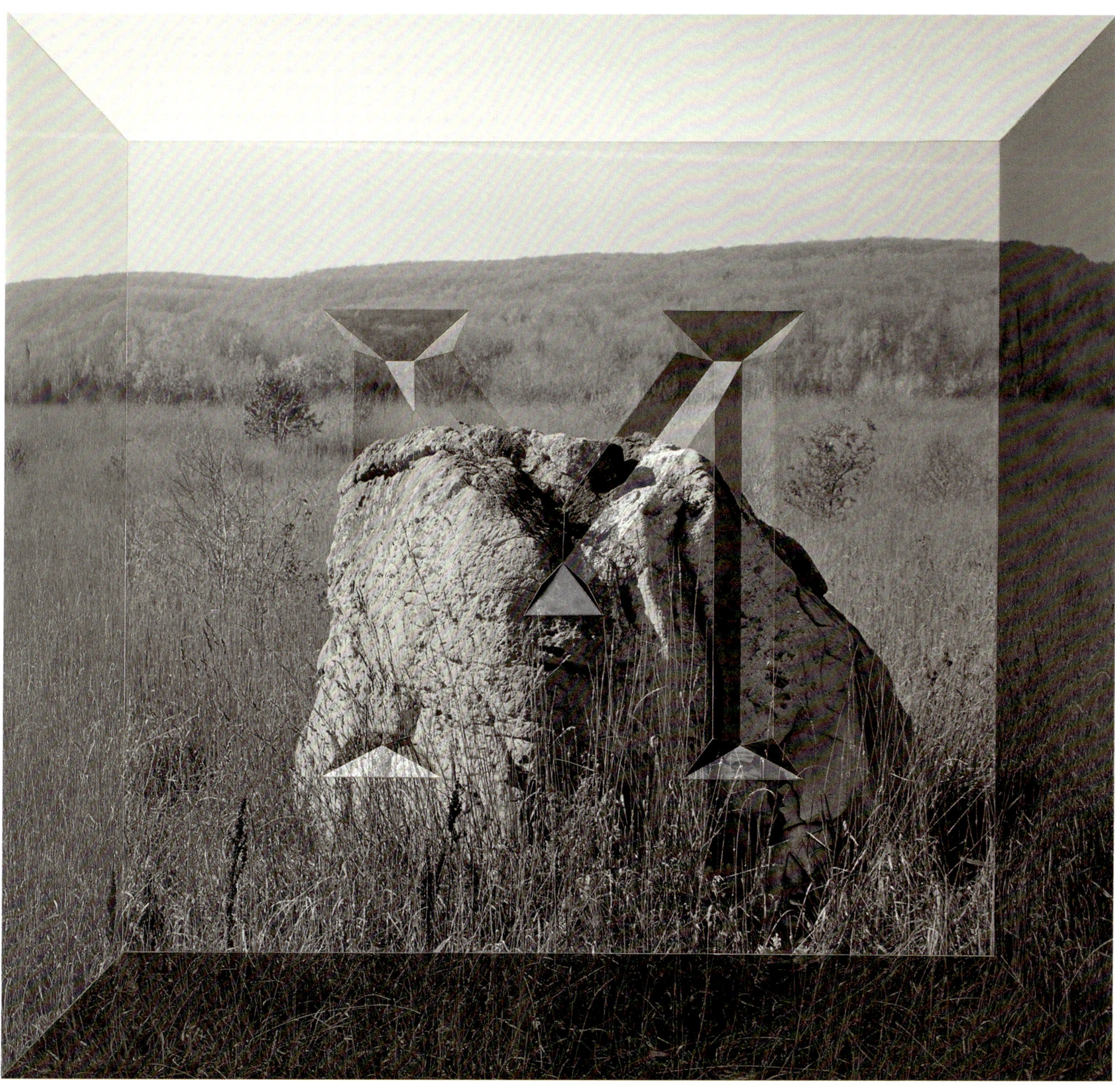

Jayce Salloum

The Ascent of Man/Acts of Consumption, 1985–1987
Videotape, slide-dissolve programs, photographs, and bookwork
Dimensions variable
Courtesy of the artist

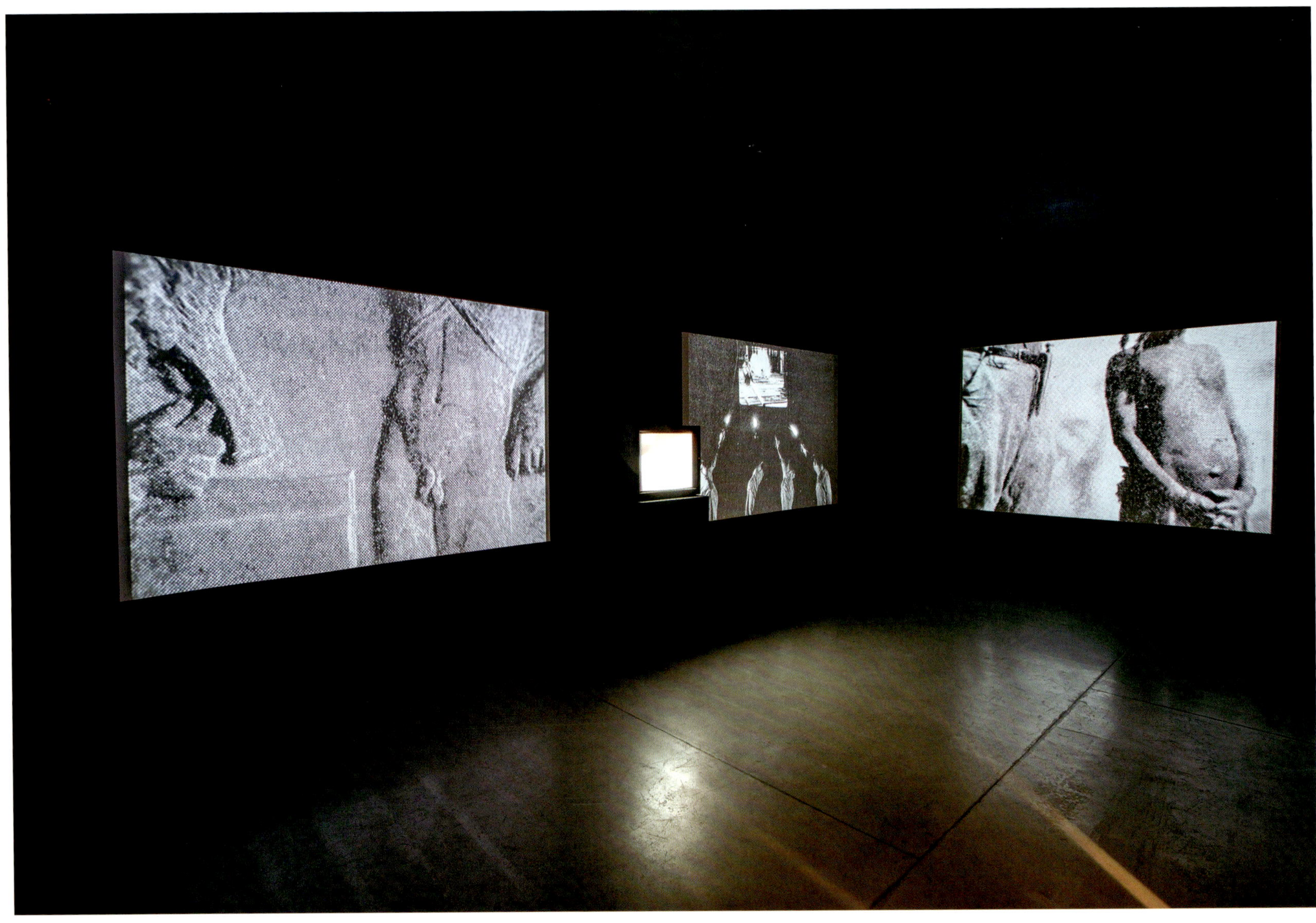

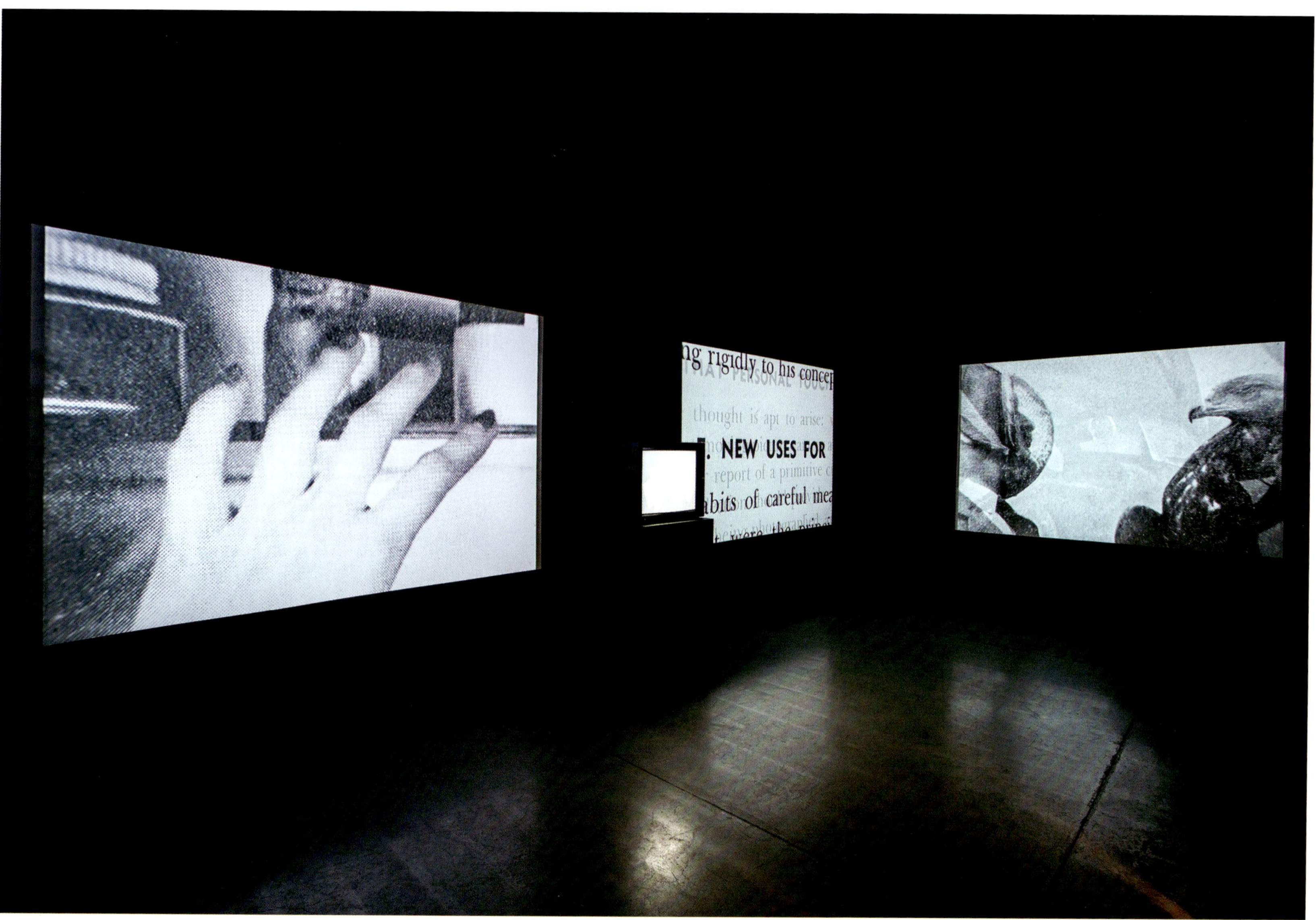
ng rigidly to his concep
thought is apt to arise:
. NEW USES FOR
report of a primitive
abits of careful mea

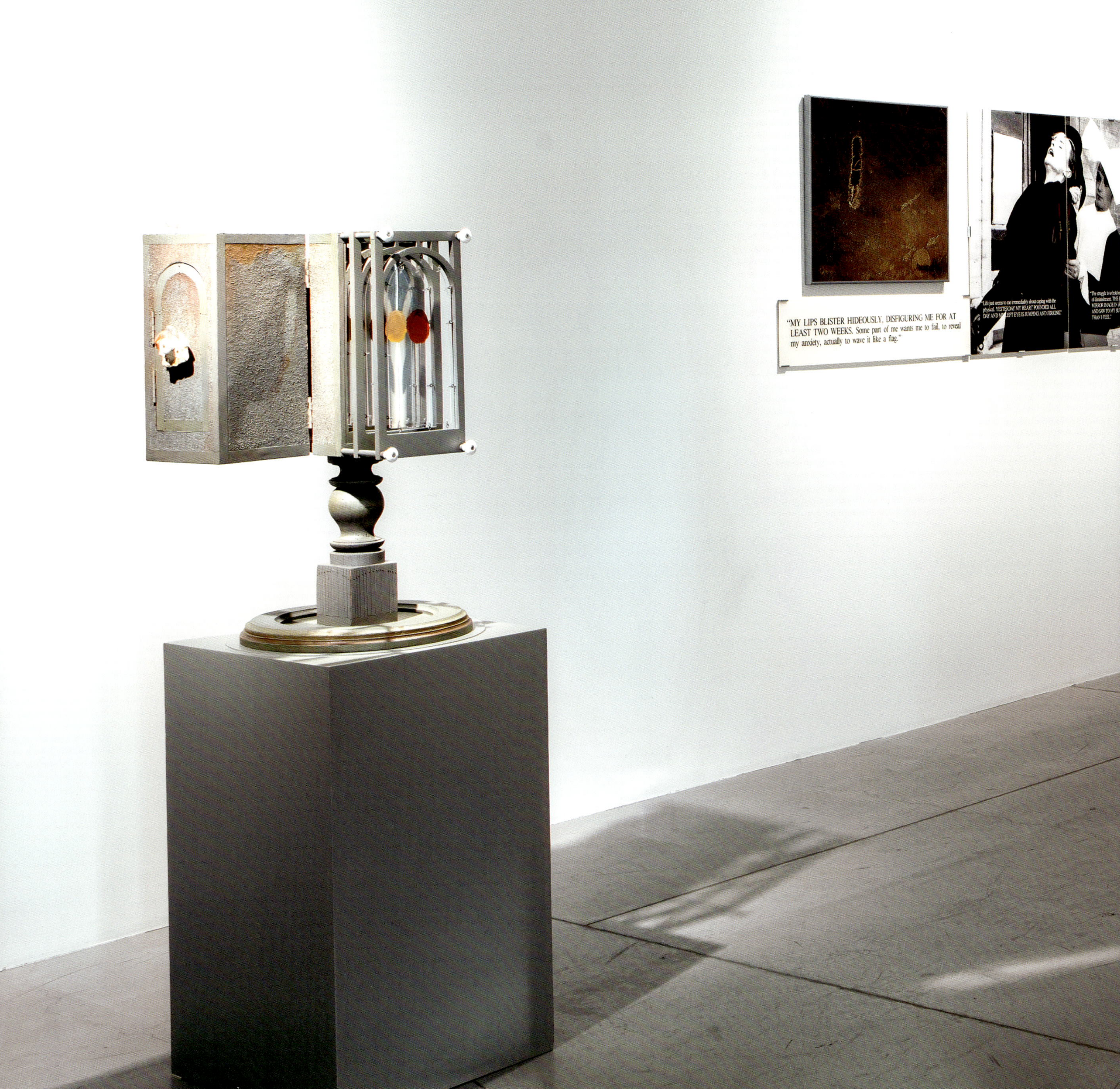
"MY LIPS BLISTER HIDEOUSLY, DISFIGURING ME FOR AT
LEAST TWO WEEKS. Some part of me wants me to fail, to reveal
my anxiety, actually to wave it like a flag."

Storytelling

Dibajimoowinan wiindimaading

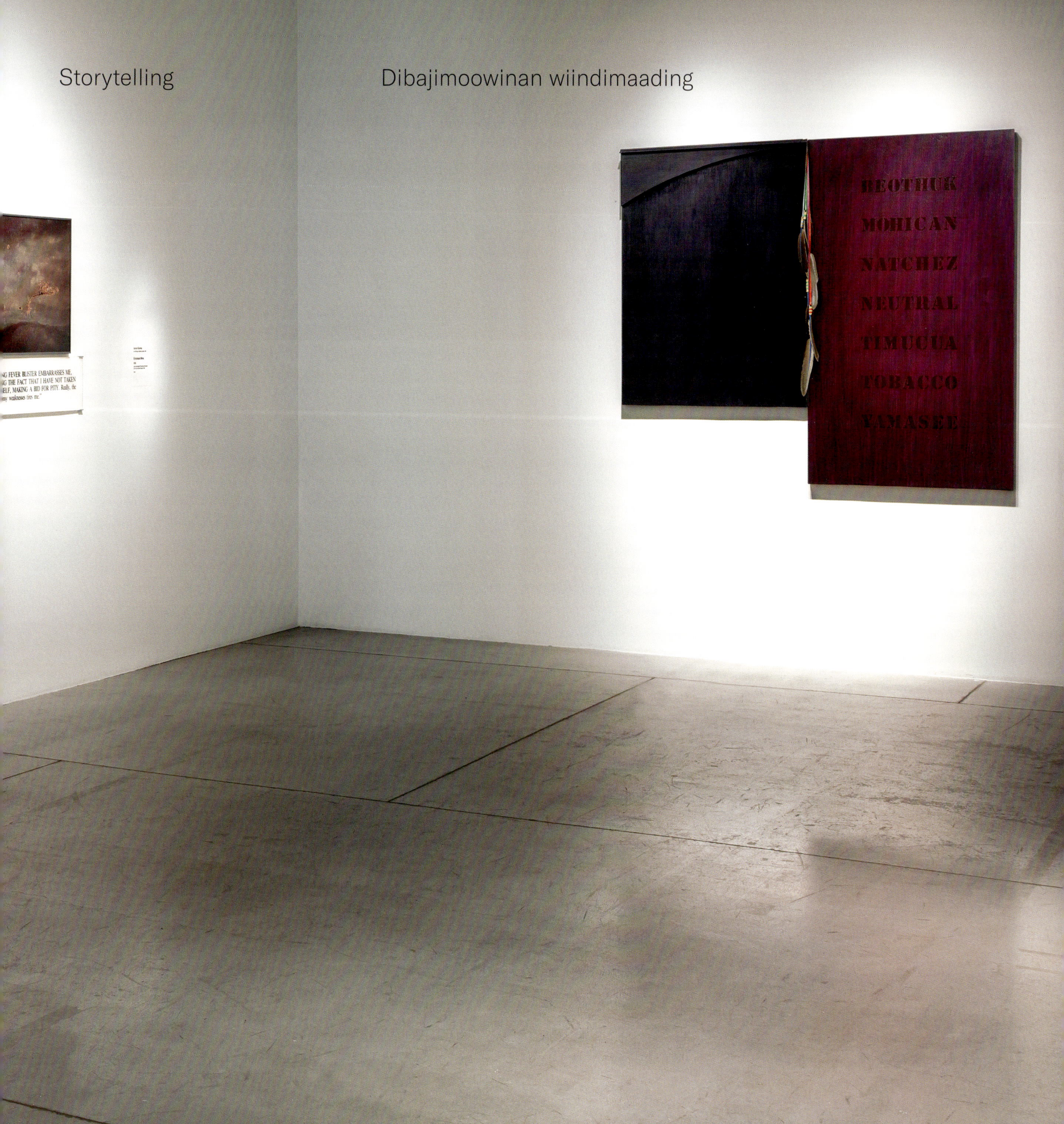

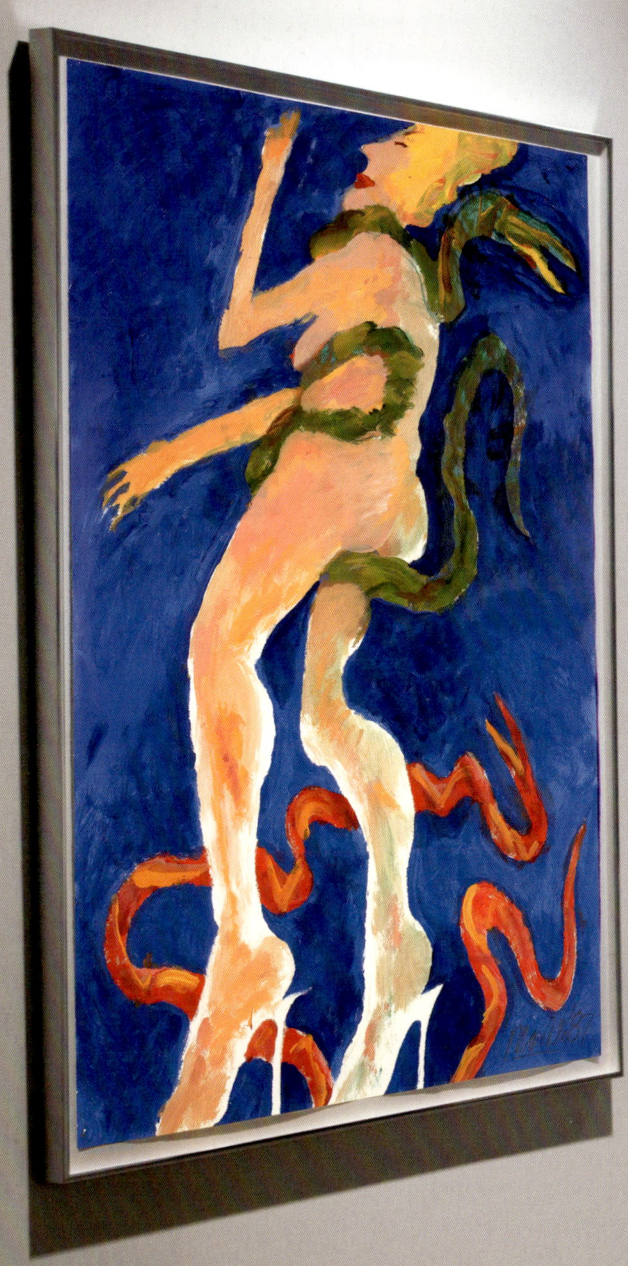

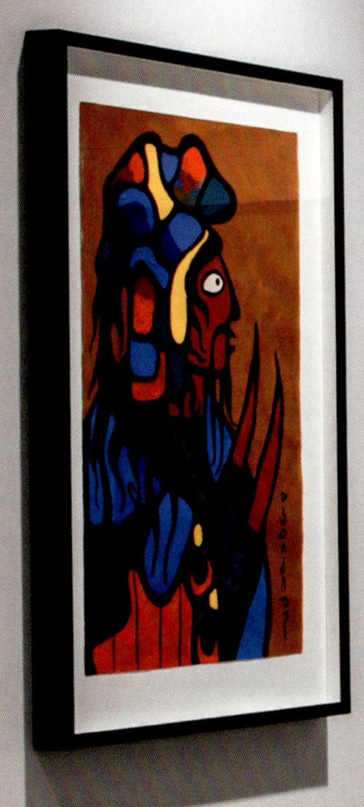

TORONTO

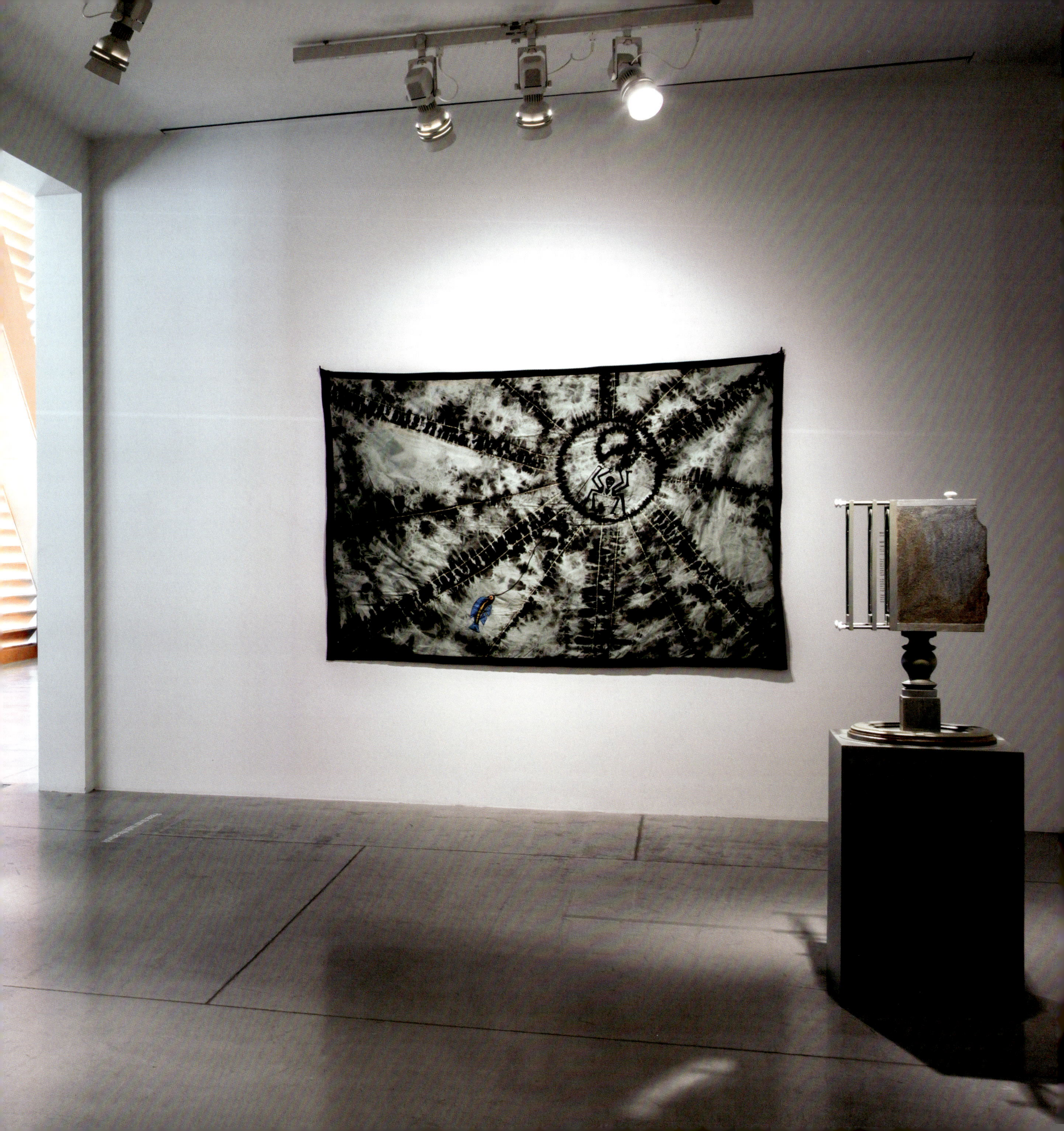

Winsom Winsom

MIRROR OF DEARTH, 1989
Dyes, ink, and paint on cotton with applique
146 × 220 cm
Art Gallery of Ontario, purchase, 2017, 2017/66

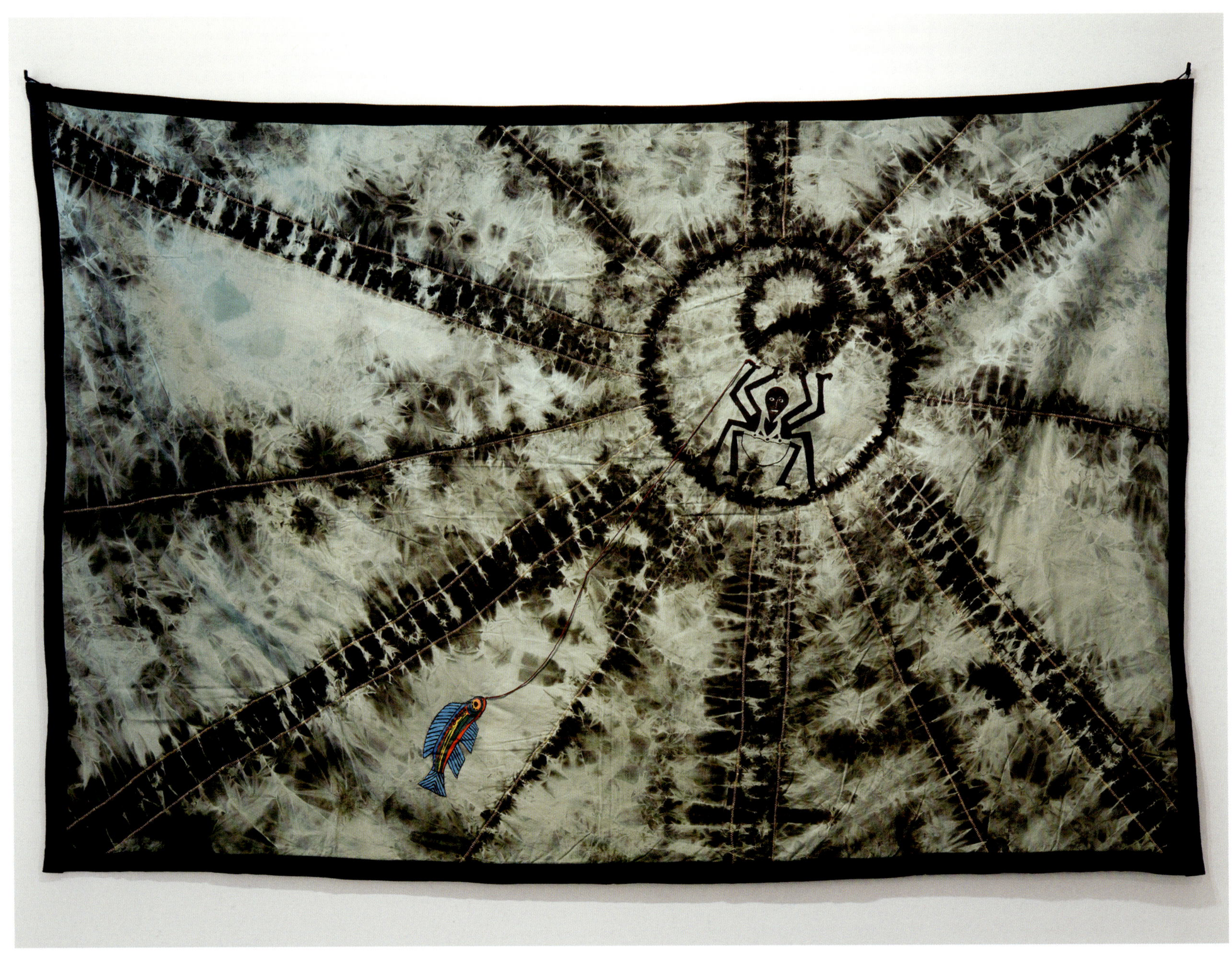

Kim Moodie

Untitled, 1984
Black ink on paper
56.7 × 76.4 cm
Art Gallery of Ontario, gift of Mary Handford, 2006, 2006/392

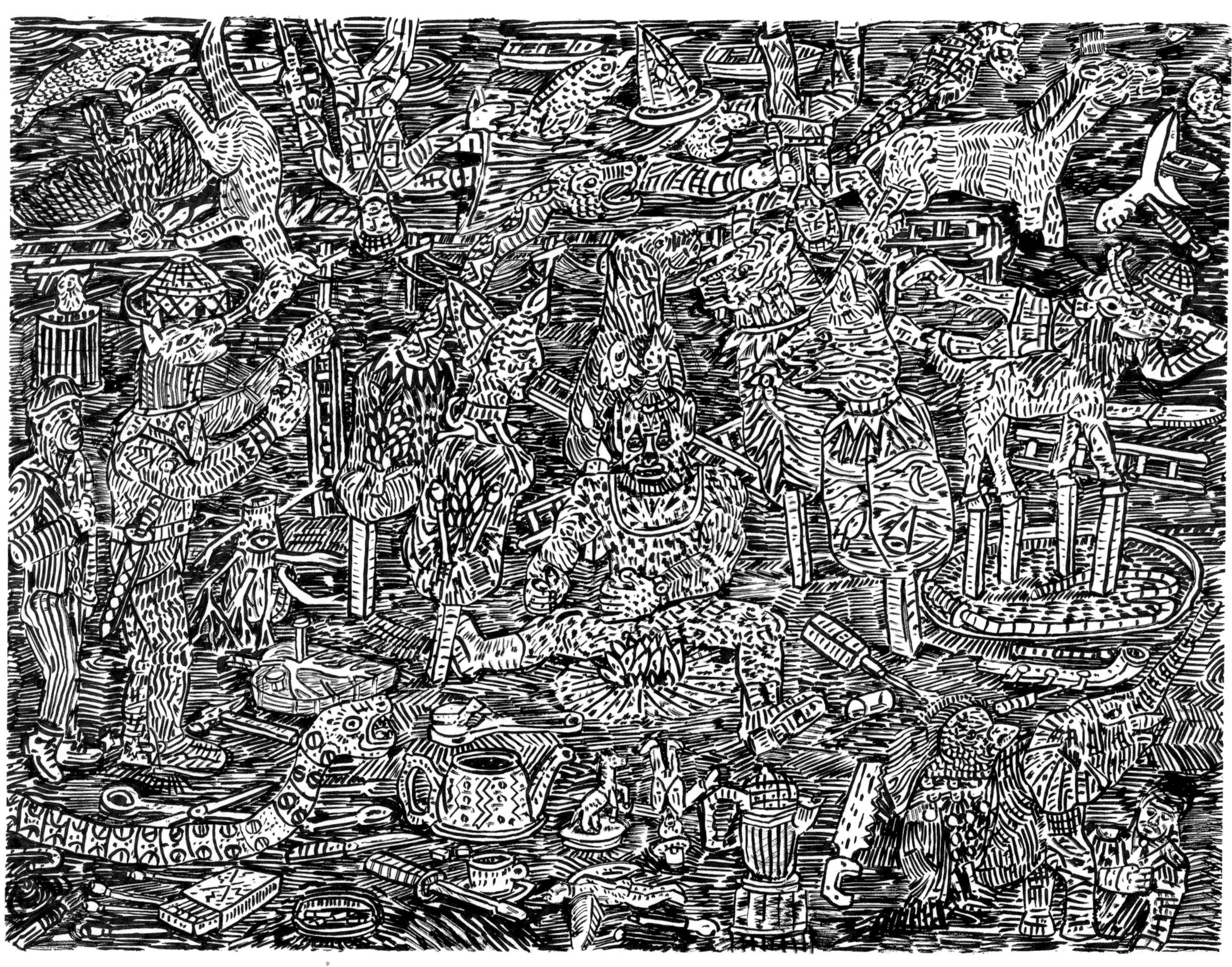

Janice Gurney

Emphasis Mine, 1985
Colour photographs, photostat, and Plexiglas
72.4 × 269.2 cm
Art Gallery of Ontario, gift of Ron and
Alice Charach, 1999, 98/655

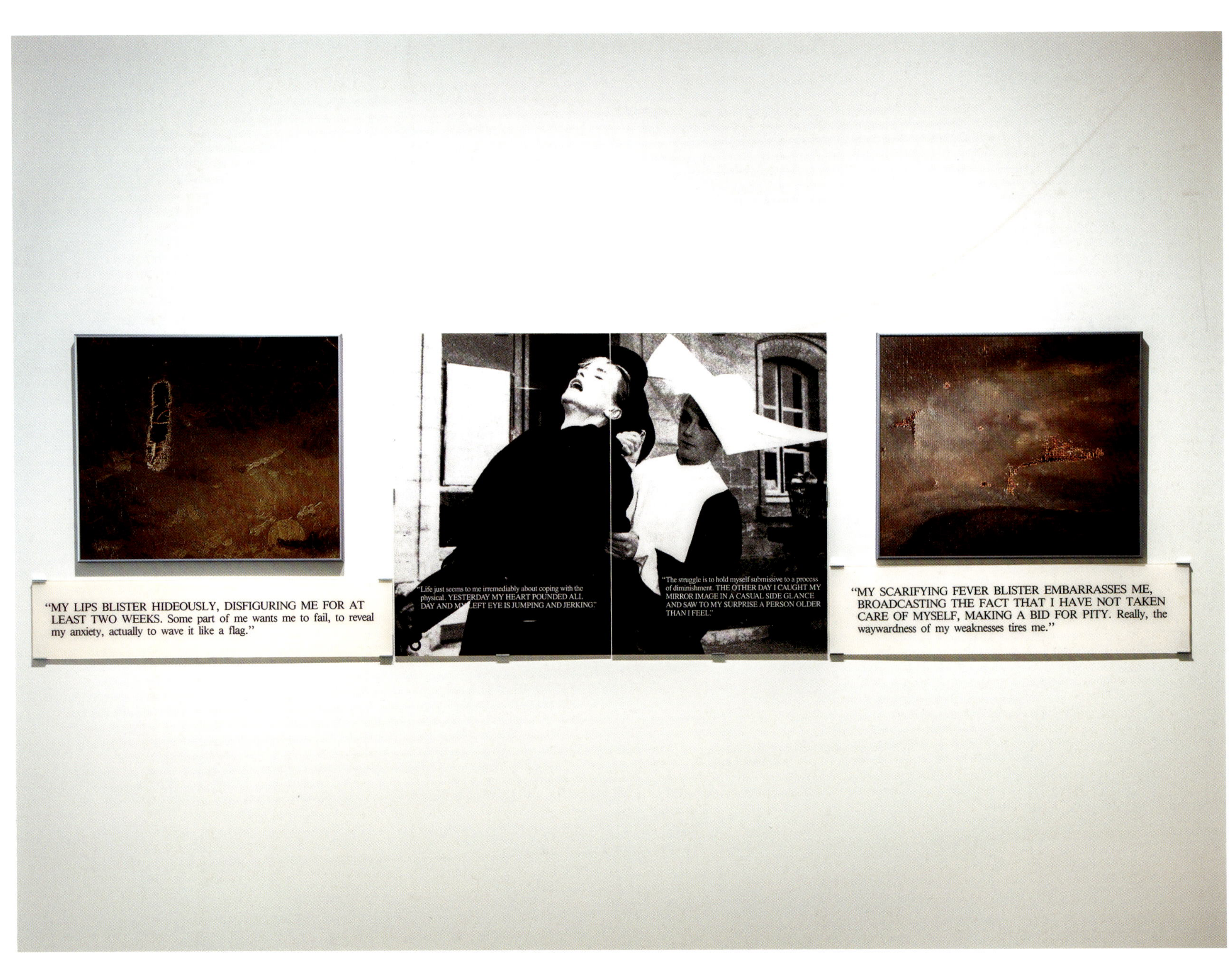

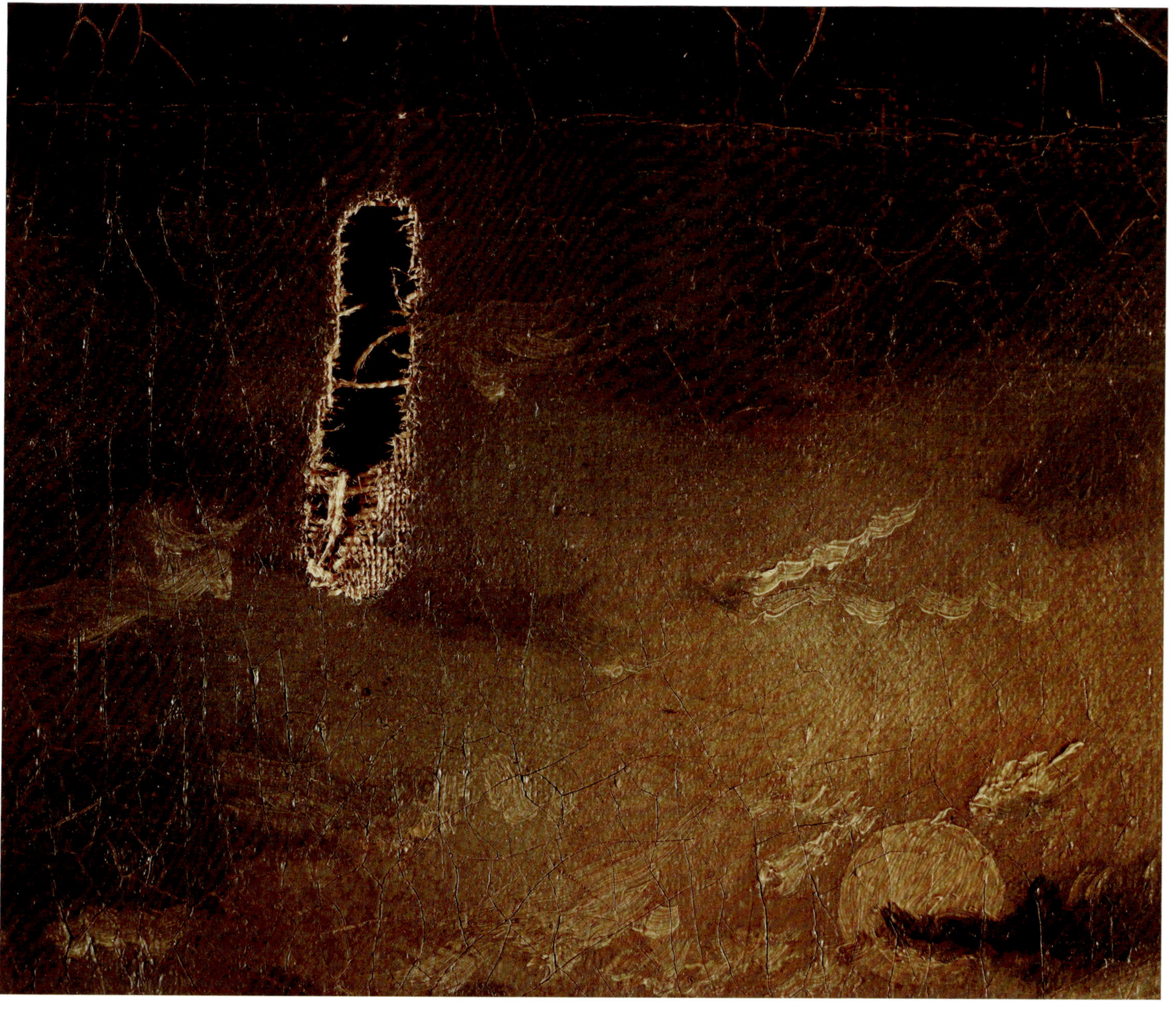

Tony Urquhart

Along the Road, 1975
Painted wood, porcelain, glazed ceramic, Plexiglas, glass, and dried flower stems
147 cm × variable
Art Gallery of Ontario, purchase with assistance from Wintario, 1979, 78/752

"I now had an art object that could double or even quadruple its space…It could change its colour, if the inside was different from the outside. It could change its texture…It could do a whole lot of other things that paintings couldn't do, yet it was essentially a painted object." —Tony Urquhart

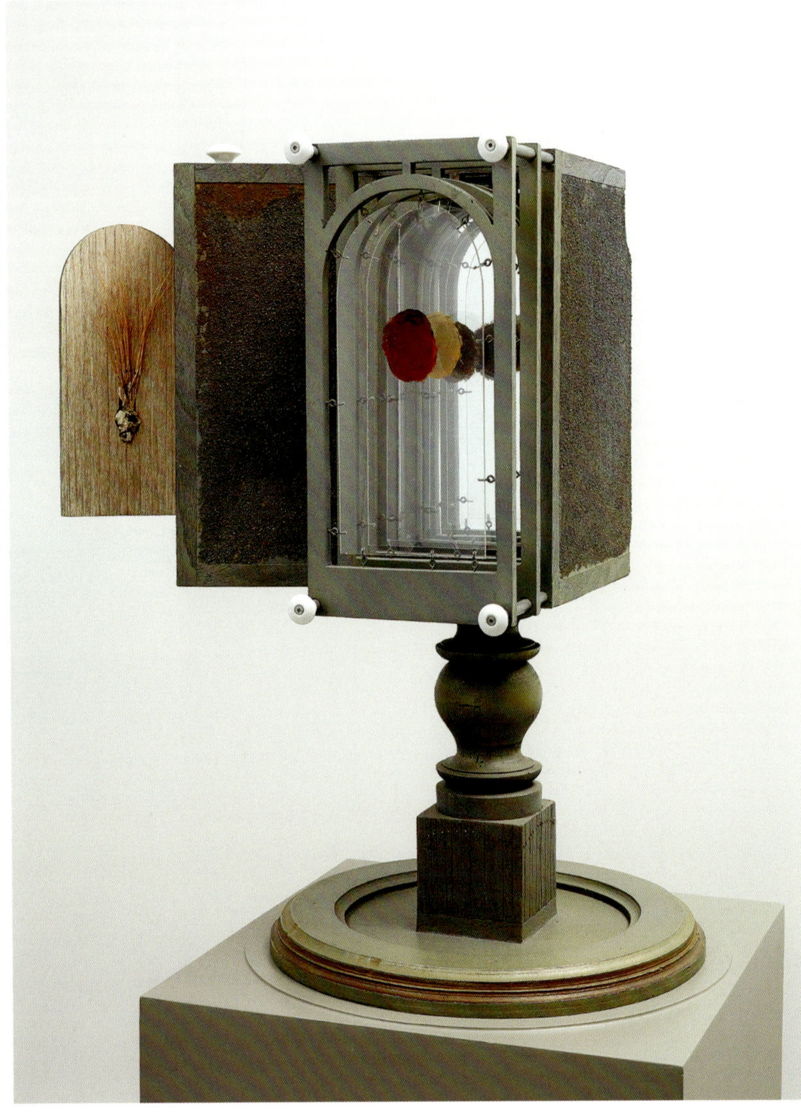

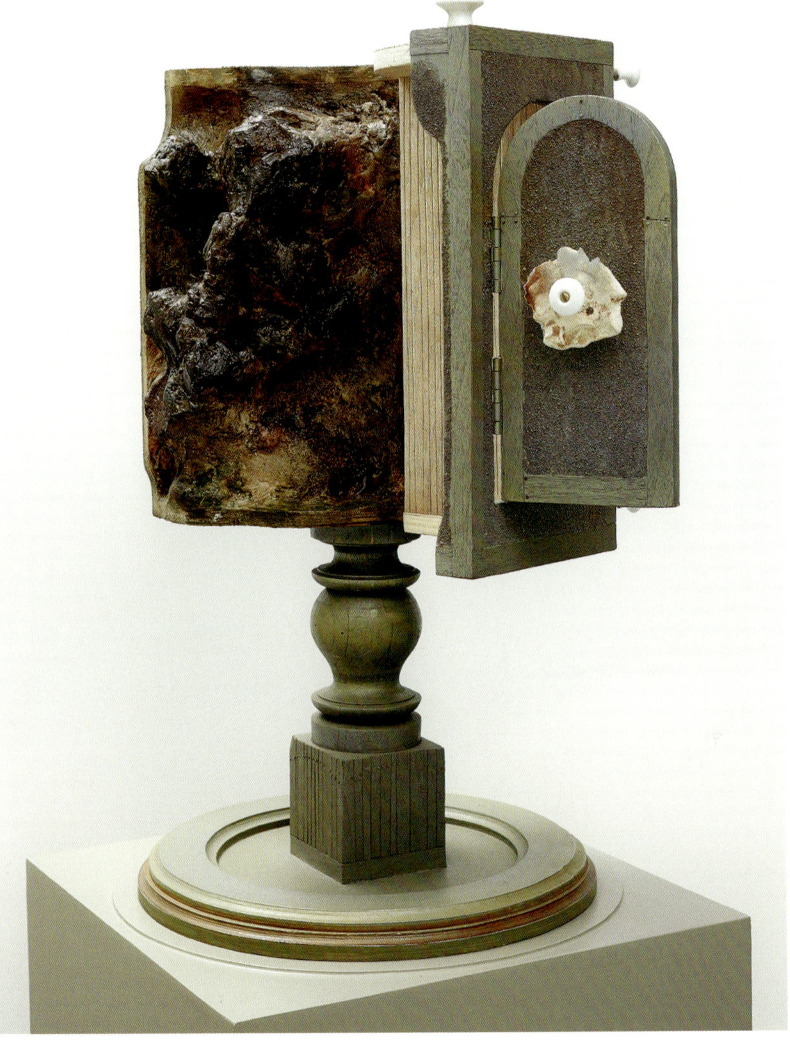

Robert Houle

In Memoriam, 1987
Oil, feathers, leather, and ribbon on plywood
137.2 × 151.9 × 9 cm
Art Gallery of Ontario, gift of Vanessa, Britney, and Nelson Niedzielski, 2000, 2000/1196

"*In Memoriam* is about the aesthetics of disappearance. Language and text are used to reference power, violence, and colonization. It is a visual citation identifying seven extinct nations as an act of vigilance against the pernicious indifference and cognitive discrimination towards First Nations." —Robert Houle

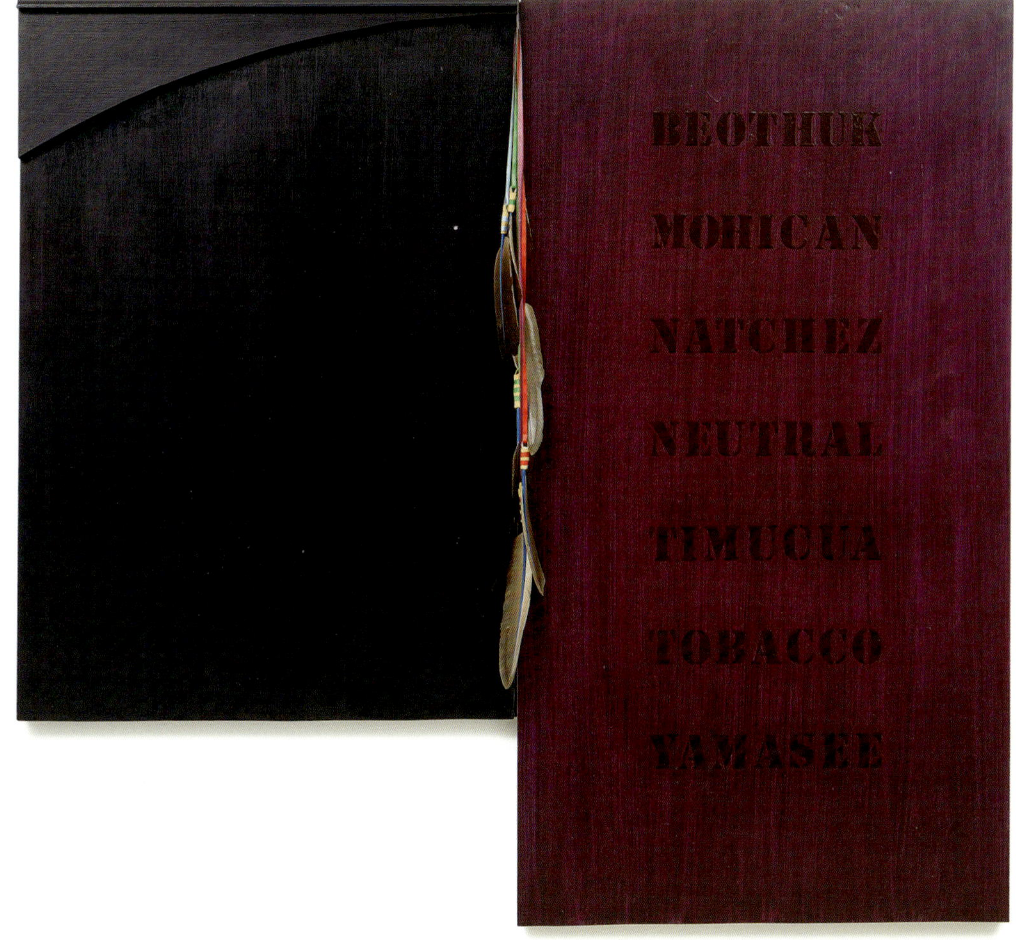

Robert Nelson Markle

Snakes Galore, 1987
Acrylic on paper
111.8 × 76 cm
Art Gallery of Ontario, gift of Marlene Markle, Holstein, Ontario, 2001, 2001/445

Art Gallery of Ontario Artist Life Member card, 1980s (not shown here)
Robert Markle fonds, E.P. Taylor Library & Archives, Art Gallery of Ontario, gift of Marlene Markle, 2004

Certificate of Indian Status, 1980s (not shown here)
Robert Markle fonds, E.P. Taylor Library & Archives, Art Gallery of Ontario, gift of Marlene Markle, 2004

John Graham Coughtry
To Robert from Graham with love, c. 1969 (not shown here)
Artist book gifted to Robert Markle
Robert Markle fonds, E.P. Taylor Library & Archives, Art Gallery of Ontario, gift of Marlene Markle, 2004

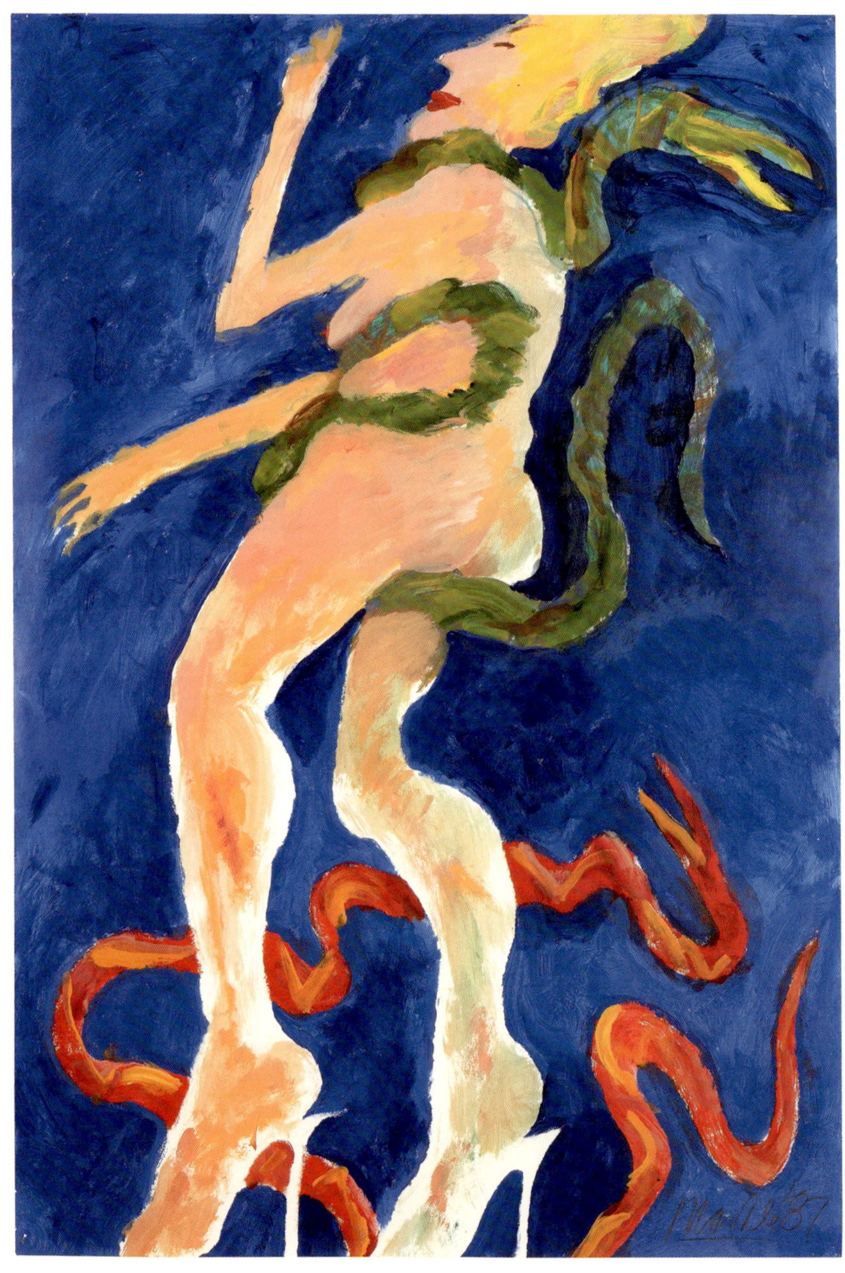

Norval Morrisseau

Ancestral Warrior, 1972
Acrylic on paper
76.3 × 56.5 cm
Art Gallery of Ontario, gift of
Dr. Peter Lewin, Toronto, 1999, 99/543

"Norval, [with] his incredible ability with the formal problems of art (colour-design-space) and his commitment to the world of his people, gives one the sense of power that only genius provides… It is sufficient to say that in the history of Canadian painting, few have, and will remain giants. Norval shall." —Jack Pollock, Toronto art dealer

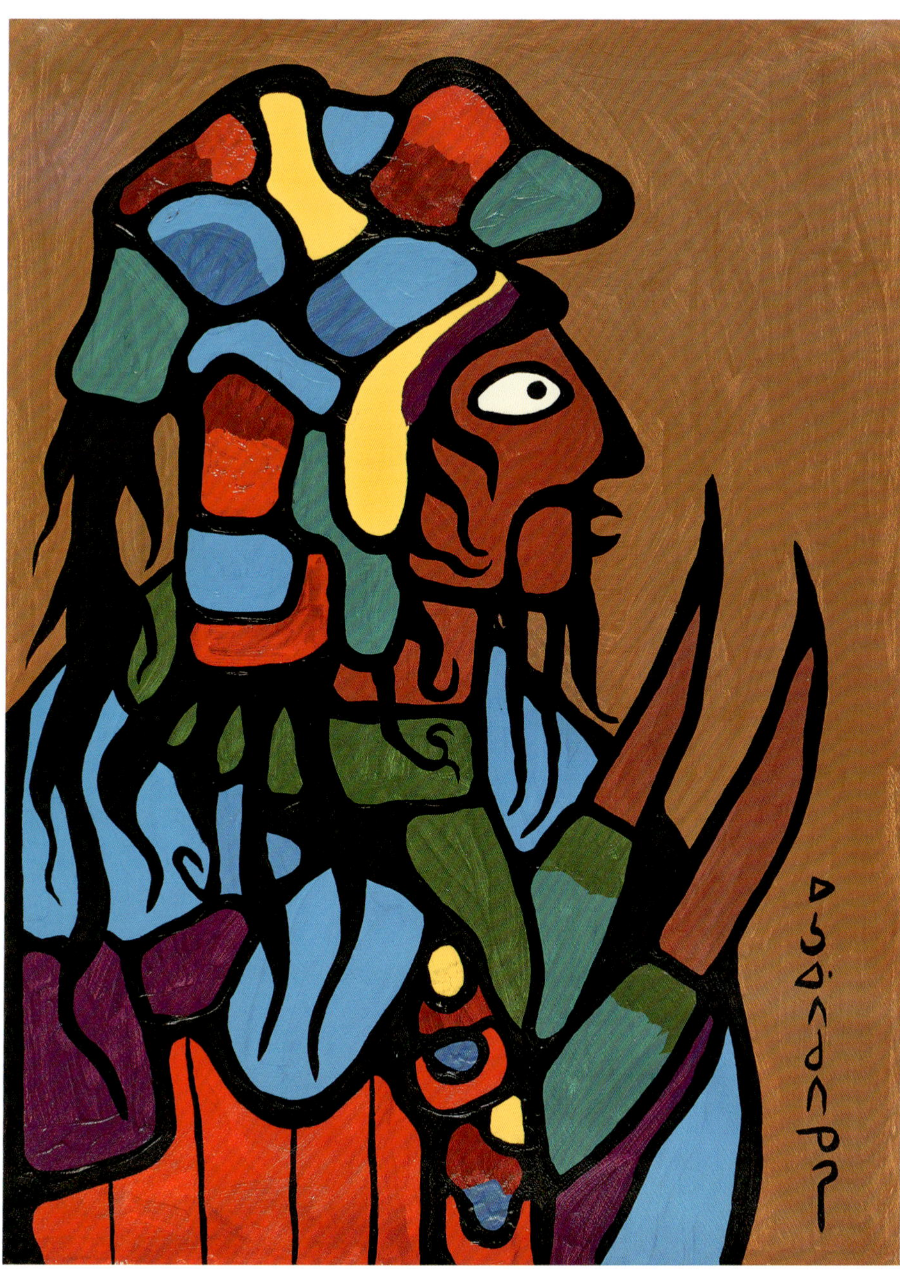

Nancy Johnson

Allies—Several Stories, Part II, 1984
Opaque watercolour on paper
55.9 × 86.4 cm each
Art Gallery of Ontario, gift from
the George W. Gilmour Perspective
Exhibition Fund, 1987, 86/287 A-J

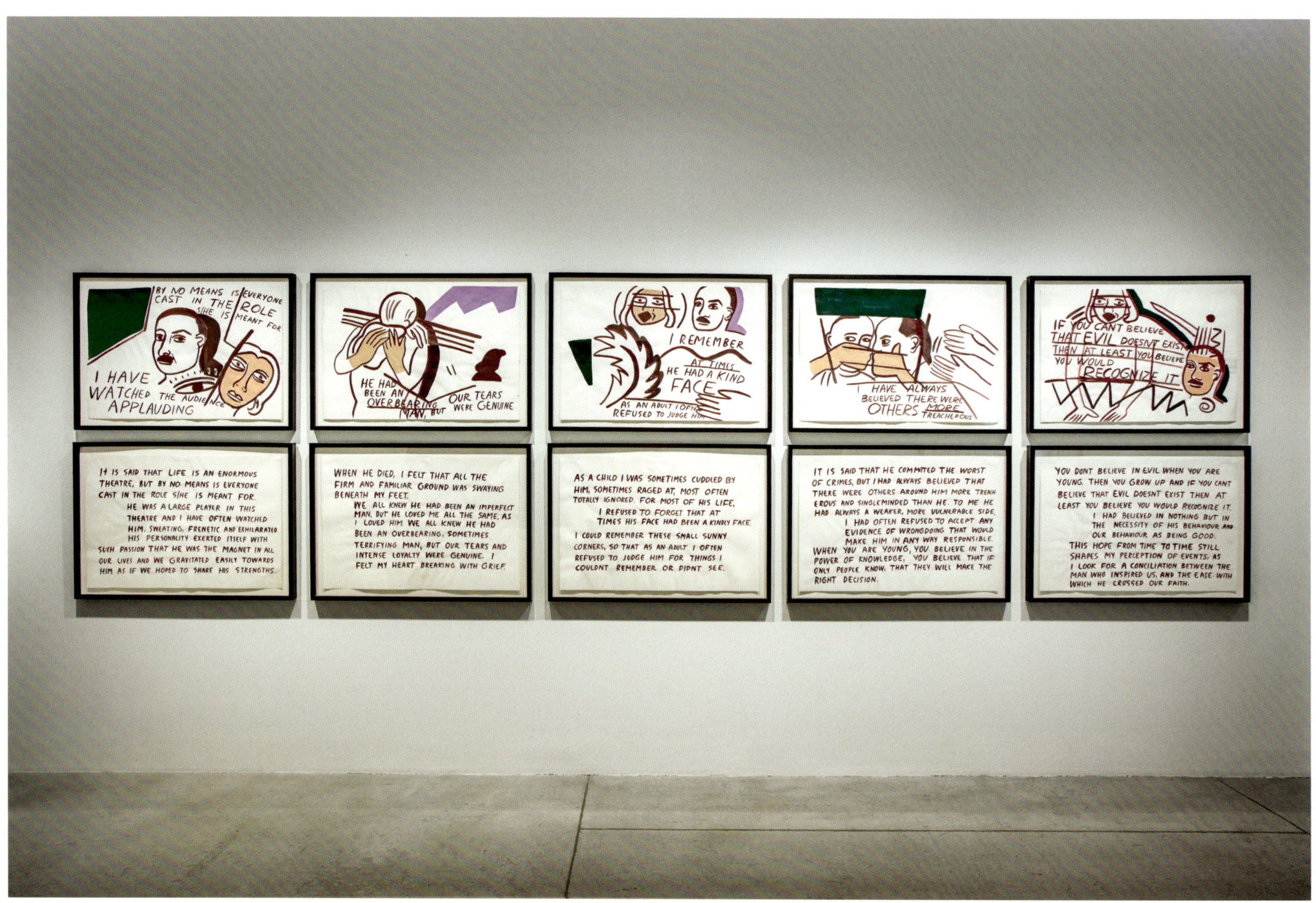

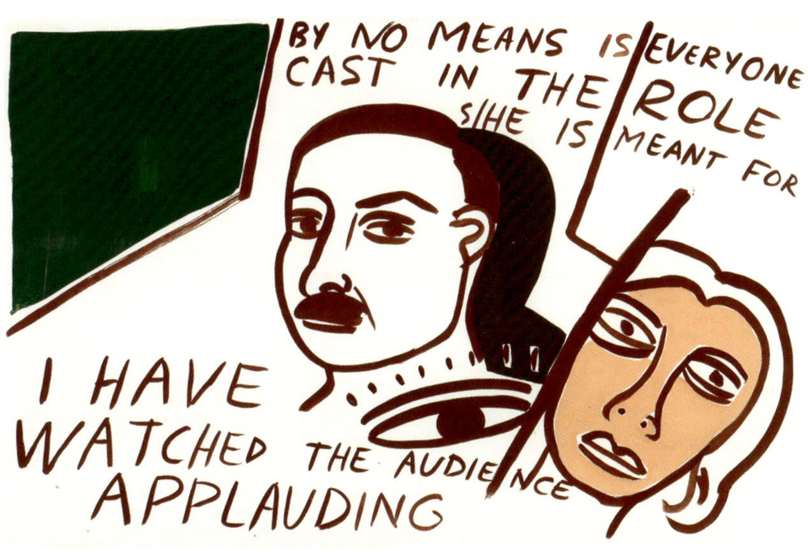

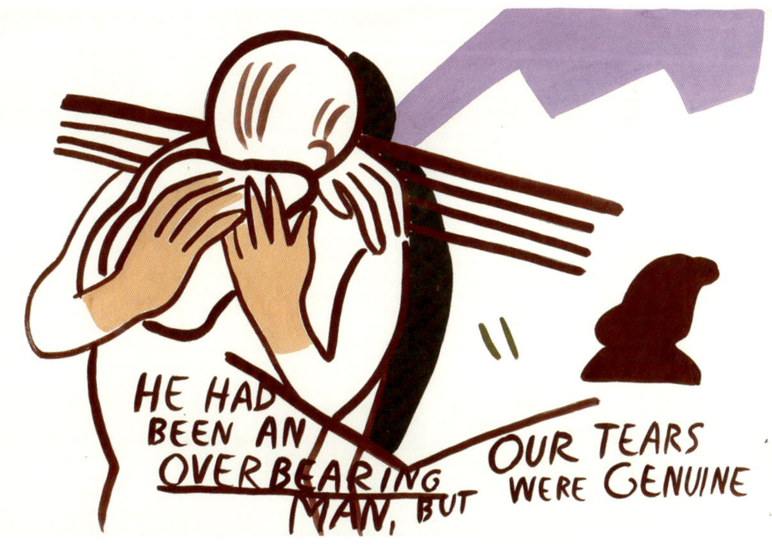

IT IS SAID THAT LIFE IS AN ENORMOUS THEATRE, BUT BY NO MEANS IS EVERYONE CAST IN THE ROLE S/HE IS MEANT FOR.

HE WAS A LARGE PLAYER IN THIS THEATRE AND I HAVE OFTEN WATCHED HIM, SWEATING, FRENETIC AND EXHILARATED.

HIS PERSONALITY EXERTED ITSELF WITH SUCH PASSION THAT HE WAS THE MAGNET IN ALL OUR LIVES AND WE GRAVITATED EASILY TOWARDS HIM AS IF WE HOPED TO SHARE HIS STRENGTHS.

WHEN HE DIED, I FELT THAT ALL THE FIRM AND FAMILIAR GROUND WAS SWAYING BENEATH MY FEET.

WE ALL KNEW HE HAD BEEN AN IMPERFECT MAN, BUT HE LOVED ME ALL THE SAME, AS I LOVED HIM. WE ALL KNEW HE HAD BEEN AN OVERBEARING, SOMETIMES TERRIFYING MAN, BUT OUR TEARS AND INTENSE LOYALTY WERE GENUINE. I FELT MY HEART BREAKING WITH GRIEF.

Douglas Walker

Untitled (Flowers of Acne), 1986
Resin-coated gelatin silver prints with marker ink
234.8 × 152.5 cm
Art Gallery of Ontario, gift of Robert and
Lynn Simpson, 1998, 98/228

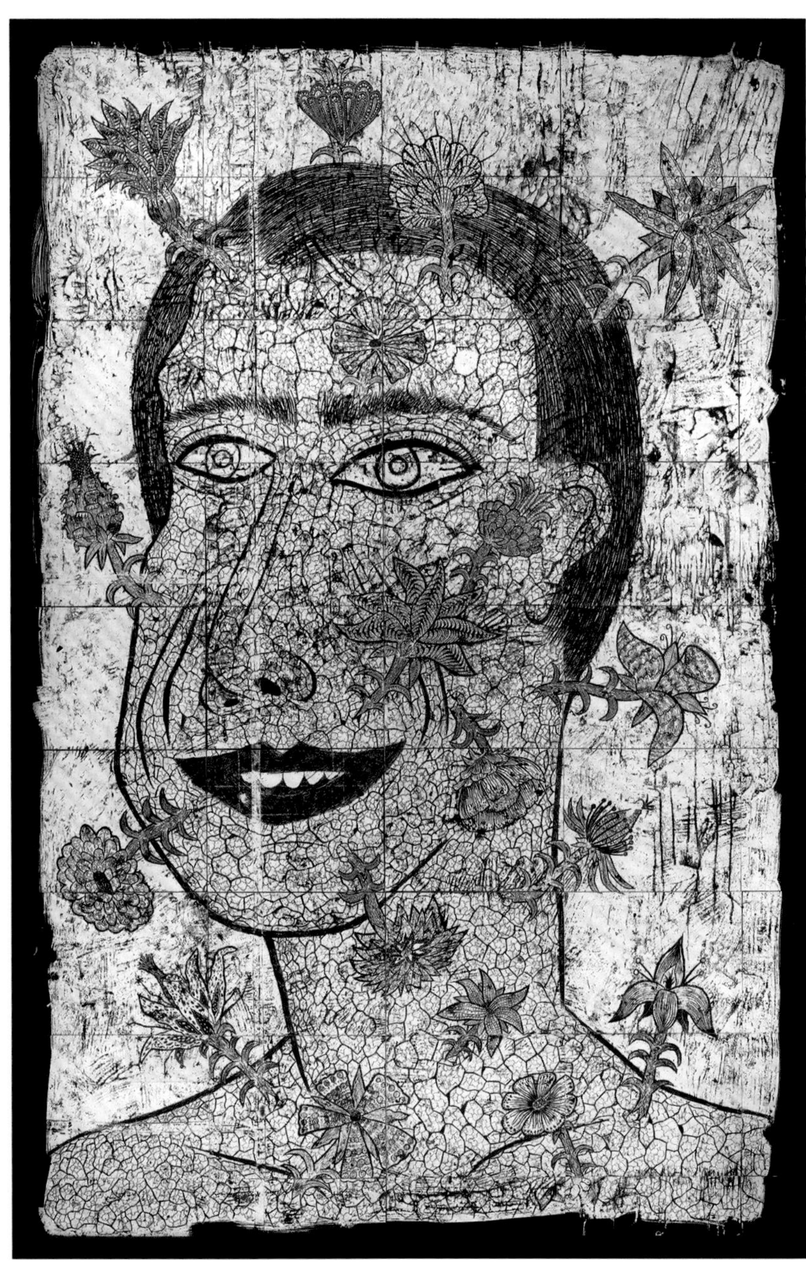

Andy Patton

The Statues, 1983
Oil on canvas
152.6 × 244 cm
Art Gallery of Ontario, purchase, 1984, 84/108

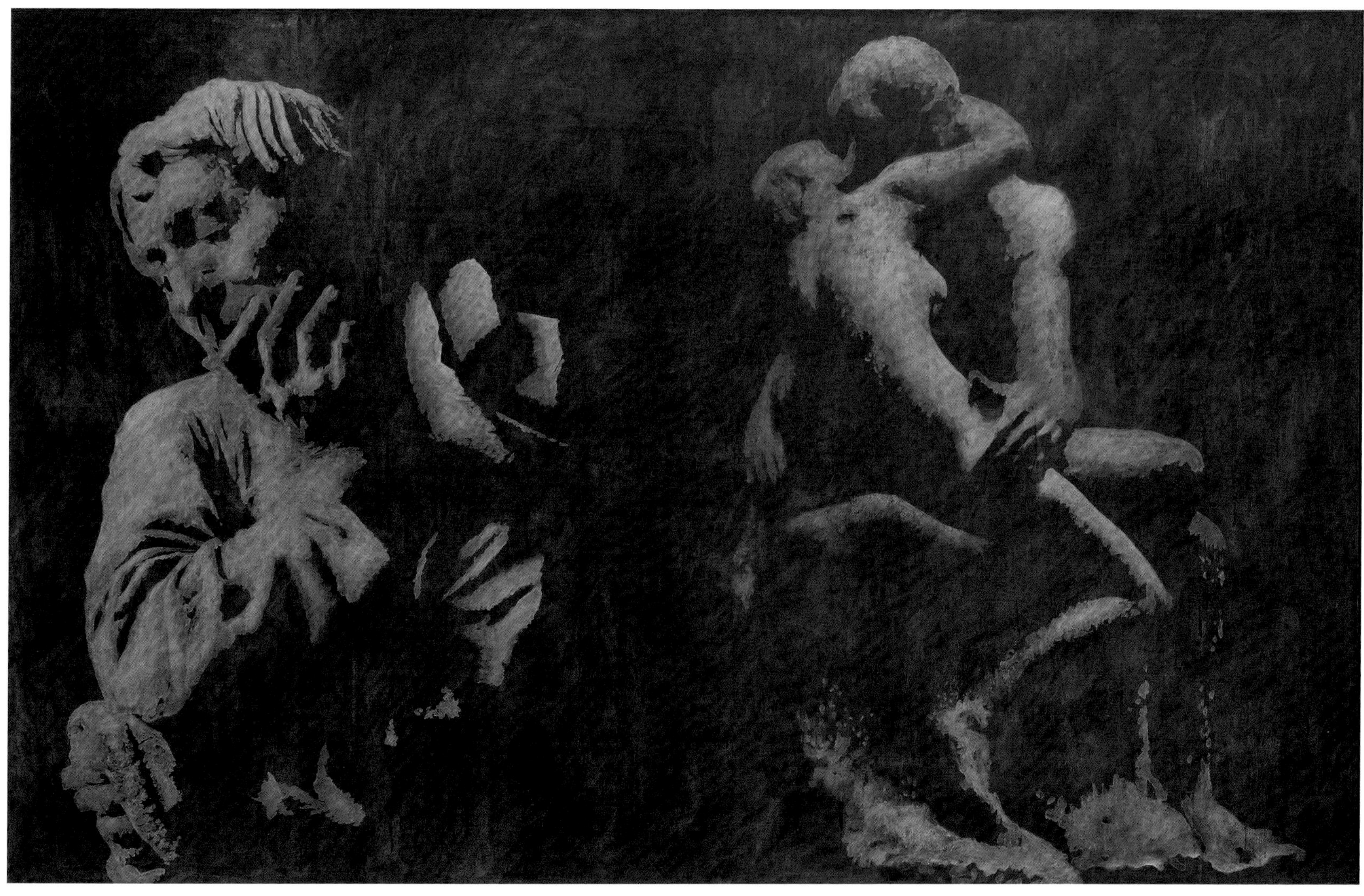

Vera Frenkel

The Business of Frightened Desires: Or, the Making of a Pornographer, 1984
Slide projector, photographic prints, and archive materials
Courtesy of the artist

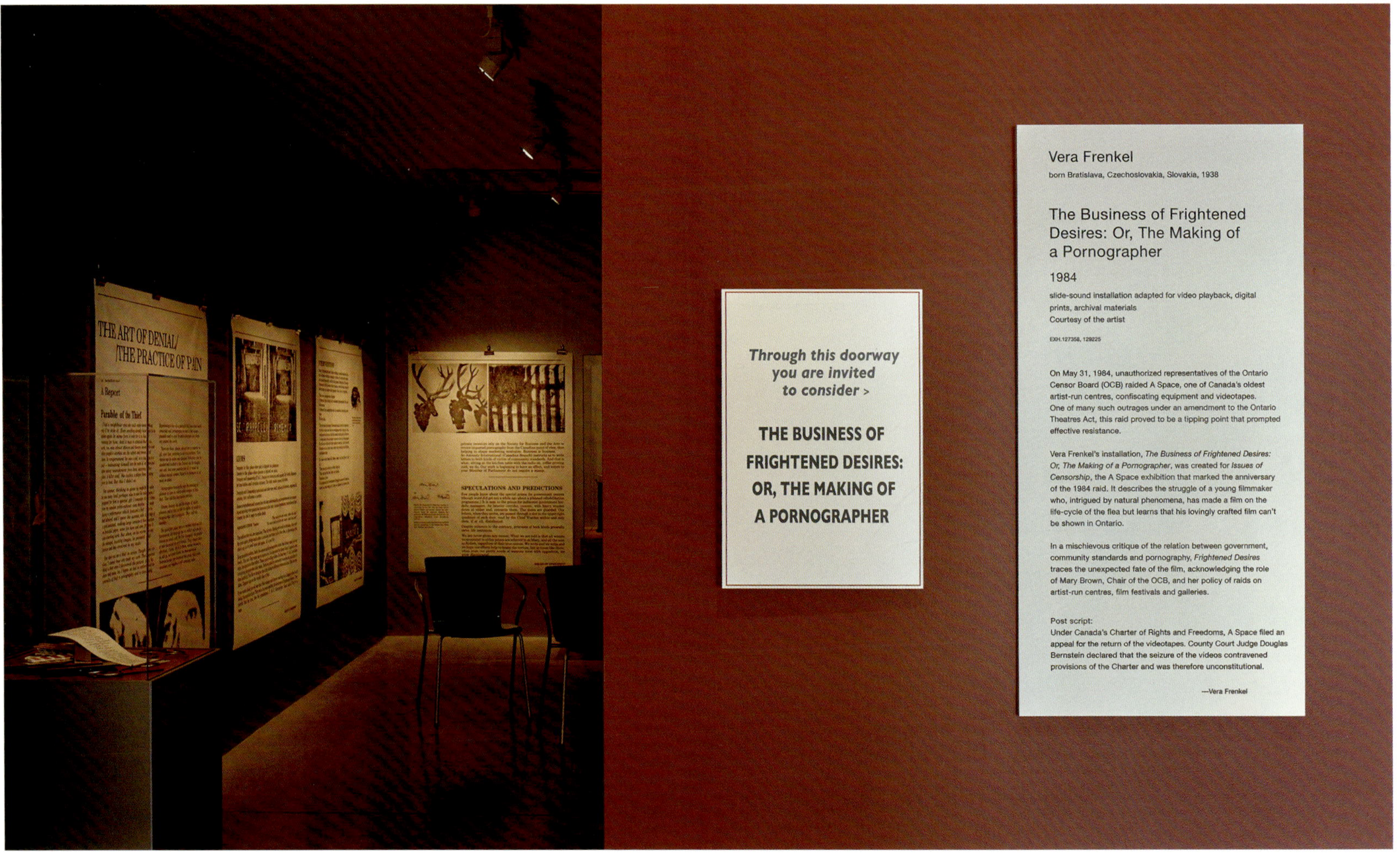

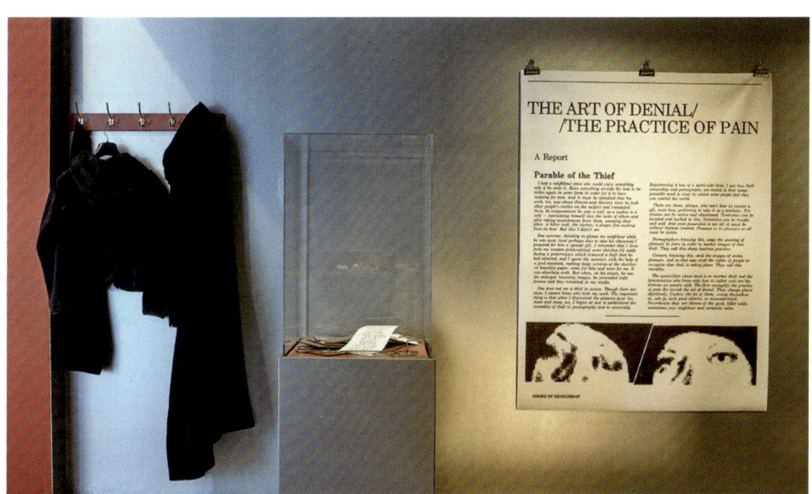
THE ART OF DENIAL/
/THE PRACTICE OF PAIN
A Report
Parable of the Thief

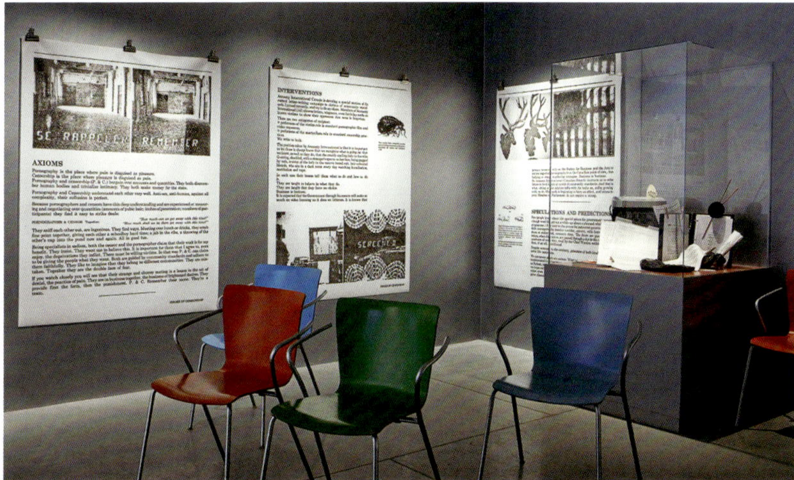
AXIOMS
INTERVENTIONS

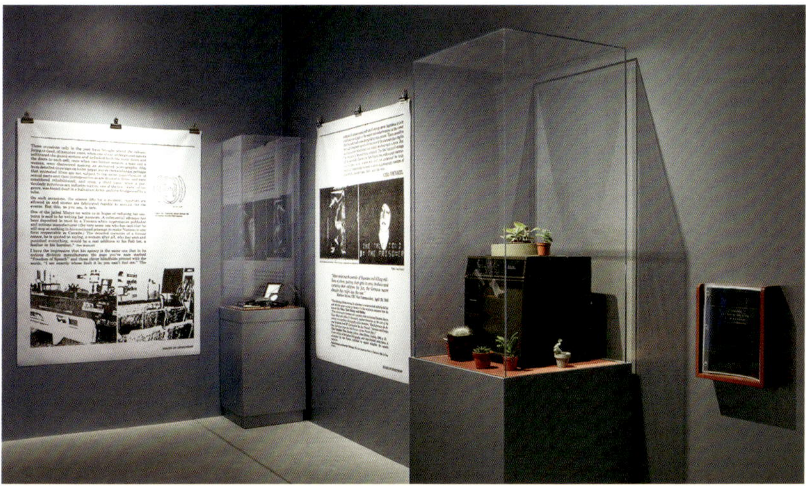

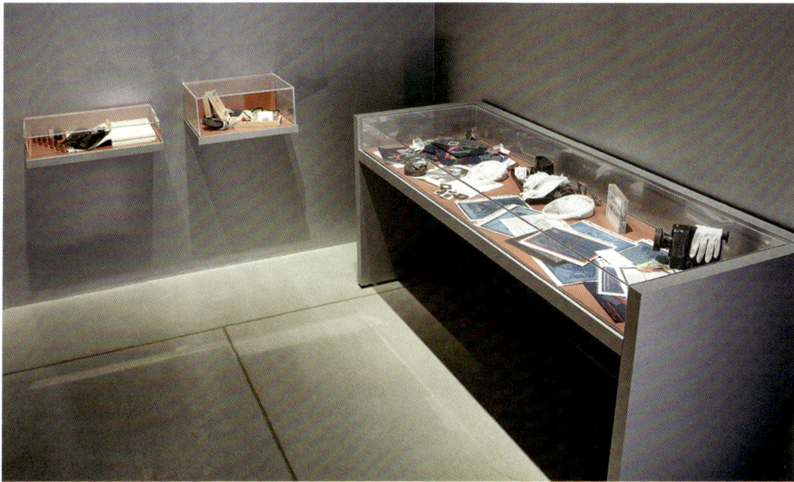

John Scott

Trans Am Apocalypse No. 3, 1998–2000
Incised text on acrylic paint on
1980 Pontiac Firebird Trans Am
129 × 184 × 504 cm
Art Gallery of Ontario, gift of Chris Poulsen,
2007, 2007/102

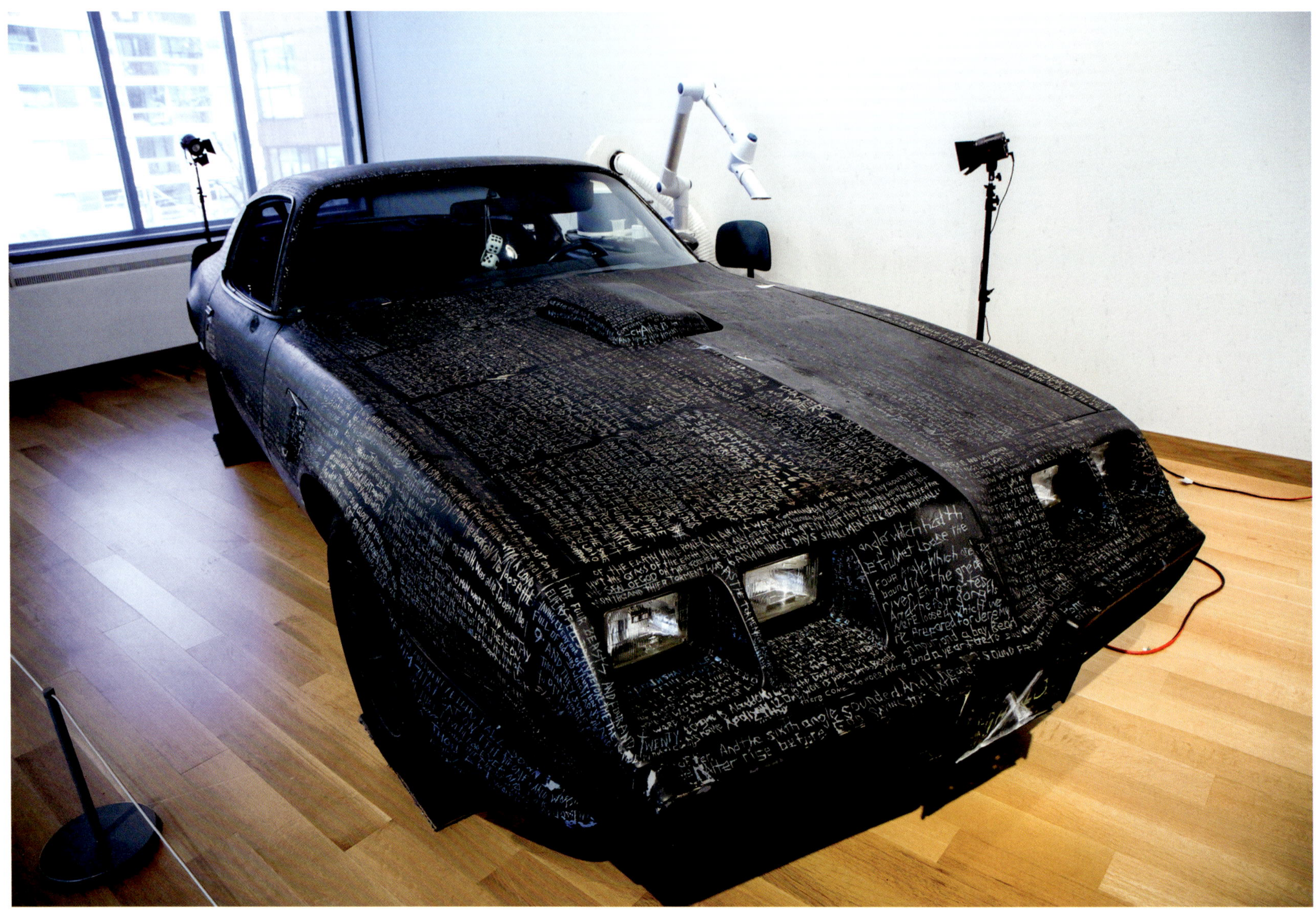

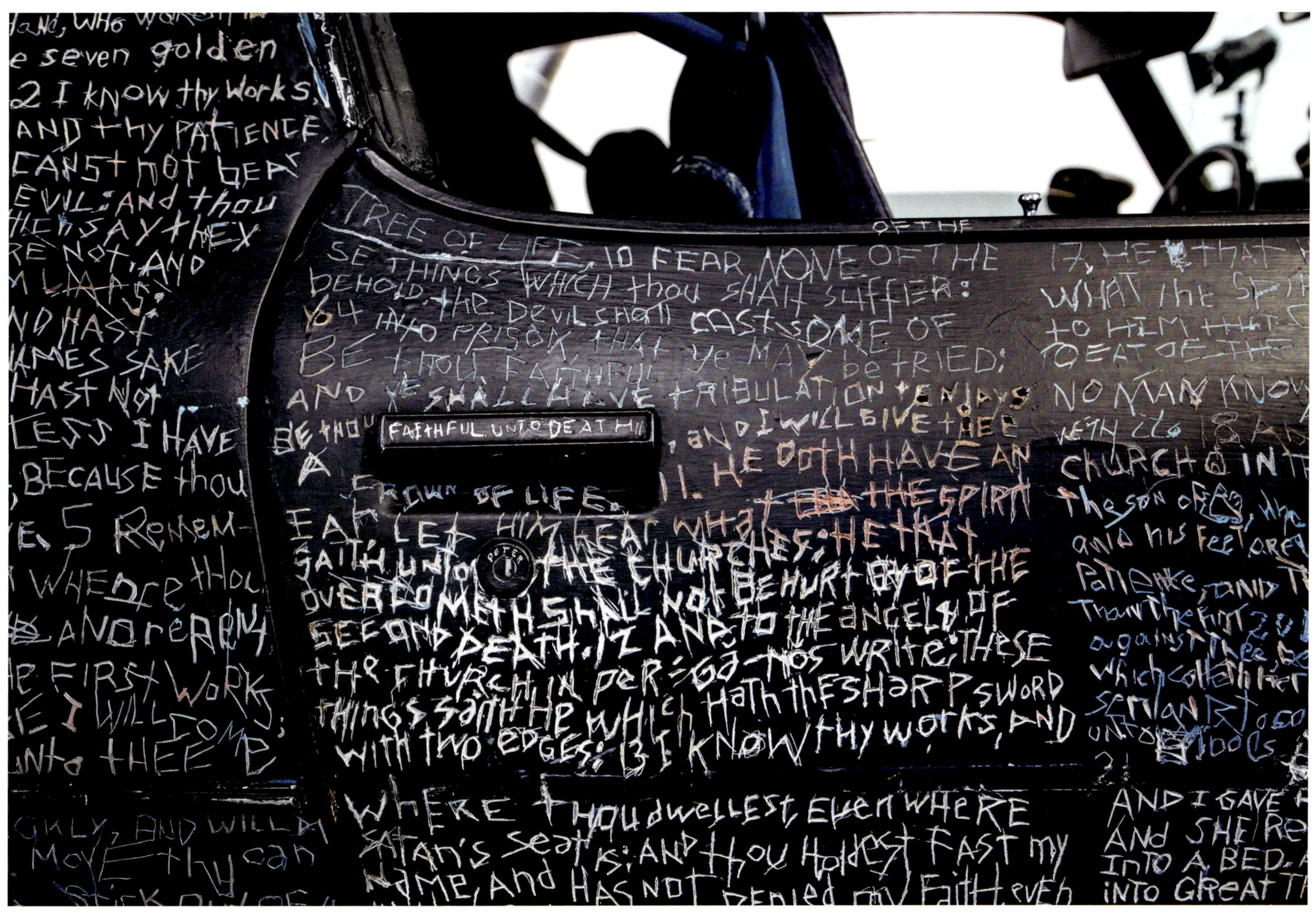
seven golden
2 I know thy works,
AND thy PATIENCE,
FAITHFUL UNTO DEATH
things saith he which hath the sharp sword
with two edges; 13 I KNOW thy works, AND
WHERE thou dwellest, even where
Satan's seat is: AND thou Holdest fast my
NO MAN KNOW
AND I GAVE
INTO GREAT

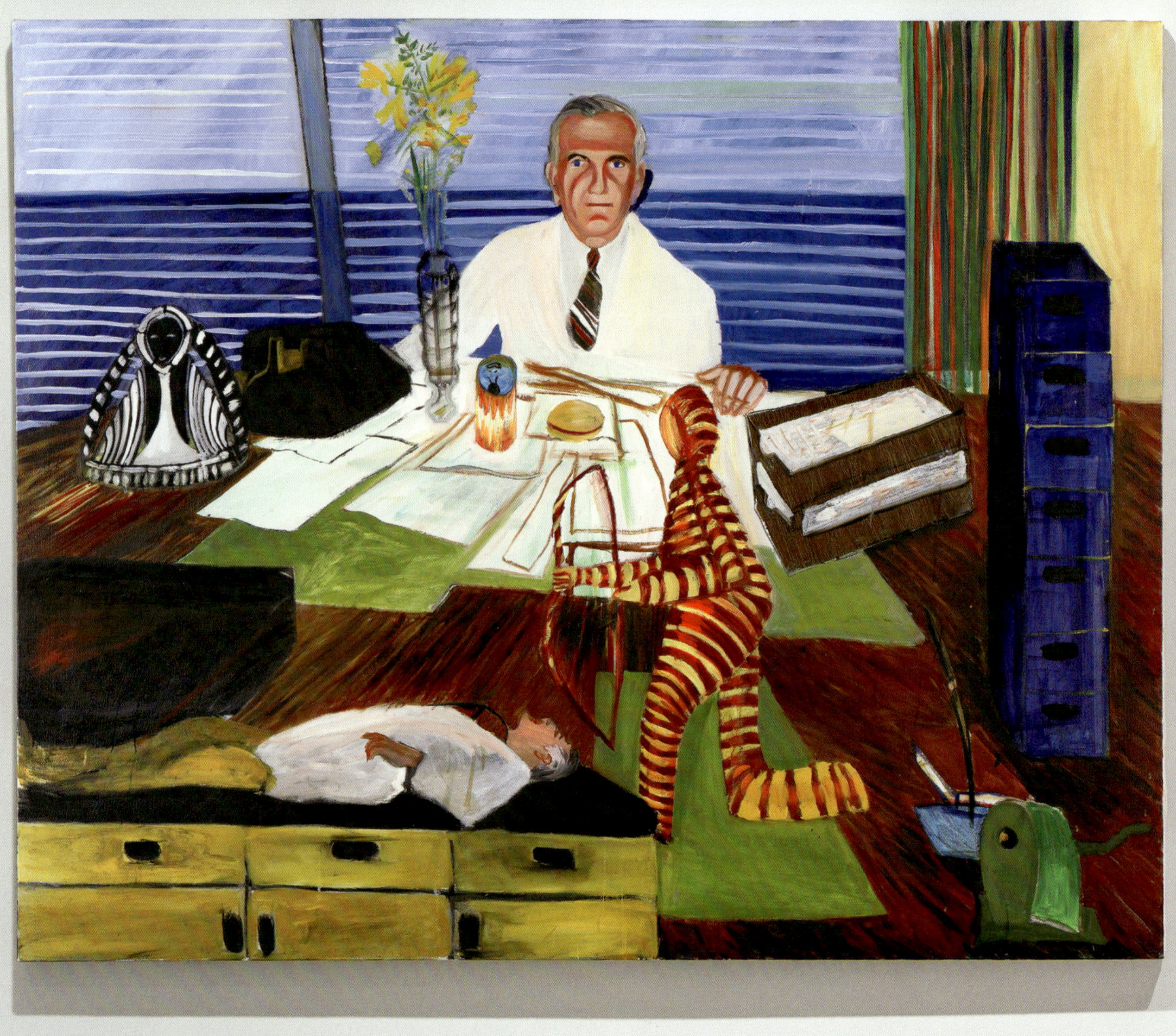
Oliver Girling
Dual Portrait of
Dr. Michael Braudo M.D.
1980

Representation

E-waabnjigaadeg

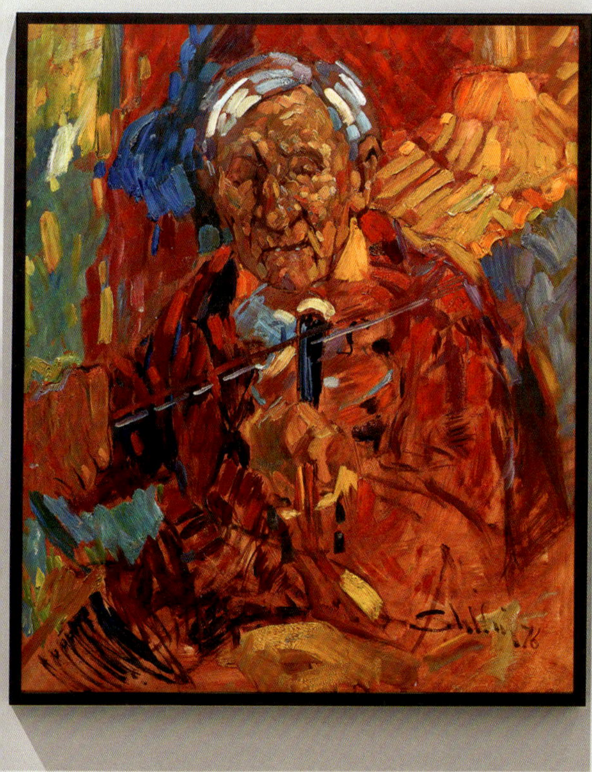

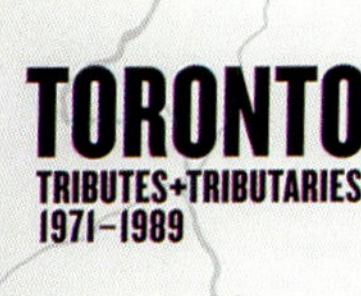

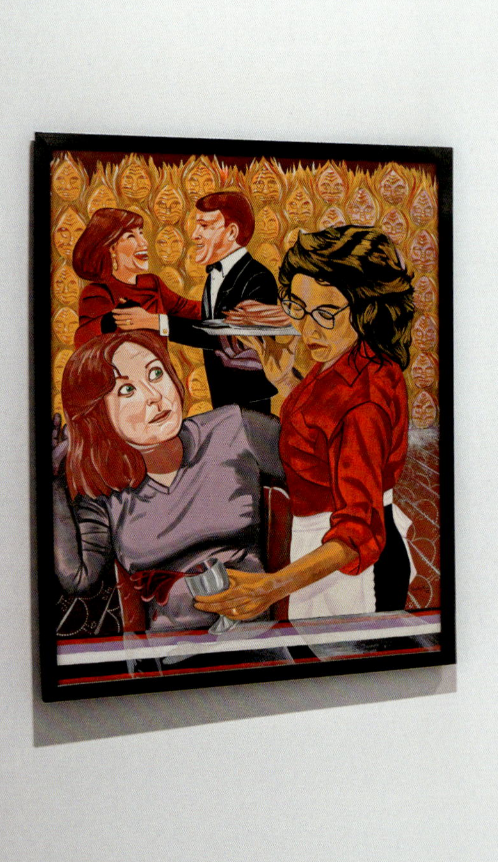

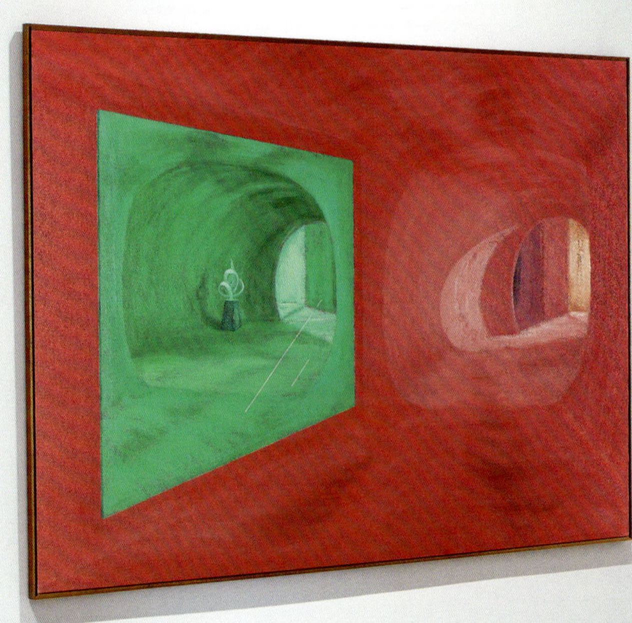

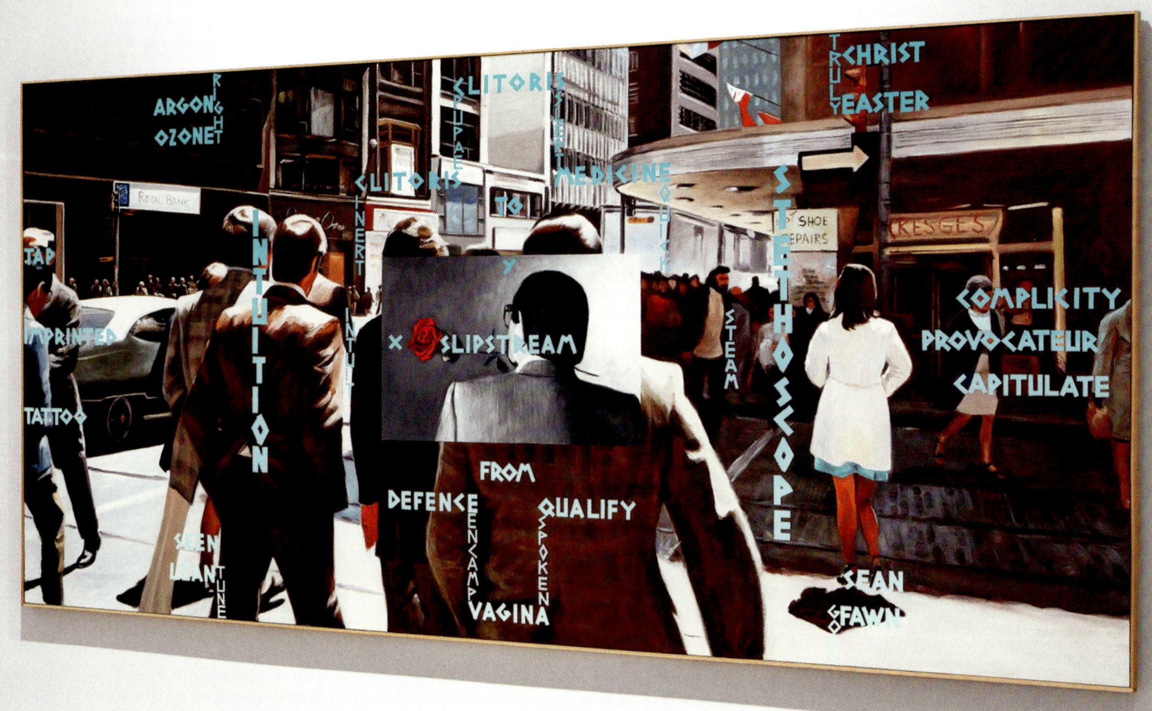

ARGON
OZONE
RIGHT
CLITORIS
CLITORIS
TRULY
CHRIST
EASTER
MEDICINE
INTUITION
INERT
TO
SHOE REPAIRS
KRESGES
STETHOSCOPE
STEAM
JAP
IMPRINTED
TATTOO
SLIPSTREAM
COMPLICITY
PROVOCATEUR
CAPITULATE
FROM
DEFENCE
ENCAMP
QUALIFY
SPOKEN
VAGINA
SEEN
LEAN
TUNE
SEAN
FAWN

Tim Jocelyn

Spaceman, Yellow, Orange & Blue, 1985
Cut coloured paper and vinyl collage on paper
40.1 × 32.5 cm
Art Gallery of Ontario, gift of Norman Garnet, 1999, 99/738

West Wind with Satellite, 1985
Cut coloured paper collage on paper
34.4 × 30.3 cm
Art Gallery of Ontario, gift of Norman Garnet, 1999, 99/739

Deer, Geese, Satellite, 1986 (not shown here)
Cut coloured and metallic-coated vinyl collage on paper
54.6 × 53.3 cm
Art Gallery of Ontario, gift of Norman Garnet, 1999, 99/740

Moose "Electrified," 1985 (not shown here)
Cut coloured paper collage on paper
45.7 × 35.6 cm
Art Gallery of Ontario, gift of Norman Garnet, 1999, 99/737

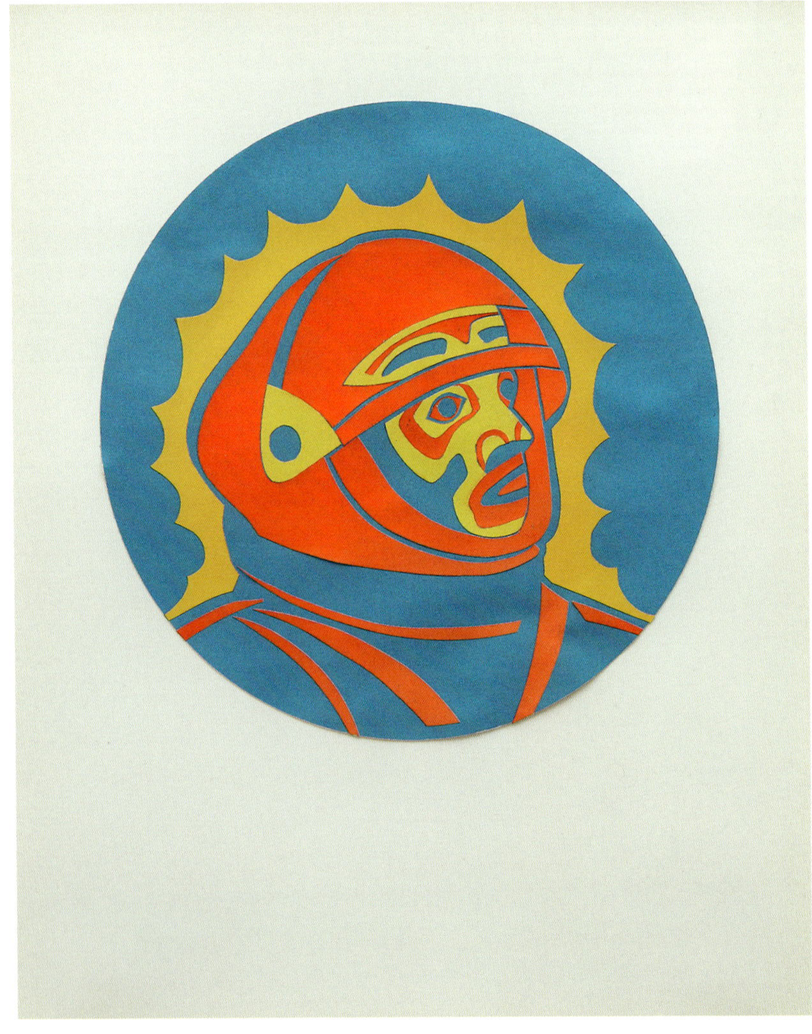

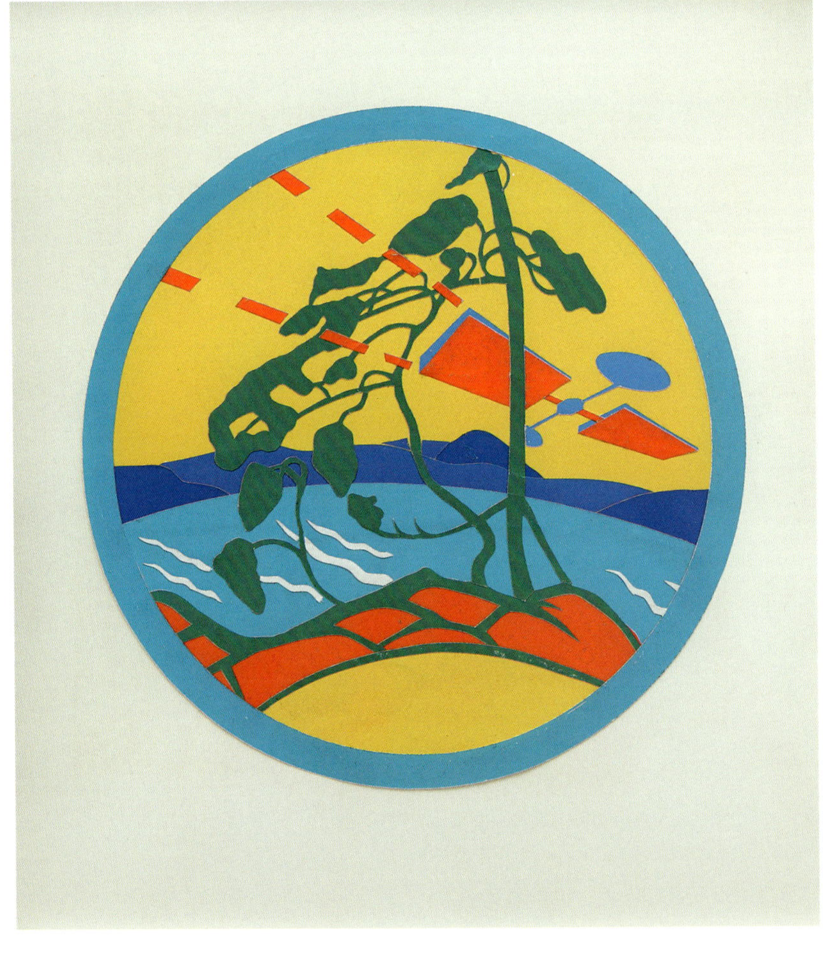

Andy Fabo

The Craft of the Contaminated, 1984
Oil, acrylic, and steel on plywood
230.8 × 182.3 cm
Art Gallery of Ontario, purchase, 1984, 84/107

"If we don't have the wherewithal for real survival we at least have the image of survival down pat. There's no point in arguing who of the artists here caught what from whom…We are all carriers and the waves incessantly pound against our raft." —Andy Fabo

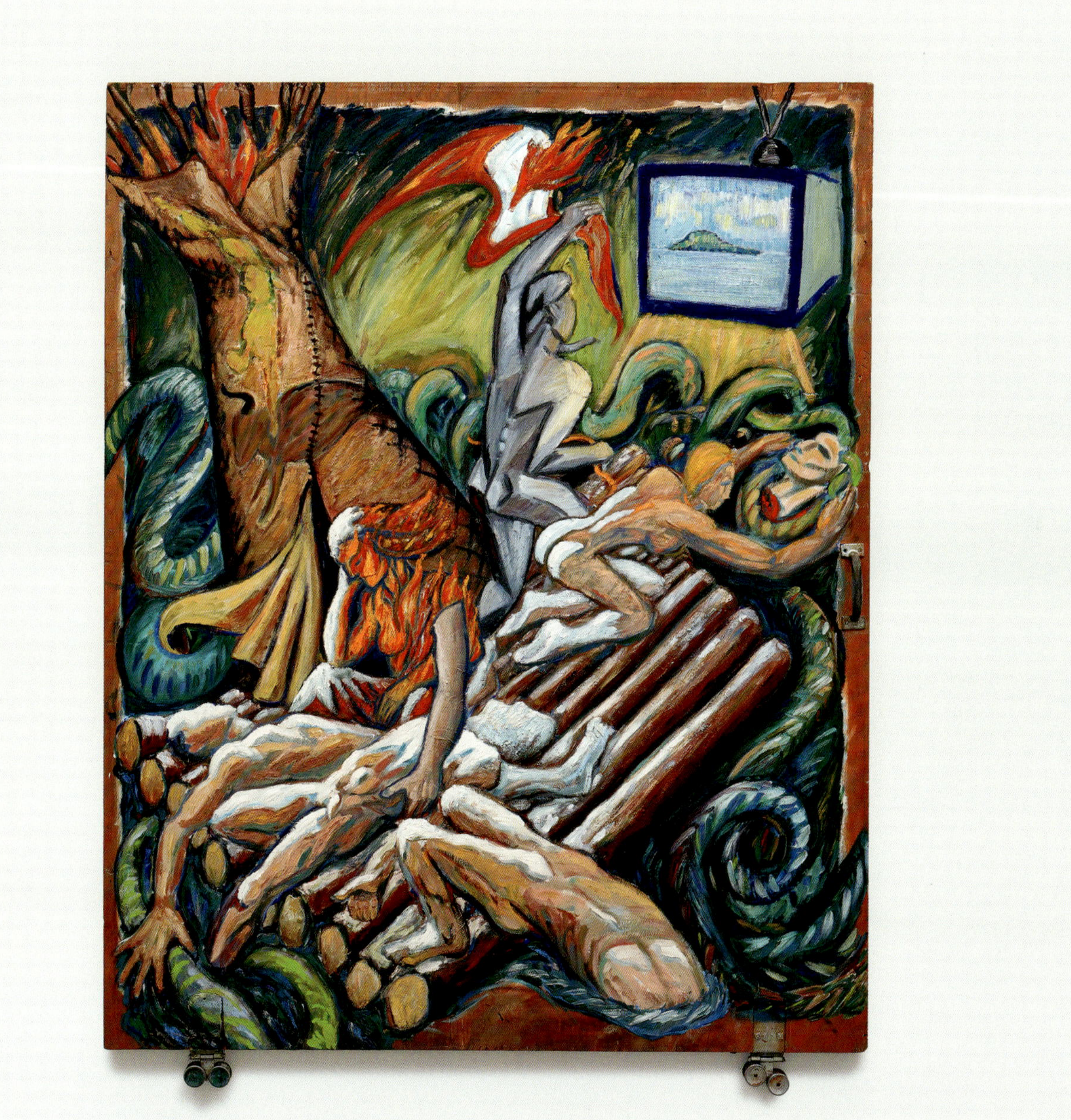

Shirley Wiitasalo

Green Mirror with Sculpture, 1986
Oil on canvas
152.4 × 213.4 cm
Art Gallery of Ontario, purchase, 1989, 89/119

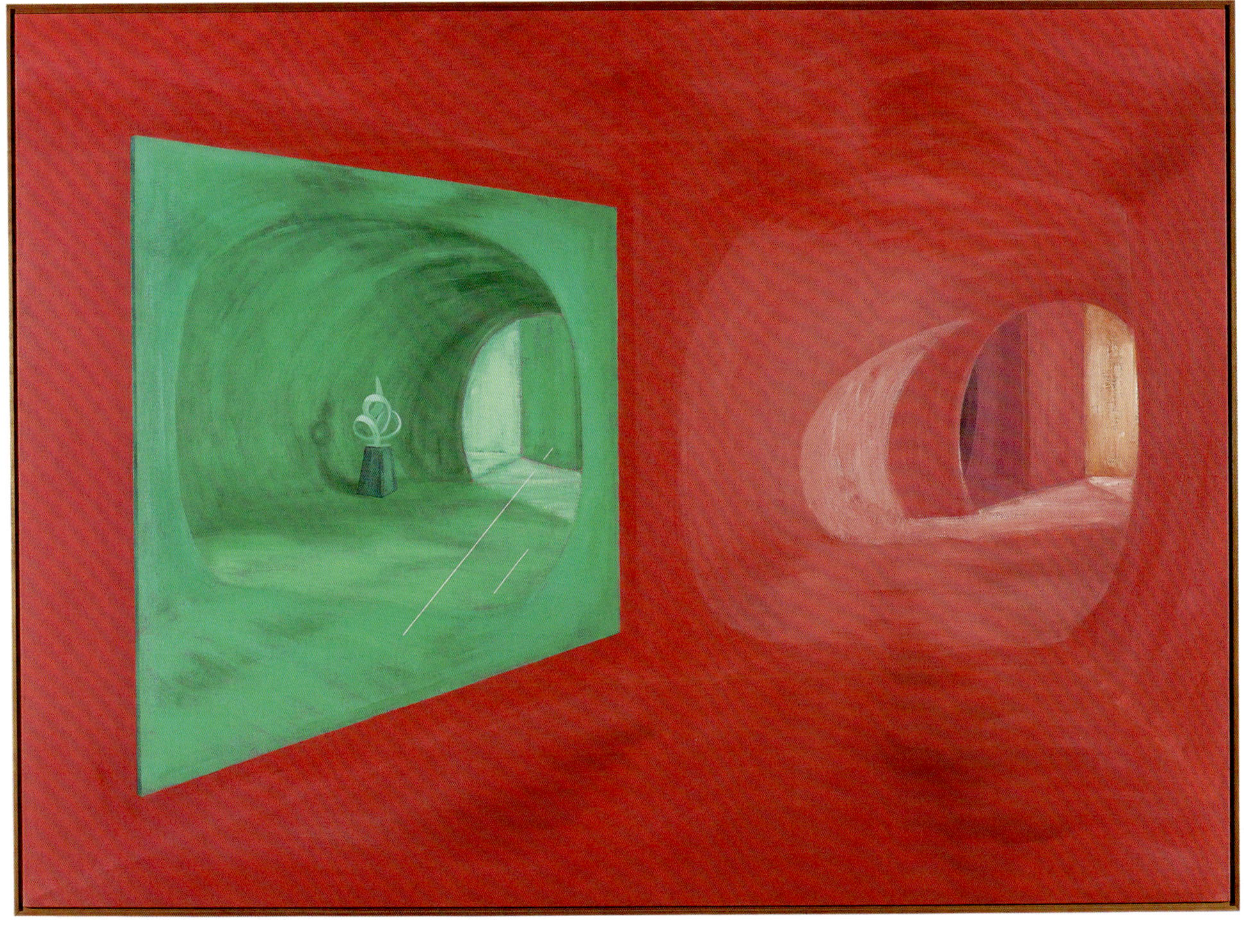

Joanne Tod

Directional Carpet, 1987
Oil and acrylic on canvas
157.5 × 320.2 cm
Art Gallery of Ontario, gift of Morris and Vivian Saffer, 1999, 99/622

"My style was shaped early on, during a time when colour field painting was in vogue. I really had to stand my ground and persevere when realist painting was not the latest flavour." —Joanne Tod

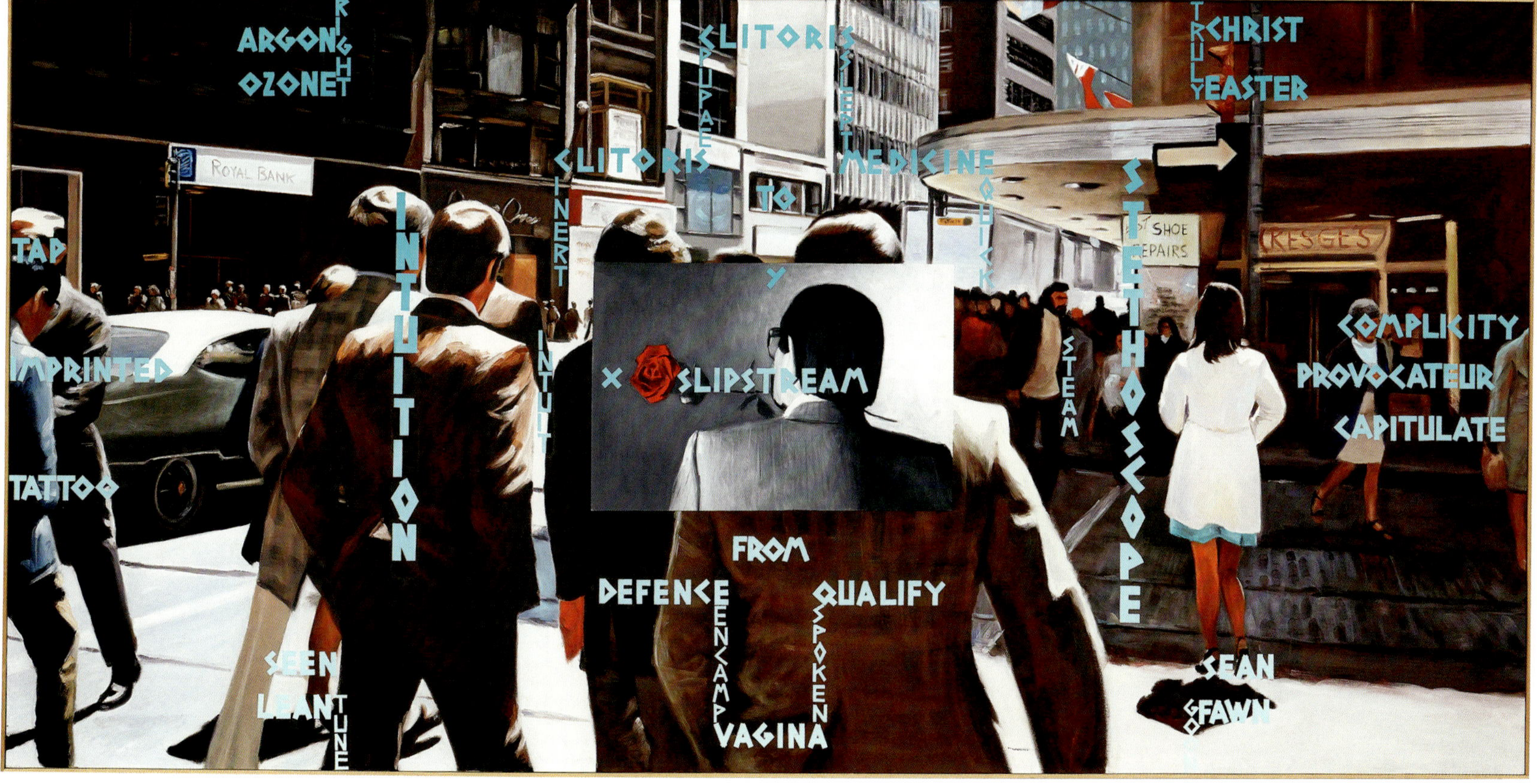

Arthur Shilling

Old Mike, 1976
Oil on hardboard
101.6 × 86 cm
Art Gallery of Ontario, gift of Dr. Michael Braudo, 2007, 2007/753

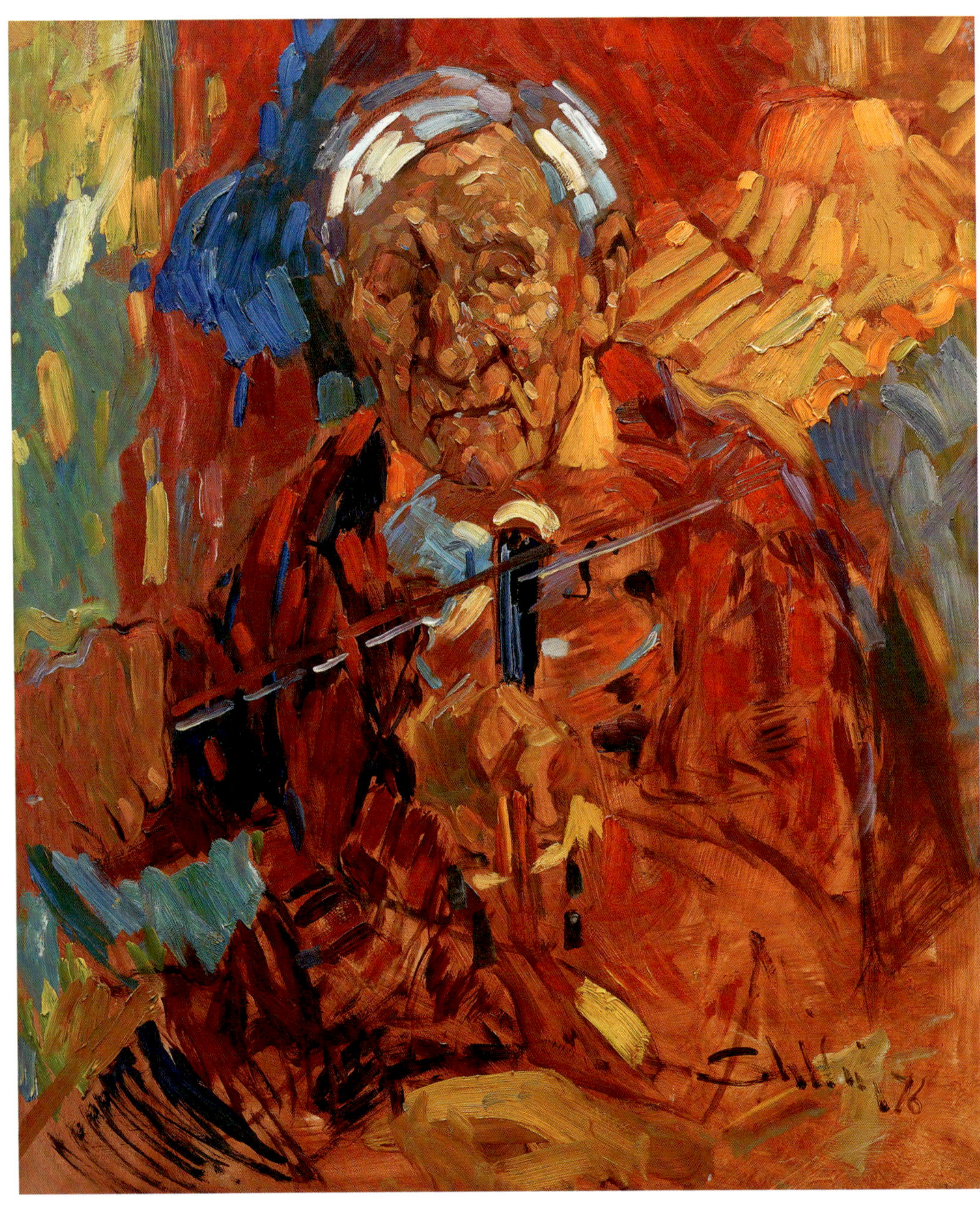

Shelley Niro

Waitress, 1986
Oil on canvas
121.9 × 91.4 cm
Collection of the artist

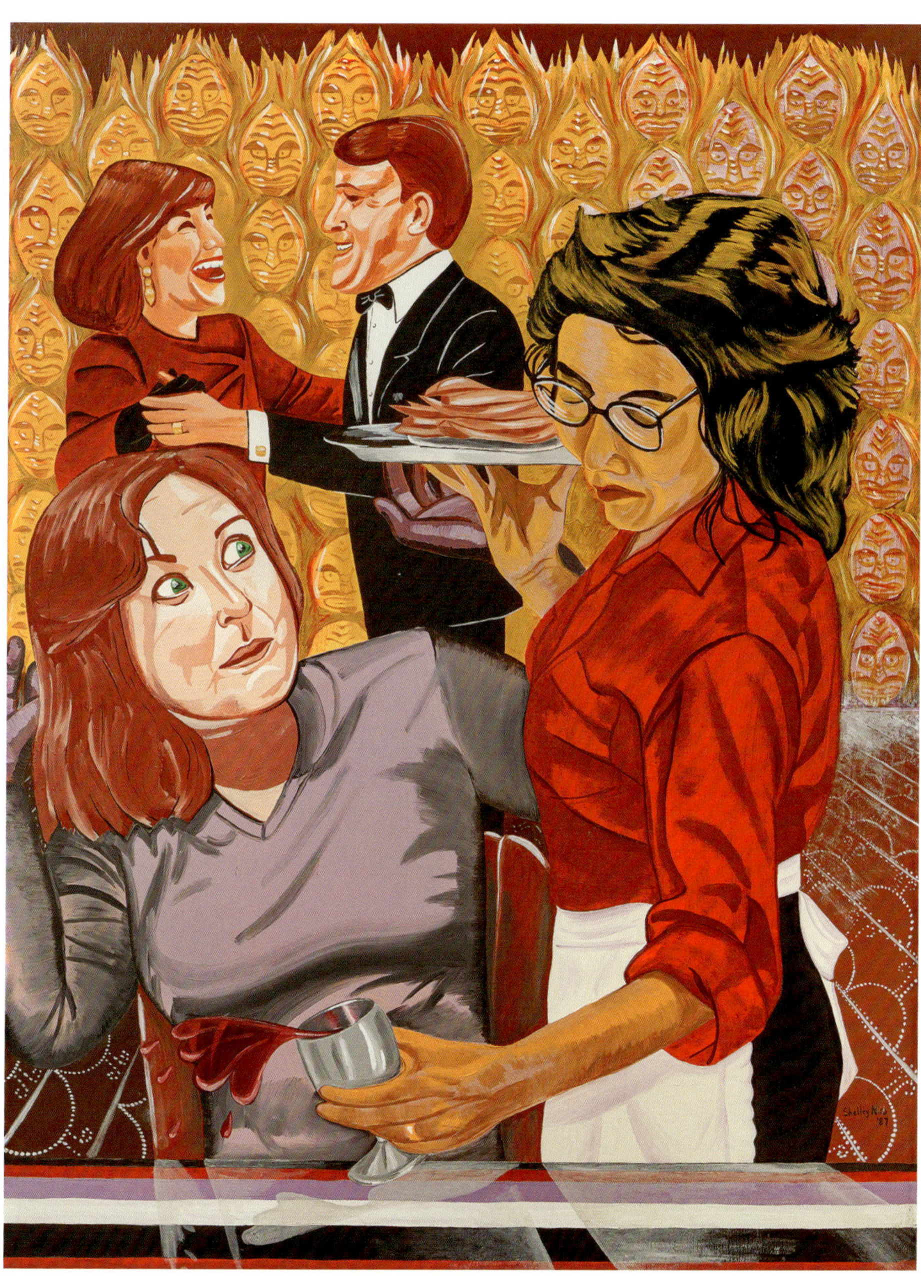

Oliver Girling

Dual Portrait of Dr. Michael Braudo M.D., 1985
Oil on canvas
152.8 × 192 cm
Art Gallery of Ontario, gift of Dr. Michael Braudo, 2007, 2007/729

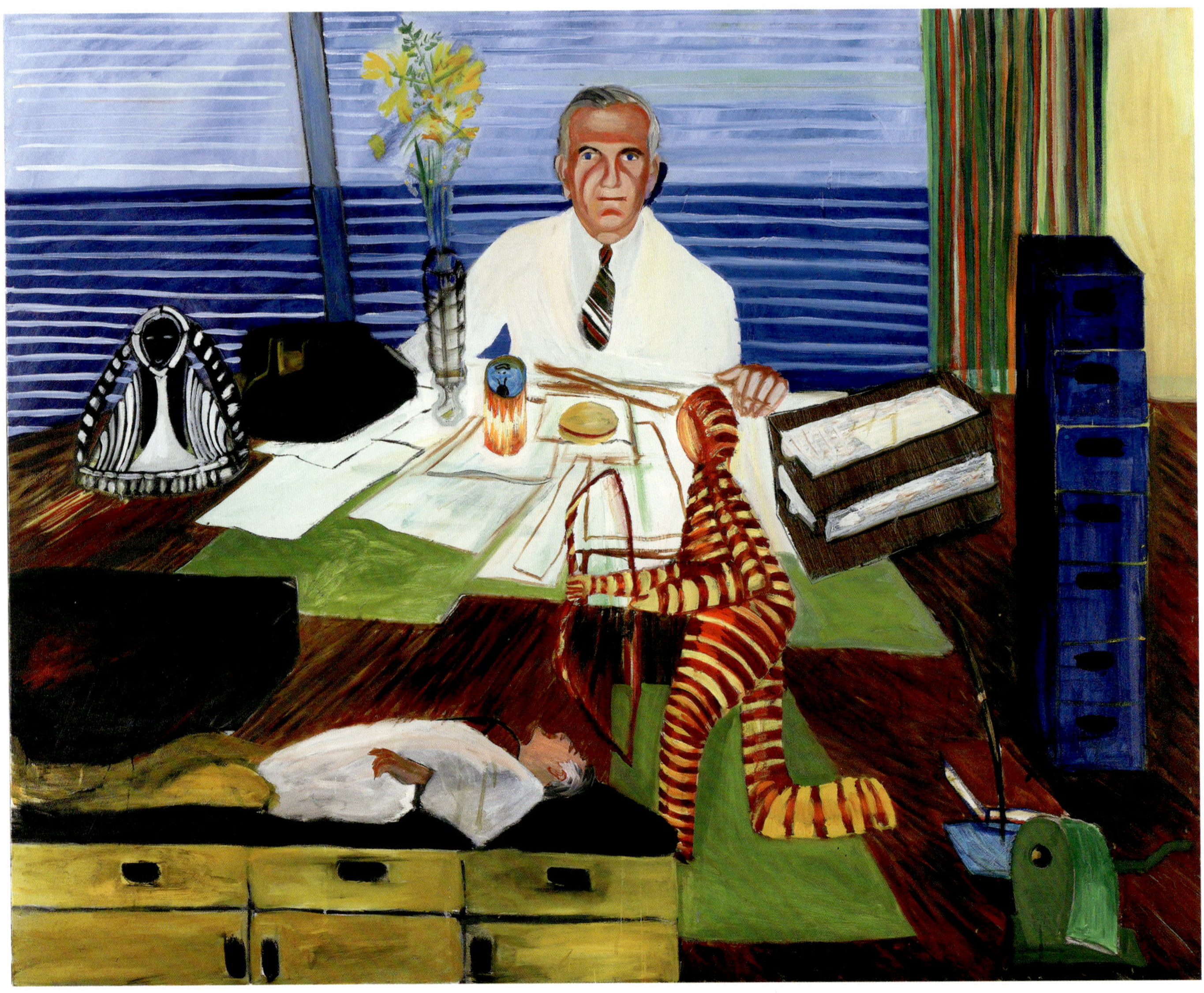

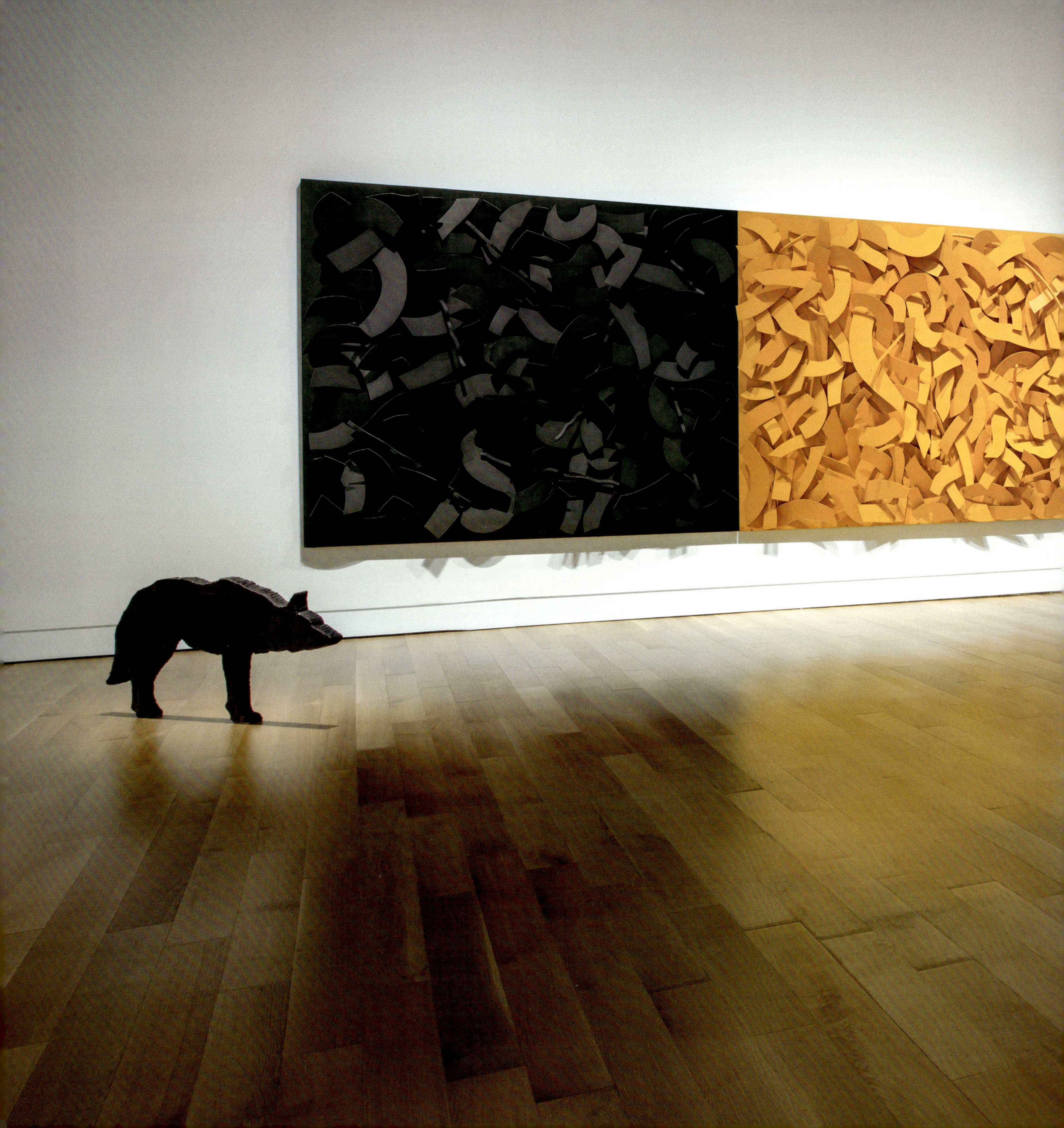

Boundless

Eko-naabing baashjeying

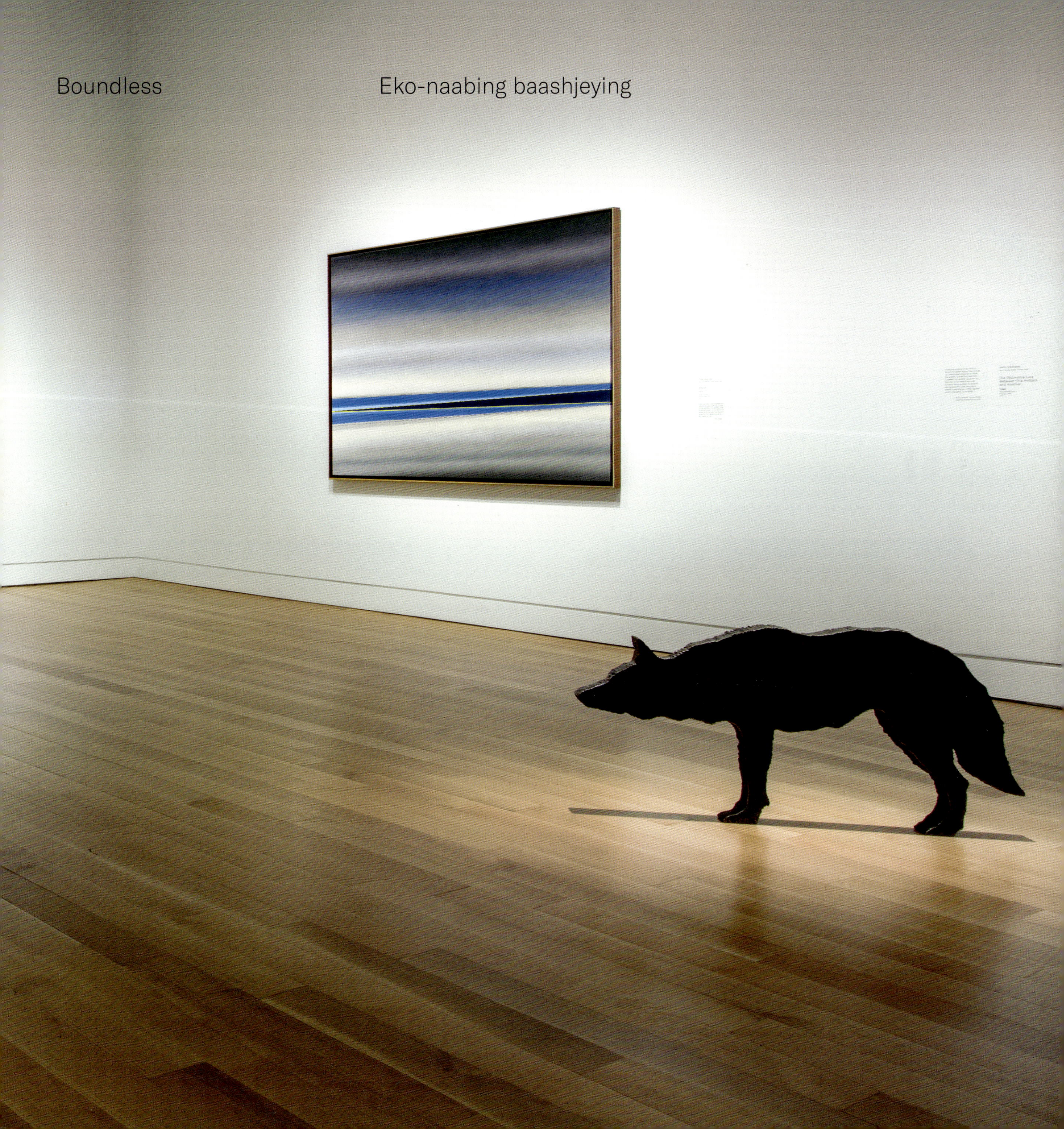

John McEwen

The Distinctive Line Between One Subject and Another, 1980
Flame-cut plate steel
54.5 × 116 × 6.4 cm and 55.5 × 116.4 × 6.4 cm
Art Gallery of Ontario, purchase, 1981, 81/73

"These two animals bring a kind of life into the gallery space. They disrupt our comfortable categories of inside and outside, animate and inanimate, movement and stillness. Because I am Wolf Clan (in the Anishinaabe clan system) I have a number of personal associations that come into play in relation to this artwork—I often feel like a wolf in the gallery, so to speak." —Wanda Nanibush, Curator, Indigenous Art, AGO

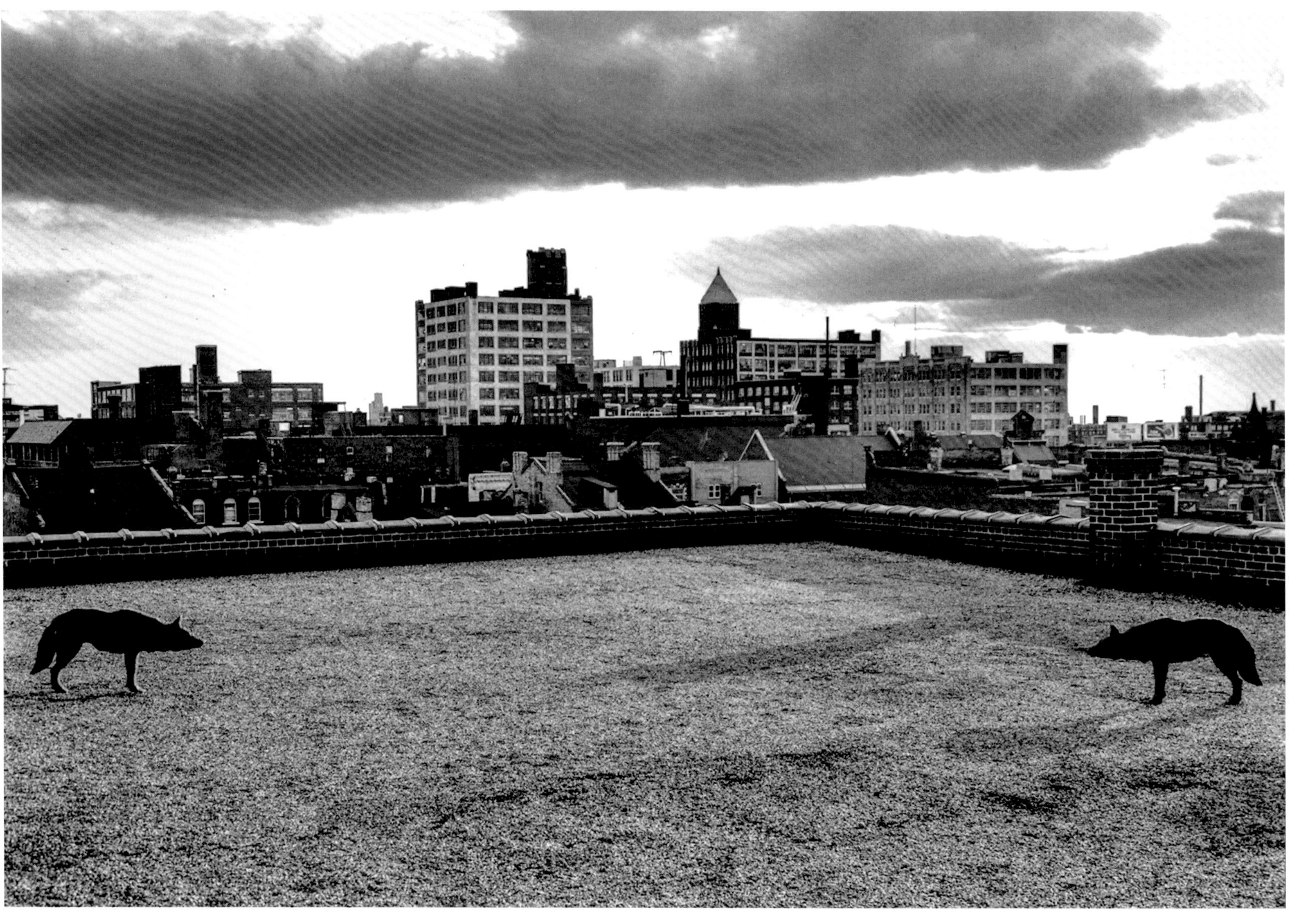

Nobuo Kubota

Folia Series #1 and *#2*, 1976
Painted plywood
96 × 198.1 × 30.5 cm
Art Gallery of Ontario, gift of the Canada Council Art Bank, 2004, 2004/815

"I get the most pleasure and the most intense involvement in art when I'm making it. When I'm thinking of it. You should talk to my wife, I kind of disappear. I'm around but I kind of disappear until it's finished."
—Nobuo Kubota

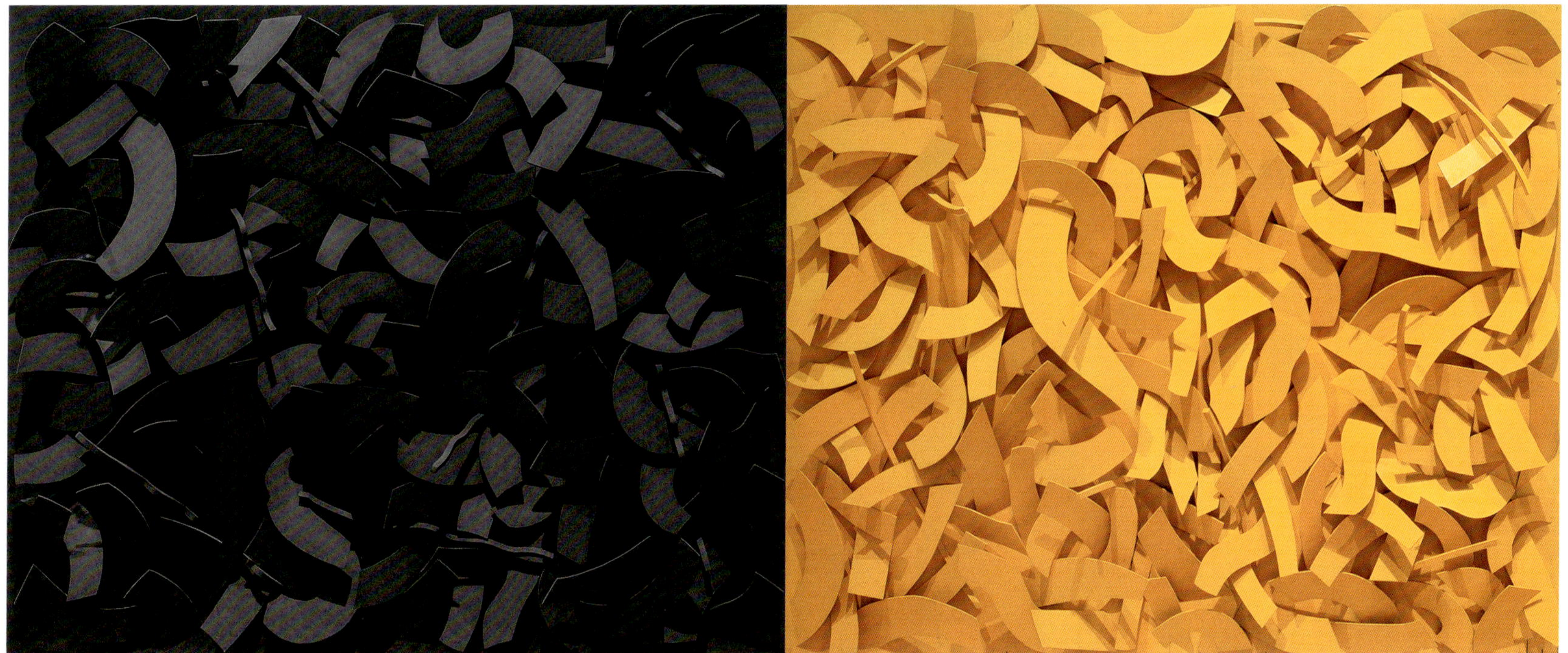

David Bolduc

Covered (for G. Iskowitz), 1988
Acrylic and graphite on canvas
127 × 203 cm
Art Gallery of Ontario, gift of Alkis Klonaridis, 1993, 93/272

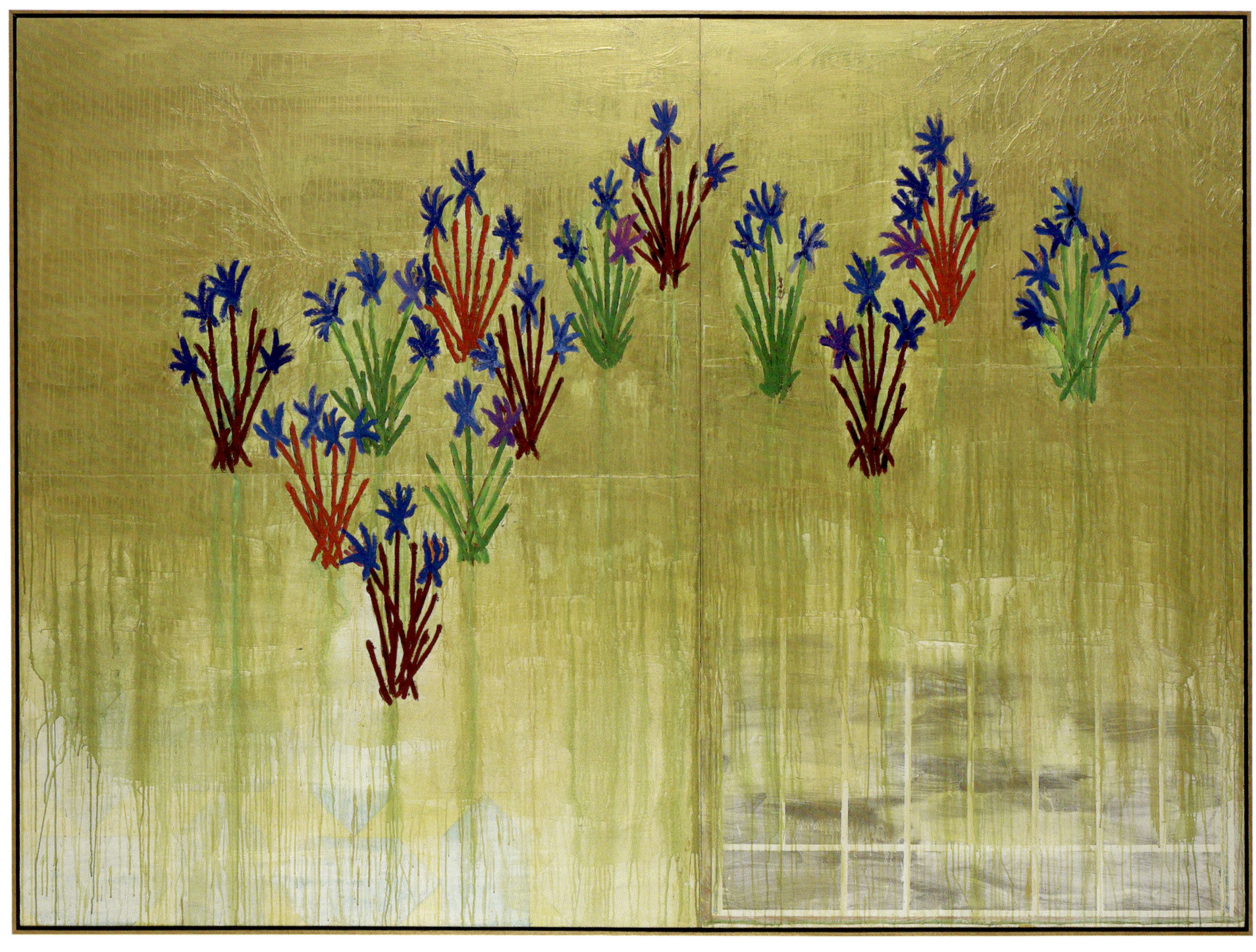

K.M. Graham

Leaf and Tree, 1976
Acrylic and chalk on canvas
177.1 × 172.1 cm
Art Gallery of Ontario, gift of Dr. Michael Braudo, 2007, 2007/730

"I didn't deliberately try to do modernist painting. That came spontaneously and intuitively, and I couldn't have been more surprised when I found out what it was all about." —K.M. Graham

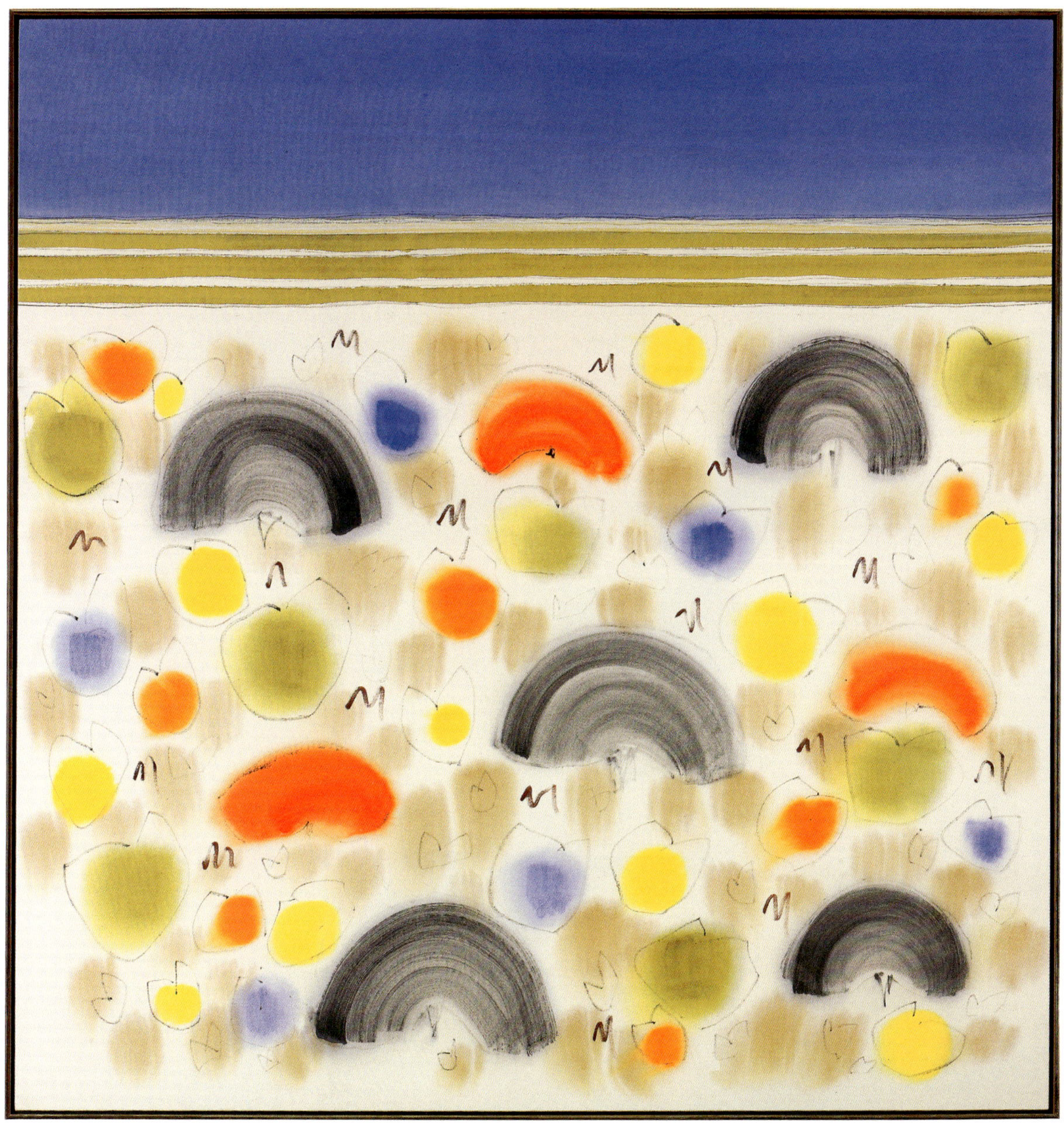

Kazuo Nakamura

Number Structure II, 1984
Oil and graphite on canvas
127 × 152.3 cm
Art Gallery of Ontario, gift of Kazuo Nakamura, Toronto, 2001, 2001/73

"In a sense, scientists and artists are doing the same thing. This world of pattern is a world we are discovering together." —Kazuo Nakamura

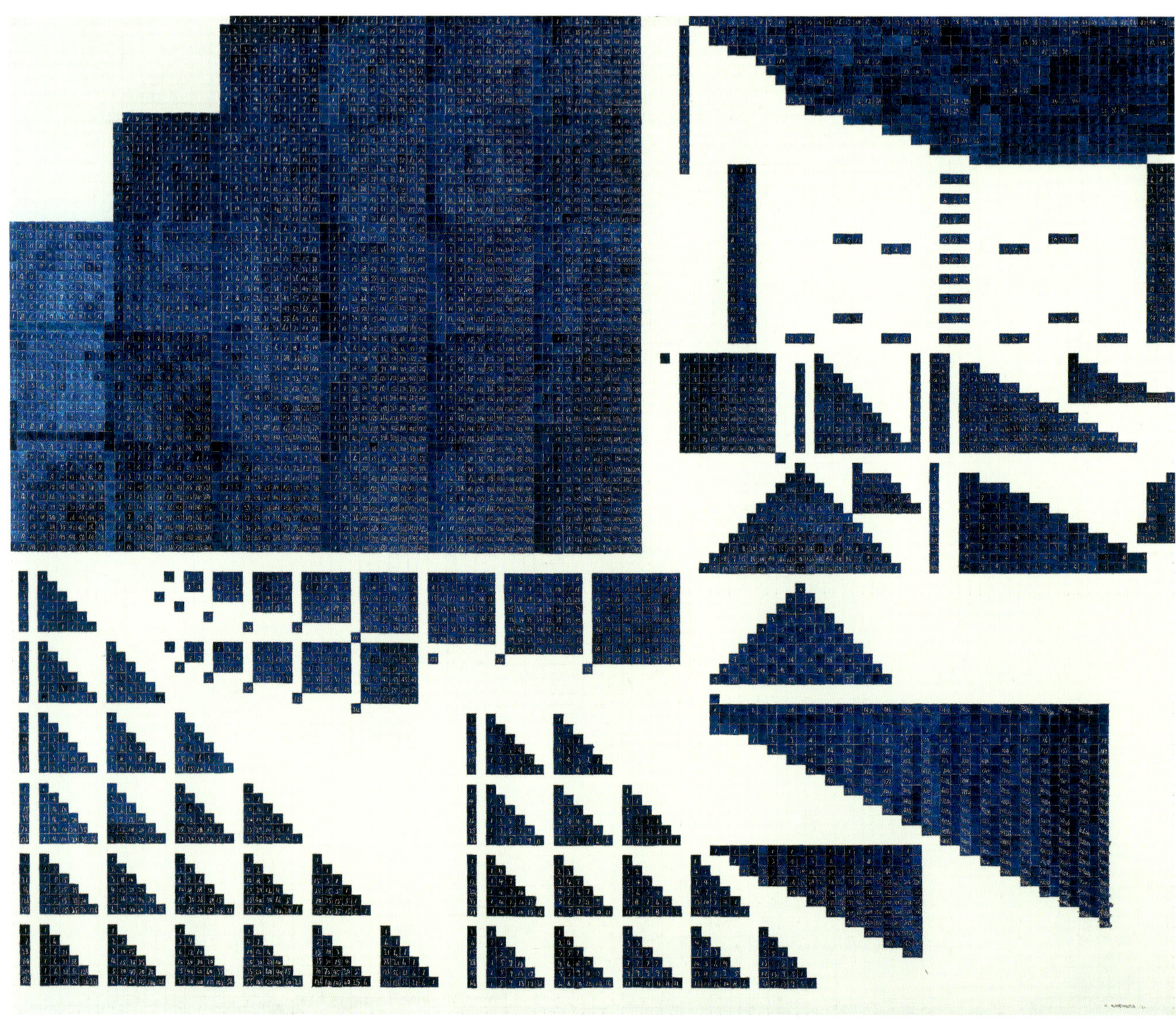

Rita Letendre

Aforim, 1975
Acrylic on canvas
137.2 × 198.1 cm
Art Gallery of Ontario, anonymous gift, 1975, 75/58

"Light and colour, and sometimes the absence of colour, have always been the key elements in my painting. With its different values, colour reflects the shades of life. But light, from the first shock of birth to the last breath of life—light is my life." —Rita Letendre

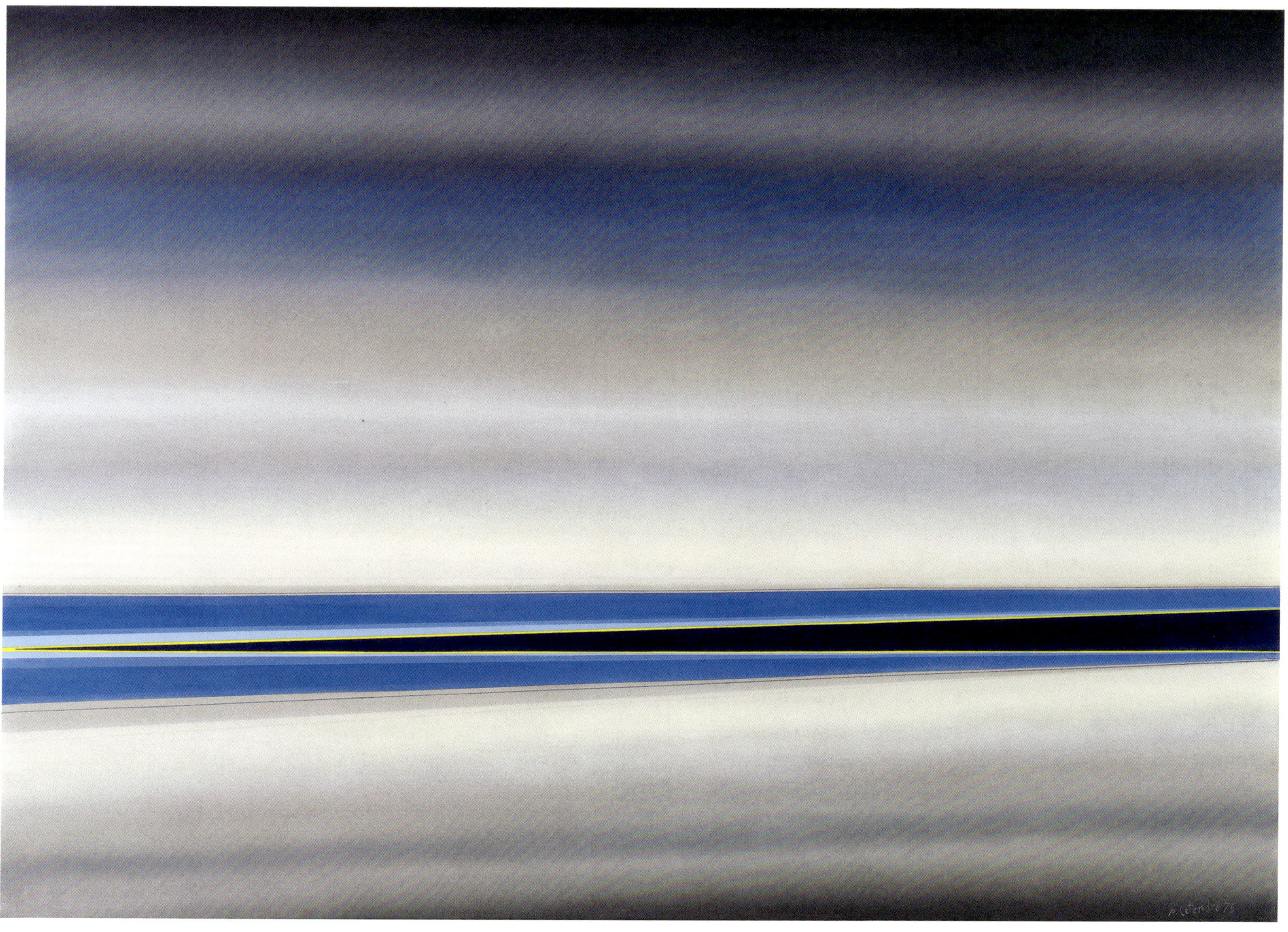

Carol Wainio

Outered, 1984
Acrylic and graphite on canvas
130.2 × 170.2 cm
Art Gallery of Ontario, gift from the George W. Gilmour Perspective Exhibition Fund, 1985, 85/11

"I am uncomfortable with certainty. I like the paintings to come apart, to show how they're made, to acknowledge their speculative origins." —Carol Wainio

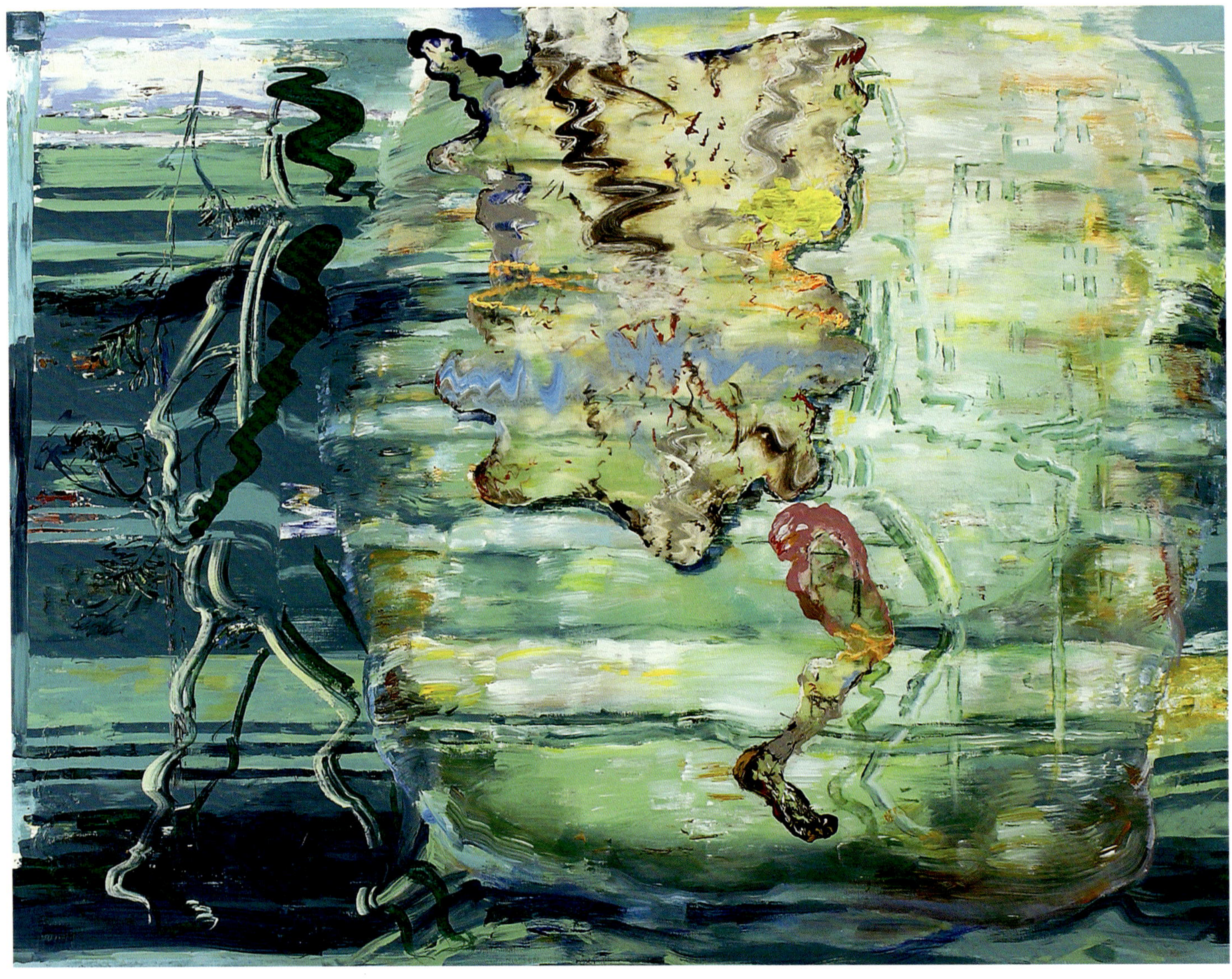

Brian Burnett

Fifteen Thousand Feet, 1983
Acrylic on canvas
213.9 × 171 cm
Art Gallery of Ontario, gift of Francis and Marvin Yontef, 2007, 2007/105

"I want the viewer to be overpowered by the painting…the viewer shouldn't feel stronger than the painting."
—Brian Burnett

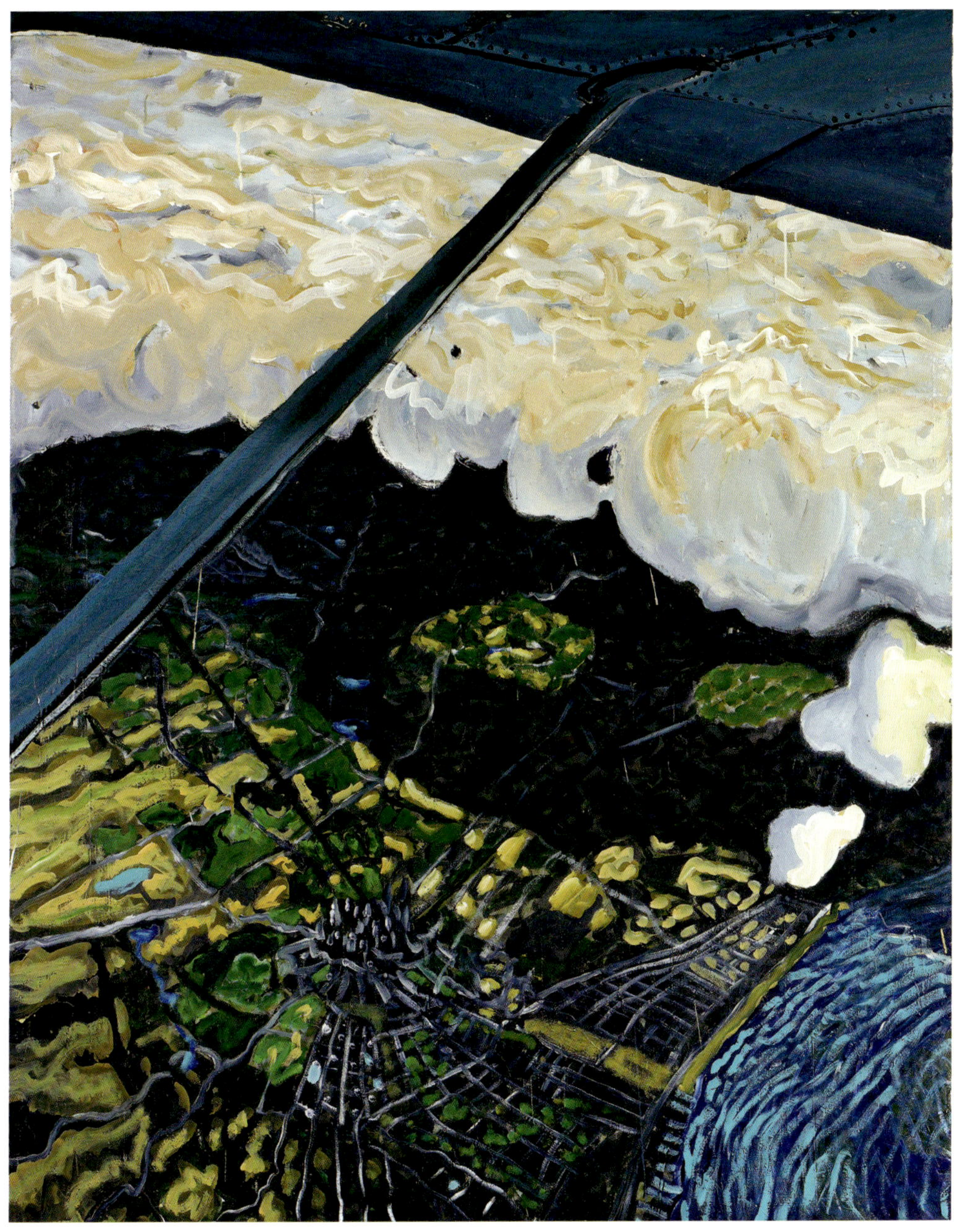

Gordon Rayner

A Night at the Opera, 1974
Wax crayon, ink, and brush over
cut printed paper collage on paper
50.3 × 65 cm
Art Gallery of Ontario, gift of Norcen Energy
Resources Limited, 1986, 86/69

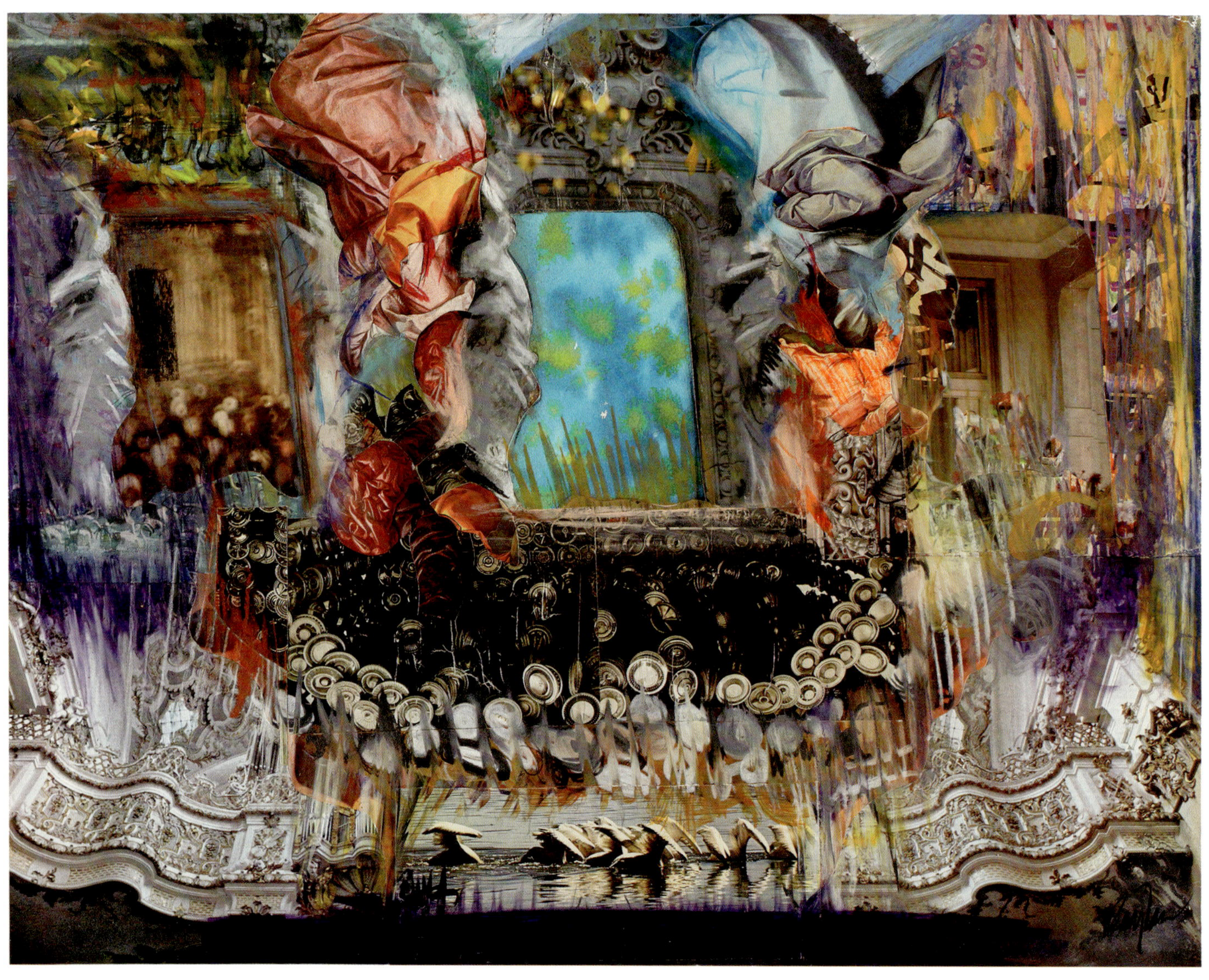

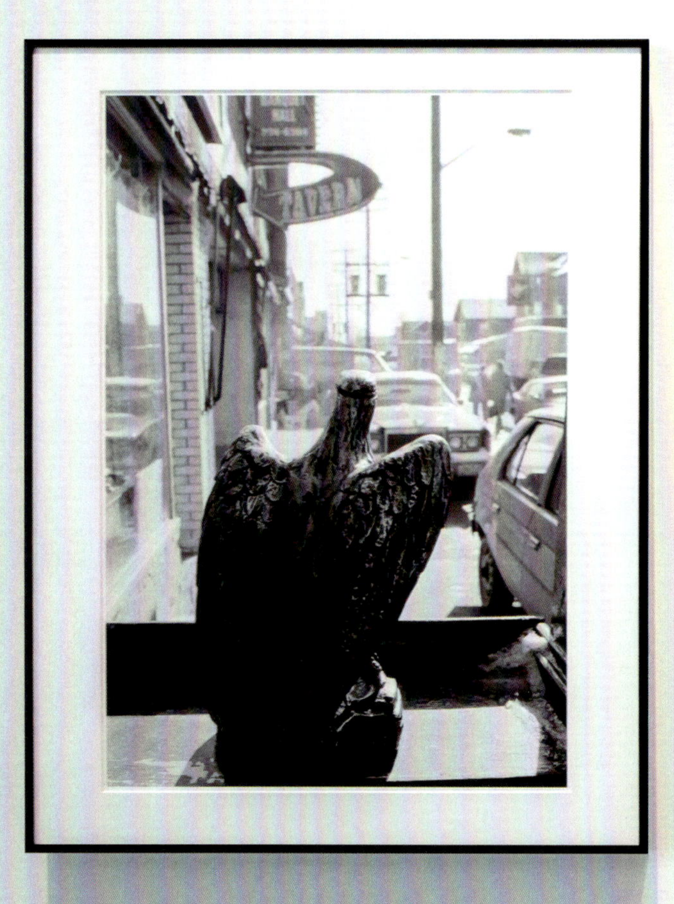
TAVERN

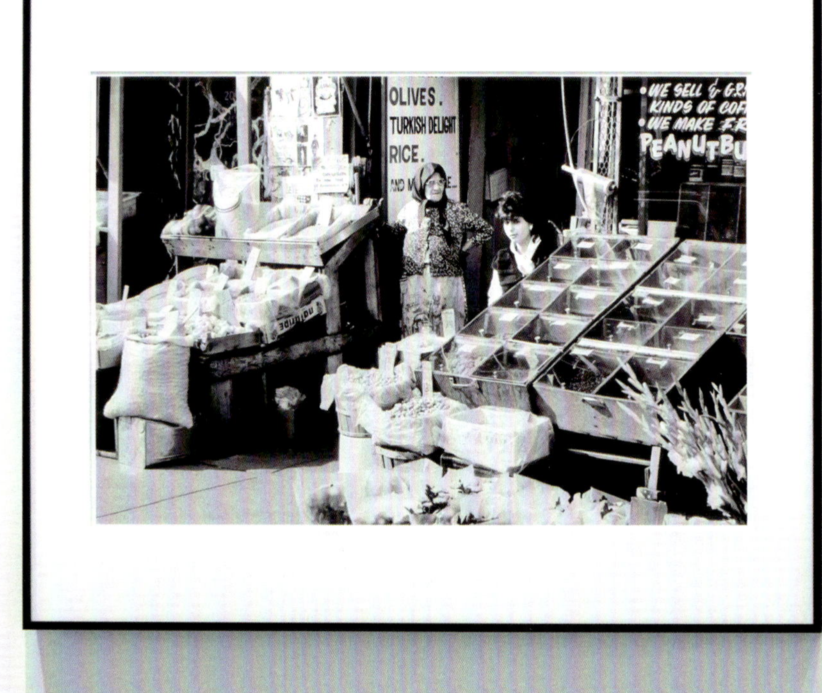
OLIVES.
TURKISH DELIGHT
RICE.

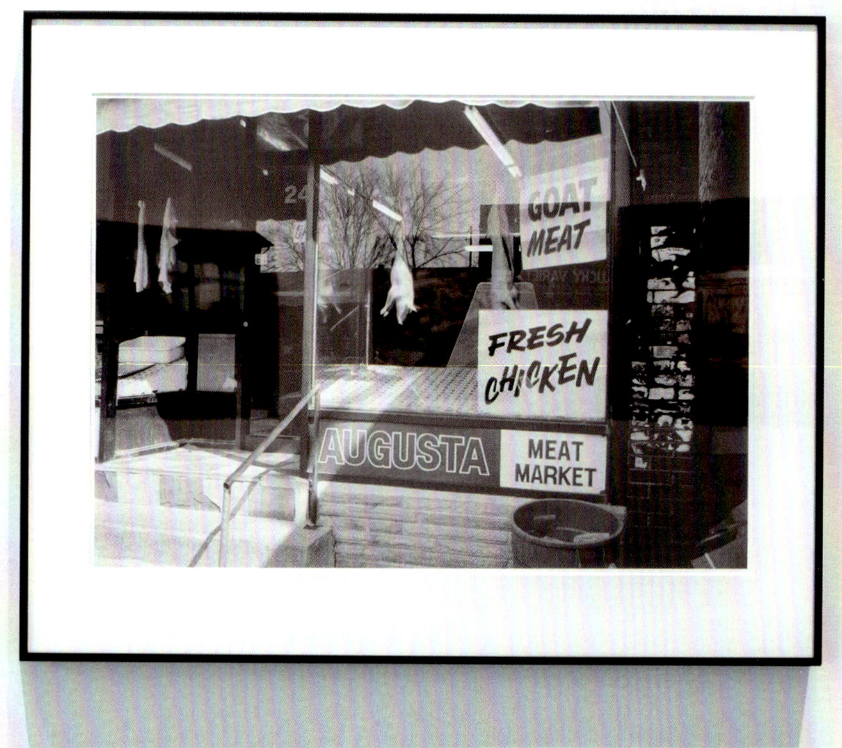
GOAT
MEAT
FRESH
CHICKEN
AUGUSTA
MEAT
MARKET

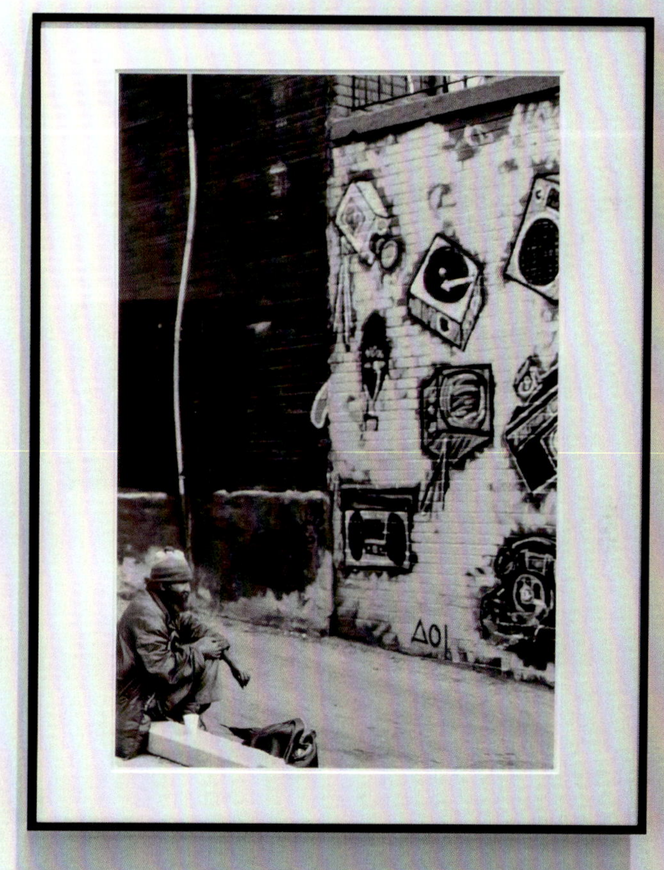

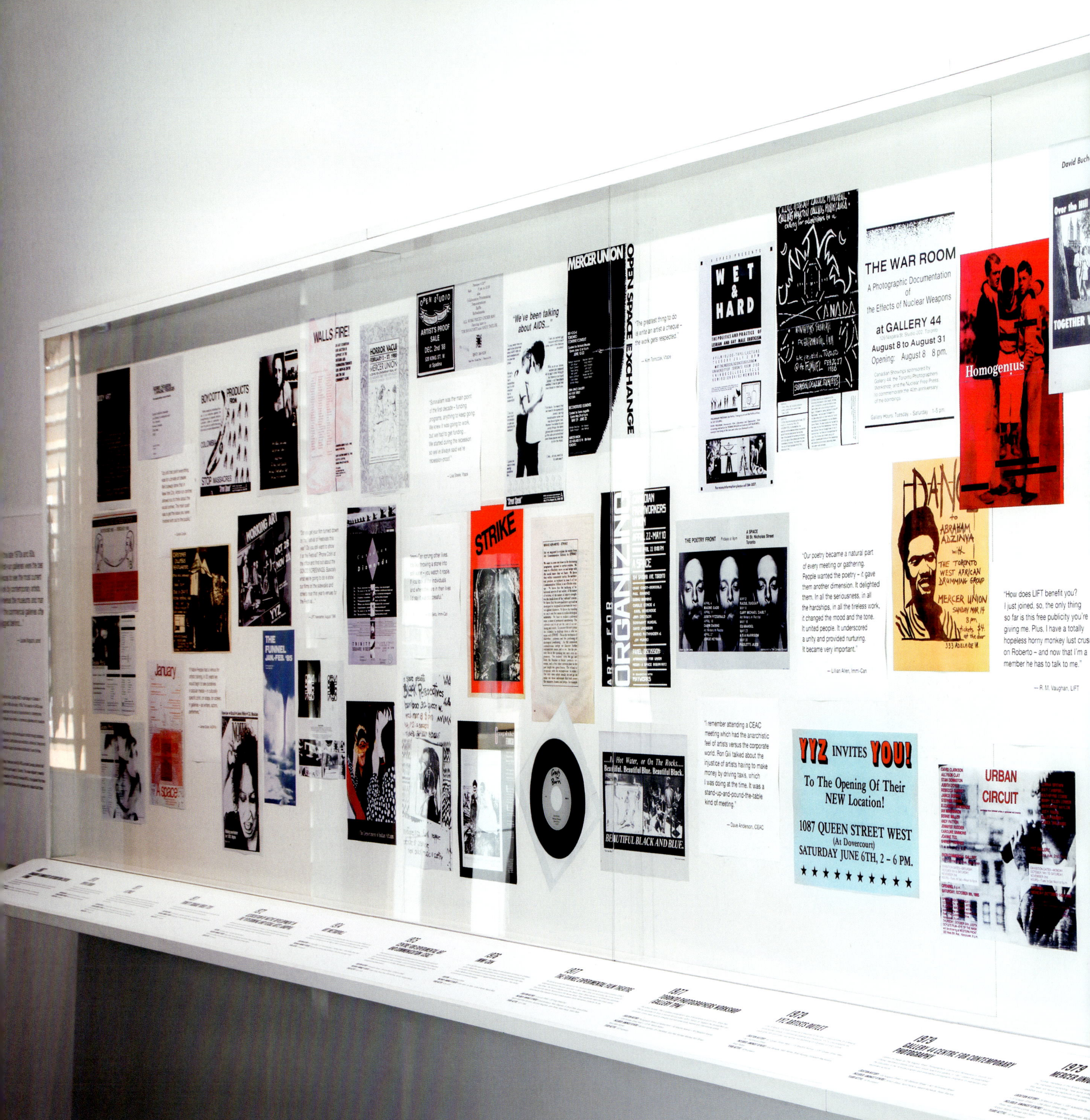

THE WAR ROOM
A Photographic Documentation of the Effects of Nuclear Weapons
at GALLERY 44
August 8 to August 31
Opening: August 8 8 pm.
Homogenius
WET & HARD
MERCER UNION
OPEN SPACE EXCHANGE
"We've been talking about AIDS..."
WALLS FIRE!
HORROR VACUI
OPEN STUDIO ARTIST'S PROOF SALE DEC. 2nd '88
BOYCOTT PRODUCTS FROM COLOMBIA STOP MASSACRES
WORKING ART
STRIKE
ART FOR ORGANIZING
THE POETRY FRONT
"Our poetry became a natural part of every meeting or gathering. People wanted the poetry – it gave them another dimension. It delighted them. In all the seriousness, in all the hardships, in all the tireless work, it changed the mood and the tone. It united people. It underscored a unity and provided nurturing. It became very important."
— Lillian Allen, Immi-Can
DANCE to ABRAHAM ADZINYA with THE TORONTO WEST AFRICAN DRUMMING GROUP MERCER UNION
333 ADELAIDE W.
"How does LIFT benefit you? I just joined, so, the only thing so far is this free publicity you're giving me. Plus, I have a totally hopeless horny monkey lust crush on Roberto – and now that I'm a member he has to talk to me."
— R. M. Vaughan, LIFT
THE FUNNEL JAN.-FEB. '85
January
A space
"I remember attending a CEAC meeting which had the anarchistic feel of artists versus the corporate world. Ron Giii talked about the injustice of artists having to make money by driving taxis, which I was doing at the time. It was a stand-up-and-pound-the-table kind of meeting."
— Dave Anderson, CEAC
...Hot Water, or On The Rocks.... Beautiful. Beautiful Blue. Beautiful Black.
BEAUTIFUL BLACK AND BLUE.
YYZ INVITES YOU!
To The Opening Of Their NEW Location!
1087 QUEEN STREET WEST
(At Dovercourt)
SATURDAY JUNE 6TH, 2 – 6 PM.
URBAN CIRCUIT
1979
YYZ ARTISTS' OUTLET
1979
GALLERY 44 CENTRE FOR CONTEMPORARY PHOTOGRAPHY
1979
MERCER UNION

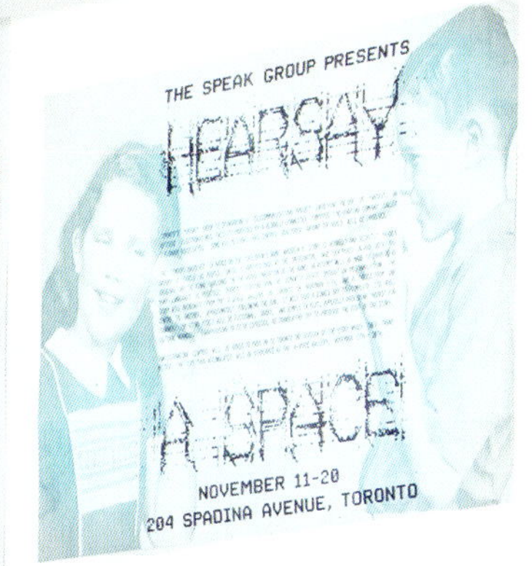

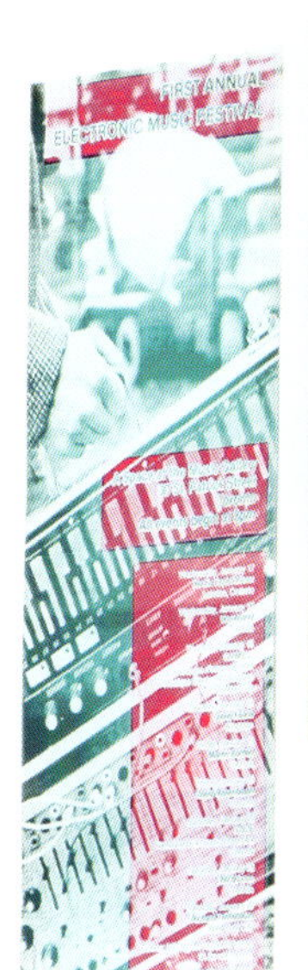

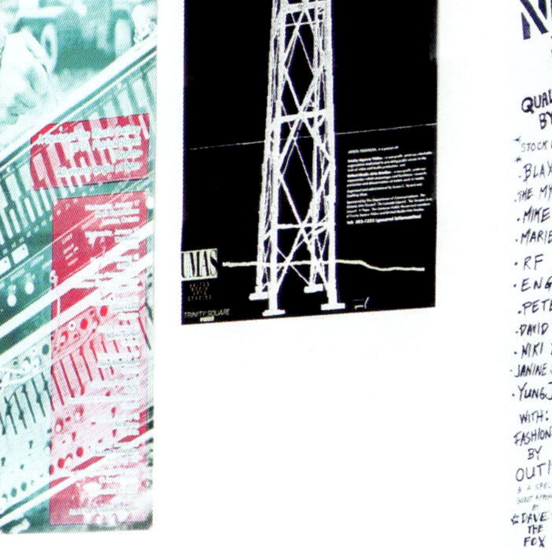

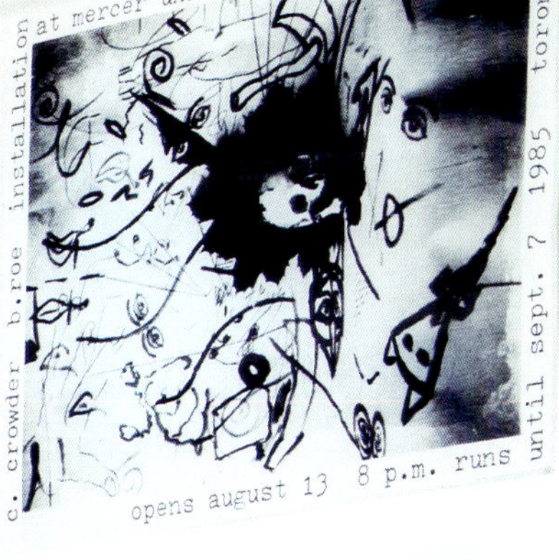

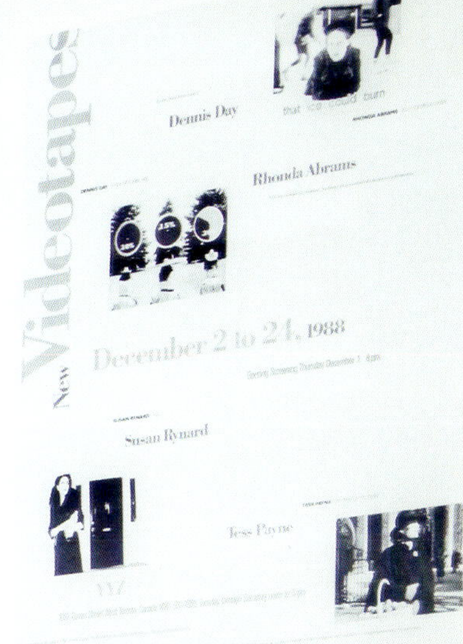

"The shift in the 1970s was very much taking on politics through art. Artists dealing with issues was a legitimate undertaking."

— Kari Beveridge

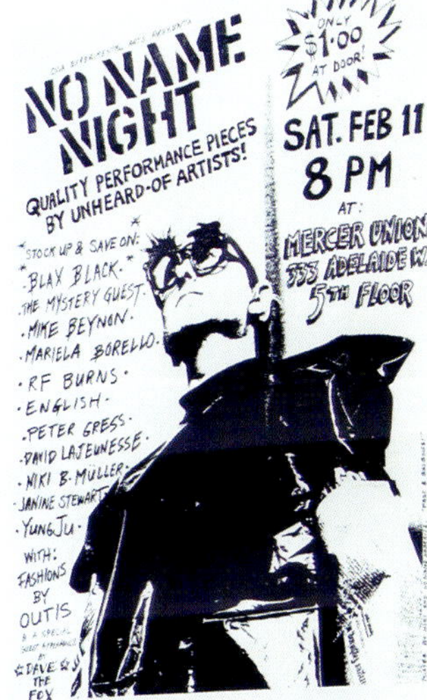

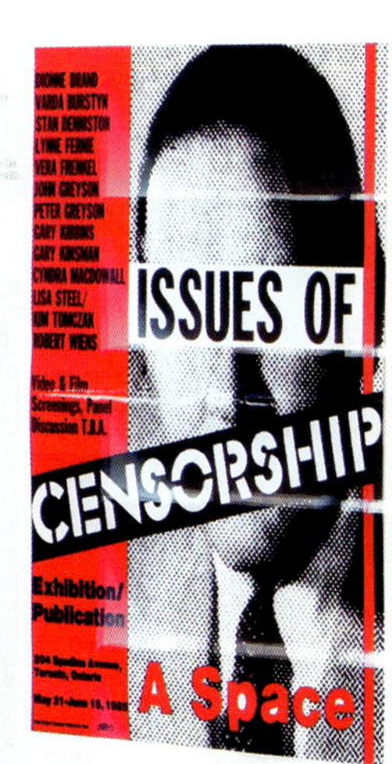

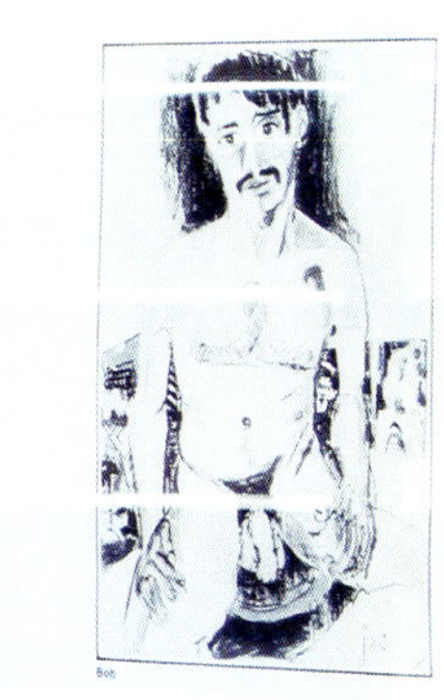

"A Space. This was the first artist-run centre in Canada we say, and why do we say that? There were of course others: Intermedia in Vancouver and short-lived spaces in Winnipeg and London, Ontario, and perhaps others, all burnt out by premature birth and/or premature ejaculation…"

— AA Bronson

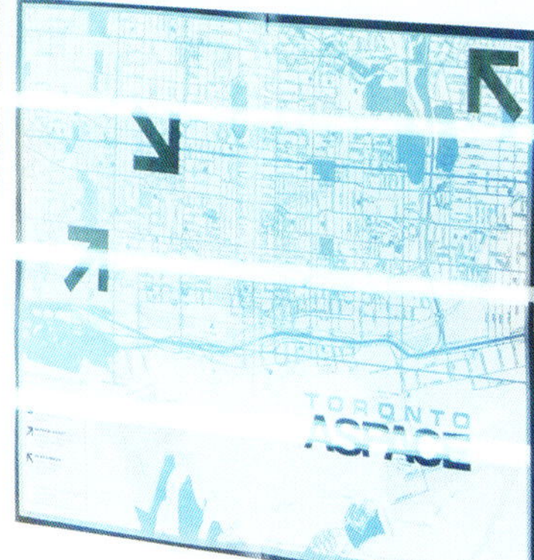

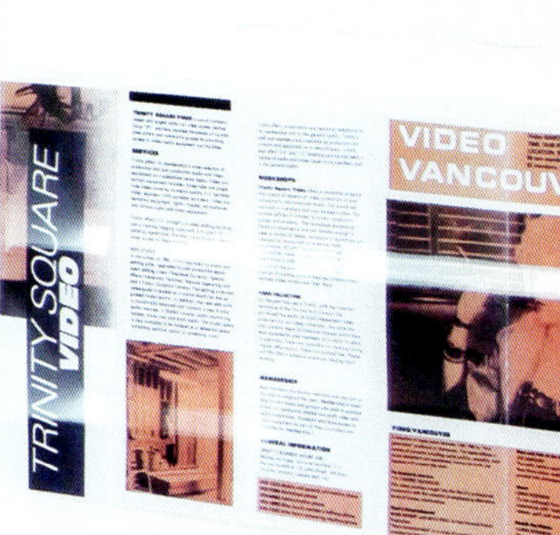

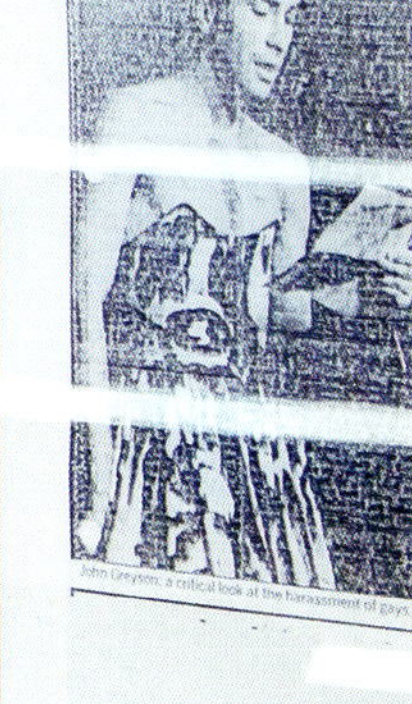

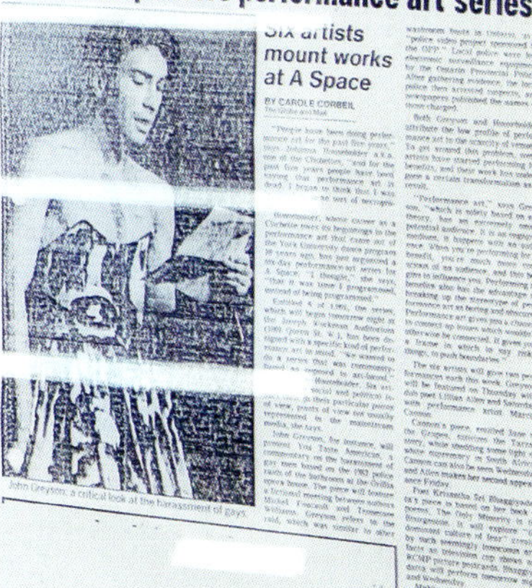

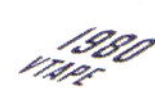

Ato Seitu

Corner Stone, 1970s
Vinyl print
50.8 × 76.2 cm
Courtesy of the artist

WOMAN WITH A SOLID SOUL

She is the woman who loves to speak of love.
When she speaks of love her eyes are
like twinkling stars;
For she possess a yearning to share herself
with one whom she can trust in tender moments.
She desires to love and to be loved.
To her, love is like poetry and poetry is love;
which is a truth that flows straight from the heart.
When she speaks of loves she glows anew like
rays of sunlight after a rainy day.

Her inner sense of beauty, through love,
is the comforting voice of self-worth that
warms the soul.
She knows that love is harmony and harmony
is love.
However, when she thinks of love she becomes
an angry black woman;
For lack of love is a bandit of her happiness
and starvation of her need.

—Ato Seitu

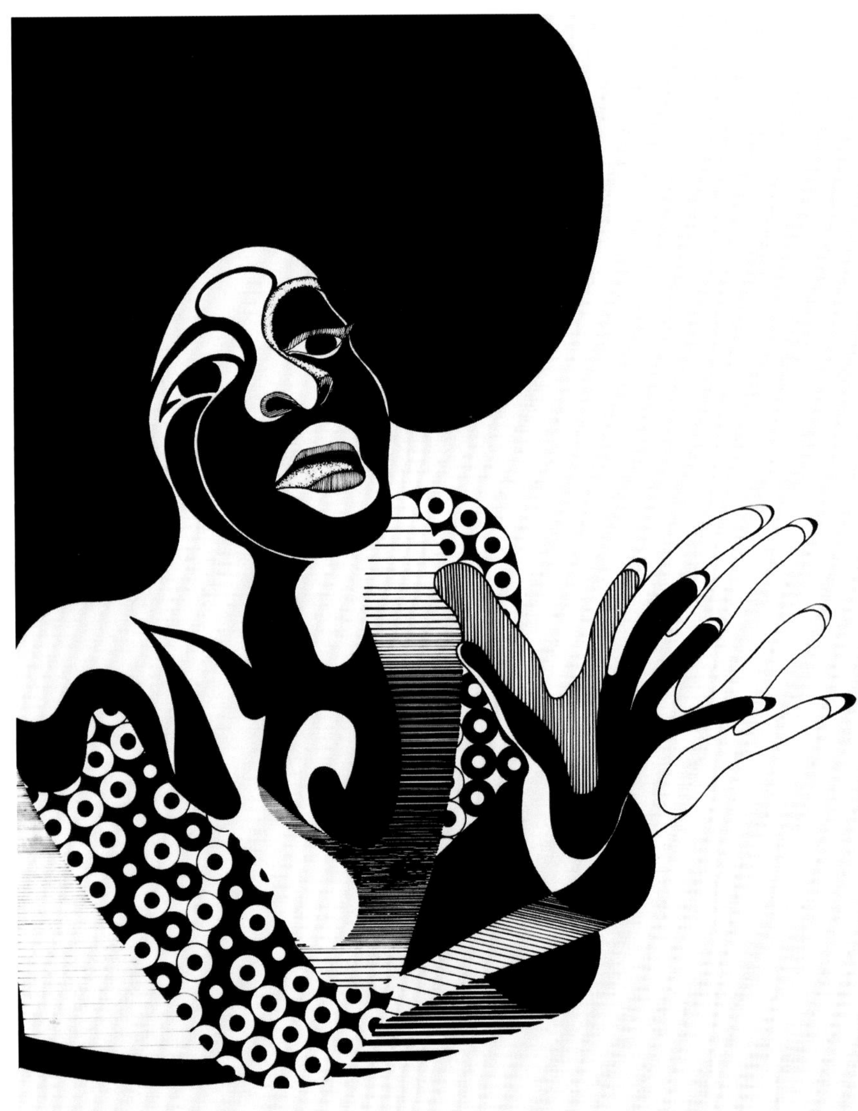

We Are the Mothers and Fathers for Our Children, 1970s
Vinyl print
76.2 × 50.8 cm
Courtesy of the artist

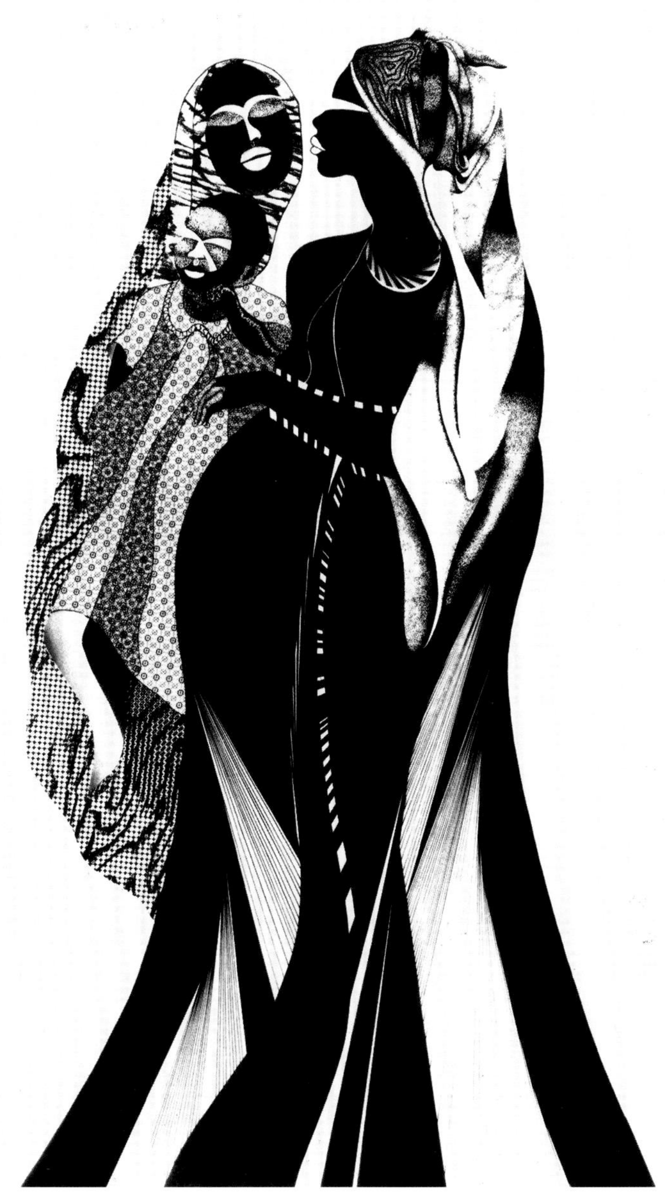

David Zapparoli

Boys Waiting for Games Room, 1989
Vinyl print
59.7 × 91.4 cm
Courtesy of the artist

Victoria Day Fun, 1991
Vinyl print
91.4 × 59.7 cm
Courtesy of the artist

Fashion Show, 1989
Vinyl print
59.7 × 91.4 cm
Courtesy of the artist

Unknown
Archival Photograph of Regent Park
Vinyl print
59.7 × 91.4 cm

Girl Painting, 1998
Vinyl print
59.7 × 91.4 cm
Courtesy of the artist

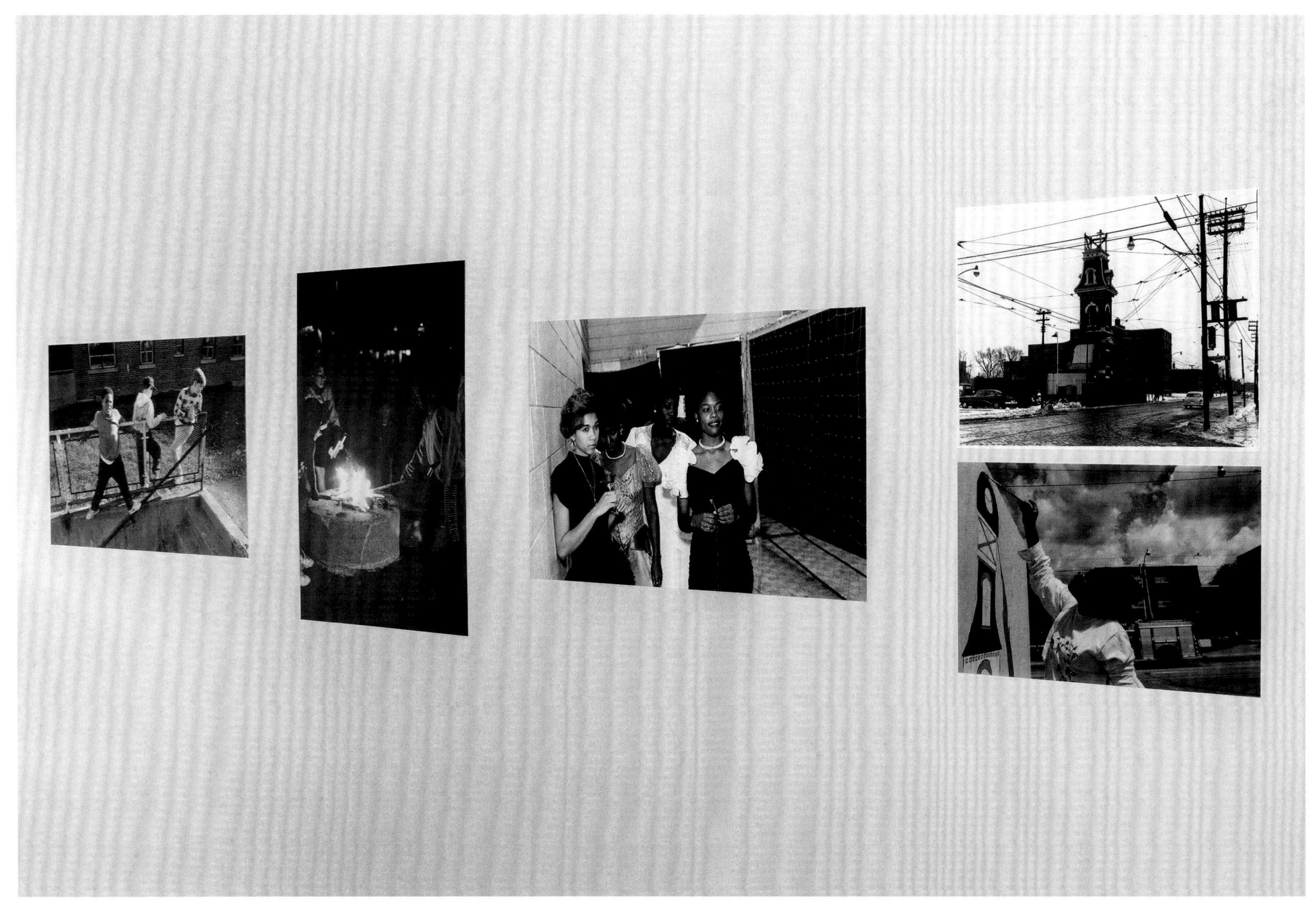

"In days gone by, I found myself in what was once Regent Park's only fast food joint, known as the Root 'n' Burger. In a moment of reflection, a woman announced 'I might be in the ghetto. But my mind ain't!' And in so doing, [she] crystallized the challenge facing many of Regent Park's residents: How to participate in the community and transcend the negativity that weighs on it.

These photographs represent my foray into revealing a community that I was a part of—yet discovering for the first time. It was a mission of enlightenment that found inspiration from the younger generation. A generation that would be the last to negotiate the hallways, sidewalks, and grassy fields of their much-maligned community before the work began on the redevelopment that would see the community transformed." —David Zapparoli

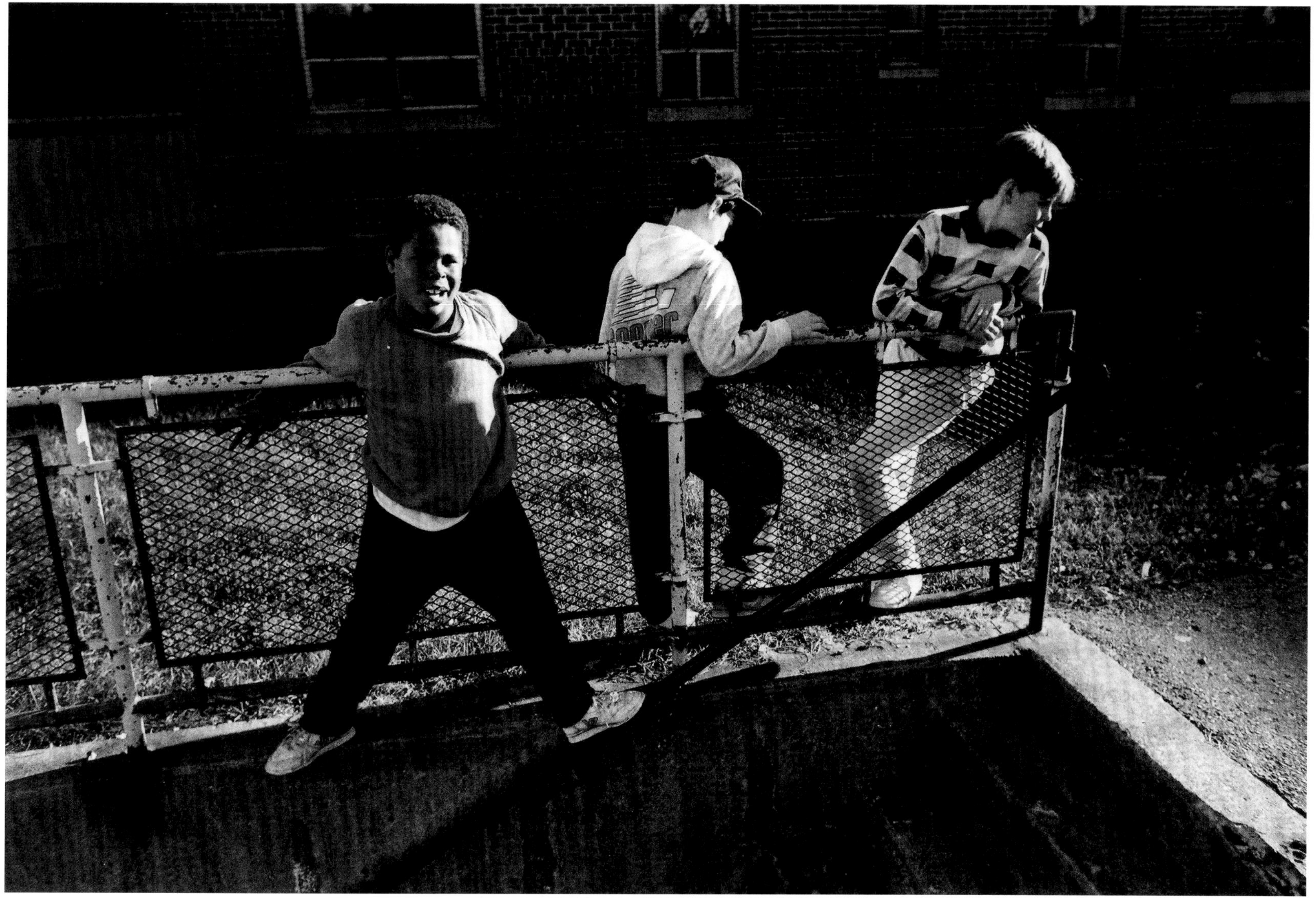

Jeff Thomas

Toronto Series: Queen St. West, 1984
Pigment print on archival paper
88.7 × 67 cm
Art Gallery of Ontario, gift of Jeff Thomas, 2016, 2016/439

Toronto Series: Queen St. West, 1984
Pigment print on archival paper
70.5 × 50.8 cm
Art Gallery of Ontario, gift of Jeff Thomas, 2016, 2016/440

Toronto Series: Queen St. West, 1984
(not shown here)
Pigment print on archival paper
70.5 × 50.8 cm
Art Gallery of Ontario, gift of Jeff Thomas, 2016, 2016/438

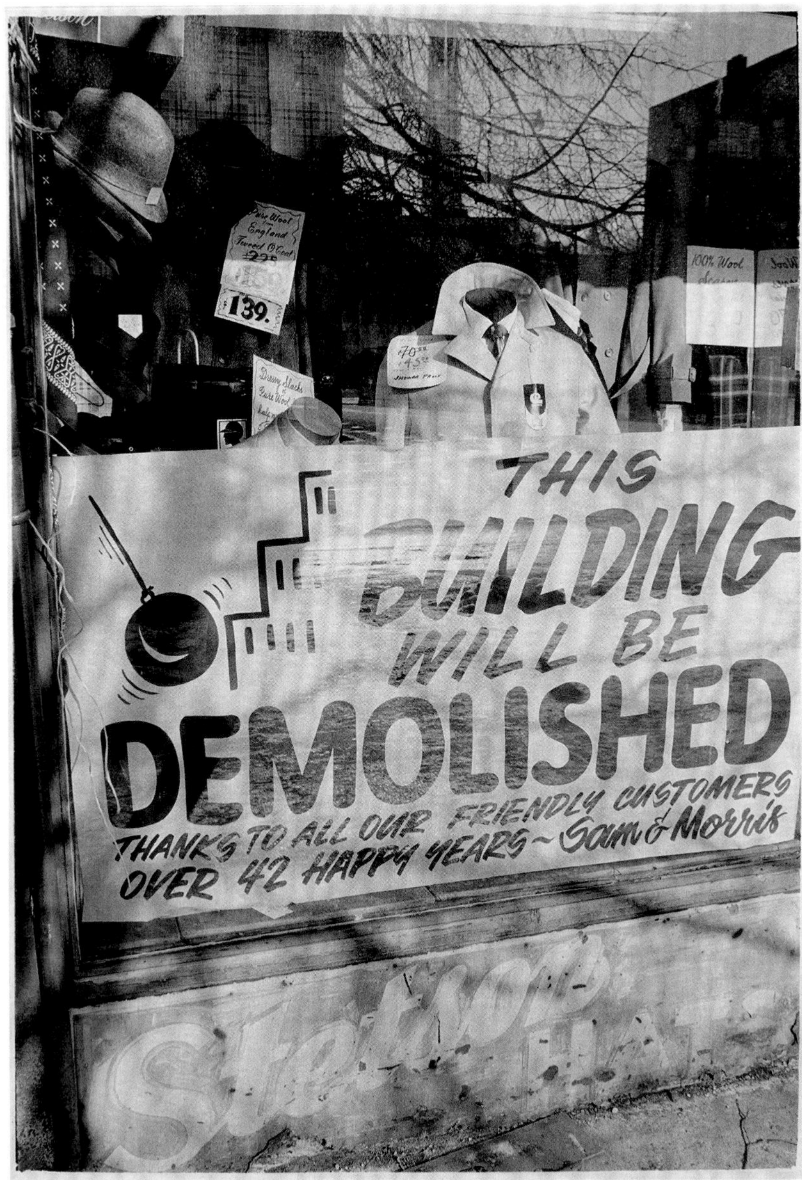

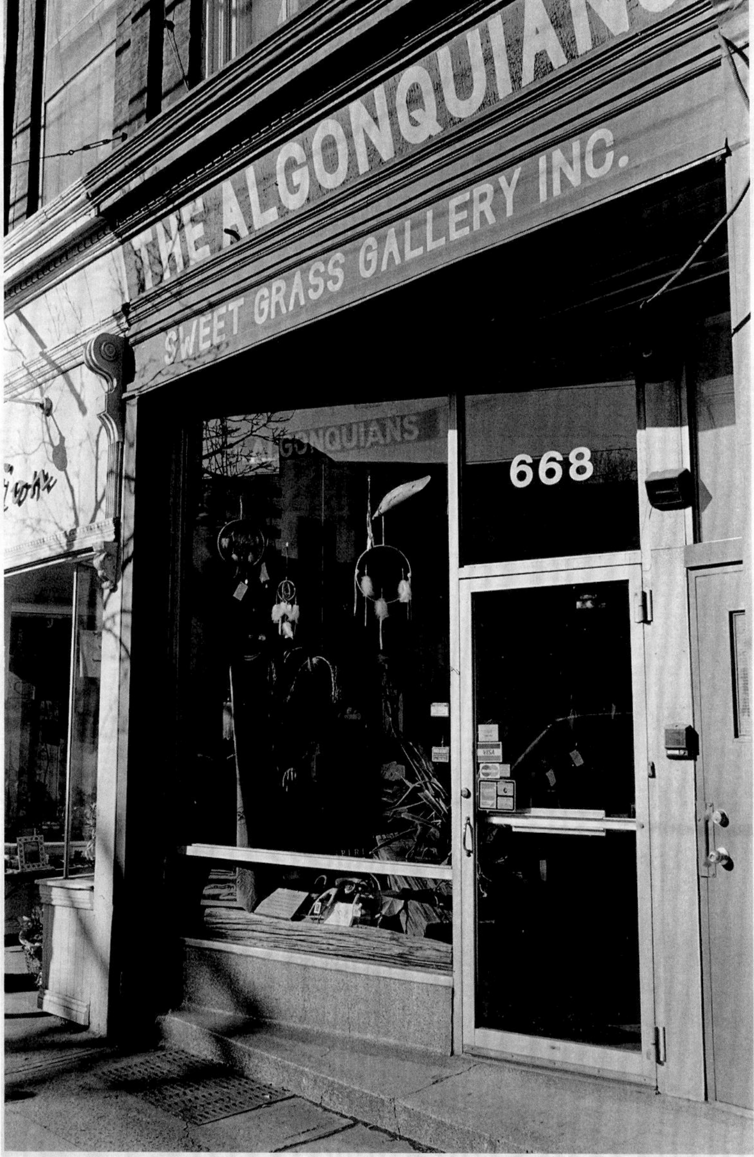

Toronto Series: Kensington Market, 1984
Pigment print on archival paper
70.5 × 50.8 cm
Art Gallery of Ontario, gift of Jeff Thomas, 2016, 2016/434

Toronto Series: Kensington Market, 1984
Pigment print on archival paper
70.5 × 50.8 cm
Art Gallery of Ontario, gift of Jeff Thomas, 2016, 2016/436

Toronto Series: Kensington Market, 1984
(not shown here)
Pigment print on archival paper
50.8 × 70.5 cm
Art Gallery of Ontario, gift of Jeff Thomas, 2016, 2016/435

Toronto Series: Kensington Market, 1984
(not shown here)
Pigment print on archival paper
50.8 × 70.5 cm
Art Gallery of Ontario, gift of Jeff Thomas, 2016, 2016/437

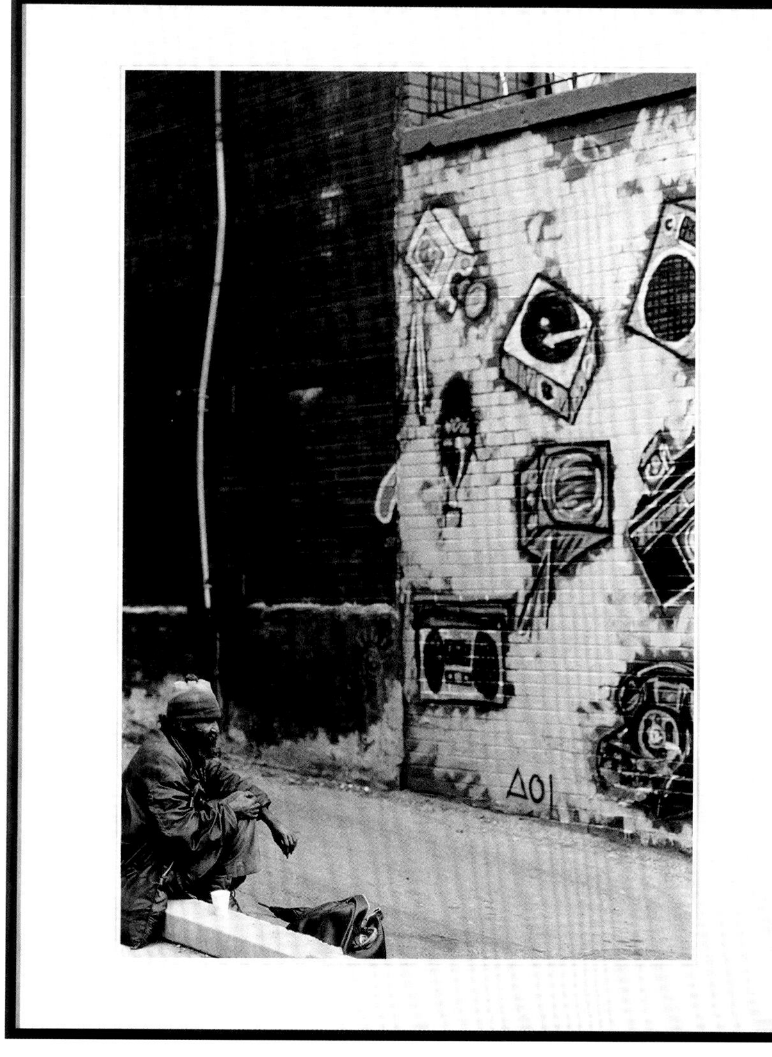

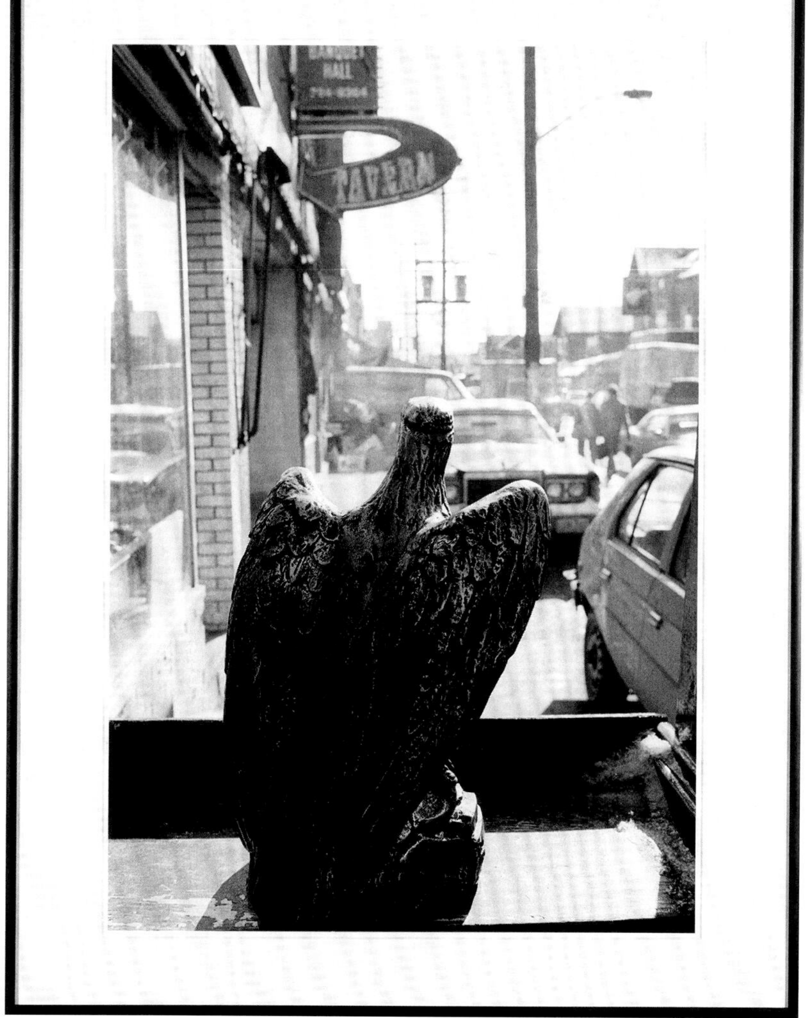

Brian Kipping

Motel Office, 1986
Oil on plywood
40.6 × 53.5 × 1.7 cm
Art Gallery of Ontario, gift of Susan Chater, Toronto, 2008, 2008/152

Subway Interior, 1983
Oil and wax on wood
31 × 38.2 × 3 cm
Art Gallery of Ontario, gift of Susan Chater, Toronto, 2008, 2008/148

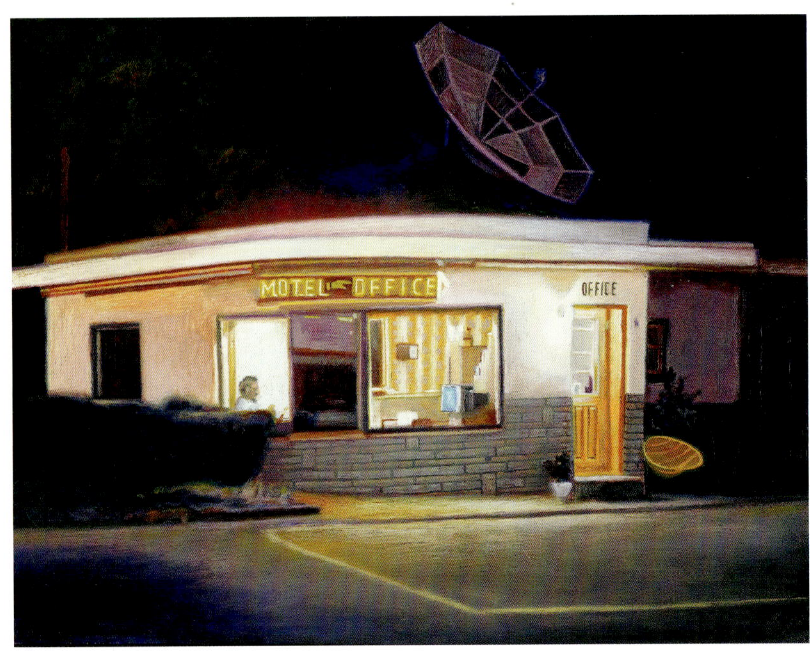

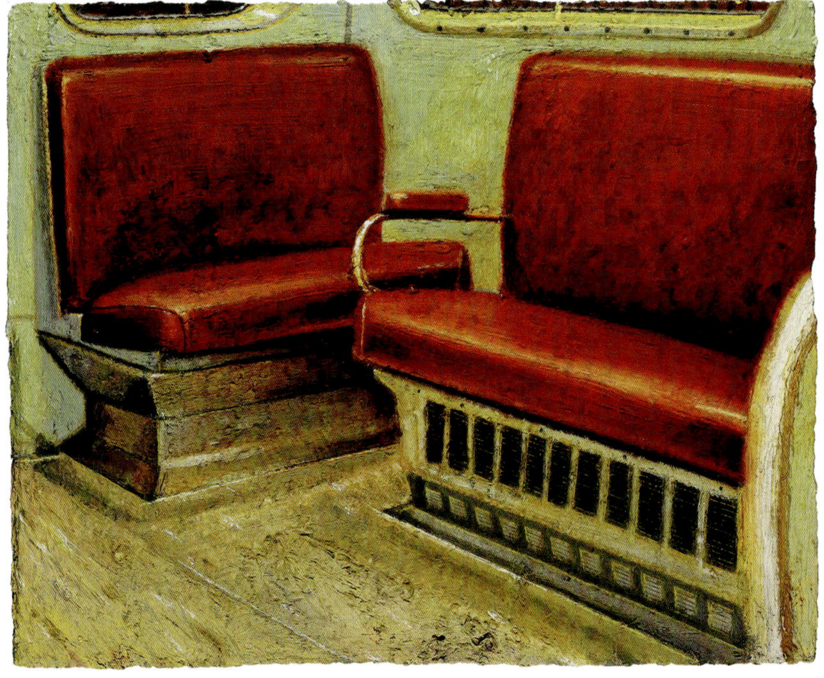

Dr. Cleaners at Night, 1984
Oil on wood
31.2 × 39.8 × 3.5 cm
Art Gallery of Ontario, gift of Susan Chater,
Toronto, 2008, 2008/149

Subway Newsstand, 1985
Oil on plywood
30.7 × 30.4 × 1.9 cm
Art Gallery of Ontario, gift of Susan Chater,
Toronto, 2008, 2008/151

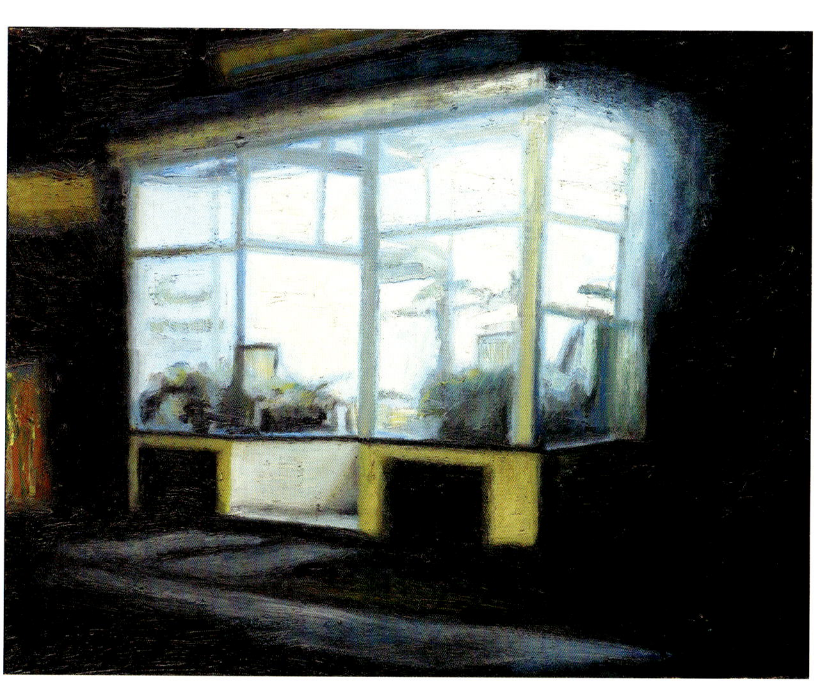

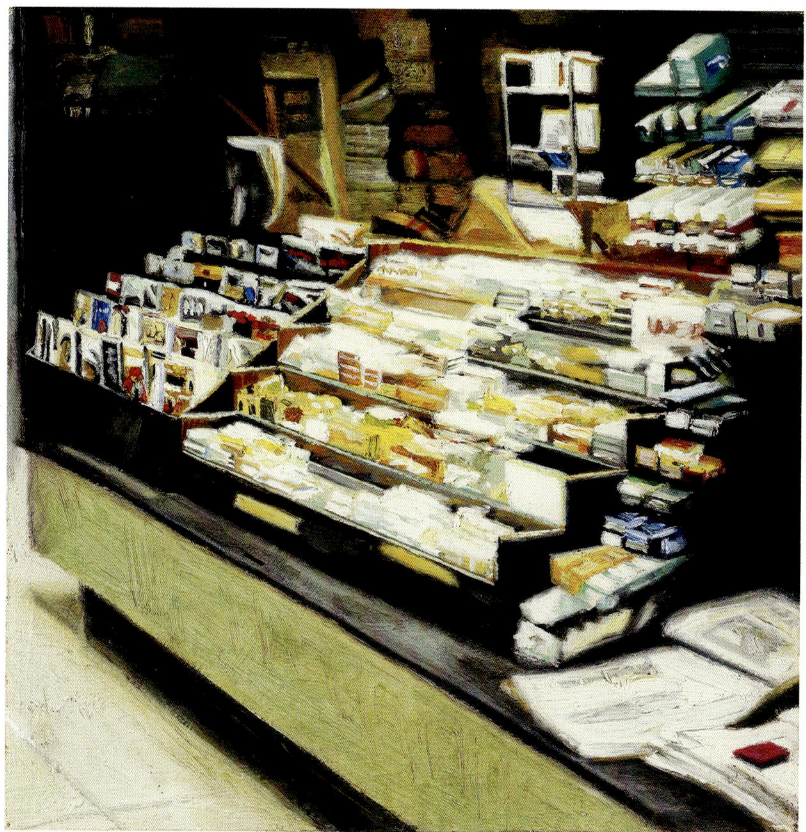

Greg Curnoe

Mariposa T.T., December 29, 1978–
February 28, 1979
Watercolour and opaque watercolour
over graphite on paper
119 × 170 cm
Art Gallery of Ontario, gift of Sheila Curnoe,
London, Ontario, 1997, 97/121

Level Book #8, February 1979 – June 1980
(not shown here)
Cycling log notebook
Greg Curnoe fonds, E.P. Taylor Library & Archives,
Art Gallery of Ontario, gift of Sheila Curnoe, 2003

"In 1992 Greg was killed when a pickup truck drove into a group of London Centennial Wheelers club riders. That morning we lost not only one of Canada's most prominent artists but also one of the nicest, most cheerful persons one could meet. Greg was always smiling and never more so than when he was riding his bike or doing his artwork."—Mike Barry, co-founder of Mariposa Bicycles

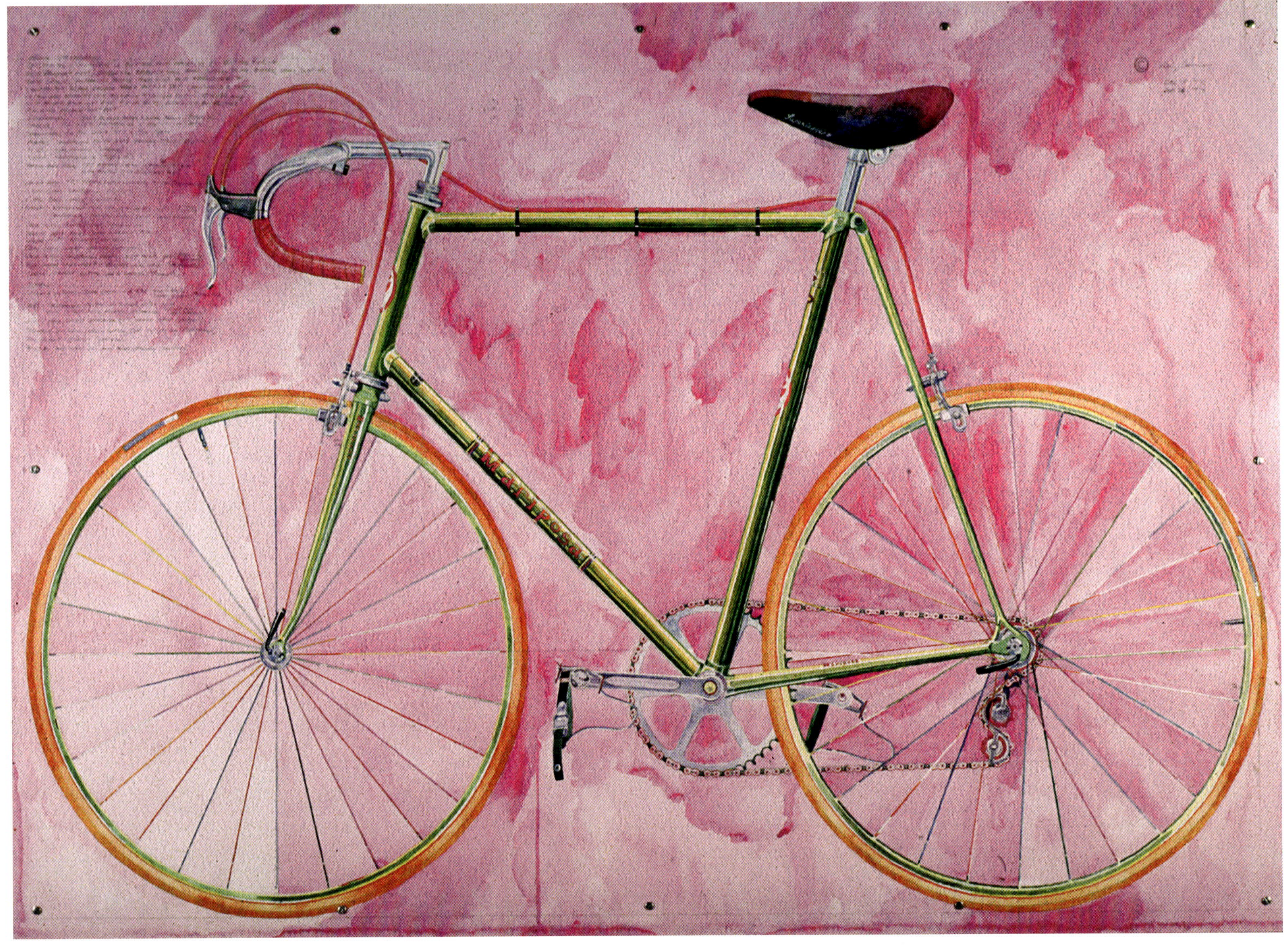

Lisa Steele and Kim Tomczak

Love^2, 1990–2008
HD video, colour, silent, 15:30 min.
Collection of the artists

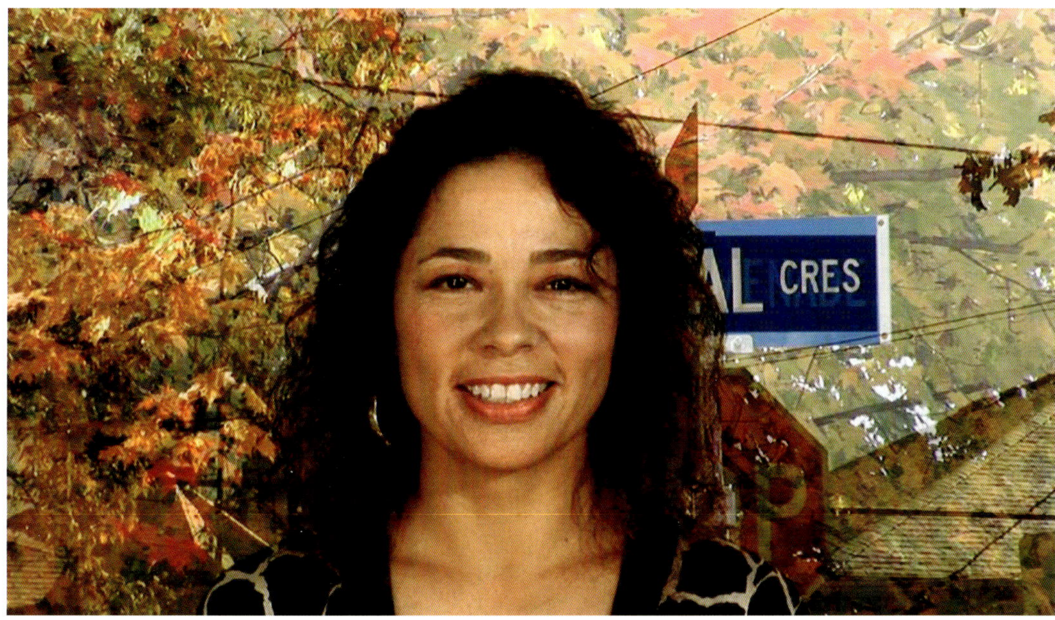

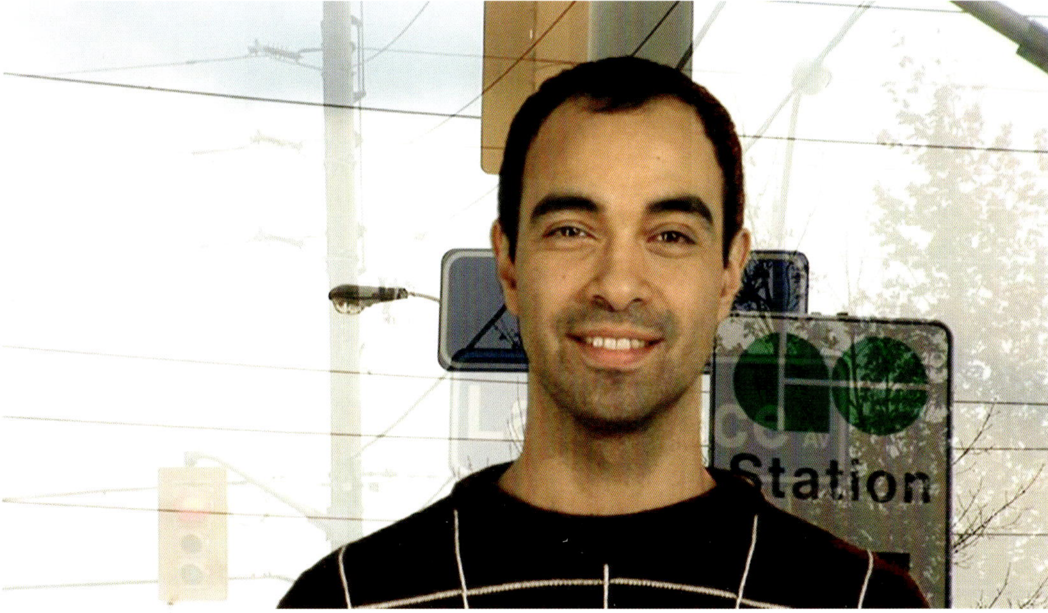

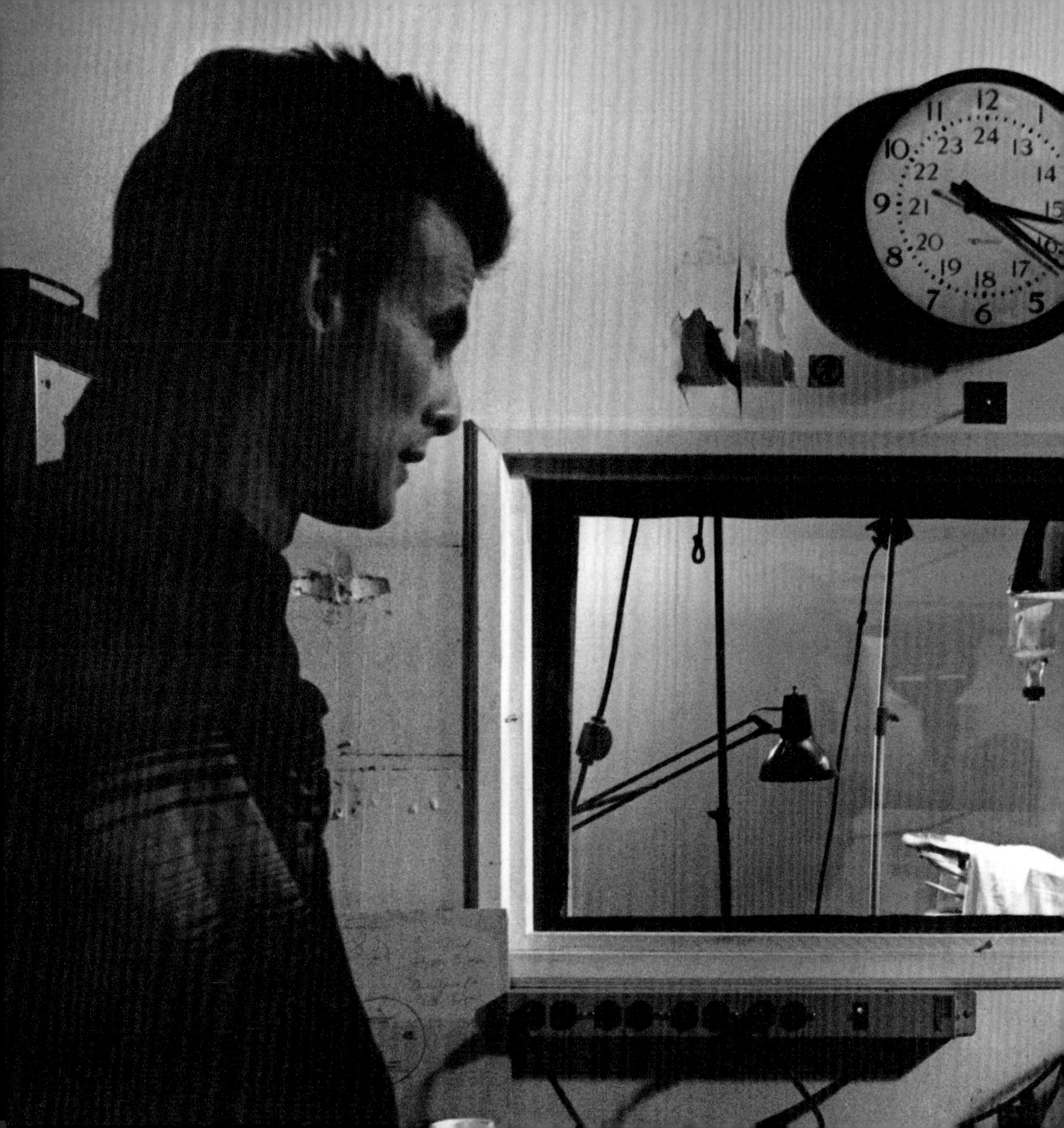

Experimental Film and Video Art

Ezhi-ndikenjigaadeg Mzinaates jigewin miiniwaa Mzinaatesjige Ntaa-nokiichigewin

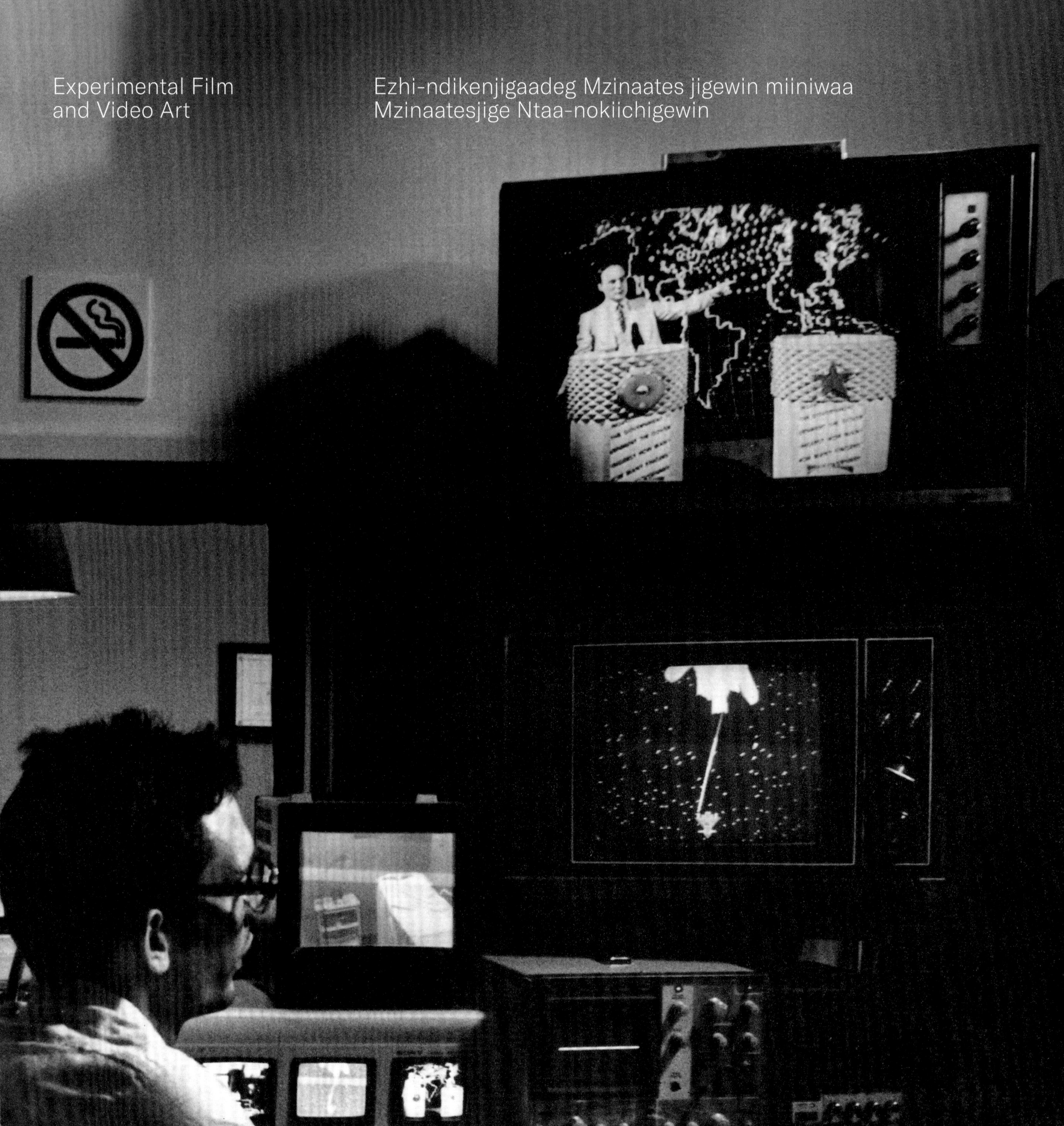

Film and Video Festival

Thursday, March 9, to Sunday, March 12, 2017
Jackman Hall, Art Gallery of Ontario

Thursday, March 9, 2017

CFMDC Presents: Personal Perspectives 1971–1979

Solidarity, 1973
Joyce Wieland

Metamorphosis, 1975
Barry Greenwald

Jim and Muggins Tour Toronto, 1978
Michael Kennedy

On the Pond, 1978
Philip Hoffman

Weather Building, 1976
Ross McLaren

She Is Away, 1976
R. Bruce Elder

Minimum Charge No Cover, 1976
Janis Cole and Holly Dale

Mondo Punk, 1978
Suzanne Naughton

Thursday, March 9, 2017

Joyce Wieland's *The Far Shore*

The Far Shore, 1976
Joyce Wieland

Friday, March 10, 2017

Bodies That Matter

D-E-S-I-R-E, 1989
Glace W. Lawrence

Turn, 1971
Stephen Cruise

Baby Dolls, 1978
Rodney Werden

Black & White, 1971
Raphael Bendahan

Hormone Warzone, 1983
Hummer Sisters

Friday, March 10, 2017

Vera Frenkel's *The Secret Life of Cornelia Lumsden: A Remarkable Story*

The Secret Life of Cornelia Lumsden: A Remarkable Story, Part 1, Her Room in Paris, 1979
Vera Frenkel

The Secret Life of Cornelia Lumsden: A Remarkable Story, Part 2, "And Now the Truth" (A Parenthesis), 1980
Vera Frenkel

Saturday, March 11, 2017

Michael Snow: *Seated Figures & So Is This*

Seated Figures, 1988
Michael Snow

So Is This, 1982
Michael Snow

Saturday, March 11, 2017

Indigenous Freedom

The Ballad of Crowfoot, 1968
Willie Dunn

Charley Squash Goes to Town, 1969
Duke Redbird

Cowboy and Indian, 1972
Don Owen

What Price an Island? 1985
Mike MacDonald

Saturday, March 11, 2017

Vtape's Toronto New Work Shows Revisited—Program 1

Out of the Blue, 1991
Richard Fung

Once Upon a Time, 1984
Randy & Berenicci

How Many Fingers?
1981
Andrew J. Paterson
and Alan Fox

AIDS PSAs, 1993
Michael Balser,
David Findlay,
Zachery Longboy, and
Mike MacDonald

Skin, 1990
Colin Campbell

Got Away in the Dying Moments, 1992
Dennis Day
(with Ian Middleton)

Another Man, 1988
Youth Against Monsterz

Saturday, March 11, 2017

Vtape's Toronto New Work Shows Revisited—Program 2

Westinghouses (Arts Seen Theme), 1976
Jane Wright

Absence, 1986
Su Rynard

Dinner, 1989
Marnie Parrell

Freeze Frame, 1983
Susan Britton

Say, 1978
Rodney Werden

It Depends, 1984
Paulette Phillips

Perils of Pedagogy, 1984
John Greyson

Scannex Man, 1981
John Watt

Part 1/Untitled, 1984
Jorge Lozano

The Long Take, 1984
Gary Kibbins

Up to Scratch, 1986
Craig Berggold
and Clive Robertson

Sunday, March 12, 2017

Eyes of the Wise

Pure Virtue, 1985
Tanya Mars

Passion: A Letter in 16mm, 1985
Patricia Rozema

Private Eyes, 1987
Lisa Steele and
Kim Tomczak

There Is in Power… Seduction, 1985
Annette Mangaard

At 99: Portrait of Tandy Murch, 1975
Deepa Mehta

Sunday, March 12, 2017

CFMDC Presents: Geographies of Self and City

Speakbody, 1980
Kay Armatage

Cityscape, 1988
Wendy Rowland,
Darlene Pratt, and
Angela Sigsworth

From Nevis To, 1987
Christene Browne

All Flesh Is Grass, 1988
Susan Oxtoby

The Bird That Chirped on Bathurst, 1981
Midi Onodera

Mine's Bedlam, 1980
Carl Brown

Now, Yours, 1982
Mike Hoolboom

Stop Darlington, 1987
Robert Kennedy
and Cal Woodruff

Waterworx (A Clear Day and No Memories), 1982
Rick Hancox

Sunday, March 12, 2017

Performance

Television's Human Nature, 1977
Tom Sherman

Tango, 1976
Susan Britton

Performance (Untitled), 1974
Tom Dean

Lily Eng, Solo Improvisation, dOCUMENTA 6, 1977
Missing Associates
(Lily Eng and
Peter Dudar)

The Myth of the Fishes, 1985
Rhonda Abrams

Making a Scene, 1984
Martha Davis

Exhibition Screening Room

Lament of the Sugar Bush Man, 1987
Rhonda Abrams

Le jardin (du Paradis): The Garden (of Paradise), 1982
Raphael Bendahan

Dangling by Their Mouths, 1981
Colin Campbell

Turn, 1971
Stephen Cruise

Stories from the Front (and Back): A True Blue Romance, 1981
Vera Frenkel

Chinese Characters, 1986
Richard Fung

Shut the Fuck Up, 1985
General Idea

Urinal, 1989
John Greyson

D-E-S-I-R-E, 1989
Glace W. Lawrence

Limited Warranty, 1983
Jorge Lozano

At 99: Portrait of Tandy Murch, 1975
Deepa Mehta

Tvideo, 1980
Tom Sherman

Private Eyes, 1987
Lisa Steele and Kim Tomczak

Baby Dolls, 1978
Rodney Werden

A and B in Ontario, 1984
Joyce Wieland and Hollis Frampton

Orientations: Lesbian & Gay Asians, 1986
Richard Fung

Rhonda Abrams

Lament of the Sugar Bush Man, 1987
video, colour, sound, 12 min.

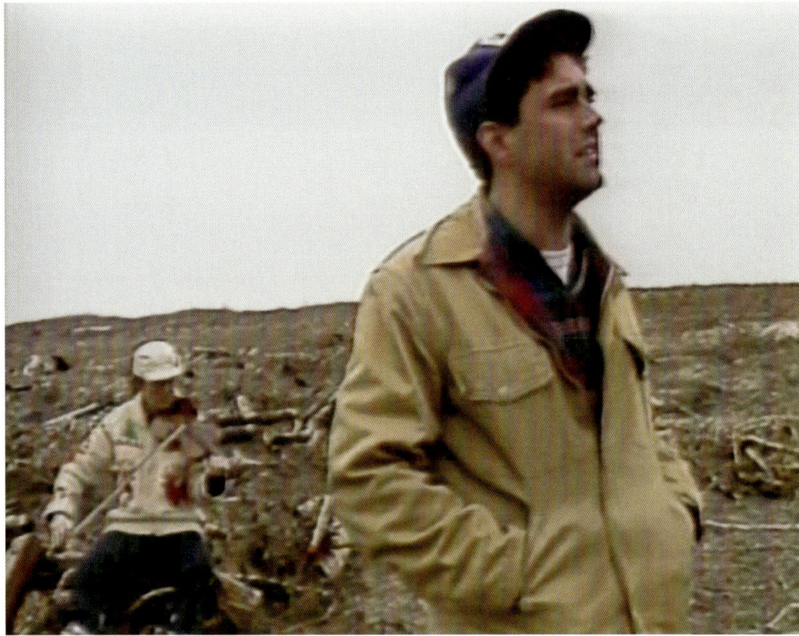

Rhonda Abrams

The Myth of the Fishes, 1985
video, colour, sound, 7:30 min.

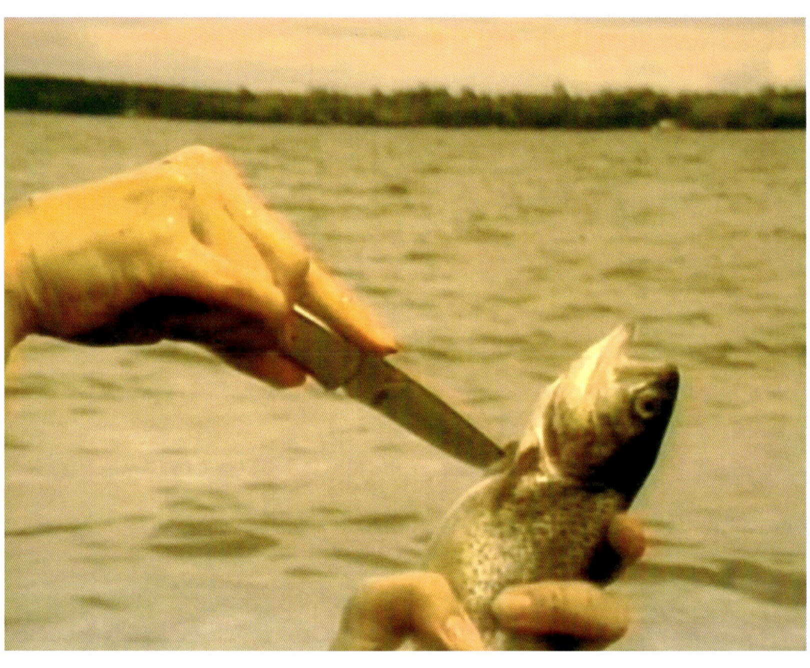

Kay Armatage

Speakbody, 1980
16mm film, colour, sound, 8 min.

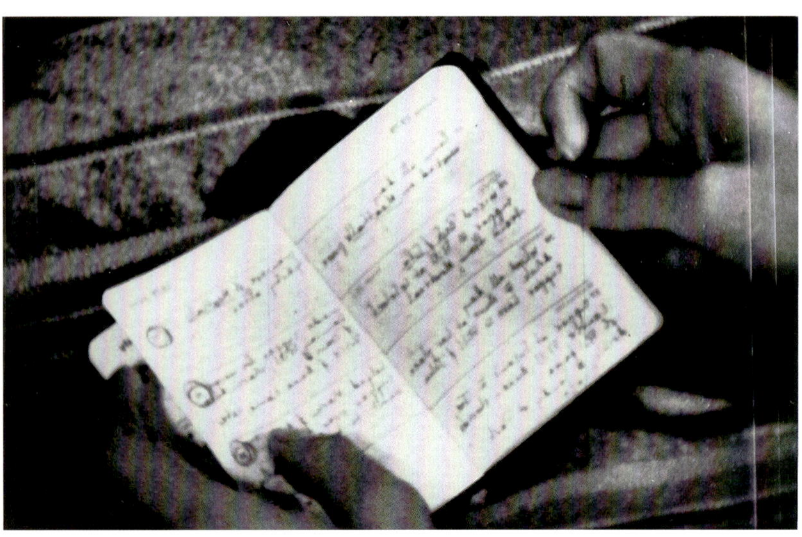

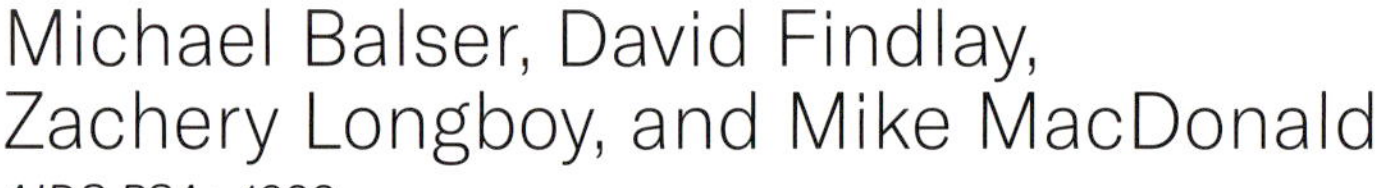

Michael Balser, David Findlay, Zachery Longboy, and Mike MacDonald

AIDS PSAs, 1993
From *Second Decade,* produced by Michael Balser
video, colour, sound, 4 × 30 sec.

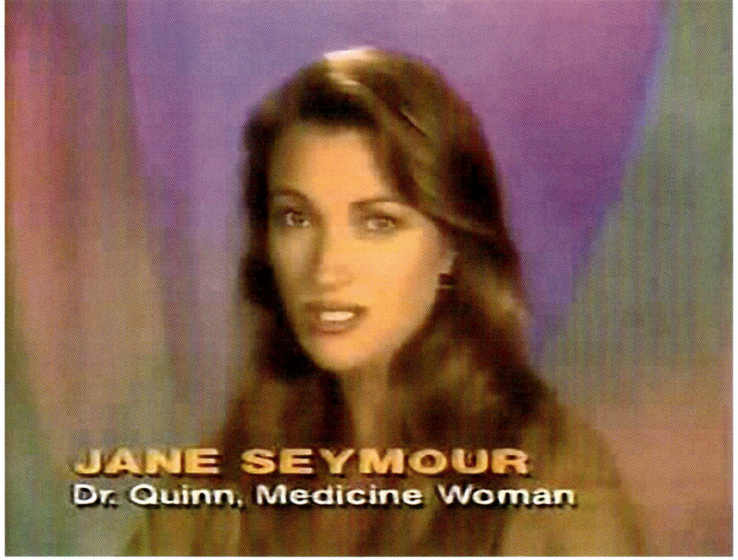

Raphael Bendahan

Le jardin (du Paradis) : The Garden (of Paradise), 1982
16mm film, colour, sound, 21:44 min.

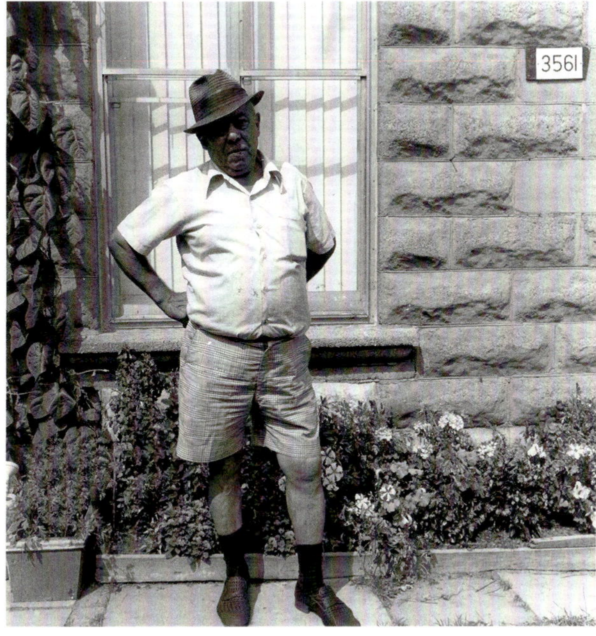

Raphael Bendahan

Black & White, 1971
16mm film, b&w, sound, 8 min.

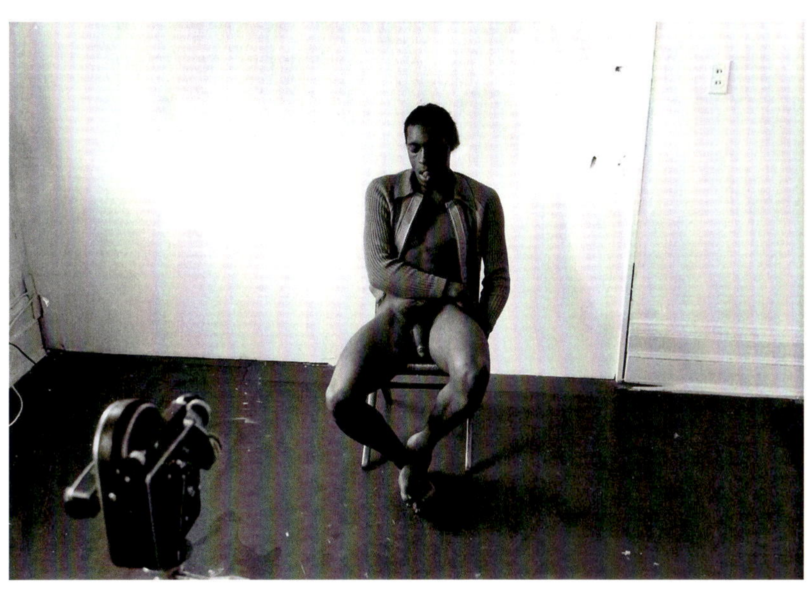

Craig Berggold and Clive Robertson

Up to Scratch, 1986
video, colour, sound, 5:30 min.

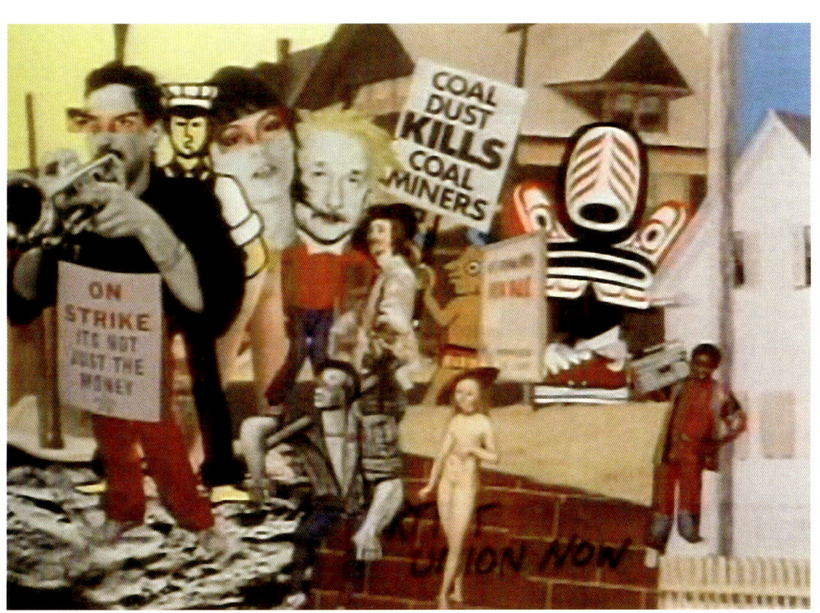

Susan Britton

Freeze Frame, 1983
video, colour, sound, 2 min.

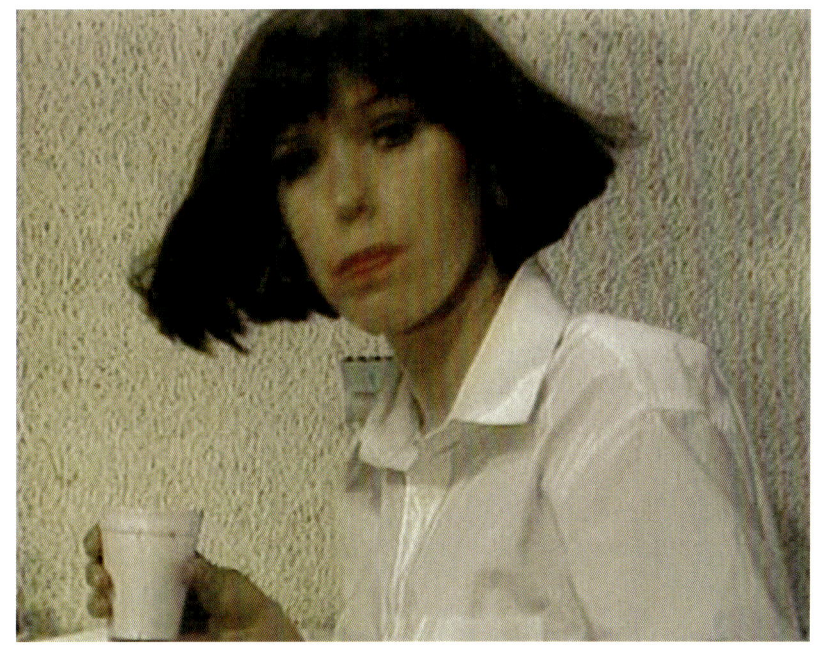

Susan Britton

Tango, 1976
video, b&w, sound, 12 min.

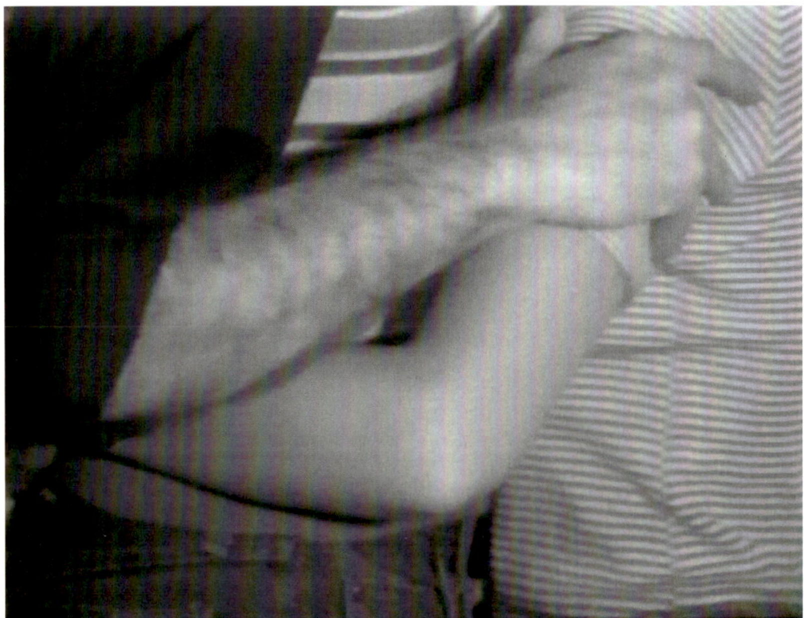

Carl Brown

Mine's Bedlam, 1980
Super 8 film, colour, sound, 8 min.

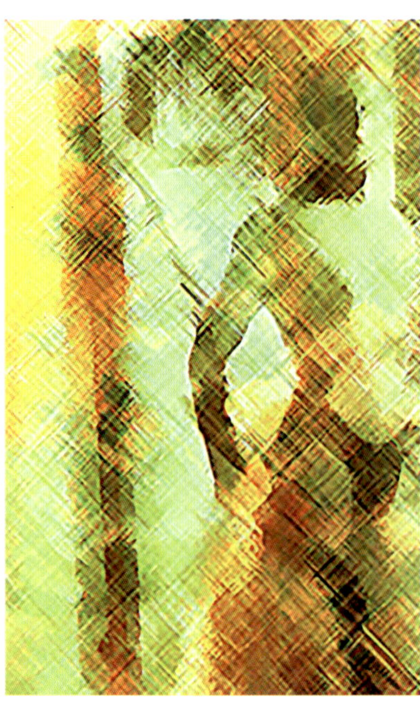

Christene Browne

From Nevis To, 1987
video, b&w, sound, 7 min.

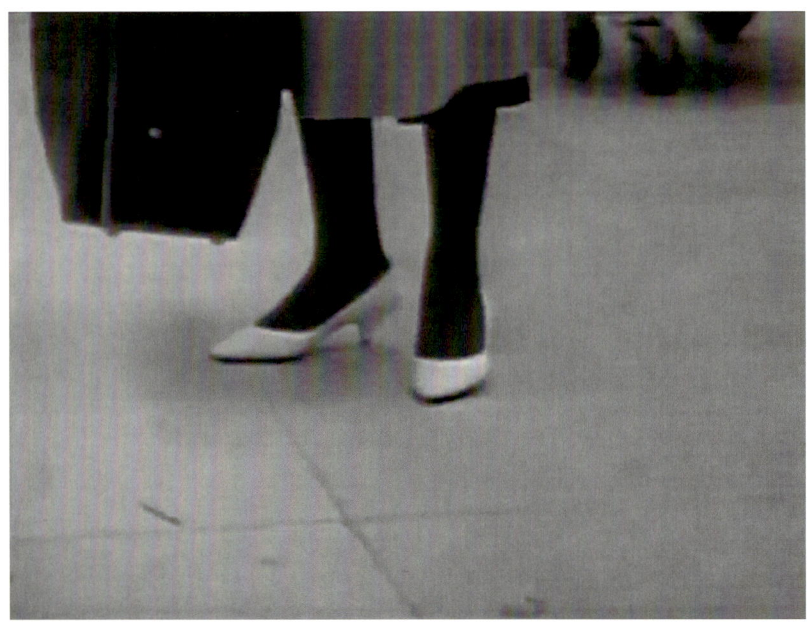

Colin Campbell

Dangling by Their Mouths, 1981
video, colour, sound, 60 min.

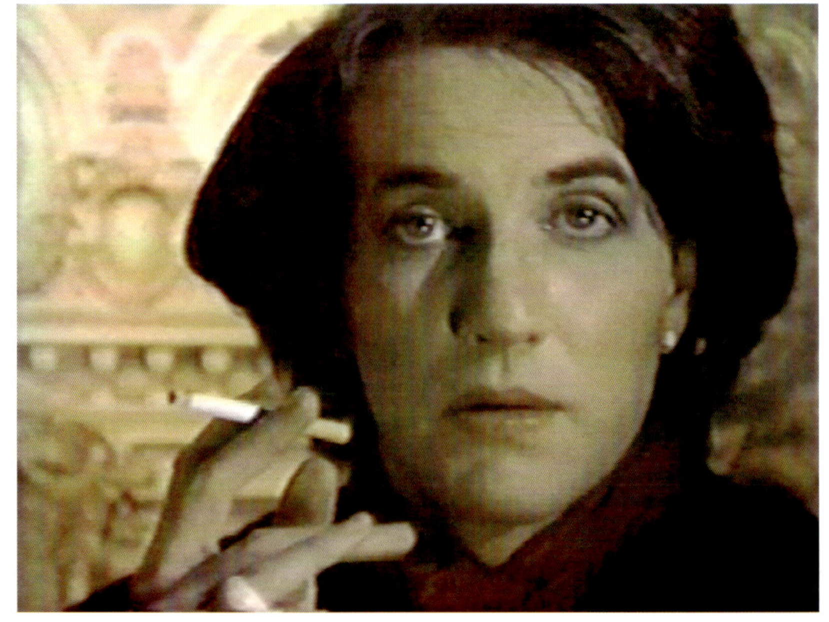

Colin Campbell

Skin, 1990
video, colour, sound, 14:50 min.

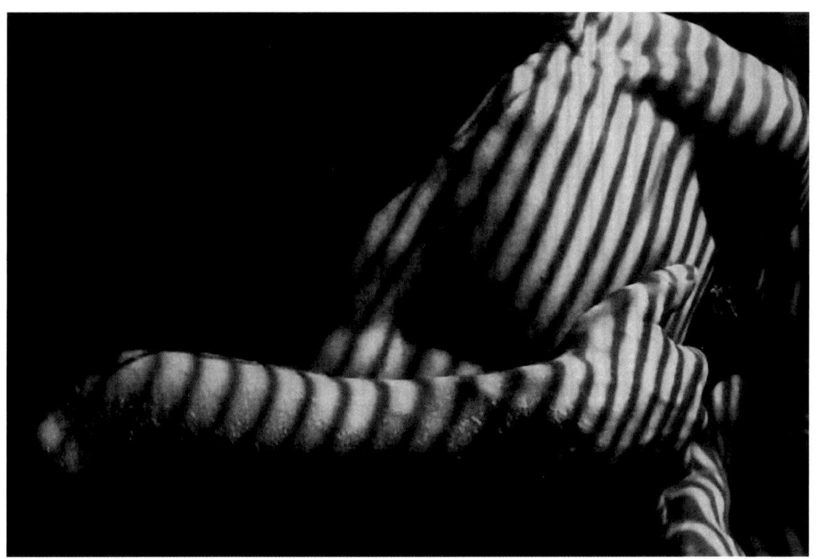

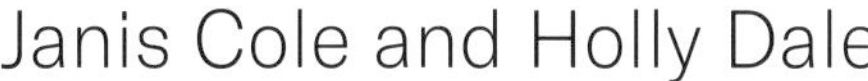

Janis Cole and Holly Dale

Minimum Charge No Cover, 1976
16mm film, colour, sound, 11 min.

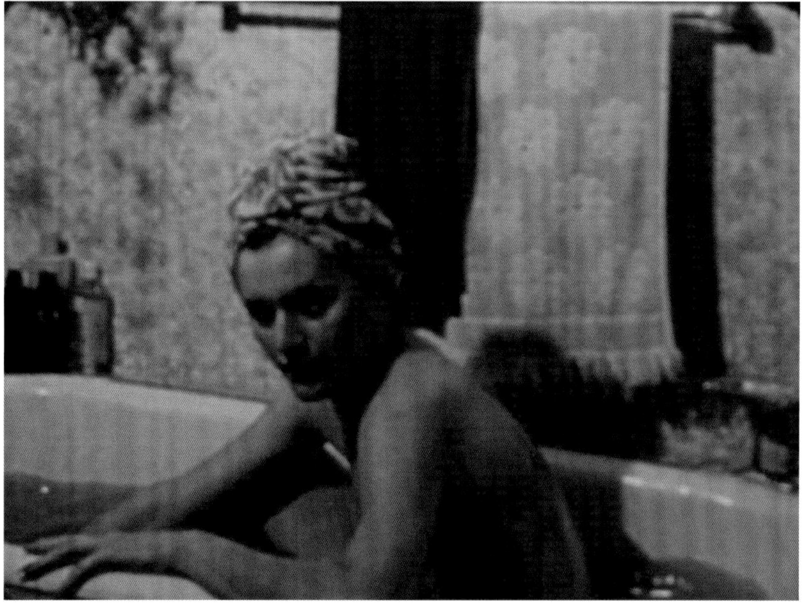

Stephen Cruise

Turn, 1971
video, b&w, sound, 6:30 min.

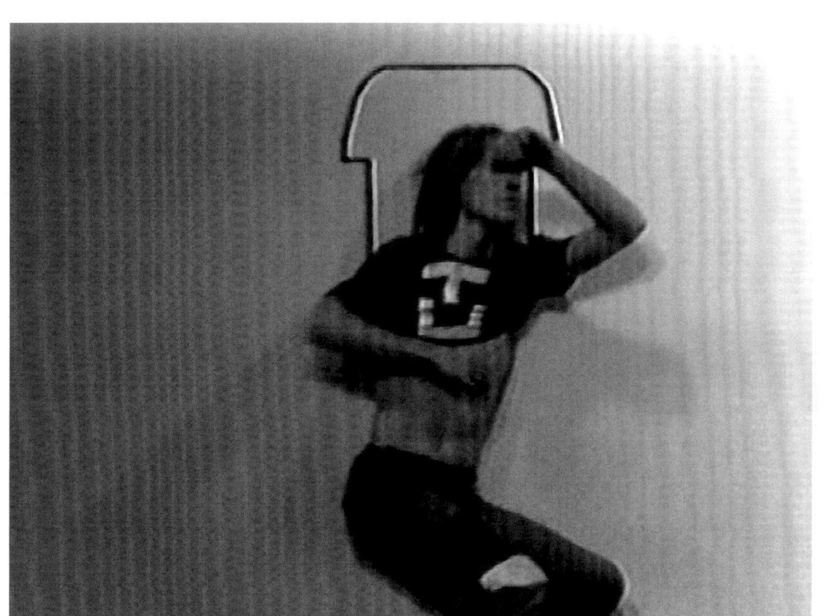

Martha Davis

Making a Scene, 1984
Super 8 film, colour, sound, 5:30 min.

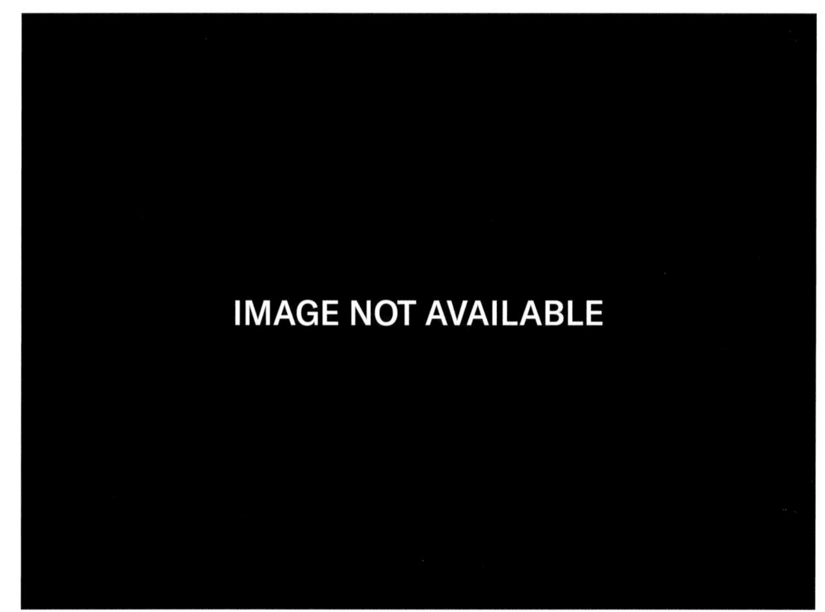

Dennis Day (with Ian Middleton)

Got Away in the Dying Moment, 1992
video, colour, sound, 4:30 min.

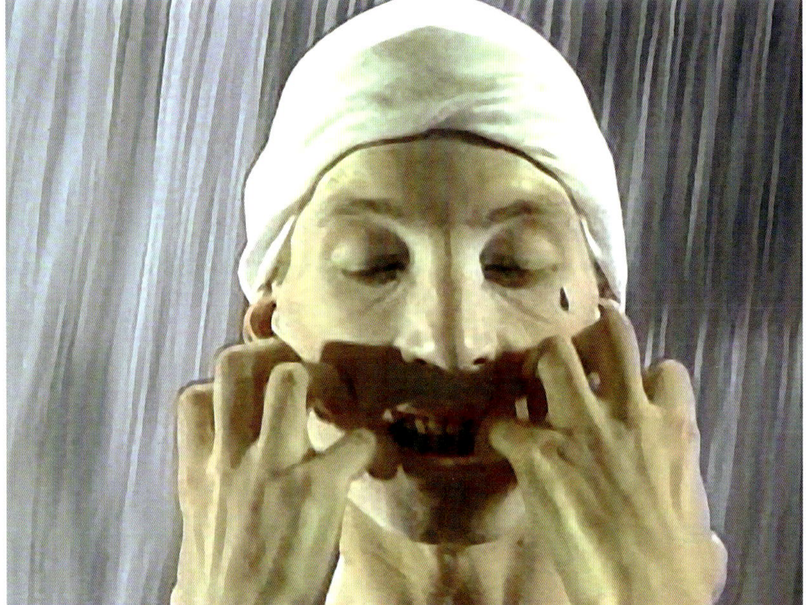

Tom Dean

Performance (Untitled), 1974
video, b&w, sound, 18:30 min.

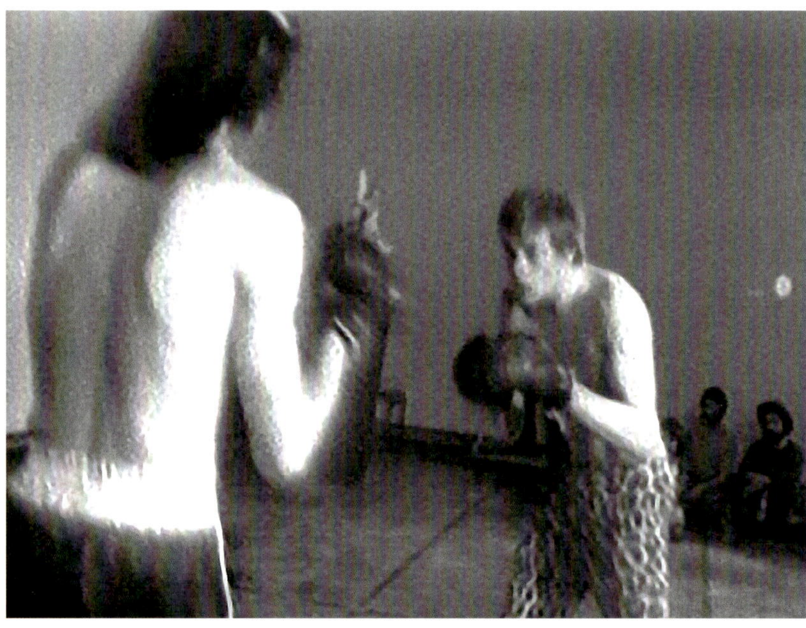

Willie Dunn

The Ballad of Crowfoot, 1968
16mm film, colour, sound, 10 min.

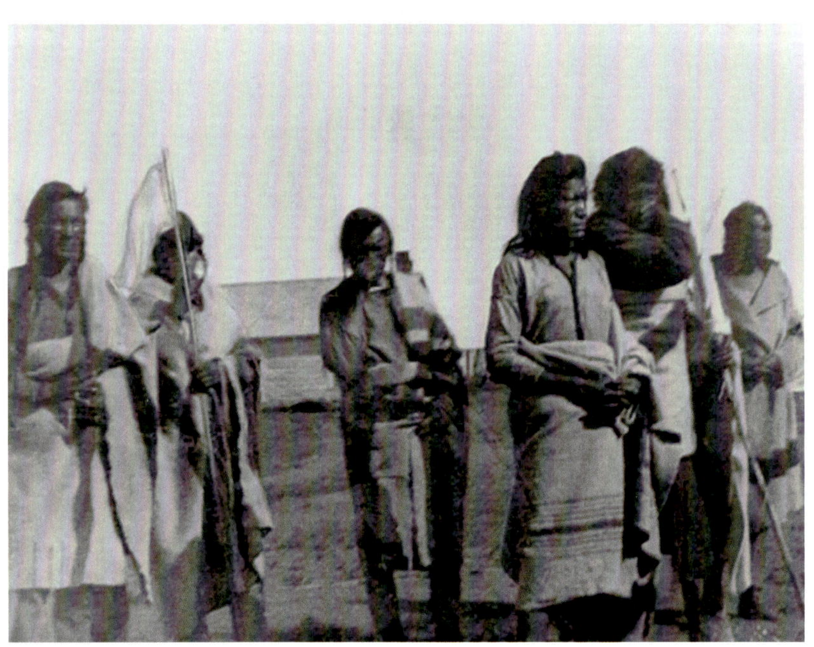

R. Bruce Elder

She Is Away, 1976
16mm film, colour, sound, 13 min.

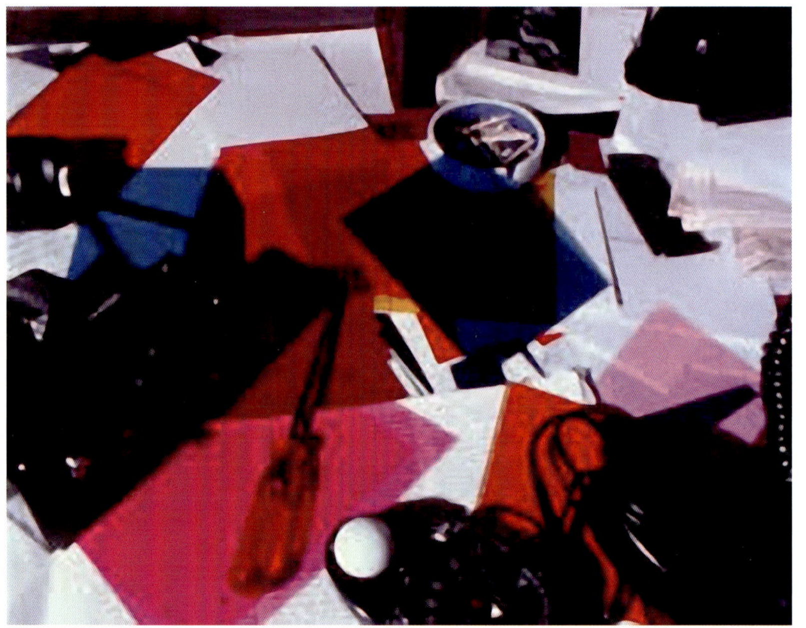

Vera Frenkel

Stories from the Front (and Back): A True Blue Romance, 1981
video, colour, sound, 60 min.

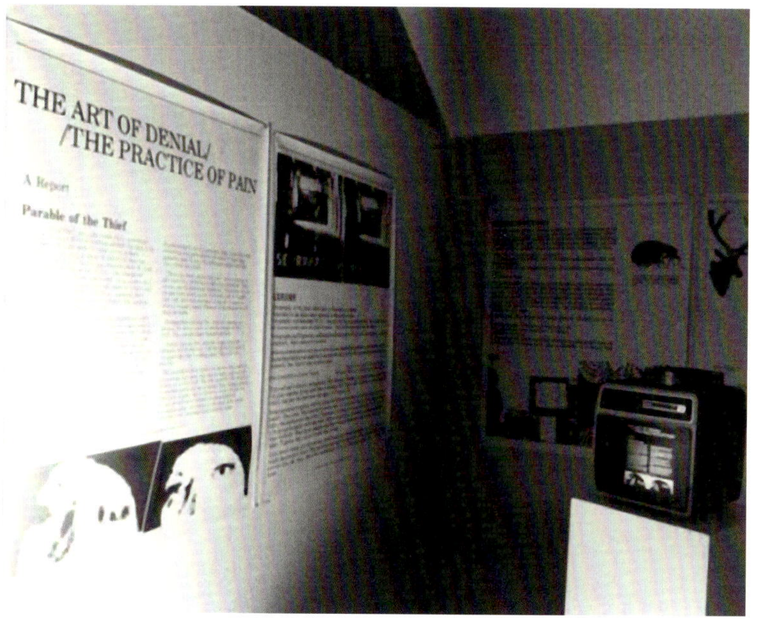

Vera Frenkel

The Secret Life of Cornelia Lumsden: A Remarkable Story, Part 1, Her Room in Paris, 1979
video, colour, sound, 60 min.

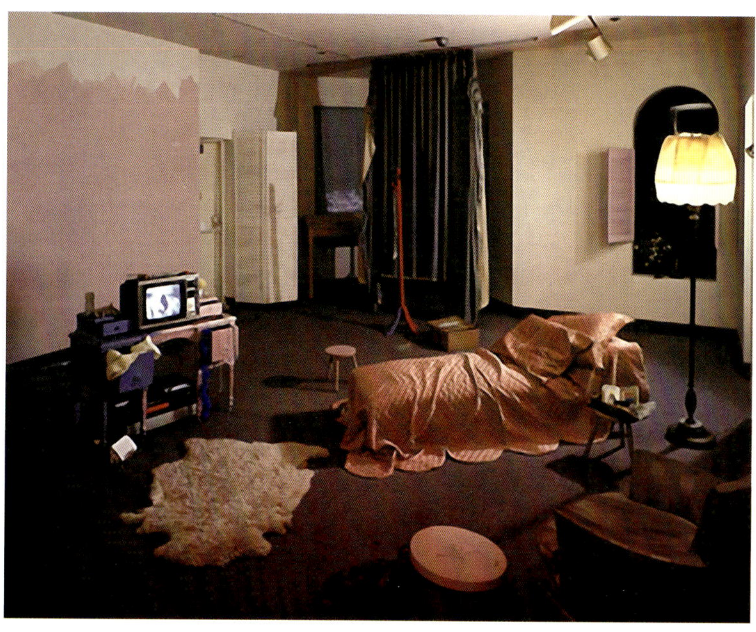

Vera Frenkel

The Secret Life of Cornelia Lumsden: A Remarkable Story, Part 2, "And Now The Truth" (A Parenthesis), 1980
video, colour, sound, 31 min.

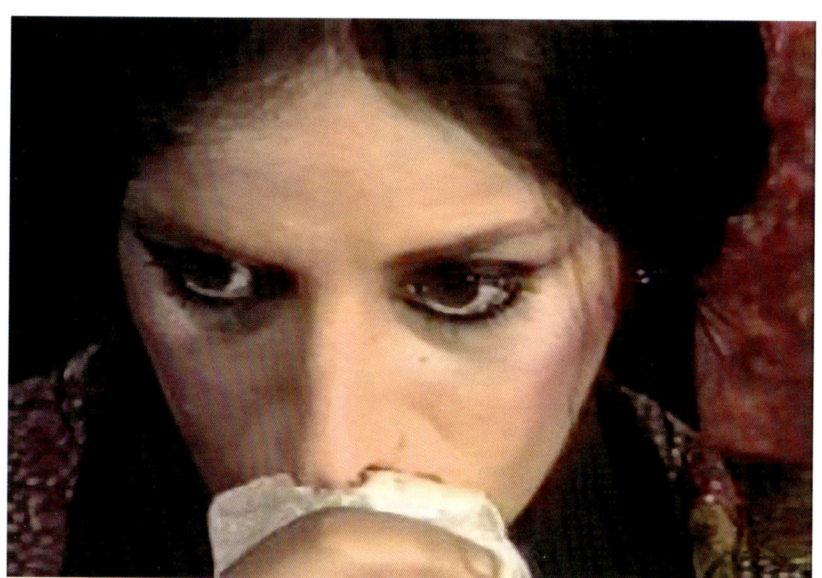

Richard Fung

Chinese Characters, 1986
video, colour, sound, 20:30 min.

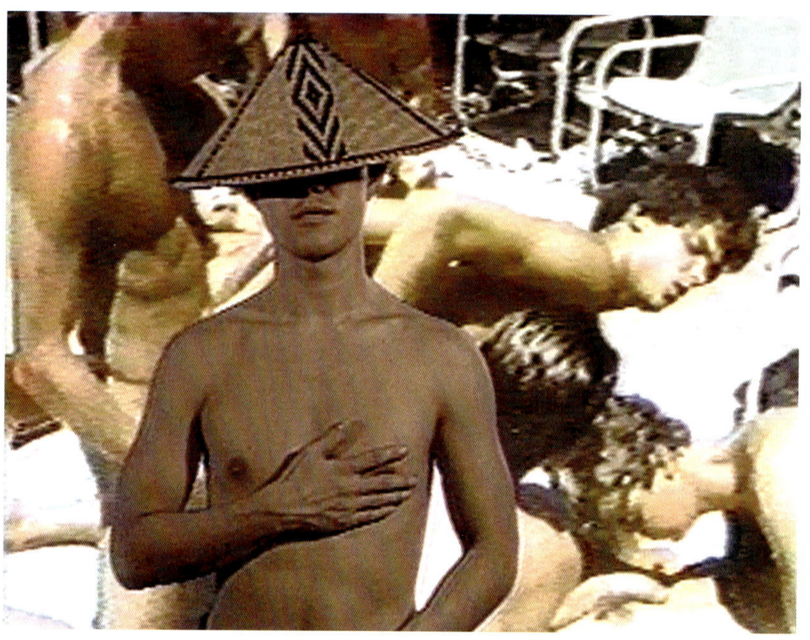

Richard Fung

Orientations: Lesbian & Gay Asians, 1986
video, colour, sound, 56 min.

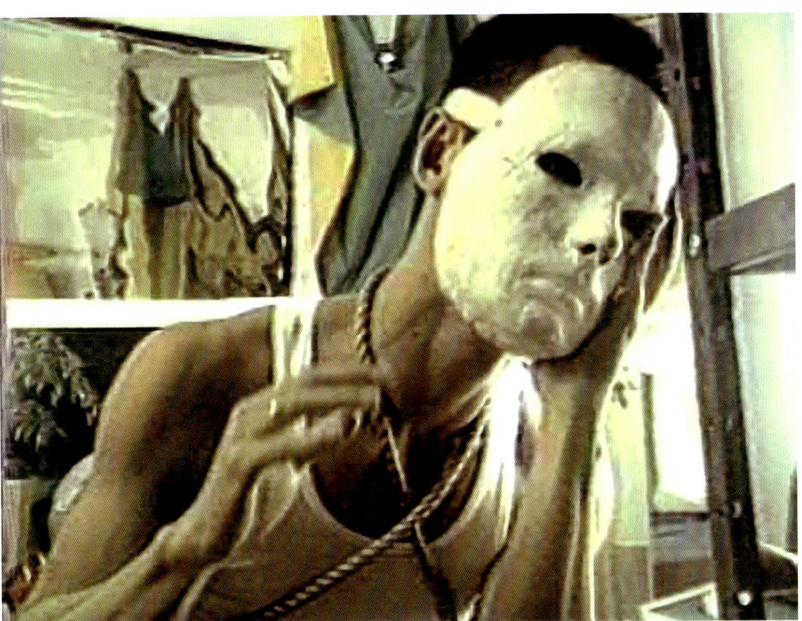

Richard Fung

Out of the Blue, 1991
video, colour, sound, 28 min.

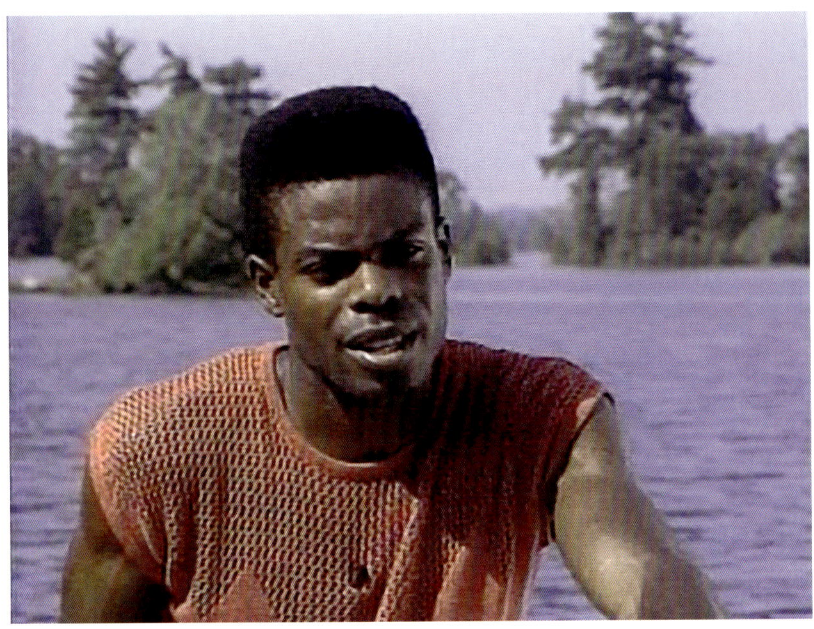

General Idea

Shut the Fuck Up, 1984
video, colour, sound, 14 min.

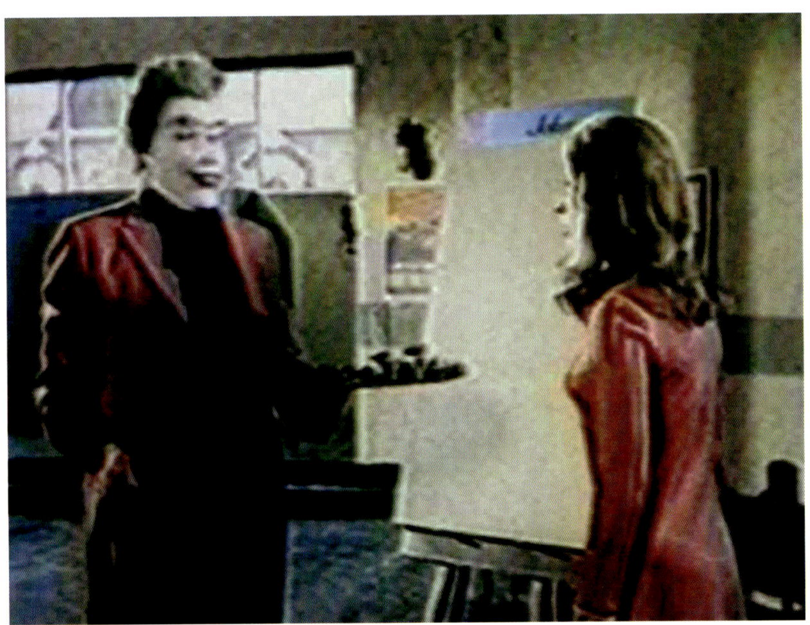

Barry Greenwald

Metamorphosis, 1975
16mm film, b&w, sound, 10:30 min.

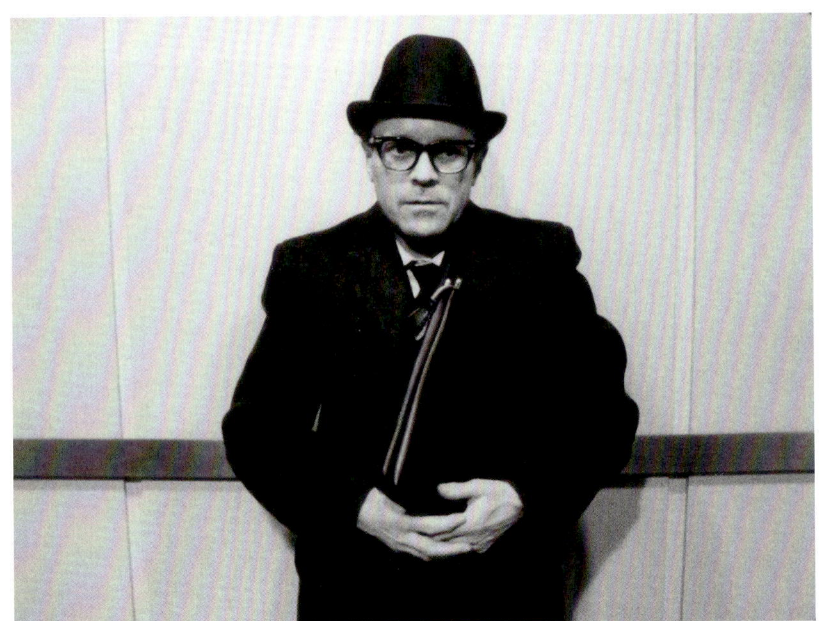

John Greyson

Perils of Pedagogy, 1984
video, colour, sound, 5 min.

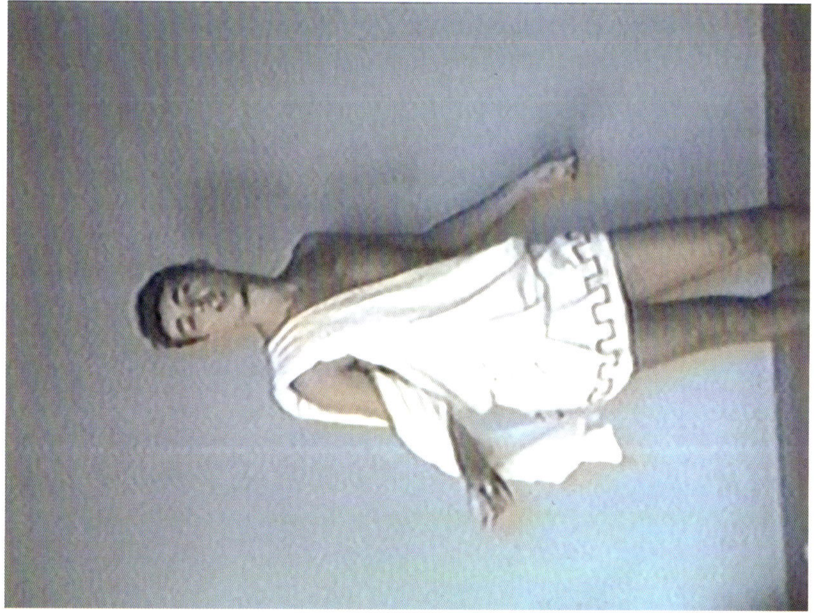

John Greyson

Urinal, 1988
16mm film, b&w, sound, 100 min.

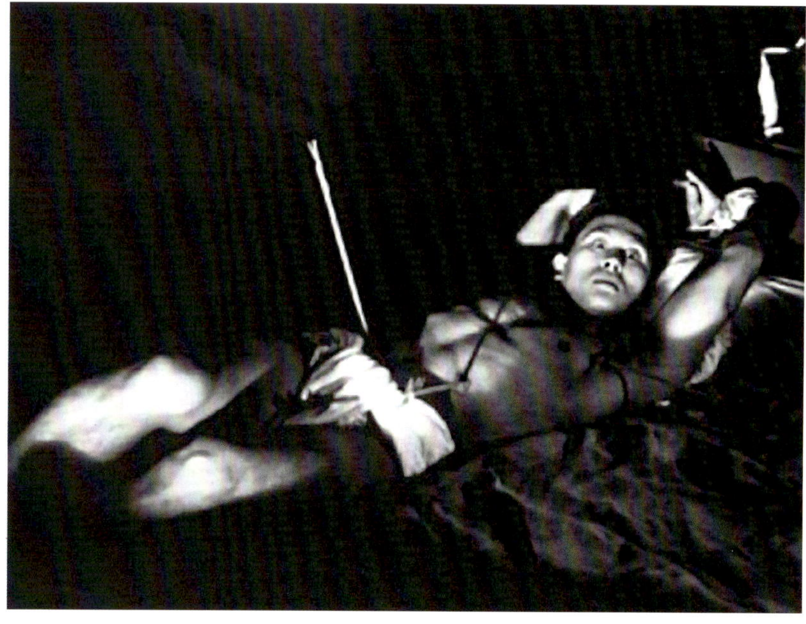

Rick Hancox

Waterworx (A Clear Day and No Memories), 1982
16mm film, colour, sound, 5:32 min.

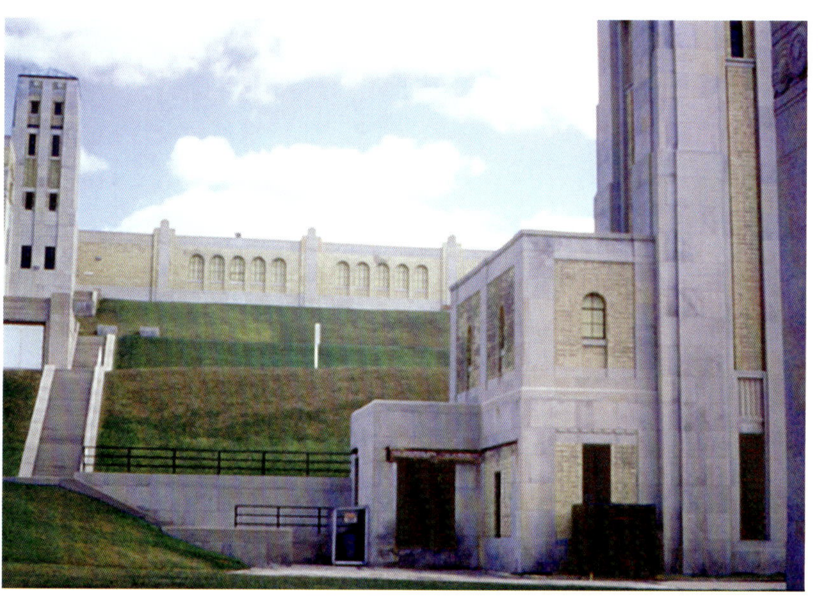

Philip Hoffman

On the Pond, 1978
16mm film, b&w, sound, 9 min.

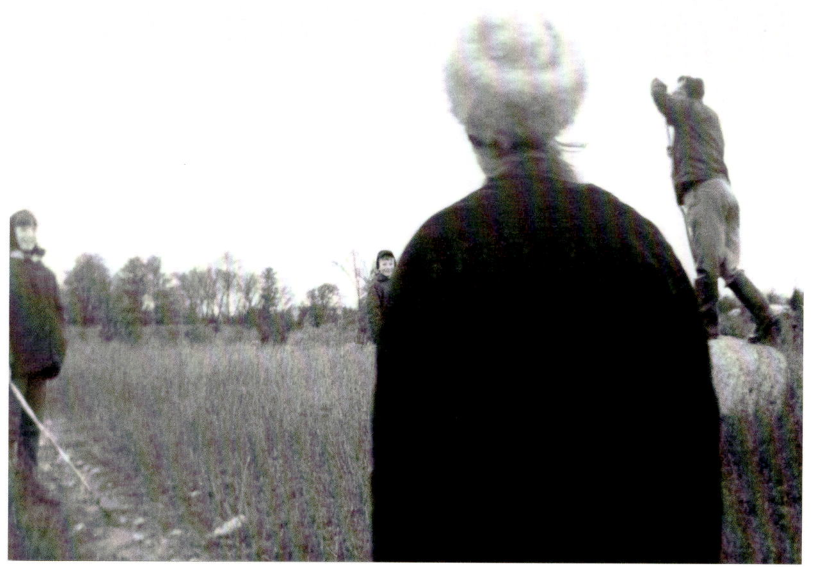

Mike Hoolboom

Now, Yours, 1982
16mm film, colour, sound, 10 min.

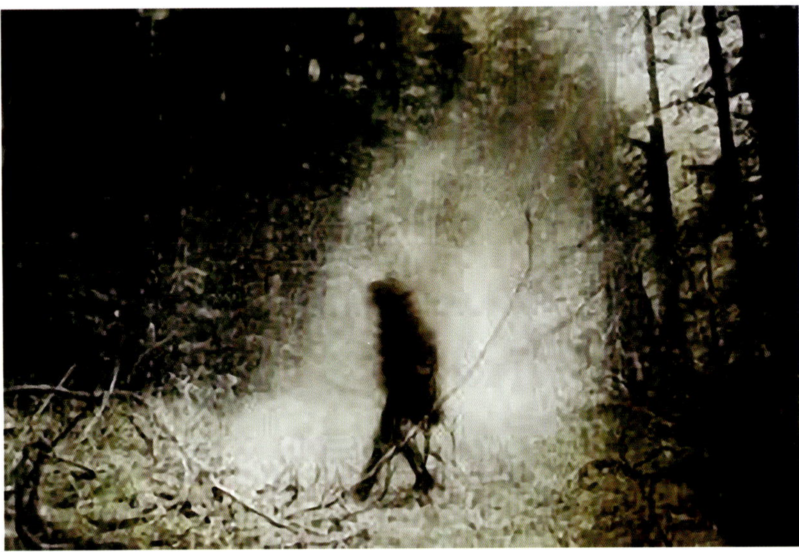

Hummer Sisters

Hormone Warzone, 1983
video, colour, sound, 11 min.

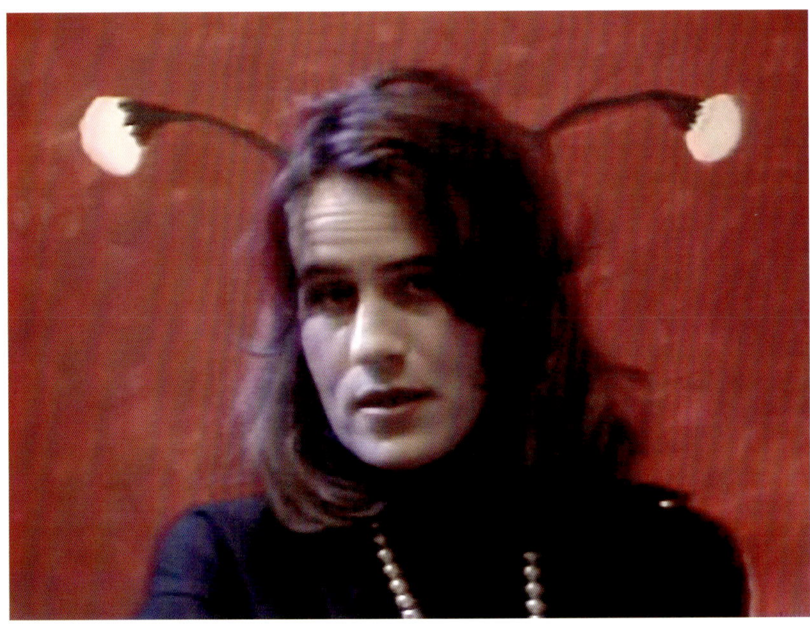

Michael Kennedy

Jim and Muggins Tour Toronto, 1978
16mm film, b&w, sound, 15 min.

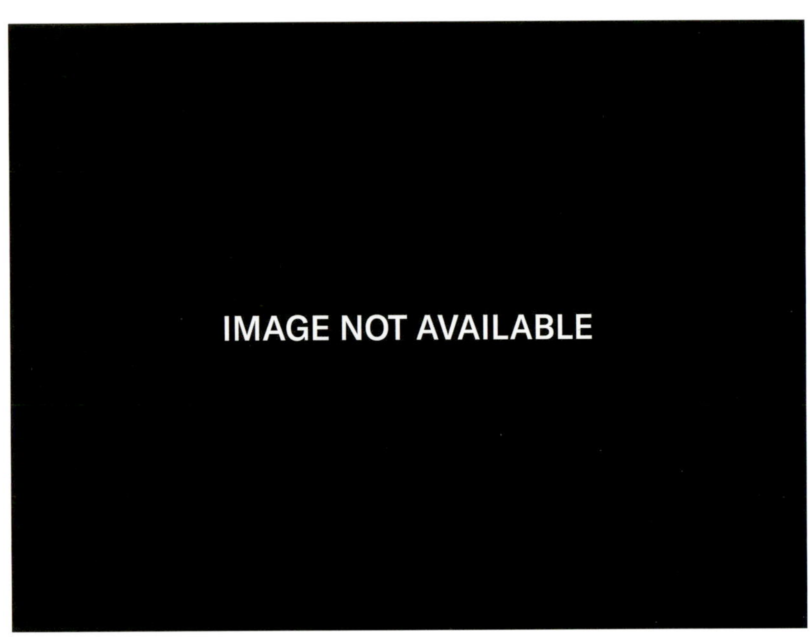

Robert Kennedy and Cal Woodruff

Stop Darlington, 1987
16mm film, colour, sound, 4 min.

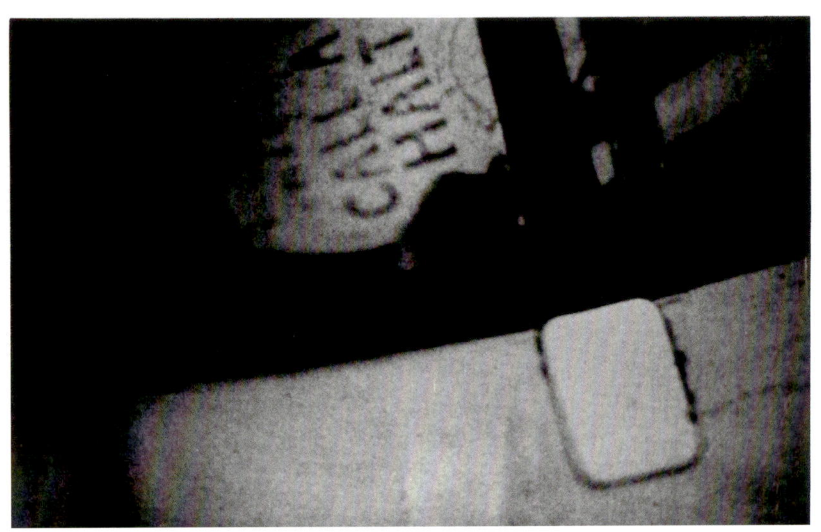

Gary Kibbins

The Long Take, 1984
video, colour, sound, 7 min.

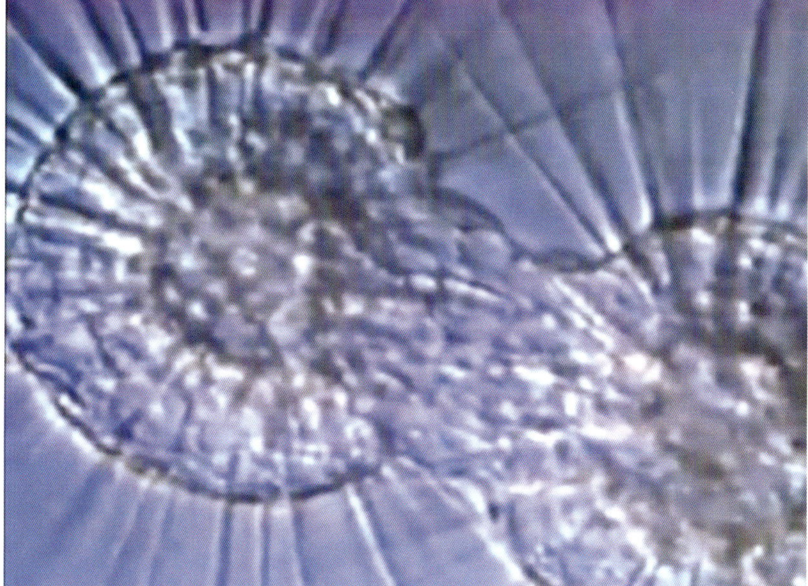

Glace W. Lawrence

D-E-S-I-R-E, 1989
video, b&w, sound, 3:30 min.

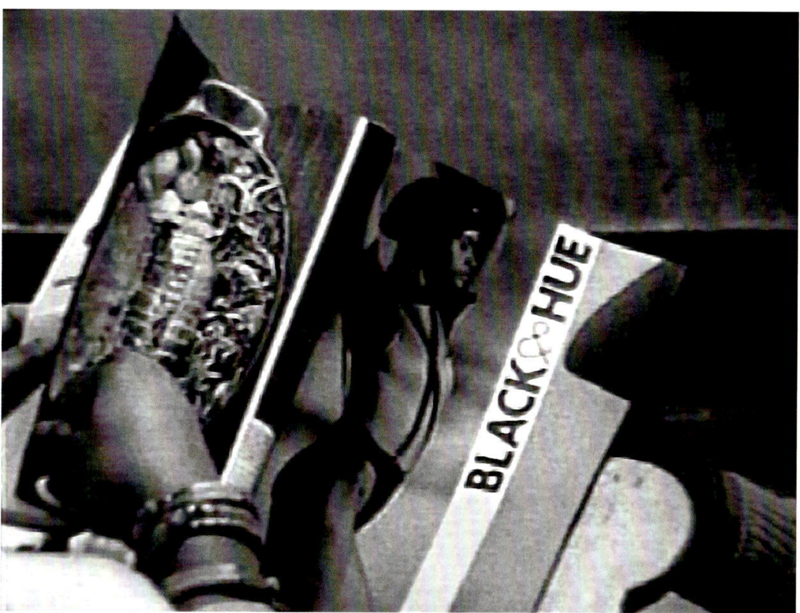

Jorge Lozano

Limited Warranty, 1983
video, colour, sound, 10 min.

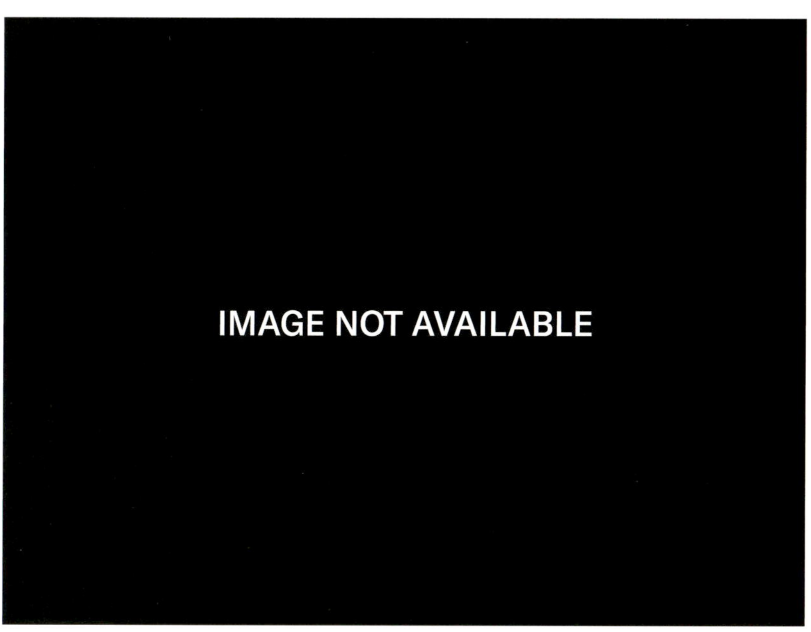

Jorge Lozano

Part 1/Untitled, 1984
video, colour, sound, 6 min.

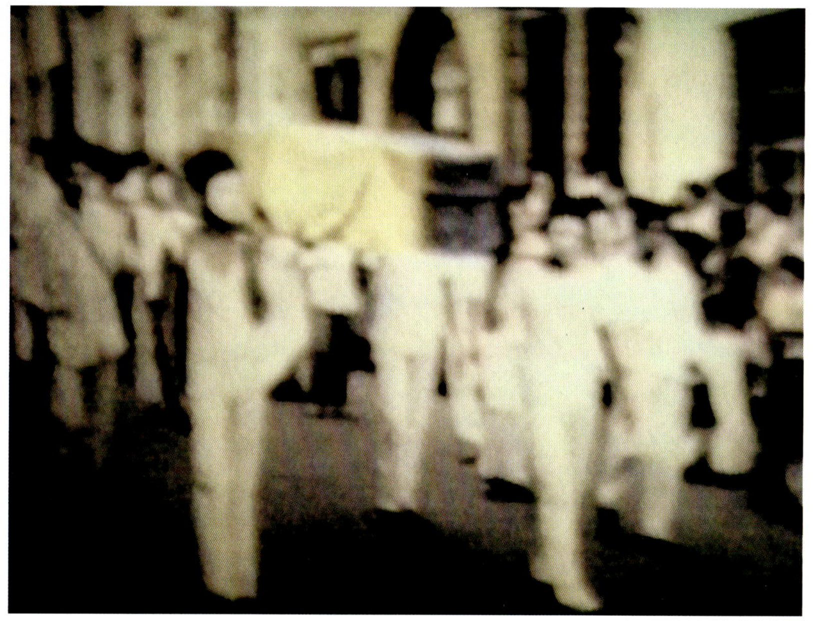

Mike MacDonald

What Price an Island?, 1985
video, colour, sound, 28 min.

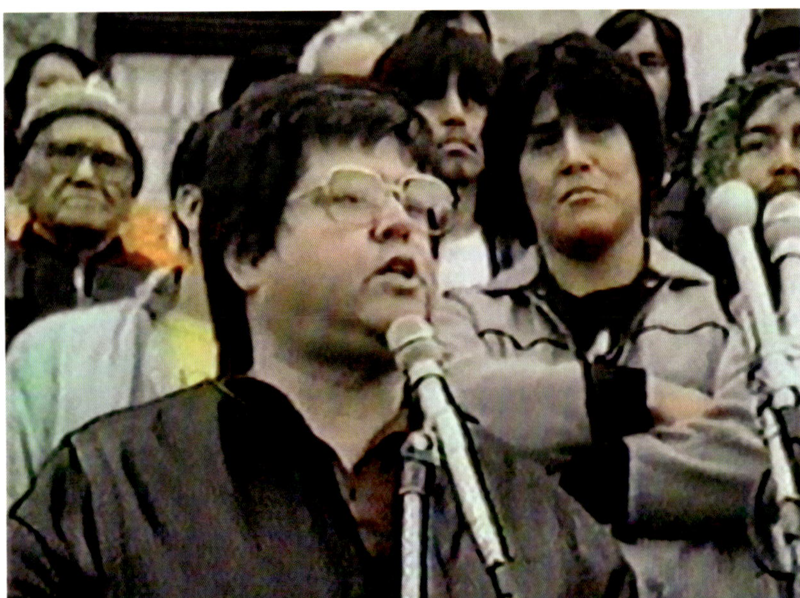

Annette Mangaard

There Is in Power...Seduction, 1985
16mm film, b&w, sound, 5 min.

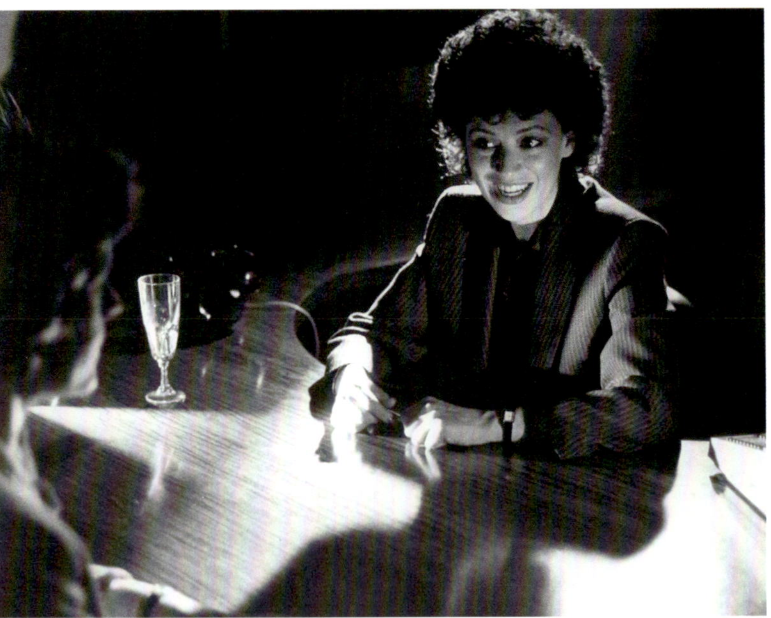

Tanya Mars

Pure Virtue, 1985
video, colour, sound, 16:30 min.

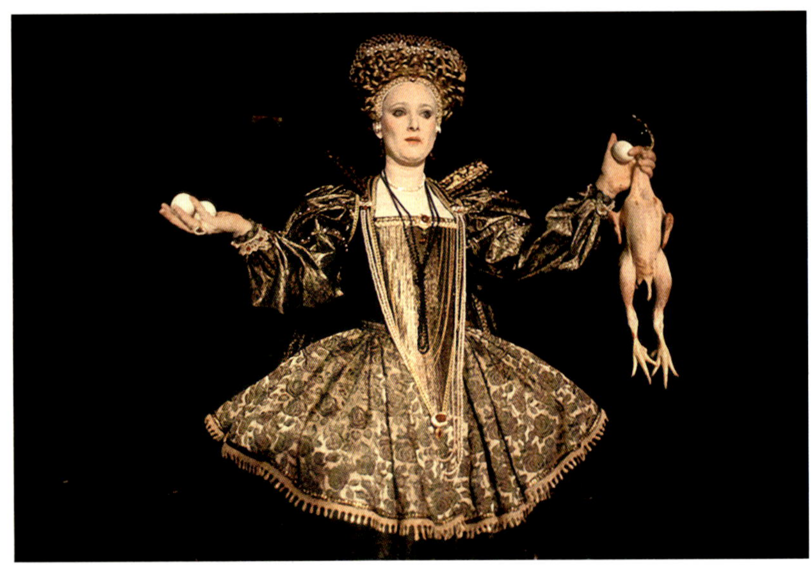

Ross McLaren

Weather Building, 1976
16mm film, colour, sound, 10 min.

Deepa Mehta

At 99: Portrait of Tandy Murch, 1975
16mm film, colour, sound, 24 min.

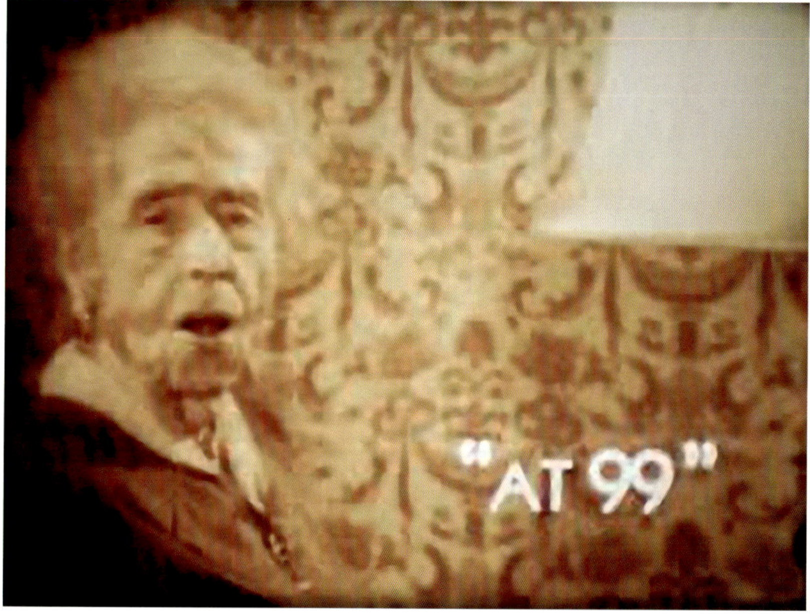

Missing Associates (Lily Eng and Peter Dudar)

Lily Eng, Solo Improvisation, dOCUMENTA 6, 1977
video, b&w, sound, 12:27 min.

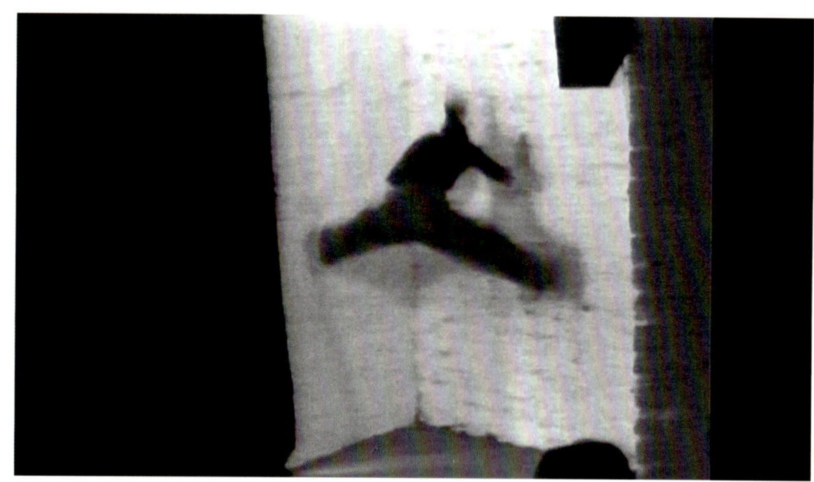

Suzanne Naughton

Mondo Punk, 1978
16mm film, colour, sound, 6 min.

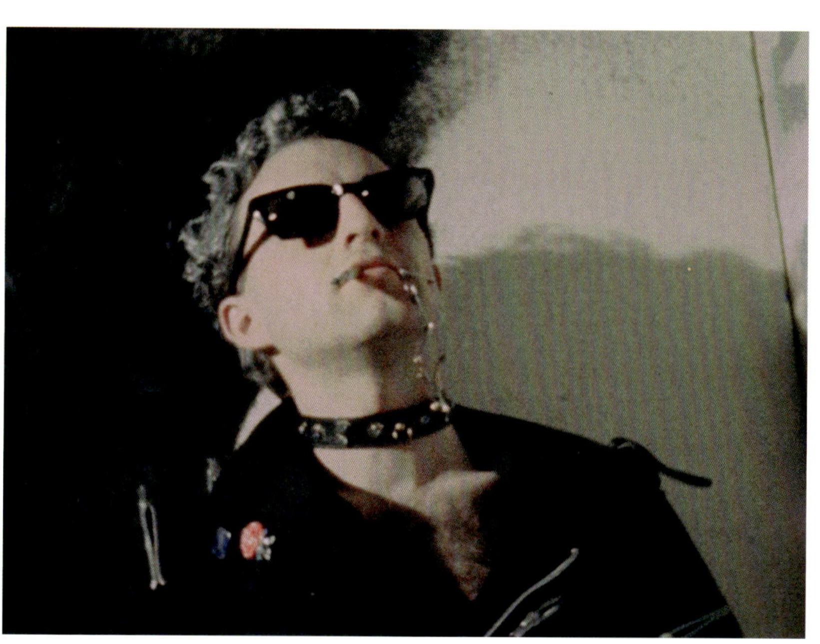

Midi Onodera

The Bird That Chirped on Bathurst, 1981
16mm film, b&w, sound, 3:40 min.

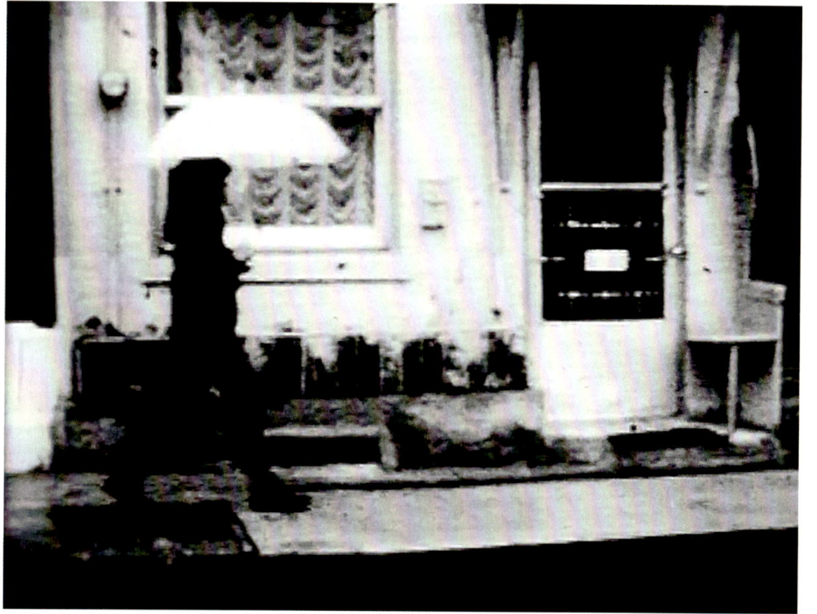

Don Owen

Cowboy and Indian, 1972
16mm film, colour, sound, 44 min.

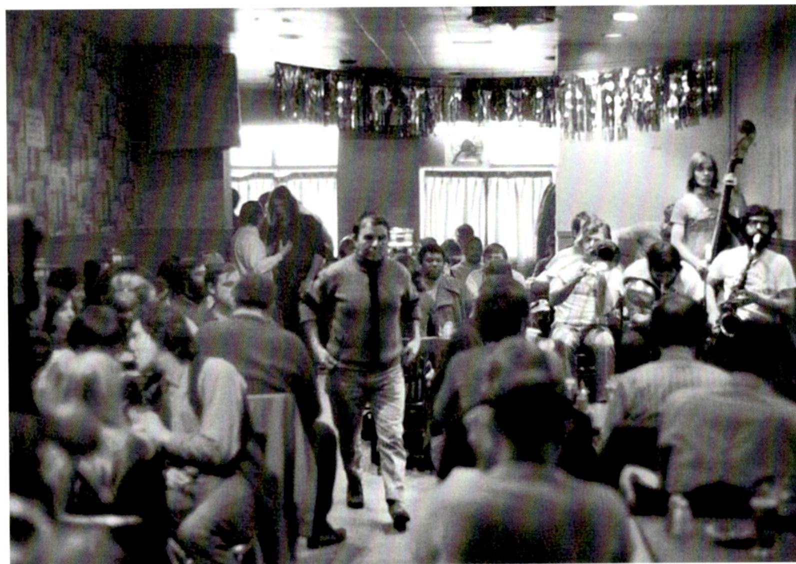

Susan Oxtoby

All Flesh Is Grass, 1988
16mm film, colour, sound, 15 min.

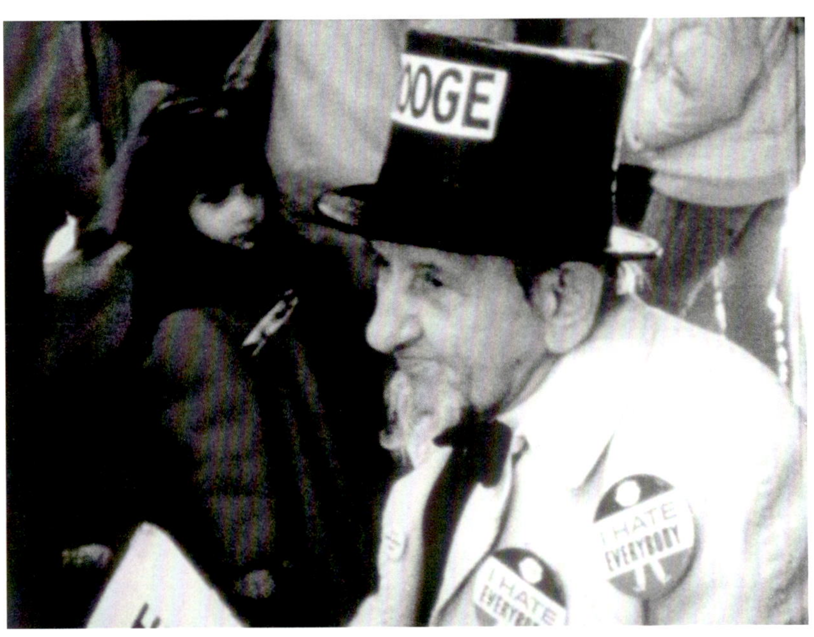

Marnie Parrell

Dinner, 1989
video, colour, sound, 4 min.

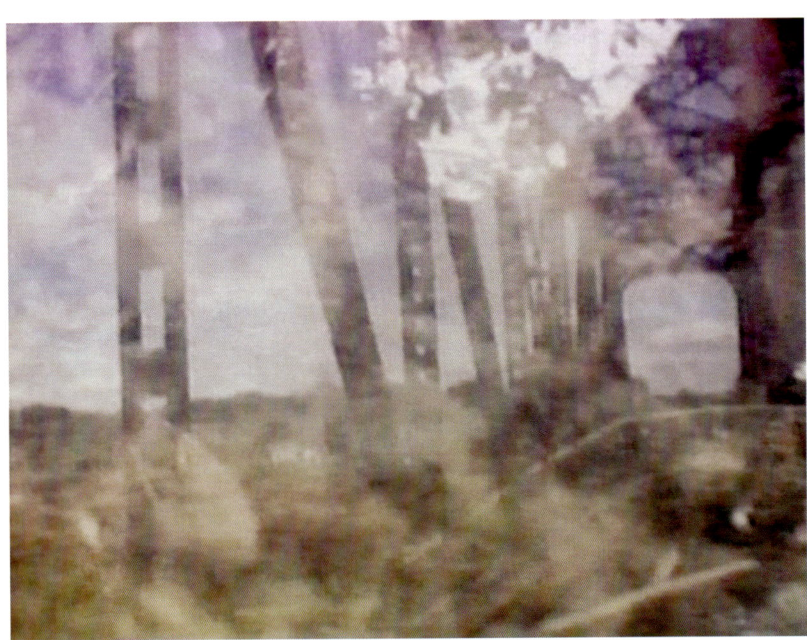

Andrew J. Paterson and Alan Fox

How Many Fingers?, 1981
video, colour, sound, 8 min.

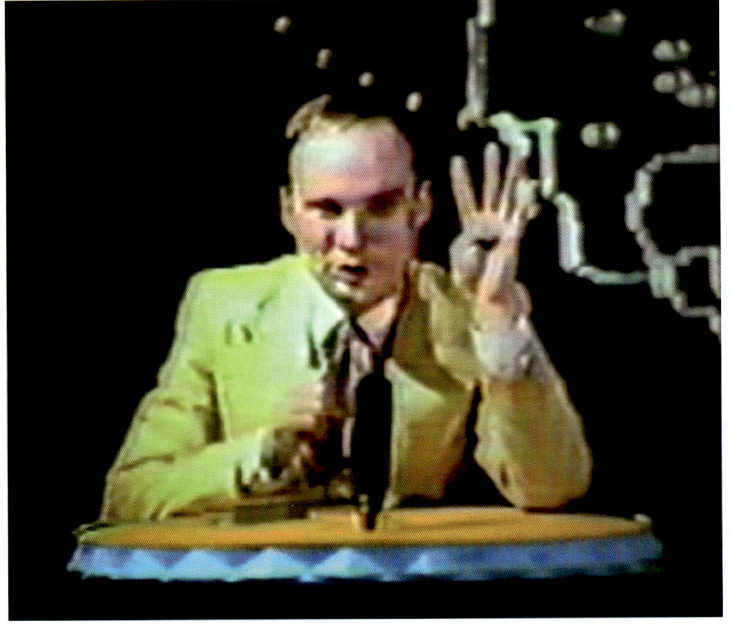

Paulette Phillips

It Depends, 1984
video, colour, sound, 29:30 min.

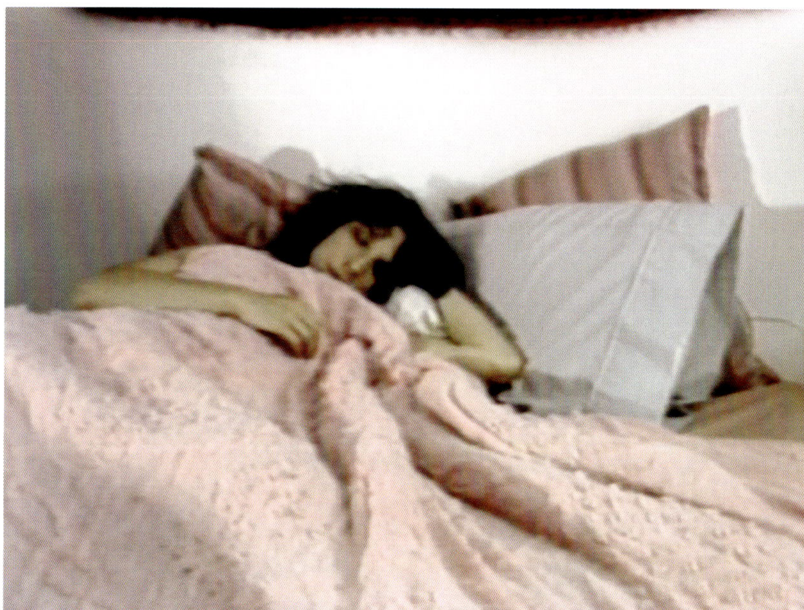

Randy & Berenicci

Once Upon a Time, 1984
video, colour, sound, 18:30 min.

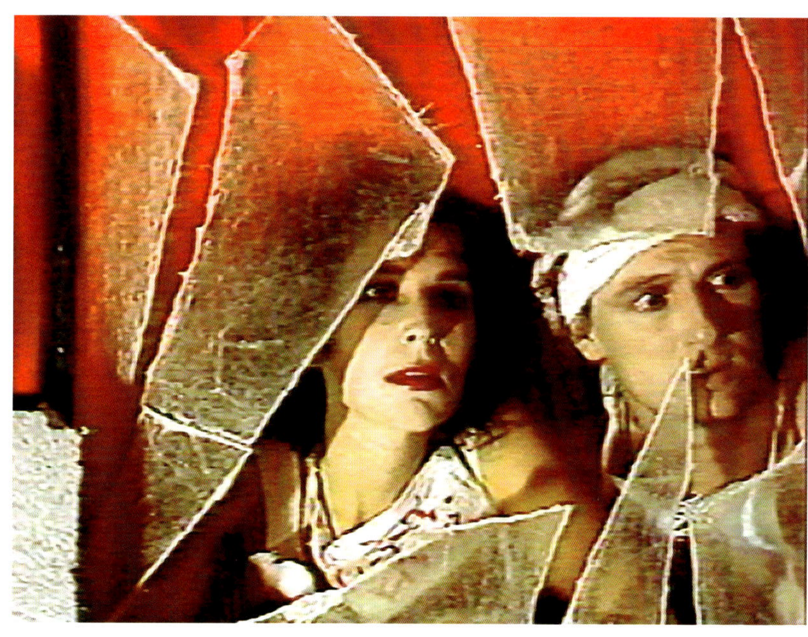

Duke Redbird

Charley Squash Goes to Town, 1969
16mm film, colour, sound, 4 min.

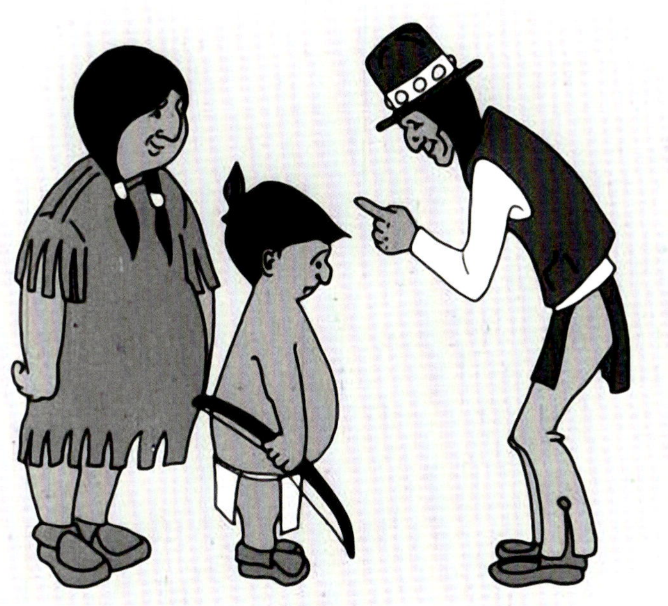

Wendy Rowland, Darlene Pratt, and Angela Sigsworth

Cityscape, 1988
16mm film, b&w, sound, 10 min.

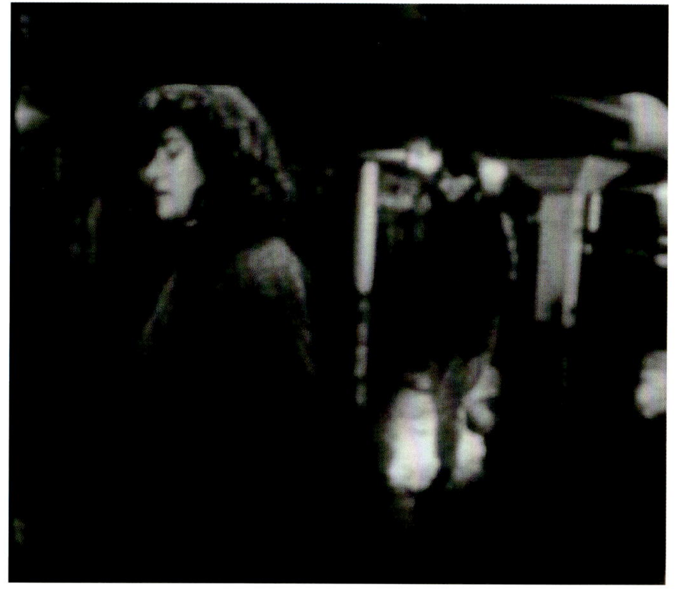

Patricia Rozema

Passion: A Letter in 16mm, 1985
16mm film, colour, sound, 28 min.

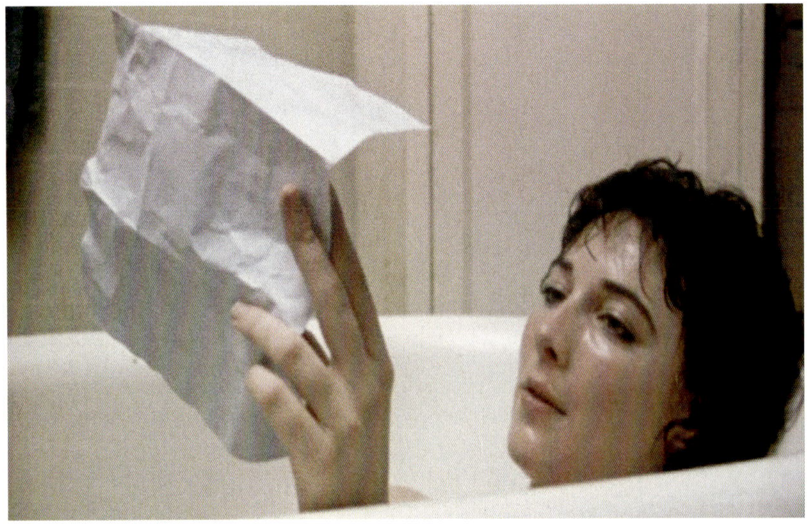

Su Rynard

Absence, 1986
video, colour, sound, 5:30 min.

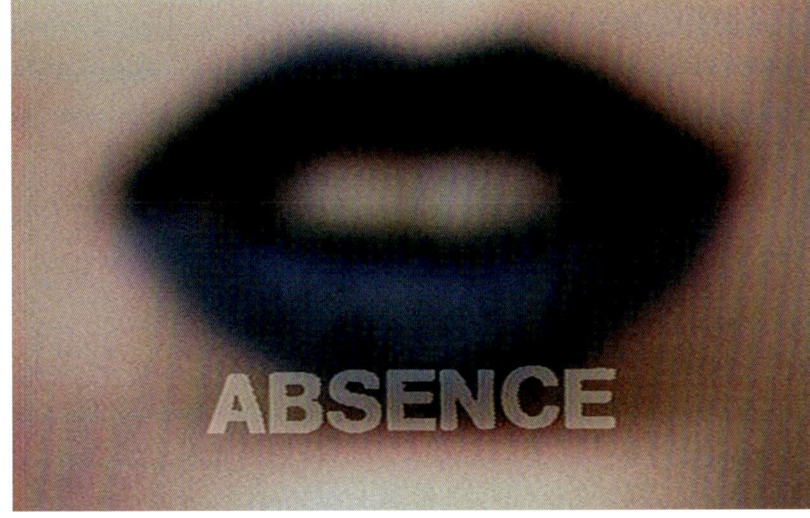

Michael Snow

Seated Figures, 1988
16mm film, colour, sound, 42 min.

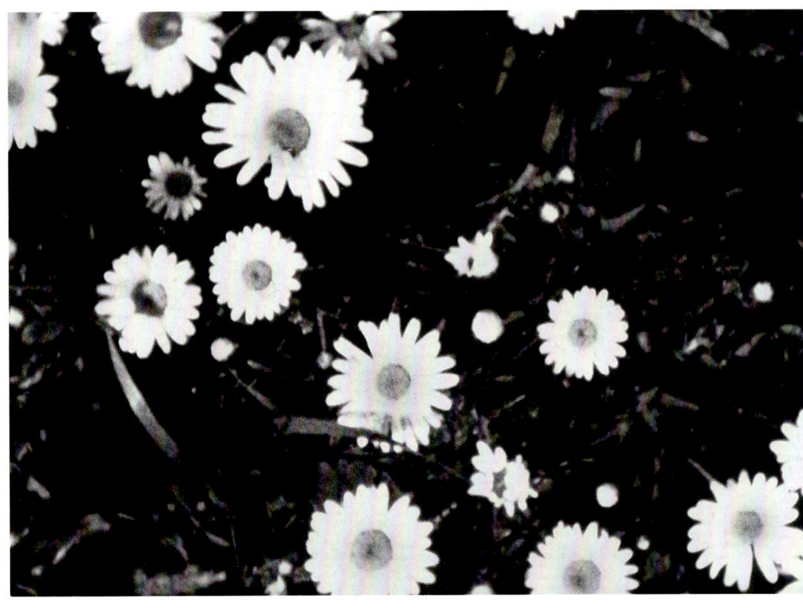

Michael Snow

So Is This, 1982
16mm film, colour, silent, 43 min.

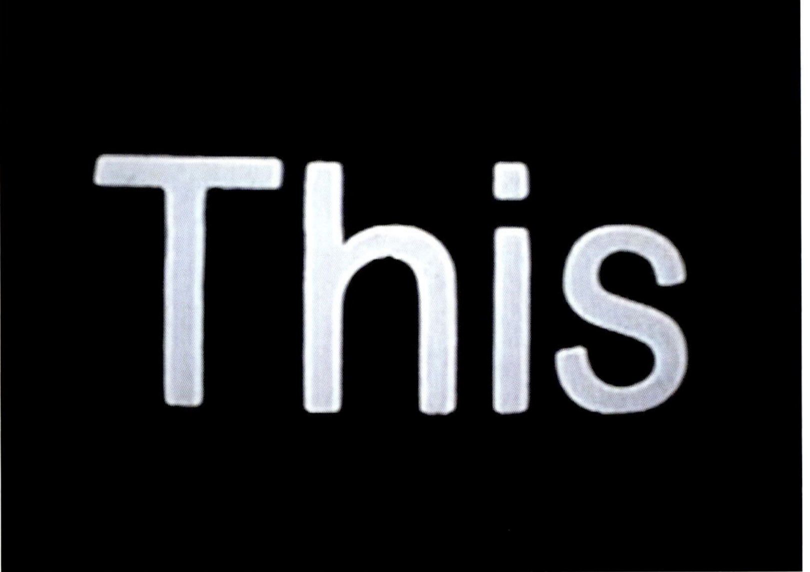

Tom Sherman

Tvideo, 1980
video, colour, sound, 28 min.

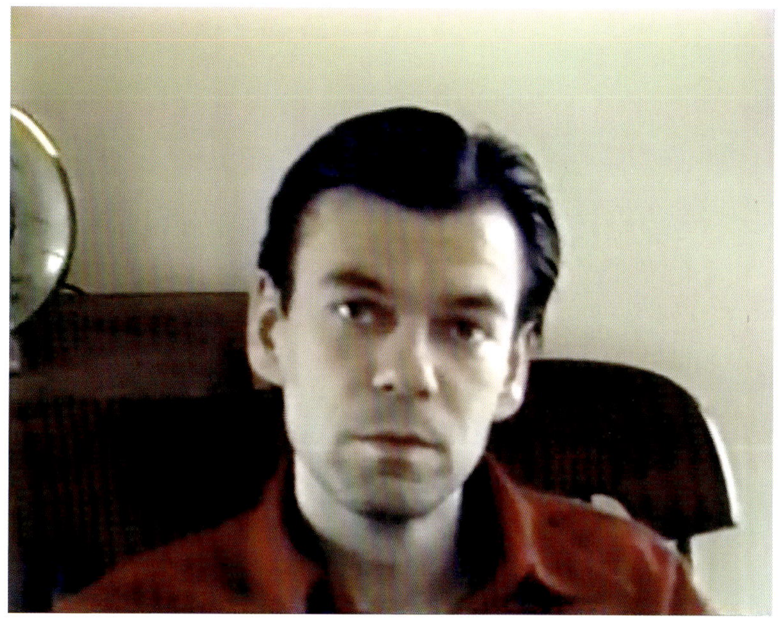

Tom Sherman

Television's Human Nature, 1977
video, colour, sound, 28 min.

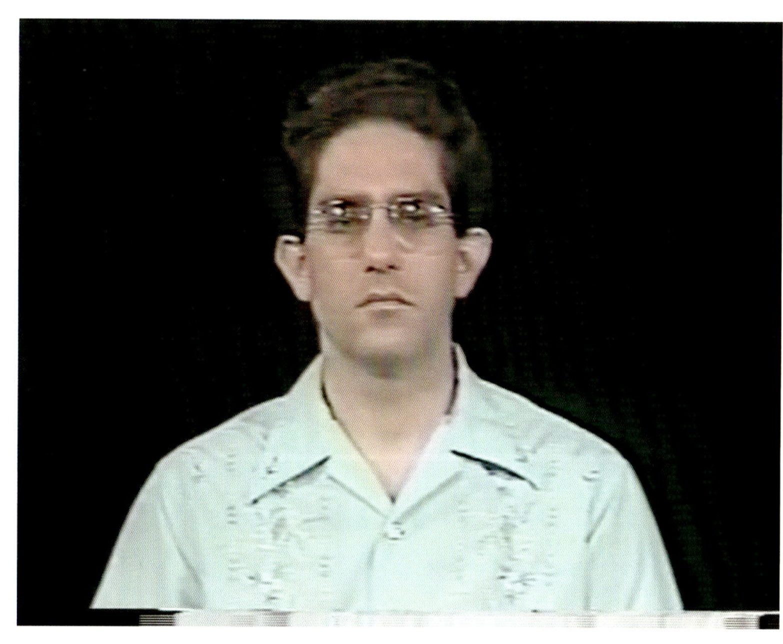

Lisa Steele and Kim Tomczak

Private Eyes, 1987
video, colour, sound, 18:29 min

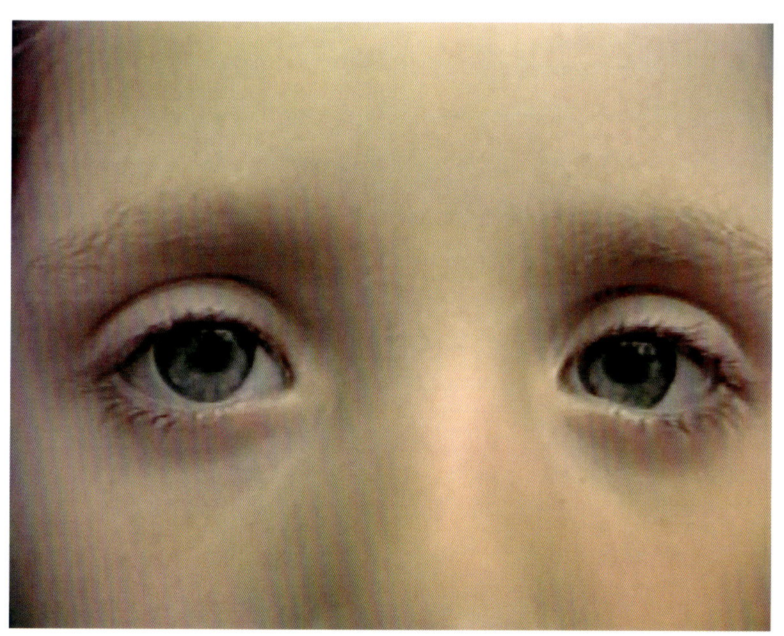

John Watt

Scannex Man, 1981
video, colour, sound, 6 min.

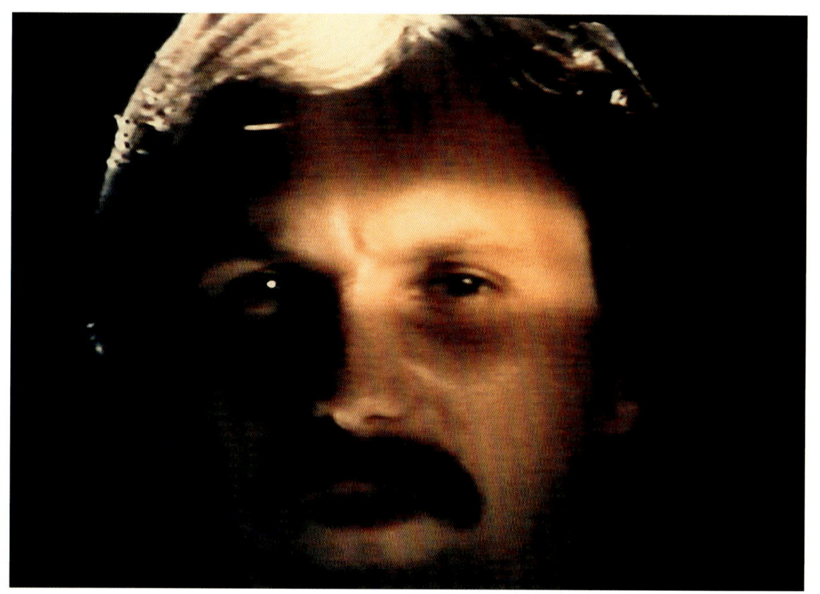

Rodney Werden

Baby Dolls, 1978
video, colour, sound, 19 min.

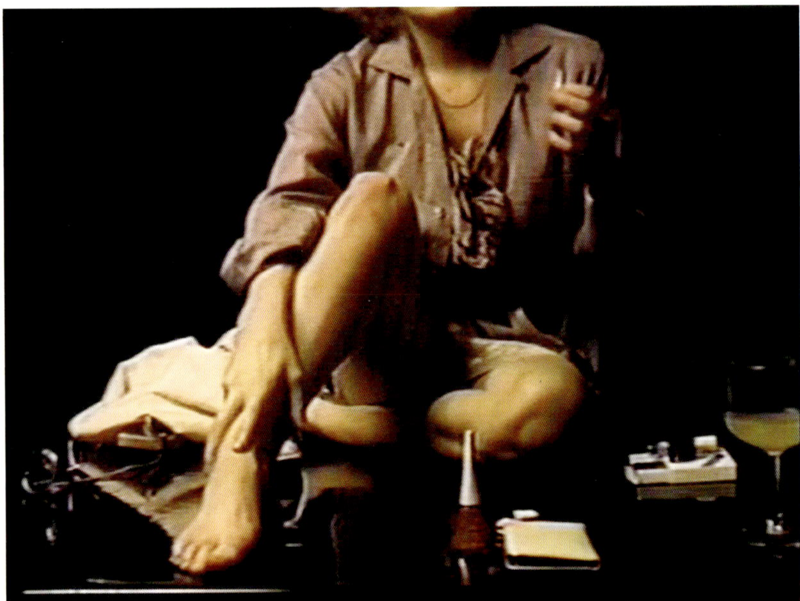

Rodney Werden

Say, 1978
video, b&w, sound, 3 min.

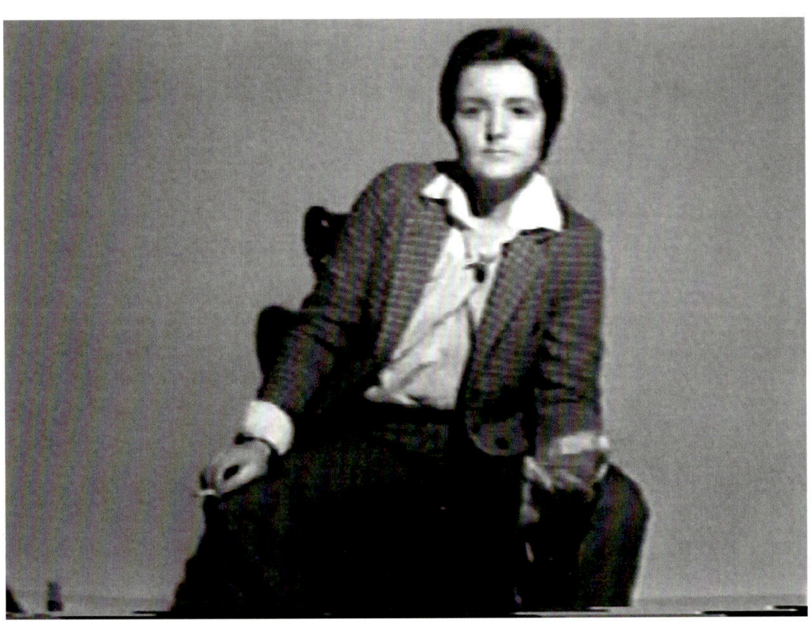

Joyce Wieland

Solidarity, 1973
16mm film, colour, sound, 10:40 min.

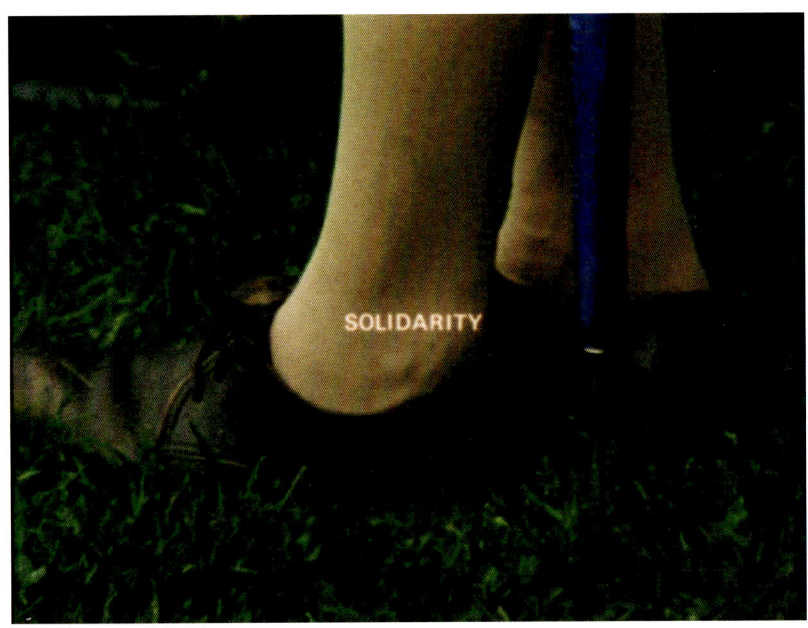

Joyce Wieland

The Far Shore, 1976
16mm film, colour, sound, 1h 45 min.

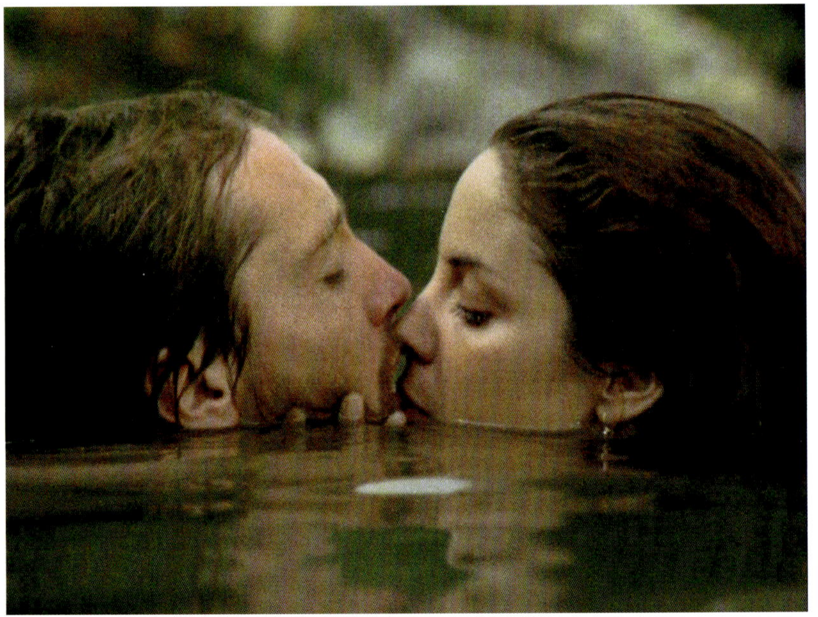

Joyce Wieland and Hollis Frampton

A and B in Ontario, 1984
16mm film, b&w, sound, 16:05 min.

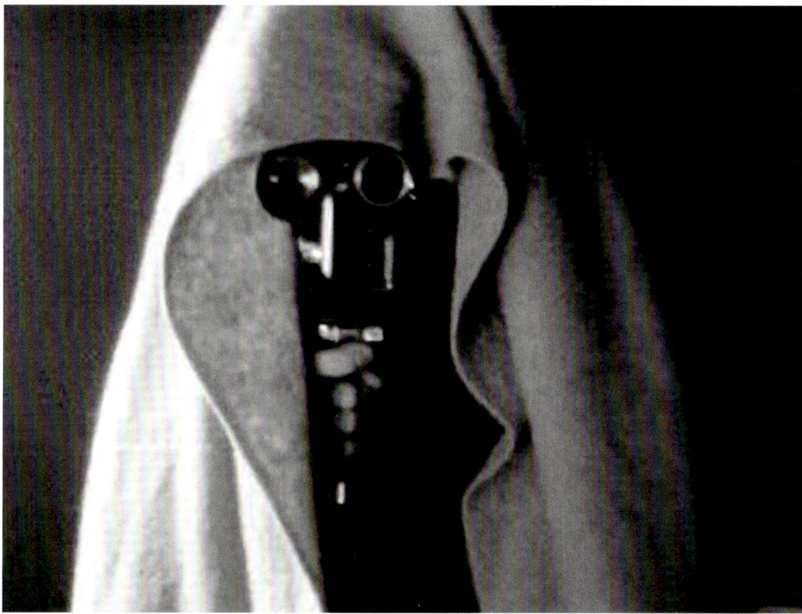

Jane Wright

Westinghouses (Arts Seen Theme), 1976
video, colour, sound, 4 min.

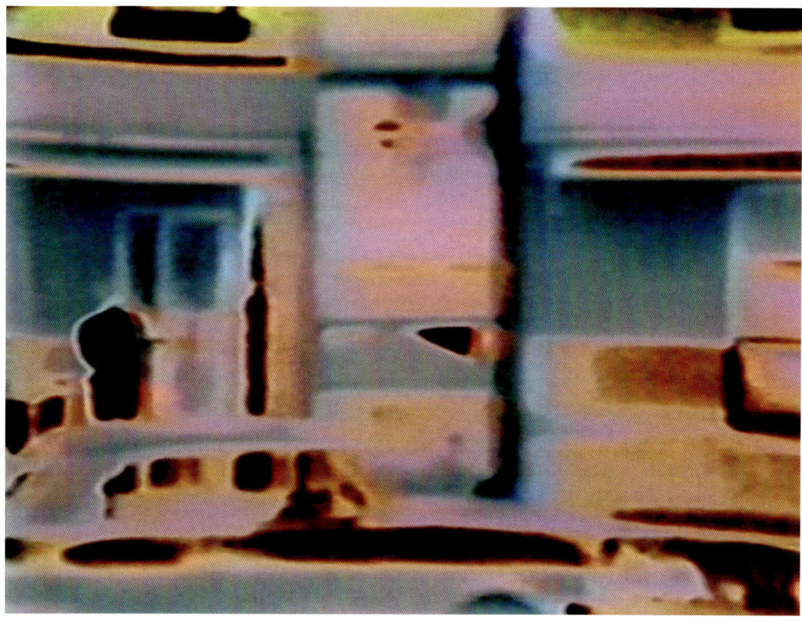

Youth Against Monsterz

Another Man, 1988
video, colour, sound, 3 min.

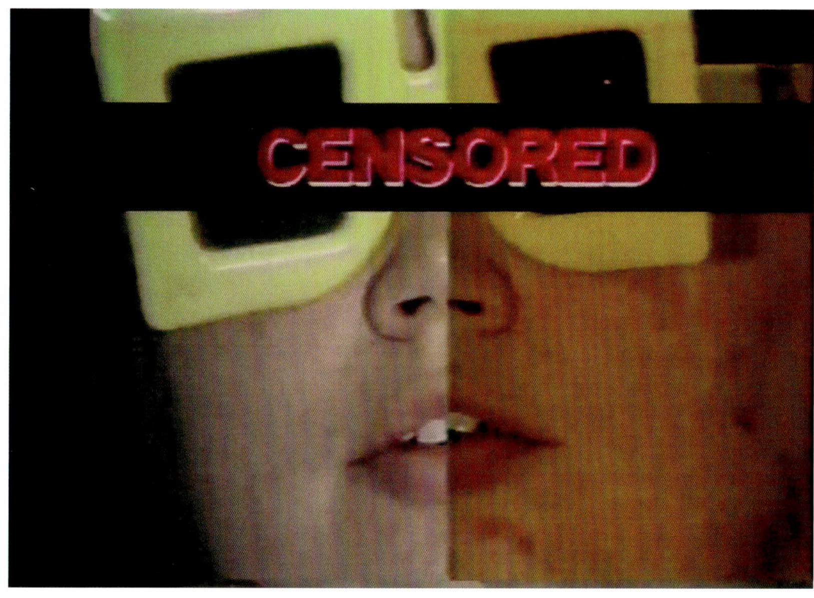

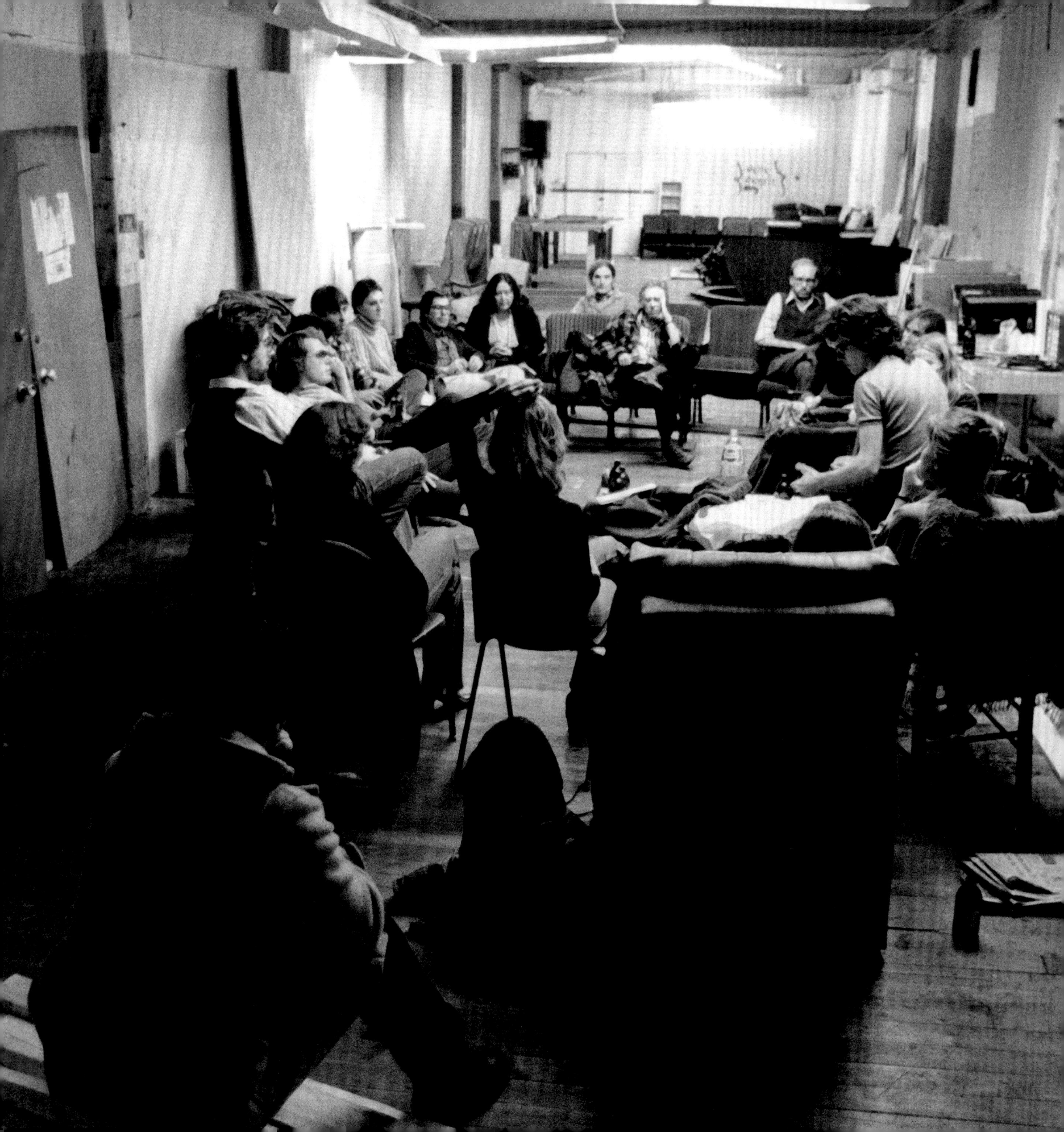

From Art to Community: The Toronto Film Scene, 1971–1989

Jim Shedden

"Toronto's development as a media arts capital has been driven by a tension between insecurity and parochialism, which has...ironically...brought out the best of the Toronto film, video, and media scene's international perspective and local energy." —Mike Zryd[1]

In the 1970s, Toronto established itself as one of the great centres of artists' film, alongside other cities like New York, San Francisco, London, Tokyo, and Berlin. One can credit the strength of the film co-op scene; the teaching of experimental film history and filmmaking in post-secondary institutions; and, of course, the strength of the films themselves. As artists' film activity has proliferated globally, Toronto remains one of the leaders in all aspects of artists' filmmaking, distribution, exhibition, research, and pedagogy.

The groundbreaking films of Michael Snow and Joyce Wieland in the 1960s were catalysts for the burgeoning movement that followed. In 1962, they moved to New York City, where Wieland made the bulk of her films, and Snow made a number of iconoclastic films that eventually became icons themselves, such as *Wavelength* (1967) and *<---> (Back and Forth)* (1969). Despite their eventful decade in New York, however, Snow and Wieland are quintessential Toronto filmmakers, who went on to make major works while living here. Upon their return to Canada in 1971, when the story of *Tributes + Tributaries* begins, they would each make terrifically ambitious films, both shot in Quebec: Snow's *La région centrale* (1971) and Wieland's *Pierre Vallières* (1972). Snow's film is an audacious three-hour record of rugged landscape and open sky in northern Quebec, shot with a mechanized robotic arm that was capable of moving in every possible direction. *Pierre Vallières* captures the Front de libération du Quebec (FLQ) leader's mouth, up close, as he delivers essays on Quebec's history, race, and feminism. Both works endure as landmarks of cinema—utterly original and iconic but still idiosyncratic.[2]

Some of their films made in Toronto include Snow's *So Is This* (1982) and *Seated Figures* (1988), which each use a single device (one-word-per-shot and tracking shots looking down only inches from the ground respectively) to provoke powerful philosophical considerations of space, time, language, presence, and absence. Wieland's *The Far Shore* (1976), loosely based on the life of the painter Tom Thomson, managed to scandalize simply because it was a conventional narrative—it was boundary-hopping in a way that was seen as a form of betrayal in certain circles. Still, critics like Marshall Delaney (a.k.a. Robert Fulford) and Barbara Halpern Martineau praised the film and saw in it an embrace of narrative that embodied Wieland's ongoing artistic concerns. As Wieland said, "I did my best to embrace the form of the feature film in this work, without compromising myself. What I had developed in my past films was stillness, the use of grain, love of light, and personal subject matter. I brought my knowledge of film and joined it to traditional form."[3]

As it turns out, *The Far Shore* anticipated a trend that would emerge in the 1980s—the embrace of literary forms (storytelling, diary, autobiography, biography, the essay) instead of the more purely cinematic approaches that defined earlier artists' films. Snow's *Wavelength*

Opposite: The first Annual General Members Meeting at the Funnel's new space, November 7, 1978, at 507 King Street E., Toronto. Photo © John Porter.

—

1. Mike Zryd, "Toronto as Experimental Film Capital," in Chris Gehman, *Explosion in the Movie Machine: Essays and Documents on Toronto Artists' Film and Video* (Toronto: YYZ, 2013).

2. R. Bruce Elder pays homage to Wieland's film in *Lamentations: A Monument to the Dead World, Part 1: The Dream of the Last Historian* (1985), only the lips in his film are those of Bart Testa performing as Augustine. The sequence serves to underscore the originality of *Pierre Vallières*.

3. Barbara Halpern Martineau, "The Far Shore: A Film about Violence; A Peaceful Film about Violence," *Cinema Canada* (April 1976): 20–23.

and *La région centrale*, for example, are classics of pure modernist cinema.[4] Later on, Snow's *So Is This* incorporates the new trend: it is a thoughtful reflection on the nature of the photographic image as it is transformed through time, but also a forceful essay about being, time, and language. Toronto filmmakers would increasingly adopt literary forms in their work, encouraged by schools and other institutions. Sheridan College's film program, for example, was an extremely fertile breeding ground for generations of film artists, most of whom embraced autobiography and poetry in their work. Filmmakers like Phil Hoffman, Richard Kerr, and Mike Hoolboom took their cues, at least in part, from their instructors Rick Hancox and Jeffrey Paull. Hancox's *House Movie* (1972), *Home for Christmas* (1978), and *Moose Jaw* (1992) are intricately resolved syntheses of experimental filmmaking and autobiography, while films like *Waterworx (A Clear Day and No Memories)* (1982) bring poetry and film together seamlessly. Hancox's students would follow in his footsteps quite directly, as with Hoffman's early work (e.g., *On the Pond,* 1978), and more obliquely in the work of Kerr, Hoolboom, and Mike Cartmell, each finding new ways of integrating literary expression into film form.

No one would call R. Bruce Elder's films narrative, but narrative moments punctuate his three longest films. For example, *Illuminated Texts* (1983) opens with a deliberately and painfully bad performance of Eugène Ionesco's *The Lesson* (1951), chaotically interrupted with intertitles of excerpts from the play, background music and sound that go in and out of audibility, and then interruptions by the devil from Peter Weiss's *Marat/Sade* (1964). All of this serves as a device for introducing some of the film's key themes: autobiography, history, mathematics, pedagogy, alienation, and evil. In fact, Elder's films, while definitely informed by Modernist precursors like Stan Brakhage and Bruce Baillie in their exquisite shooting style and polyphonic montage constructions, also allow the incursion of the literary—probably more than almost any other film artist—especially in the form of poetry, philosophy, autobiography, and the essay.

D.I.Y. Institutions

Generally speaking, Toronto film artists have had ambivalent relationships to institutions, eschewing especially the National Film Board of Canada (NFB) and the CBC, which is why considerations of artists' films don't normally look at work produced by those institutions (apart from the work of Arthur Lipsett and Norman McLaren at the NFB). However, a number of extremely compelling, innovative works featuring Indigenous artists either in front of or behind the camera were produced at the NFB in the late 1960s and early 1970s. Willie Dunn's *The Ballad of Crowfoot* (1968) is a montage of archival photos, etchings, and newspaper clippings, set to Dunn's ballad about Crowfoot, or Isapo-Muxika, Blackfoot warrior and chief of the Siksika First Nation, associated with the North-West Rebellion of 1885. Duke Redbird's animated film *Charley Squash Goes to Town* (1969) is based on his comic strip character who indeed goes to town, but returns to the reserve after realizing he prefers the way of life of his own people. *Cowboy and Indian* (1972), directed by the prolific NFB giant Don Owen, is a non-linear documentary about "the Indian" Robert Markle (Mohawk) and the "cowboy" Gordon Rayner—both visual artists, teachers, and jazz musicians. The film is one of the highlights of the NFB's history, combining its characteristically high production values with a freeform sense of narrative, weaving us through the artists' creative lives, their relationship with each other, and life in the city and life on the farm.

Outside of the NFB, the prevailing D.I.Y. spirit led to a number of ad-hoc organizations becoming miniature institutions unto themselves over time. These organizations helped facilitate production (e.g., the Funnel, the Toronto Filmmakers Co-Operative, and the Liaison of Independent Filmmakers Toronto); distribution (the Canadian Filmmakers Distribution Centre); and exhibition (the Funnel, the Innis Film Society, Pleasure Dome, etc.). Further, many films would be funded by the Canada Council, the Ontario Arts Council, and the Toronto Arts Council. The Art Gallery of Ontario, the Festival of Festivals (now the Toronto International

4. However, filmmaker and critic R. Bruce Elder has persuasively argued that they are quintessentially postmodern. R. Bruce Elder, *Image and Identity: Reflections on Canadian Film and Culture* (Waterloo, Ontario: Wilfrid Laurier University Press, 1989).

Film Festival), Harbourfront Centre, and other large cultural institutions showed artists' films, including many Toronto works. Even the Goethe-Institut Toronto, funded by the Government of Germany, became a big supporter of Toronto filmmakers through creative and collaborative programming.

This level of organizational support didn't change the fact that Toronto film is ultimately a D.I.Y. culture. As a case in point, John Porter, one of the key personalities involved in the Funnel, has made over 300 Super 8 films, almost single-handedly documented the Toronto scene during this period, organized many screenings, and collaborated with the feminist postpunk band Fifth Column, making films for them and projecting at their performances. Fifth Column had been showing their own films and others borrowed from the library at their performances but saw Porter's work at the Funnel and became enamoured of its punk energy. In the end, Porter projected films at most Fifth Column performances from 1982 to 1992, including at the Funnel, the Poor Alex Theatre, Larry's Hideaway, Lee's Palace, the Beverley Tavern, the Concert Hall, and in venues in New York City, Pittsburgh, Montreal, Guelph, London (Ontario), Ann Arbor, and so on. As further evidence of Toronto's fertile and cross-disciplinary scene at the time, in addition to making films, a number of members of Fifth Column (including G.B. Jones and Caroline Azar), with a handful of other artists, writers, and filmmakers, published the dynamic and influential fanzine *Hide*, which mixed articles on the Toronto music scene and on international artists, like Bush Tetras and Glenn Branca, with features on filmmakers like Kenneth Anger, Ross McLaren, and Vivienne Dick.

In his extensive writing on the Toronto film scene, Mike Zryd has argued that in order to understand its history, one must examine the development of the institutions that support it. In addition to production, distribution, and exhibition organizations, Zryd contends that we need to consider academic institutions and the various ways they nurture not only filmmakers but also film critics, programmers and curators, teachers, and appreciative audiences.[5] Since those institutions, for the most part, are not primarily dedicated to artists' film, we need to appreciate the maverick individuals who have carved out spaces for such work and, in so doing, have had significant influence on the life of film art in Toronto. I've already acknowledged Sheridan College, but one would also have to look at various instructors and professors like Ross McLaren at the Ontario College of Art (now OCAD University); R. Bruce Elder at Ryerson Polytechnic Institute (now Ryerson University); Kay Armatage and Bart Testa at the University of Toronto; and Kathy Elder, Librarian at the Sound and Moving Image Library at York University, where she has consistently made a space for experimental, documentary, and other artisanal forms of filmmaking.

1989: A Case Study

Our story ends in 1989, with a tale of two film festivals. That year, the International Experimental Film Congress was held in Toronto.[6] An ambitious gathering—quite probably the last of its kind—of experimental filmmakers, scholars, students, curators, programmers, and others interested in the art of film, the Congress proved to be controversial. In the catalogue accompanying the Congress, its organizers state, "We have limited ourselves to aesthetic concerns…We thought it more important for filmmakers to reflect on those aspects of their work that set them apart from the other arts, and indeed from other branches of the cinema."[7] The Congress's framework was called into question by a petition signed by many in the experimental film community, for failing "to reflect the vitality and breadth, the vulnerability and urgency of current oppositional practice in the media, render[ing] nothing but obeisance to a moribund officialdom."[8] In other words, many in the community objected to what they perceived as the Congress's Modernist bias and its lack of sufficient engagement with more explicitly social, political, and aesthetically hybrid voices in the community.

By contrast, a year before, the first ever Images Festival of Independent Film and Video took place. The festival's mandate was somewhat a response to the Toronto International Film Festival, as a showcase of both film and video (almost no festivals in the world showed video

5. Mike Zryd, "The Academy and the Avant-Garde: A Relationship of Dependence and Resistance," in *Cinema Journal* 45, no. 2 (Winter 2006): 17–42.

6. I was the sole paid employee of the Experimental Film Congress at the time.

7. International Experimental Film Congress catalogue (Toronto: Art Gallery of Ontario, 1989), 10.

8. "Open Letter to the Experimental Film Congress (May 1989)," *The Independent Film and Video Monthly* 12, no. 8, 1989.

at that time), and eventually defining itself as a showcase for "artistic excellence in contemporary moving image culture through screenings, exhibitions, and performances, providing artists with a supportive forum in which to present their work and make professional connections with the media arts community."[9] As it turns out, Images paved the way for the future in Toronto. At the time, there were just two film festivals, whereas now there are more than a hundred, suggesting the great need not only for original film content but for community. Furthermore, Images paved the way for radical diversity, whereby the kind of experimental film celebrated by the Congress is shown alongside video art, documentaries, political films, animation, independent narrative film, rock videos, and media arts installations. As artist and programmer Andrew J. Paterson put it, "The Images Festival has become a host umbrella, protecting or sheltering a coterie of subcultures within a non-homogenous but seemingly interconnected moving image culture."[10]

While the inaugural Images Festival and the Congress were taking place, cataclysmic changes were taking place around the world. Politically speaking, 1989 was the year of the fatwah against Salman Rushdie, the Tiananmen Square massacre (which took place on June 4, the last day of the Congress), the wave of revolutions in Eastern Europe, the *Exxon Valdez* oil spill, the first democratic elections in Brazil, Nelson Mandela's first meeting with P.W. Botha, and the beginning of the "culture wars" (including the cancellation of Robert Mapplethorpe's show by the Corcoran Gallery of Art). In the world of artists' film and video, this period of global upheaval had the effect of intensifying the already political orientation of much of the work being produced, as well as the infrastructure in which films and tapes were exhibited and discussed. Dozens of festivals, venues, and organizations focusing on anti-racism, queer identity, AIDS activism, and other progressive frameworks emerged, from the community-run Euclid Theatre (1989–1993) to Inside Out LGBT Film Festival (1991–present) and Desh Pardesh (1990–2001), a festival of South Asian arts.

Amidst these massive changes, two almost invisible technological innovations would turn out to be revolutionary: in 1989, Tim Berners-Lee wrote the code for Hypertext Transfer Protocol, the foundation of the World Wide Web, and H.261, the first viable digital encoding standard for video was developed. It wasn't clear until about a decade later, but these innovations would have a profound effect on the production, distribution, and exhibition of artists' film. Jonas Mekas described the times optimistically: "When the old forms began collapsing and falling away though exhaustion and repetition, a new sensibility is born… things are starting to be born anew. New content needs new forms, new technologies. That is what is happening right now with the internet and digital technology. We have had 40 years of regurgitating the same old stuff and there is a necessity for change. Necessity is what matters."[11]

9. "Mandate and Mission," Images Festival website, November 2017, available online.

10. Andrew J. Paterson, "Expanding Moving Pictures: 1988–2012," 25th Annual Images Festival catalogue, 2012, 37.

11. Sean O'Hagan, "Jonas Mekas: The Man Who Inspired Andy Warhol to Make Films," *Guardian*, December 1, 2012, available online.

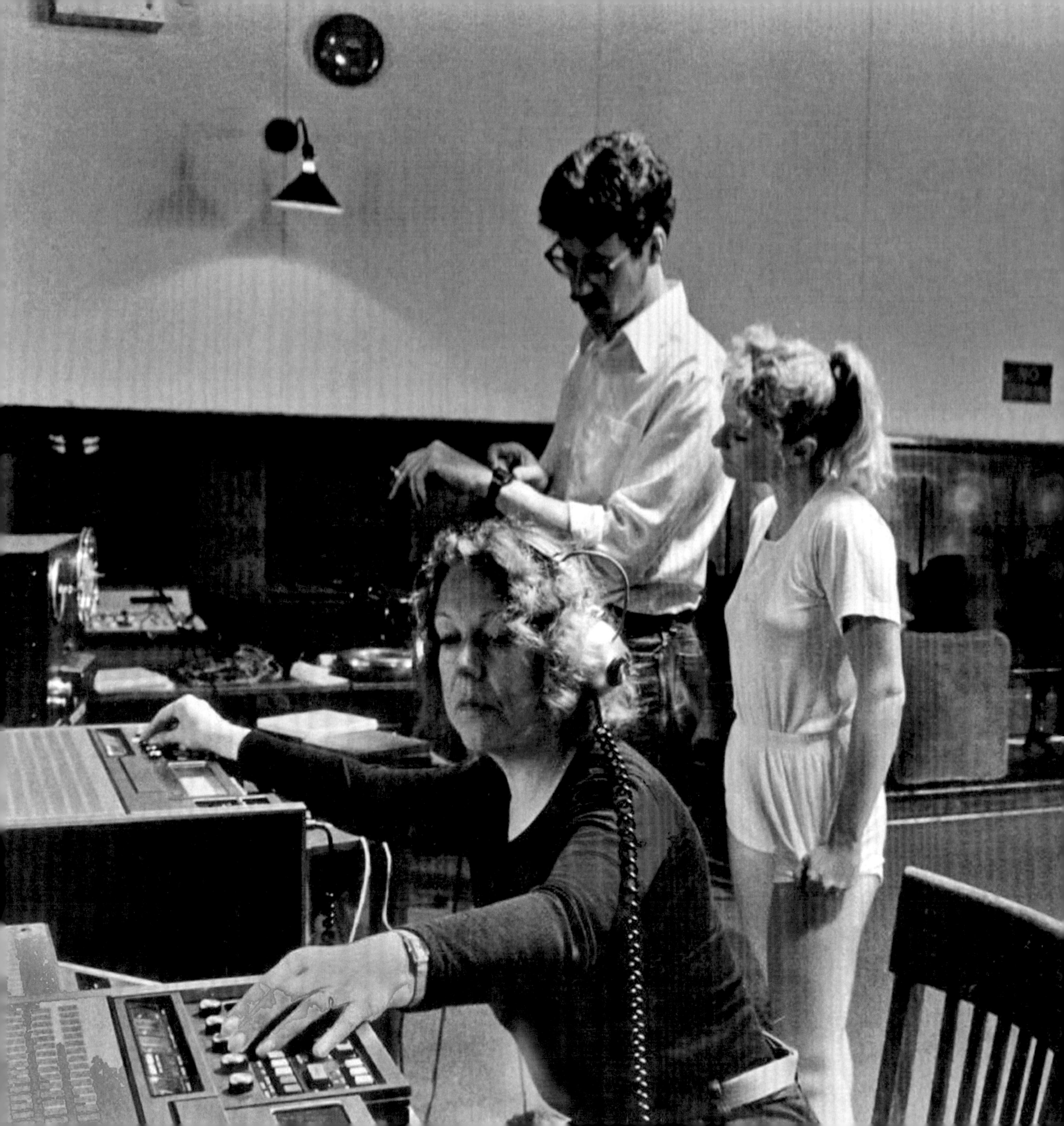

Toronto Video: Making Waves

Peggy Gale

Since its beginnings in the very late 1960s, artists' video has been unruly and difficult to classify. It has been a tool for political activism, social intervention, and documentation, and has provided a new means of representation and expression, a process-oriented and relatively ephemeral time-based alternative to the gallery-dealer profit motive of object production. At first, video offered a free exchange—a disposable "what if." Much later, by contrast, it became valued as limited-edition artwork destined for private collections and museum display or storage. Early video was sometimes not recorded at all—when presented as live-action camera-to-monitor or live-to-cable or television, for example—and yet other times it was produced on open-reel half-inch videotape for exchange or exhibition. Later, VHS and Beta or ¾-inch U-matic cassettes became standard, then digital recordings (DVDs), and later again, digital files for sharing online. Flirty, transitory, often frustrating, at times moving and beautiful, video is a distillation of energy into specific visual and aural (physical) experience.

Independent video arrived early in Toronto, alongside its appearance in Vancouver, Montreal, Halifax, and, soon enough, "everywhere else"—Calgary, Edmonton, Winnipeg, Guelph, Ottawa, Quebec City, and, in 1986, Igloolik, Nunavut.[1] The years bracketing *Toronto: Tributes + Tributaries*, 1971 to 1989, mark the defining moment and high point for video by artists.

From its earliest days, the artist-run centre A Space (founded in 1970) had simple equipment—camera, monitor, and playback deck for half-inch reel-to-reel videotape—and the first exhibition in its original location at 85 St. Nicholas Street included video from Halifax by NSCAD students Ian Murray, Doug Waterman, and Tim Zuck. In 1970 and 1971, Vito Acconci and Dennis Oppenheim were invited from New York for week-long artists' residencies, where they produced important early video works; video was opening up to an international energy and curiosity far different from the otherwise local interests of most painters and sculptors. At the same time, Trinity Square Video (founded in 1971) saw video as a tool for community action, offering portable production equipment and access to the new cable television. Lawrence and Miriam Adams opened a performance and video space first known as 15 Dancers on George Street in 1972; over several years and name changes they were important players in presenting and documenting dance works, and later, cable programming and archiving.[2]

Opposite: Vera Frenkel editing *Stories from the Front (and the Back)* with onlookers Elizabeth Chitty and Patrick Ready, 1981, at the Western Front, Vancouver. Photo © Cornelia Wyngaarde.

---

1. Details of dates and locations for independent video production and distribution are outlined in Peggy Gale, "An Other Videoscape," in *Magnetic North*, ed. Jenny Lion (Minneapolis: University of Minnesota Press; Winnipeg: Video Pool; Minneapolis: Walker Art Center, 2000), 342–345, with additional discussion of individual works on pages 345–360. In response to the growing interest in the medium, I would write "Video has captured our imagination," *Parachute* 7 (Summer 1977), 16–18, subsequently reprinted for the exhibition *In Video*, ed. Peggy Gale (Halifax: Dalhousie Art Gallery, 1977), n.p., and in *Video re/View: The (best) Source for Critical Writings on Canadian Artists' Video*, eds. Peggy Gale and Lisa Steele (Toronto: Art Metropole/Vtape, 1996), 114–120.

2. Names and iterations include 15 Dancers at 155A George St. (1972–1974), 15 Dance Laboratorium (1974–1980), and Visus Foundation (with Terry McGlade, 1974) for dance-video works and recordings, which later became Studio Two (1980–1982) for an ongoing collaboration with Rogers Cable Television via direct underground cable link. In 1981 they argued (unsuccessfully) for their own cable channel and in 1982 established the Arts Television Centre at 142 George Street, continuing to 1990. See Peggy Gale, "All These Years: Early Toronto Video," in *Explosion in the Movie Machine: Essays and Documents on Toronto Artists' Film and Video*, ed. Chris Gehman (Toronto: Images Festival and Liaison of Independent Filmmakers of Toronto, 2013), 52–71; see particularly pages 56–57.

But as Tom Sherman has noted, "In 1972 there were only three places to screen video in Toronto: A Space, Trinity Square Video, and TVOntario [known then as Ontario Educational Communications Authority]."[3] It was the artist-run centres like CEAC (1973–1978),[4] Art Metropole (founded 1974), YYZ (founded 1979), Charles Street Video (separated from A Space in 1981), and Vtape (founded 1983) that established further and ongoing support systems for production, exhibition, distribution, and publishing associated with artists' video. As active as these centres were, they remained relatively invisible to the general public. With the opening of *Videoscape* at the Art Gallery of Ontario (November 20, 1974–April 1, 1975), artists' video found its first above-ground home in Toronto.

More than forty years after its publication, the *Videoscape* catalogue feels both innocently assertive and vaguely unprofessional. Of the fifty-four artists included, some state simply their name and the work's title, while others give an earnest, poetic ramble or, rarely, an eloquent and structured text. My own essay, "A New Medium," proposes that "Artists have turned to video for its openness, its range of possibilities still undefined by either established traditions or authoritative criticism, and they have adapted its functions to their own expressive needs." These statements, I believe, remain true for those years, though video art itself would blossom over the next two decades into the mixed digital and moving image culture that effectively obliterated its original boundaries. By 2017, we can hardly recognize the incandescence felt by those first artists for this then-new opportunity. In the earliest years, artists shared their videos with friends or presented them simply in studios and small gallery spaces; by the mid-1970s, they wanted to be paid for their work, and distribution systems were established by Art Metropole and Vtape in Toronto, along with others elsewhere. Now, Facebook, Twitter, YouTube, and other media claim virtually infinite access to virtually anything. Collection and dispersal of image and experience are ubiquitous: a gift economy.

Selections for *Toronto: Tributes + Tributaries* replicate the many-branched and fluid categories for the medium, though the sheer number of works produced during the period precludes the appearance of some of my personal favourites. Video has always had roots entwined in both performance and conceptual art, and this is evident in the works included in the exhibition. Many early "performance" works were created *solely* for the video camera, the artist alone in the studio, like Colin Campbell's *Sackville, I'm Yours* (1972), Lisa Steele's *Birthday Suit—With Scars and Defects* (1974), and Noel Harding's wordless, tactile, and sculptural *Three Pieces for Circuits* (1973). We call these works, simply, video. They are intimate, often revealing dialogues with the camera that implicate the viewer in personal relationships: video as mirror and diary.

By the mid-1970s, narrative works had become a Toronto hallmark. Scripts became more common as time passed, often taking on political issues, as in Rodney Werden's revelatory *Baby Dolls* (1978) or John Greyson's campy *Perils of Pedagogy* (1984), a foretaste of his later feature-length films. Formalist experimentation with synesthetic, feedback looped, and colourized video has been rare in Toronto's history, despite the early examples of Marty Dunn's *Genesis* (1974) and Jane Wright's *Electronic Sunsets* series (1974) and *Westinghouses* (1976). A more "real" world seems to be the city's preference.

Video's ideal viewing environments continue to change. Early, single-channel artist-and-camera solo works are best in intimate surroundings or for small groups on comfortable chairs or couches. Marion Lewis, for example, arranged a weekly series at A Space in 1978 called *Another Quiet Night in Front of the TV* within the larger *VideoCabaret* installation on the gallery's ground floor. Art Metropole had its own living-room environment for screening works in its early days, and a similar arrangement was made for small, in-gallery single-monitor programs like *New Narratives for Living Room Viewing* at the Art Gallery of Ontario (1982). It wasn't until the early 1980s that video projection became a reasonable alternative to simple monitor(s) for screenings; until then, the high cost and terrible quality of projectors made them highly problematic. As digital overtook analog formats, museums began to reconsider their options. New equipment was purchased, installations began to appear more

3. Tom Sherman, email to author, November 30, 2011, in Peggy Gale, "All These Years: Early Toronto Video."

4. In 1973 the Centre for Experimental Art and Communication (CEAC) opened, moving to 15 Duncan Street in 1976 with an intense program of production and presentation of video and performance works and films, plus library and archives. CEAC vanished abruptly in 1978 when its federal and provincial funding (and equipment holdings) were withdrawn in response to the publication of a manifesto in its newspaper *STRIKE*, advocating "leg shooting/knee capping to accelerate the demise of the old system." Public funds would not continue for an organization that "has taken a position in support of terrorism" (quoted from a letter to Amerigo Marras by Timothy Porteous, associate director of the Canada Council). See Dot Tuer, "The CEAC Was Banned in Canada," first published in *C Magazine* 11 (Fall 1986), 22–37, and reprinted in Dot Tuer, *Mining the Media Archive* (Toronto: YYZ Books 2005), 54–90.

often, and "the big screen" became a reference rather than the home-style television monitor. Bigger, now, is always better, and audiences have changed, too.

As evident in *Toronto: Tributes + Tributaries*, distinctions may usefully be made between a cinema-theatre setting for public programs with a seated audience, and video-based installations in a gallery or museum context, designed for a mobile viewer who considers a work perhaps briefly before moving on. Jayce Salloum's *The Ascent of Man/Acts of Consumption* (1985–1987) is a good example of the latter, assembled from his vast collections of audio, television, film and print sources.

But all of the divisions noted in this essay are fluid. "Video" may also take over a TV context, or become social or philosophical commentary. This becomes evident in General Idea's *Pilot* (1977), commissioned by TVOntario, while remaining a true artist's video work, a comprehensive and witty self-portrait. Gary Kibbins's elegant *The Long Take* (1984) parses how words shift meaning as context varies. *Working the Double Shift* (1984) by Lisa Steele and Kim Tomczak interrogates mass media's take on contemporary home life in a critical and political assembly of images and text.

Video in Toronto, 1971 to 1989, is a rolling terrain with moveable boundaries. Varied and complex, charming and difficult; overall, well worth investigation.

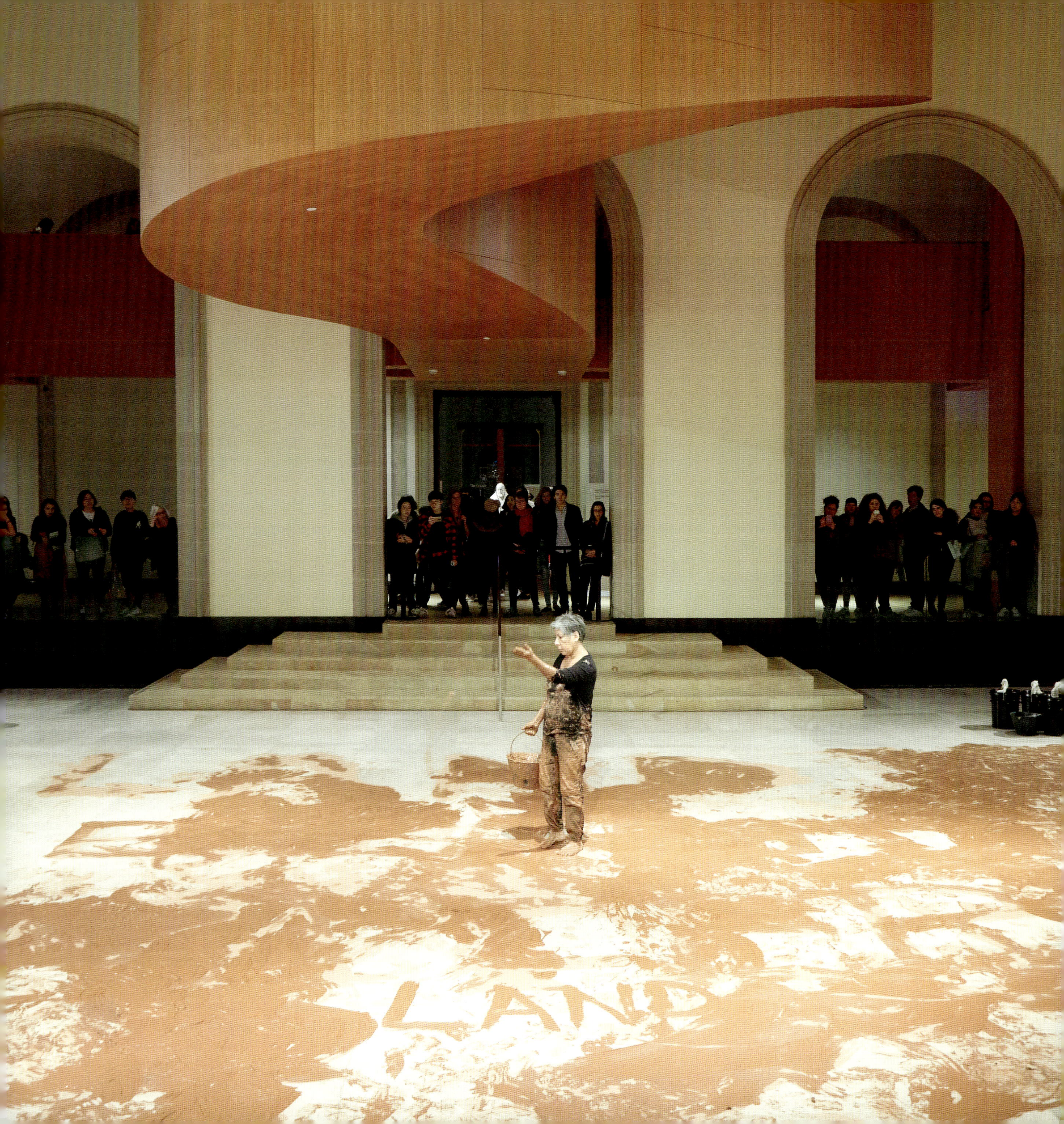
LAND

Performance as History's Antidote and Future's Contemporary: Reflections on *Toronto: Tributes + Tributaries* "In Performance" Series

Bojana Stancic

Between October 1 and November 13, 2016, the "In Performance" series was presented in conjunction with the Art Gallery of Ontario's exhibition *Toronto: Tributes + Tributaries, 1971–1989*. Organized by curator Wanda Nanibush, director of public programs Sean O'Neill, and me, "In Performance" included seven projects in almost as many weeks. During this period, the museum's building became uniquely porous in its use of space—from the fourth-floor contemporary exhibition space, to the modernist Signy Eaton gallery on the second level, to the central, sky-lit Walker Court. The series also permeated the Gallery's regular programming platforms, including the yearly all-night contemporary art event, Nuit Blanche; the AGO's signature program, the monthly art party First Thursdays; free Wednesday Nights, and select AGO Friday Nights. This porosity put on full display the multi-dimensionality and vitality not only of the exhibition but also of performance as an art form.

By presenting the work of artists who were active during the exhibition's time frame as well as their contemporary counterparts, the performance series made available to present-day Toronto audiences the vibrant histories and potential futures of the city's art landscapes. The act of looking backward and forward simultaneously bracketed the immediacy of the present—*the* crucial aspect of performance practice—and articulated the series' complex relationship to the contemporary moment. As the overlapping of concerns, histories, and bodies became visible, the interpretation of the exhibition itself expanded. The series paid tribute where it was due, and displayed resilience in the face of the contemporary conditions of both art and history. It was clear to both programmers and visitors that we were experiencing a different form of exhibition—uncontained, embodied, and filled with a different kind of urgency. I have tried to recollect these events in the following pages, from the perspective of programmer, producer, and audience—or rather, witness.

Opposite: Rebecca Belmore performing *untitled*, Walker Court, AGO, 2016. © Rebecca Belmore.

Rebecca Belmore

Crucial to the *Tributes + Tributaries* time frame was Rebecca Belmore's *Rising to the Occasion* (1987–1991), comprising the famous dress she wore in various performances. It felt important and symbolic, then, to launch the "In Performance" series with her new work. While the dress was presented in a museological setting in the AGO's Contemporary Tower, Belmore's continuing explorations of its thematic concerns were rearticulated in real time, and on the artist's real body on October 1, 2016, in a new performance as part of Nuit Blanche Toronto. *untitled* took place in Walker Court (the gallery's central interior courtyard), spanned twelve hours, and was witnessed by as many as 20,000 visitors. In this durational work, the artist mixed fifty pounds of clay with water and used it to draw, write, and paint, resurfacing the marble floor and making it seem as if nature had burst into the building. This gesture, a form of protest, demonstrated Belmore's purposeful effort in not only calling attention to the transformative power of these materials (land and water) but also enunciating their political interdependency and environmental urgency. The labour of her performance, its duration and location, served to decentralize historical narratives and reclaim institutional space, but not without major effort and toll on the body itself. Her significant, physical efforts were felt immediately by amplified sounds from the microphone attached to her shirt, as well as by the accumulation of marks left on her clothes, as clay was progressively plied over the course of the night.

untitled, 2016
Saturday, October 1, 2016, sunset to sunrise

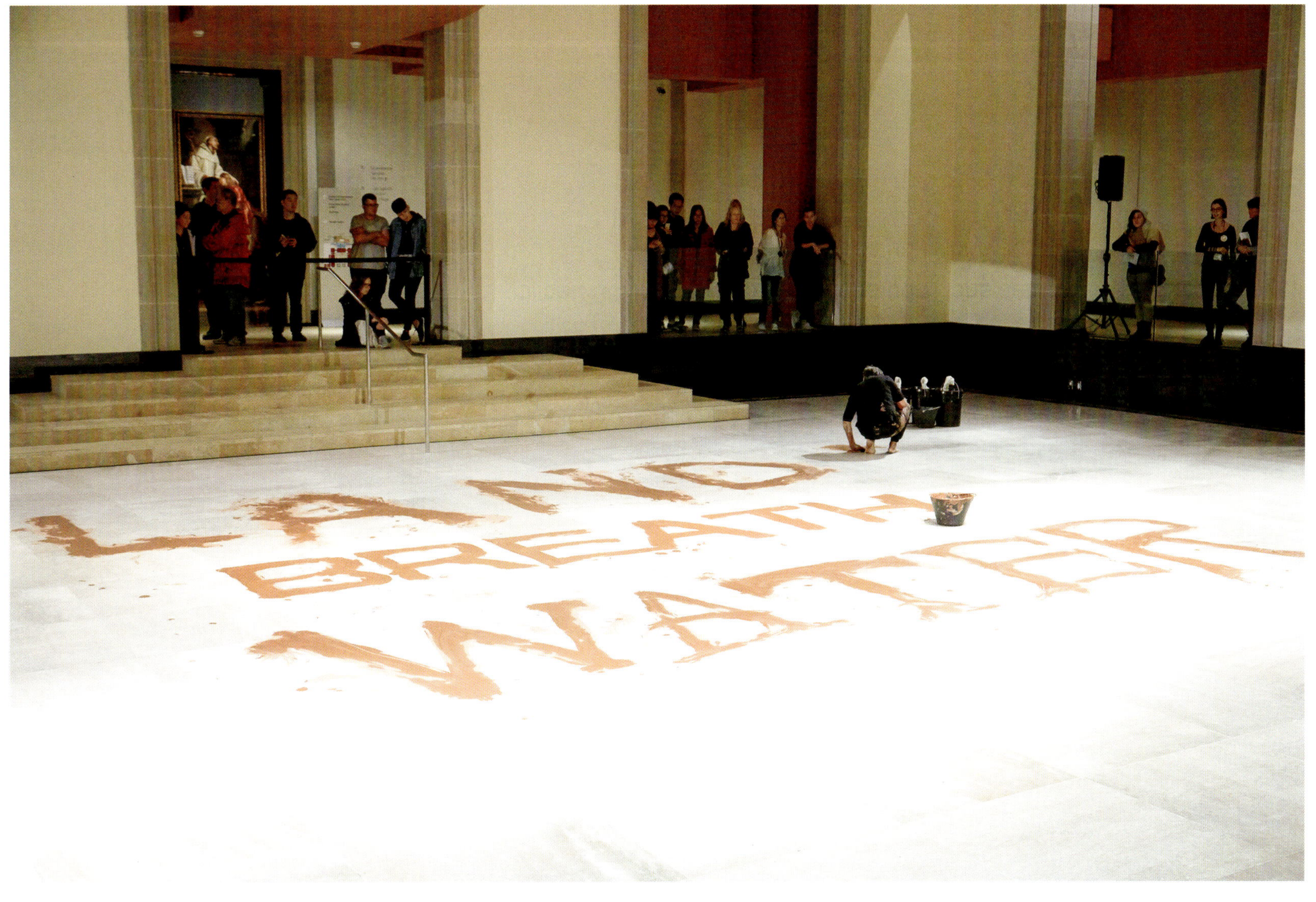

Walter Scott

Following Nuit Blanche, First Thursdays presented a new performance by Artist in Residence Walter Scott, *This Is Not Prose*, as part of October's program. Scott is an interdisciplinary artist whose use of the graphic novel form to express conceptual, absurd, and existential angst (in both the art world and the real world) is best illustrated in his popular comic book series *Wendy*. Not dissimilar from Belmore's process-based performance in its approach, although addressing different issues in content, Scott's piece focused on the continuous effort embodied in the creative instinct, and the vulnerability of the creative process. The artist set up a table in a vast empty gallery, on which sat a laptop whose screen was projected in a live-feed stream behind him. On his laptop he typed, erased, and edited the titular "Not Prose" (or poetry) in real time. The fragility of live articulation of thoughts and experiences is not often glimpsed in traditional gallery settings, and this staging opened, for the audience, the complex experience of navigating between witnessing performance and creating performance. This limbo between process and product was further underscored by extra-curricular efforts in a variety of computer/internet-based distractions (courtesy of YouTube and Google) in the real, and artful, effort to create the work.

This Is Not Prose, 2016
Thursday, October 6, 8 pm

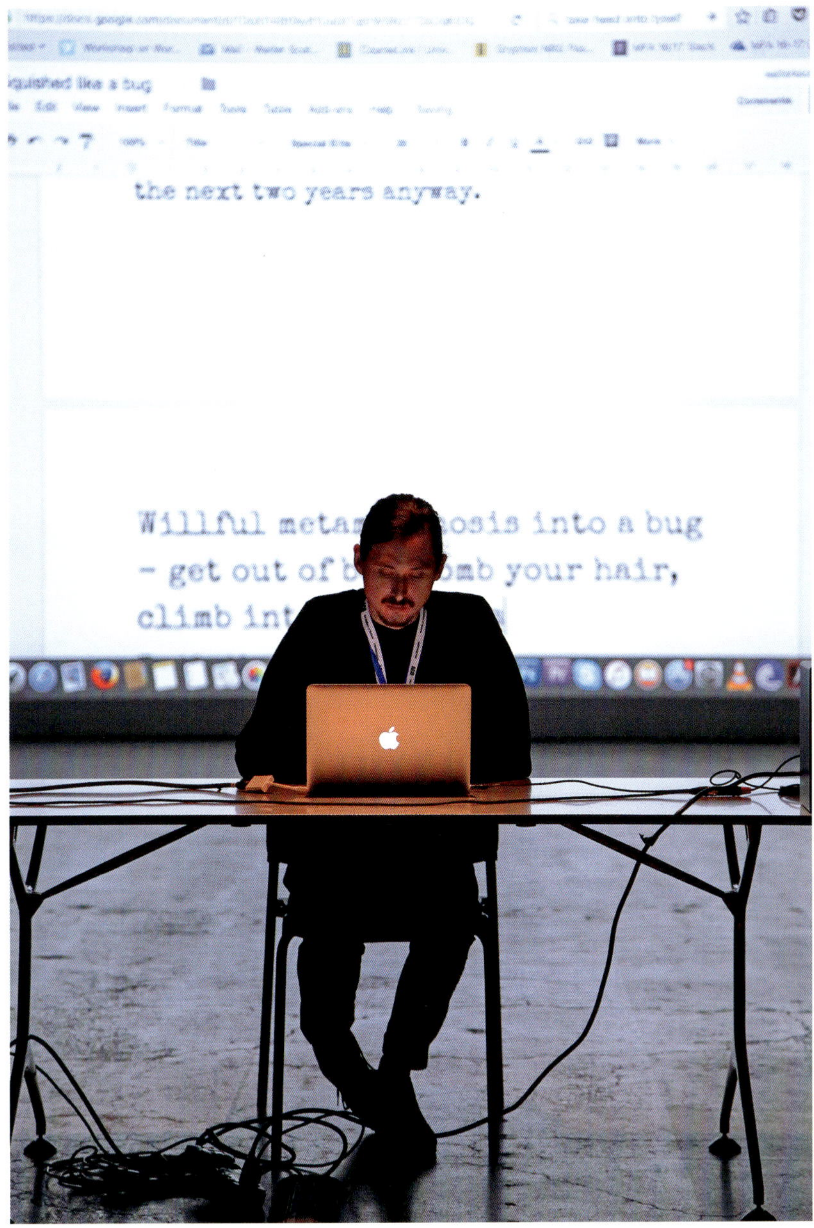

Louise Liliefeldt

The intimacy of Walter Scott's piece was rearticulated by Louise Liliefeldt's performance *WHAT DOES IT MEAN TO FORGET?* Liliefeldt's performance, however, like much of her work, was shaped by the body—both hers and, in a more symbolic way, her partner Diane McGrath's. In a space sculpted by light and peppered with a few symbolic objects, McGrath's listless body was dragged across the room, Liliefeldt marking its passage with tape outlines on the floor. The artist also used chalk and bloody handprints on the walls, creating a haunting sense of the ephemerality and fragility of being. Liliefeldt is an established figure on the Toronto performance art scene and her work spans several decades, but she has paused for the last seven years to support her ailing parents. Liliefeldt uses identity and heritage as source material for her work, and this return to artmaking was no different, taking as starting point the deterioration of her father's physical capacity. The idea of memory as identity, and its loss as death, touched upon the personal and formal qualities of performative practice, and the gestural and physical transformation of bodies, time, and space.

WHAT DOES IT MEAN TO FORGET?, 2016
Wednesday, October 19, 6 pm

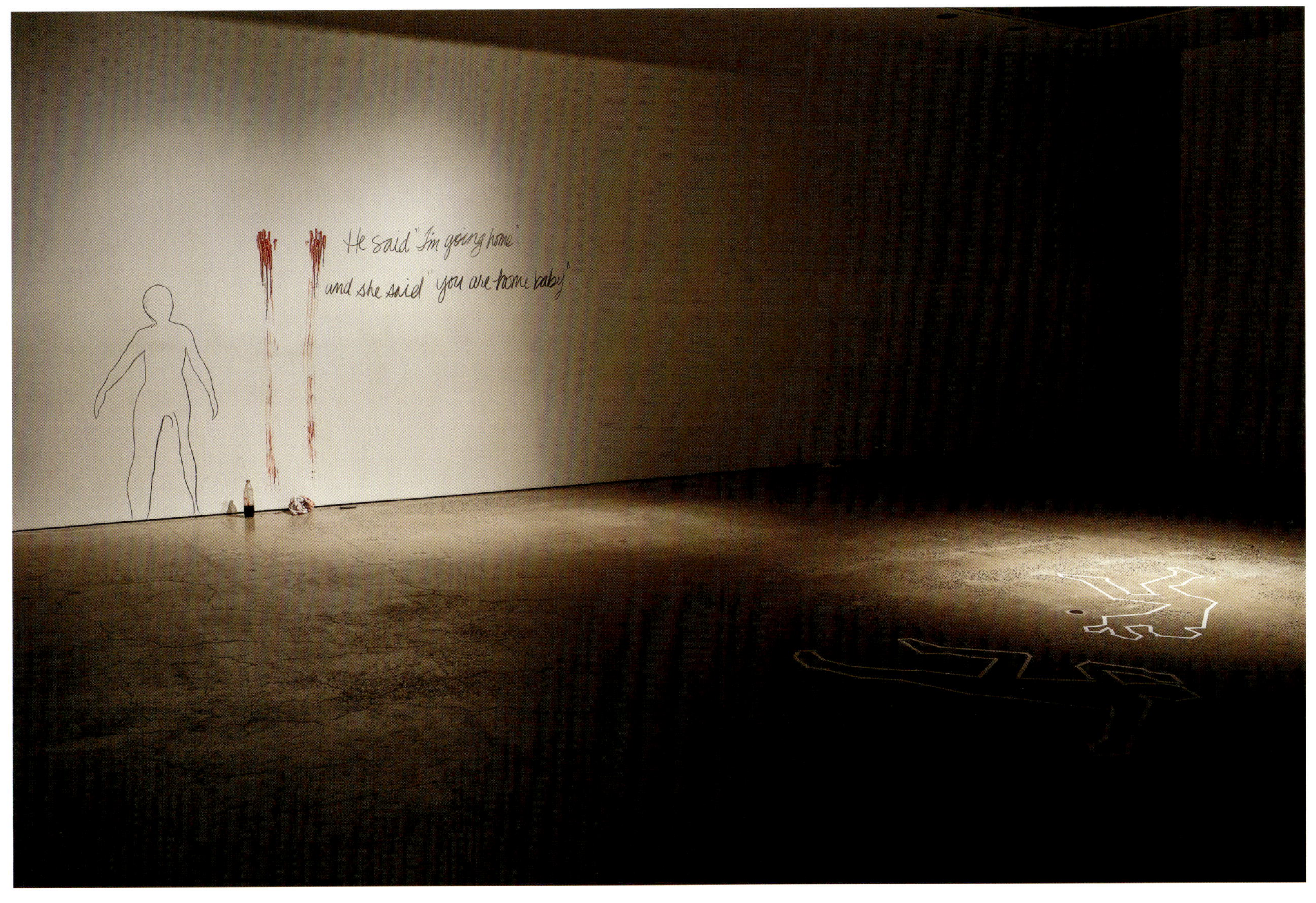

Johanna Householder

Johanna Householder's contribution to the series, *Residuals,* had a different tone from the previous performances but was no less shaped by questions of performative materiality. It brought together two of her past works, *8-Legged Dancing* (1978–2016) and *Verbatim II: Badiou/Cobain* (2007–2008), re-performed on one unforgettable Wednesday night. Householder, as part of the performance art group The Clichettes, was already present in *Tributes + Tributaries*, through the gallery installation of video and props—"residuals" of the group's historic performances. For "In Performance," *8-Legged Dancing* was restaged with collaborator Bee Pallomina, who performed to a text read out loud by Householder's daughter. The text and the title refer to the formal qualities of essay writing that bureaucrats in pre-revolutionary China were required to follow—the elaborate "8-legged" structure, demonstrating elite training. The second half of the evening consisted of a staged conversation about the nature of presence between Householder-live-in-Toronto and Householder-the-Badiou-translator, present in video, interacting across time, space, and media. The culminating act was an electrifying lip synch of a Nirvana-styled pop song with backup singers Christina Zeidler and Allyson Mitchell.

Along with her collaborators that night, Householder is known for fostering community, whether as pioneering founder of seminal performance art festival 7a*11d, or as anthologizer of two volumes of performance art by Canadian women (*Caught in the Act,* 2004, and *More Caught in the Act,* 2016). In thinking about legacies, it's worthwhile to note that both Liliefeldt and Householder have occupied pedagogical positions, tutoring new generations of performance art students during their various tenures at University of Toronto and OCAD University respectively.

Residuals, 2016
Wednesday, November 2, 2016, 7 pm

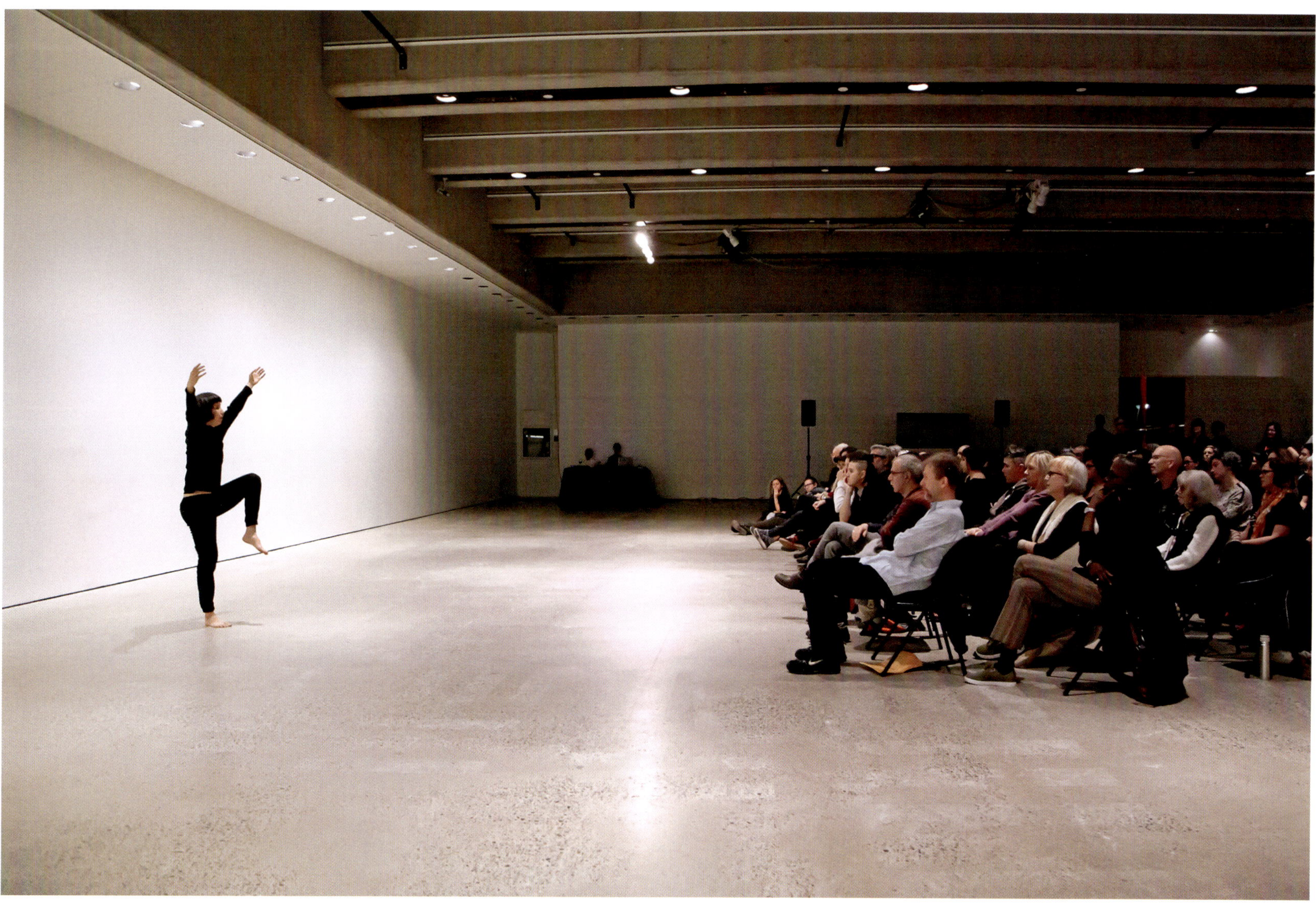

Keith Cole

While Keith Cole has a non-institutional practice that extends decades, he has studied under Johanna Householder's tutelage in recent years. Cole presented his work *#HashtagGallerySlut,* channelling Tom Thomson and David Buchan as two poles of the Canadian art historical landscape. In his own idiosyncratic language, he enumerates the playful possibilities of animating history and, better yet, the dynamic interplay made possible by live performance itself:

*Tom/David project onto me
*I am a projection of Tom/David
They project themselves onto me from the grave and I project
myself onto them from the living.
What is more important? To create a universe as Tom/David did
OR is sustaining that created universe (ie: me) so that others can
gain from it?

Cole's piece was the only one performed twice—not an easy feat for a performance art work, especially considering the intensity of the action—the artist's repetitive drowning in a water-filled canoe situated in the middle of the room. Cole here was channelling David Buchan's work of servitude (Buchan had cleaned houses as a side job), the articulation of which included a crude master directing the narrative. This was combined symbolically with Tom Thomson's death by drowning in a canoe, also denoted by the blue colour of Cole's vessel, and set in front of Thomson-esque projected landscapes. Cole's entire practice, historically and in this commissioned work, relies on an insistence on queering institutional and historical spaces—which, in this rendition, also meant including the glamour of drag queen Maria Del Monte's emotional lip synch, alluding to Cole's, Buchan's, and possibly Thomson's sexuality as an important part of their artistic identities.

#HashTagGallery Slut, 2016
Wednesday, October 26, 7 pm
Saturday, October 29, 2 pm

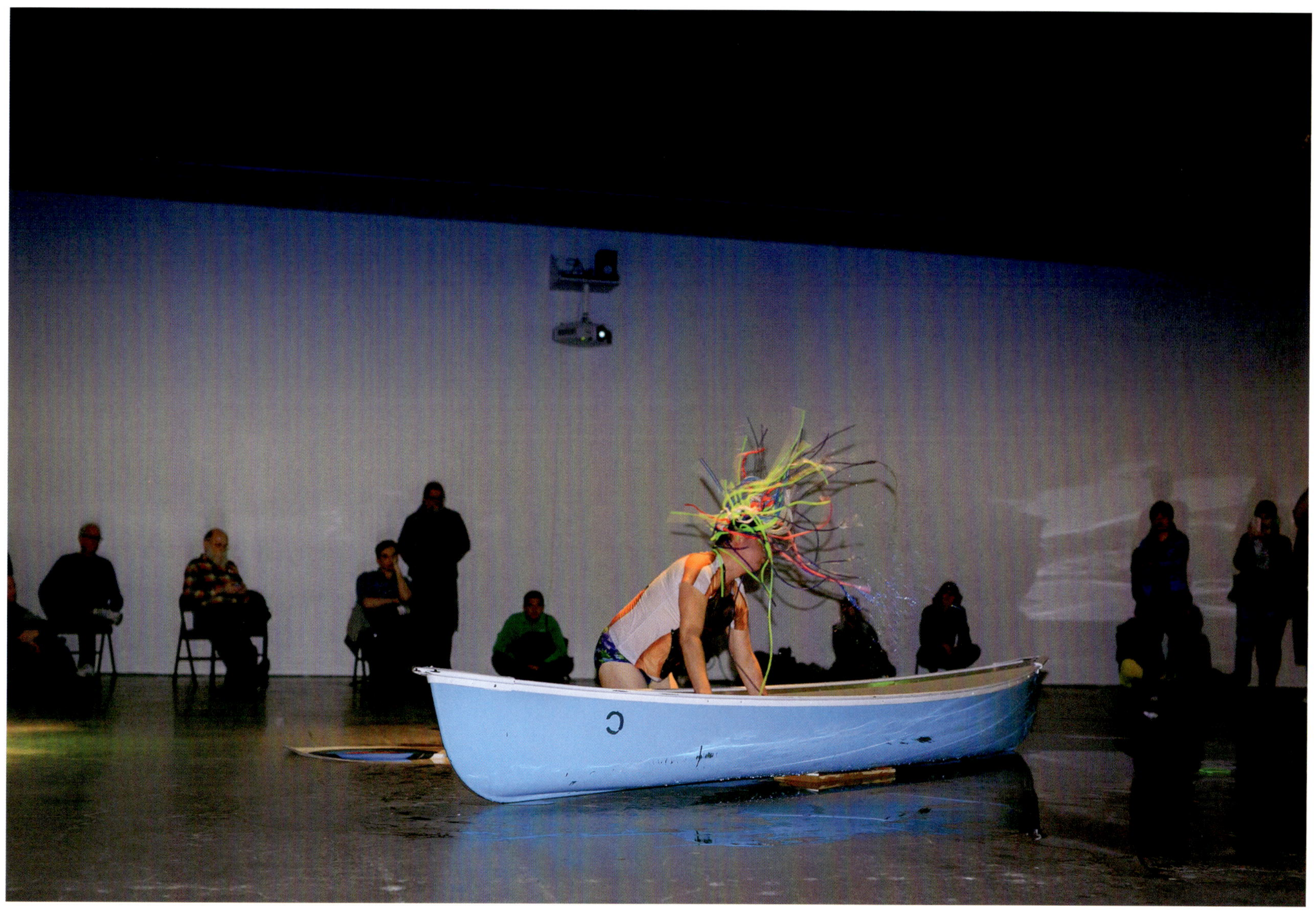

Lillian Allen

While the majority of the performances in the series took place in Signy Eaton gallery, a not-quite-white-cube space on the second floor, we did go back to Walker Court for a rapturous performance by Lillian Allen and the Revolutionary Tea Party band, whose sounds inaugurated the exhibition experience on the fourth floor. A beloved, political artist, Lillian has been working for the last four decades pioneering dub poetry in Canada. Her performance on October 28, 2016, was the culmination of a series of Friday Night programs, for which Allen herself had curated historic and emerging voices in poetry and performance, informed by her work as professor of creative writing at OCAD University. When Allen took the stage with her band of seasoned Toronto players, led by long-time Parachute Club guitarist Dave Gray, the energy of dub, and of social and political currency in the mixture of words and music, truly felt revolutionary. As embodied as it was poetic, the inspiration and the potential to change never felt historical, but rather, as urgent as all her performances over the last four decades.

Join the Revolutionary Tea Party—We Are as Beautiful as our Poetry, 2016
Friday, October 28, 7:30 pm

Lillian Allen guest-curated a four-week series of poetry, music, and spoken word events in Walker Court that culminated in her performance.

October 7: Penn Kemp, Paul Dutton, Karen Lee with Conlin Delbaere-Sawchuk, Kahsenniyo, Lacey Hill, Jennifer Alicia

October 14: Duke Redbird, Larissa Lai, Robert Priest, Catherine Black

October 21: Clifton Joseph and Special Interest Group, Margaret Christakos, Motion, Carrianne Leung, Samantha Goldman with Wolfgang Gray

October 28: Lillian Allen and the Revolutionary Tea Party with Janet Rogers and Amani, Samantha Goldman with Wolfgang Gray

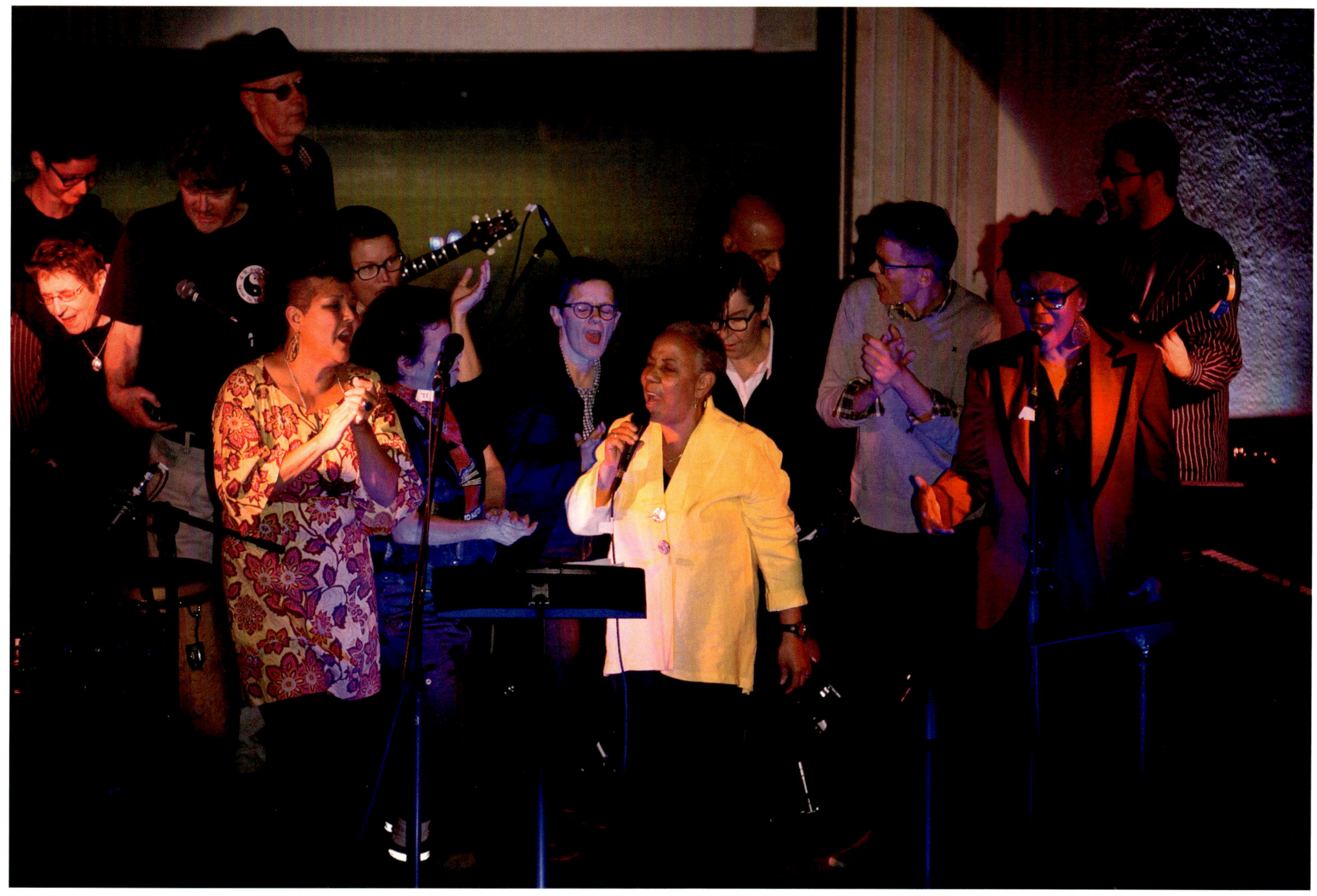

Ame Henderson and Evan Webber

The series closed with a very unconventional performance, within the already unconventional practice of performance art—the *performance encyclopaedia*, originated by Ame Henderson and Evan Webber. In essence, it was a microcosm of the working principles of the "In Performance" series, an invitation to define the present through the experience of the individual and collective past(s). For a week, invited artists worked in public, defining language about performance and making visible the writing process itself. The conclusion was a public presentation of a book that compiled the writing by the participants, printed for the benefit of a temporary community on a Sunday afternoon. It was then retired forever—the book cannot be read again—in the ultimate act of performance ephemerality.

The *performance encyclopaedia* included artists and thinkers who addressed contemporary concerns; some, like Lillian Allen, Johanna Householder, Wanda Nanibush, Sean O'Neill, and me, took part in the "In Performance" series. It felt like an important send-off to this unique program, and a clear reminder that working in performance, as in much of contemporary praxis, demands a contemporary stance with constantly evolving vocabularies that can hardly be immune to personal, historical, or political conditions.

In Closing

As I remember the series, the process, and the conversations with the artists, I remember the ambition or modesty of the different approaches—just a table, just some lighting, just some clay. Each event, however, was imbued with effort and a clarity of tasks, that, in a certain way, is easy to enumerate in words, yet will always be in excess of description and documentation. The tension and the fragility in each performance—the audiences who stumbled in and those who were there twenty minutes before doors opened, the communities that were built and those that were nurtured—cross the line between artist and spectator, but also between history and present.

performance encyclopaedia, 2016
Tuesday, November 8, 10:30 am–4:30 pm
Wednesday, November 9, 3:30–8:30 pm
Thursday, November 10, 10:30 am–4:30 pm
Friday, November 11, 10:30 am–4:30 pm
Saturday, November 12, 10:30 am–4:30 pm
Performance: Sunday, November 13, 2 pm

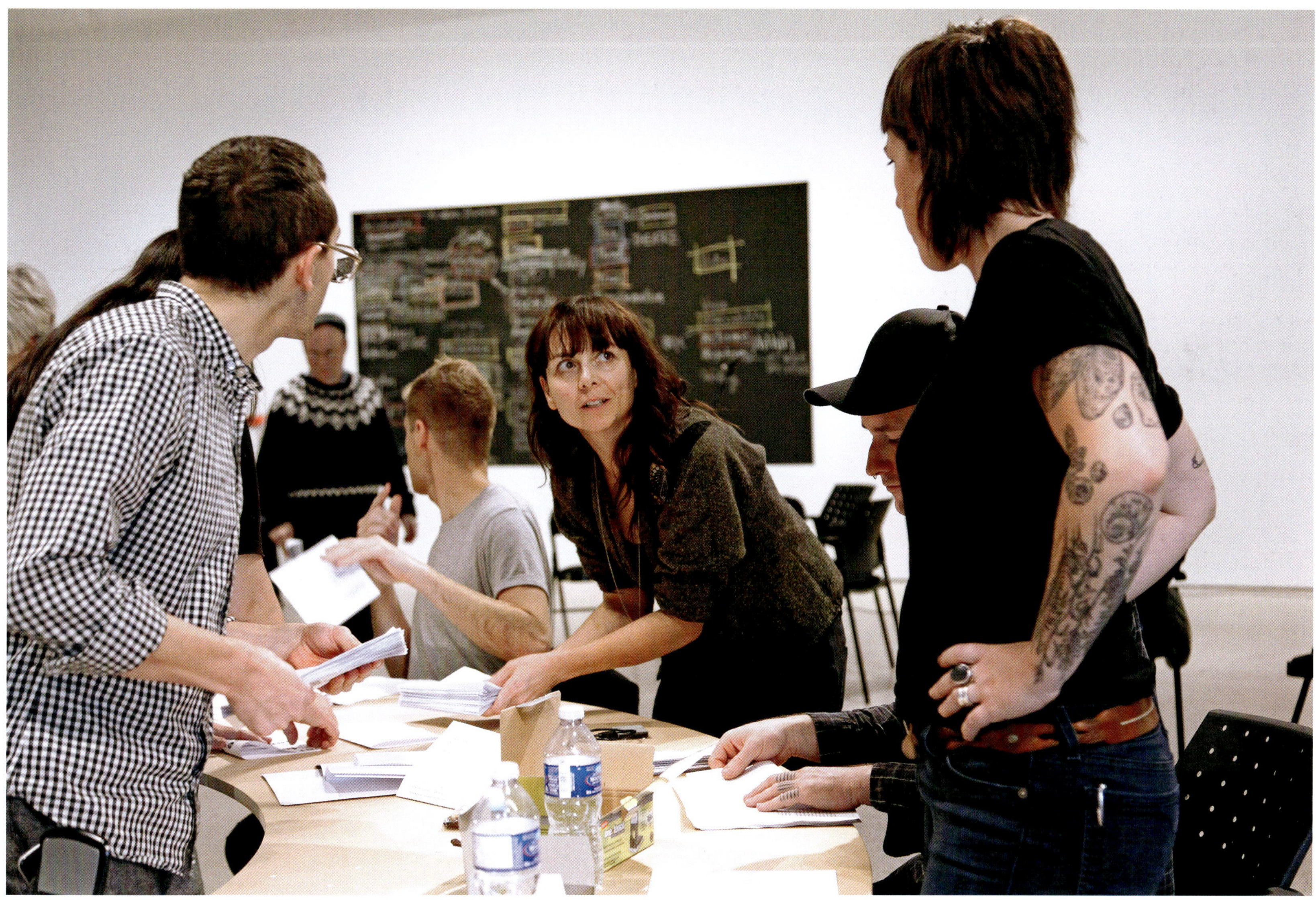

Sources for artists' quotes

Page 28
Jeff Thomas: from the artist statement on his website, May 2016.

Page 29
Lillian Allen: from the video interview "What Is Dub Poetry?" *Different Knowings Speaker's Series*, December 1, 2010, McMaster University, 6:55 min., available online.

Page 36
General Idea: from an interview with Louise Dompierre, Felix Partz, "Interview with AA Bronson, Felix Partz, and Jorge Zontal" (New York City, Friday, July 26, 1991), in *General Idea: Haute Culture; A Retrospective, 1969–1994* (Zurich: JRP/Ringier, 2011), 165.

Page 39
Rebecca Belmore: from an interview with Wanda Nanibush, "An Interview with Rebecca Belmore," *Decolonization: Indigeneity, Education & Society* 3, no. 1 (2014): 214, available online.

Page 45
Tim Whiten: quoted in Robert James Belton, *Sights of Resistance: Approaches to Canadian Visual Culture* (Calgary: University of Calgary Press, 2001), 314.

Page 66
Ron Benner: from an interview with Barbara Fischer, "An Interview with Ron Benner," in *Ron Benner: Gardens of a Colonial Present* (London, Ontario: Museum London, 2008), 103.

Page 67
Louise Noguchi: from an interview with David Fujino, "An Interview with Louise Noguchi," *The Bulletin: A Journal of Japanese Canadian Community, History and Culture*, January 8, 2014, available online.

Page 69
Duke Redbird: poem previously published in *Loveshine and Red Wine* (Cutler, Ontario: Woodland Studios Publishing, 1981).

Page 85
Robert Fones: from email correspondence with Wanda Nanibush, September 2016.

Page 96
Tony Urquhart: from the video interview "Painted Objects," directed by Linda Corbett, for *CCCA Canadian Art Database*, 2005, 8:25 min., available online.

Page 97
Robert Houle: from email correspondence with Wanda Nanibush, September 2016.

Page 99
Norval Morrisseau: Jack Pollock, "Norval Morrisseau: A View from His Agent," *TAWOW* 4, no. 4 (1974): 5-6.

Page 113
Andy Fabo: from "Nationalism/Internationalism/Regionalism," *c magazine*, Fall 1984, available online.

Page 115
Joanne Tod: from an interview with Brian Morgan, "Cover Artist Gallery: Joanne Tod," *The Walrus*, November 2010, available online.

Page 122
John McEwen: Wanda Nanibush quoted from email correspondence with John McEwen, April 2016.

Page 123
Nobuo Kubota: from the video interview "Essence," directed by Linda Corbett, for *CCCA Canadian Art Database*, 2007, 3:05 min., available online.

Page 125
K.M. Graham: quoted in Noreen Shanahan, "Celebrated Painter of Landscapes Took up Her Brush and Palette at 50," *Globe and Mail*, September 16, 2008, available online.

Page 126
Kazuo Nakamura: quoted in Roald Nasgaard, *Abstract Painting in Canada* (Vancouver: Douglas & McIntyre; Halifax: Art Gallery of Nova Scotia, 2007), 115.

Page 127
Rita Letendre: quoted in Gaston Roberge, ed., *Rita Letendre: Woman of Light* (Laval, Quebec: Belle Publisher, 1997), 22.

Page 128
Carol Wainio: quoted in Michèle Thériault, "Carol Wainio: Contemporary Registers" (Joliette, Quebec: Musée d'art de Joliette, 2000), 41.

Page 129
Brian Burnett: quoted in Mike Johnston, "Show Reflects Powerful Vision," *Whitby Free Press*, October 8, 1986, available online.

Page 136
Ato Seitu: poem, previously unpublished, 1970s.

Page 139
David Zapparoli: artist text, previously unpublished, 2016.

Page 144
Greg Curnoe: Mike Barry, "Greg Curnoe and His Mariposas," *Dandyhorse Magazine*, Spring 2009, available online.

Exhibition

Toronto: Tributes + Tributaries, 1971–1989
Art Gallery of Ontario
Toronto, Ontario, Canada
September 29, 2016–May 22, 2017

Toronto: Tributes + Tributaries, 1971–1989 was organized by the Art Gallery of Ontario. This exhibition was supported by government partners Ontario150 and the Canada Council for the Arts.

Art Gallery of Ontario
317 Dundas Street West
Toronto, Ontario M5T 1G4
Canada
www.ago.ca

Curated by
Wanda Nanibush

Project Managers
Malene Hjørngaard
Valentine Moreno

Interpretation
Laura Robb

Curatorial Administrative Assistant
Donna Austria

Translators (Anishinaabemowin)
Isadore Toulouse
Shirley Williams

Editor
Gina Badger

Design and Graphics
Marilyn Bouma-Pyper
Jim Bourke
Malene Hjørngaard
Karen Sung

Public Programming and Learning
Sarah Febbraro
Julia Galvez
Linda Lee
Jane Lott
Kathleen McLean
Johnson Ngo
Deborah Nolan
Sean O'Neill
Paola Poletto
Annie Roper
Keri Ryan
Melissa Smith
Bojana Stancic
Carrie Swartz

Conservation
Christine Fillion
Sherry Phillips
Sjoukje van der Laan
Sandra Webster-Cook
Joan Weir
Katharine Whitman

Registration
Alison Beckett
Cindy Brouse
Jerry Drozdowsky
Tim Hardacre
Joel Herman
Dale Mahar
Curtis Strilchuk

Media Production
Matthew Scott
Danny Winchester

Logistics and Art Services
Michael Beynon
Scott Cameron
Corinne Carlson
Patric Colosimo
Randal Fedje
Tina Giovinazzo
Brian Groombridge
Roland Hardy
Iain Hoadley
Matthew Janisse
Ruth Jones
Charles Kettle
David Kinsman
Jason Laudadio
Alison Lindsay
Paul Mathiesen
Doug Moore
Ben Oakley
John O'Leary
Jacques Oule
Angelo Pedari
Brent Roe
Sonia Sakamoto-Jog
Sabine Schaefer
Julie Seddon
Damian Seguin
Jelena Sisko
Craig Whiteside
Darin Yorston
Tanya Zhilinsky

Publication

Published in 2018 by the Art Gallery of Ontario.
Copyright © 2018 Art Gallery of Ontario. Artworks copyright the individual artists or their estates.
Unless otherwise noted, all photography by the Art Gallery of Ontario.

Every effort has been made to trace ownership of visual and written material used in this book. Errors or omissions will be corrected in subsequent printings provided notification is sent to the publisher.

All rights reserved. No part of this publication may be reproduced, stored in a retrieval system or transmitted, in any form or by any means, without the prior written consent of the publisher or a licence from the Canadian Copyright Agency (Access Copyright). For a copyright licence, visit www.accesscopyright.ca or call 1-800-893-5777.

The Art Gallery of Ontario is partially funded by the Ontario Ministry of Culture. Additional operating support is received from the City of Toronto, the Department of Canadian Heritage and the Canada Council for the Arts.

Contemporary programming at the Art Gallery of Ontario is supported by

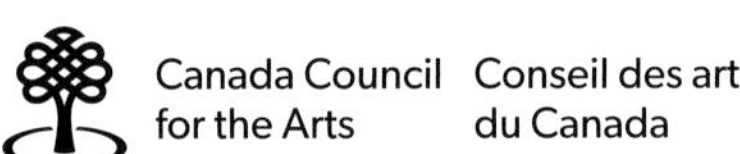

This publication was generously supported by the Sorel Etrog Publication Fund.

Printed and bound in Canada
10 9 8 7 6 5 4 3 2 1

Library and Archives Canada Cataloguing in Publication
Toronto (2017)

Toronto: tributes + tributaries, 1971–1989.
Catalogue of an exhibition held at the Art Gallery of Ontario from September 29, 2016 to May 22, 2017.

ISBN 978-1-894243-88-9 (softcover)

1. Art, Canadian—Ontario—Toronto—20th century—Exhibitions.

2. Exhibition catalogs.
I. Gale, Peggy, 1944–, writer of added commentary
II. Shedden, Jim, 1963–, writer of added commentary
III. Stancic, Bojana, 1979–, writer of added commentary
IV. Nanibush, Wanda organizer
V. Art Gallery of Ontario, issuing body, host institution
VI. Title.
VII. Title: Tributes + tributaries, 1971–1989.

N6547.T67T72 2017 709.71074'713541 C2017-905398-1

Edited by
Wanda Nanibush

Managing Editor
Jim Shedden

Production Editors
Gina Badger
Amy Lam

Photography
Craig Boyko
Christina Gapic
Ian Lefebvre
Leah Maghanoy
Jennifer Rowsom
Dean Tomlinson
Sean Weaver

Image Research
Robyn Lew

Rights and Reproduction
Tracy Mallon-Jensen

Translators (Anishinaabemowin)
Isadore Toulouse
Shirley Williams

Proofreader
Judy Phillips

Design
The Office of Gilbert Li

Pre-Press
Type A Print Inc.

Printing and Binding
Friesens, Canada

Cover
Shelley Niro
Waitress, 1986
Oil on canvas
121.9 × 91.4 cm
Collection of the artist
© Shelley Niro

Pages 132–133
Jeff Thomas
Toronto Series: Kensington Market, 1984
Pigment prints on archival paper
70.5 × 50.8 cm or 50.8 × 70.5 cm each
Art Gallery of Ontario, gift of Jeff Thomas, 2016, 2016/434-437
© Jeff Thomas

Pages 134–135
Timeline of artist-run centre activity in Toronto, 1971 to 1989

Pages 146-147
Andrew J. Paterson and Alan Fox's *How Many Fingers* in production at Trinity Square Video, September 1981
Photo © Meg Thornton, courtesy of Trinity Square Video

Page 200
Robert Houle, map of Garrison Creek, Trinity Bellwoods Park, Toronto
© Robert Houle

Pages 28, 140–141
© Jeff Thomas

Page 29
© Lillian Allen

Pages 30–31
© Carole Condé and
Karl Beveridge

Pages 36–37
© General Idea

Pages 38–39
© Rebecca Belmore

Pages 40–41
© Will Gorlitz

Page 42
© Colette Whiten

Page 43
© Ron Giii

Pages 44–45
© Tim Whiten
Documentation photos
© Grant McLeod
© Helena Wilson

Page 46
© Ian Carr-Harris

Page 47
© Murray Favro

Pages 48–49
© Louise Garfield,
Janice Hladki, and
Johanna Householder

Pages 54–55
© Barbara Astman

Pages 56–57
© Suzy Lake
Page 58
© Estate of Arnaud Maggs/
SODRAC (2018)

Page 59
© Lisa Steele

Pages 60–61
© David Rasmus

Page 64
© Jamelie Hassan

Page 65
© Catharine MacTavish

Page 66
© Ron Benner

Page 67
© Louise Noguchi

Page 68
© Noel Harding

Page 69
© Duke Redbird

Page 70
© Kim Kozzi and
Dai Skuse

Page 71
© Estate of Robert Flack

Page 72
© Shelagh Alexander

Page 73
© John Massey

Page 74
© National Gallery
of Canada, Ottawa

Page 75
© Stephen Andrews

Pages 80–81
© June Clark

Pages 82–83
© Robin John Collyer

Page 84
© Michael Snow

Page 85
© Robert Fones

Pages 86–87
© Jayce Salloum

Page 92
© Winsom Winsom

Page 93
© Kim Moodie

Pages 94–95
© Janice Gurney

Page 96
© Tony Urquhart

Page 97
© Robert Houle

Page 98
© Estate of
Robert Nelson Markle

Page 99
© Estate of
Norval Morrisseau

Pages 100–101
© Nancy Johnson

Page 102
© Douglas Walker

Page 103
© Andy Patton

Pages 104–105
© Vera Frenkel

Pages 106–107
© John Scott

Page 112
© Estate of
Tim Jocelyn

Page 113
© Andy Fabo

Page 114
© Shirley Wiitasalo

Page 115
© Joanne Tod

Page 116
© Estate of
Arthur Shilling

Page 117
© Shelley Niro

Page 118
© Oliver Girling

Page 122
© John McEwen
Photo © James A.
Chambers

Page 123
© Nobuo Kubota

Page 124
© Estate of
David Bolduc

Page 125
© Estate of
Kathleen Graham

Page 126
© Estate of
Kazuo Nakamura

Page 127
© Rita Letendre

Page 128
© Carol Wainio

Page 129
© Brian Burnett

Page 130
© Estate of
Gordon Rayner

Pages 136–137
© Ato Seitu

Pages 138–139
© David Zapparoli

Pages 142–143
© Estate of Brian Kipping

Page 144
© Estate of Greg Curnoe/
SODRAC (2018)

Page 145
© Lisa Steele and
Kim Tomczak

Pages 152–169
All films and videos
copyright the individual
artists or their estates.

Page 183
© Rebecca Belmore

Page 185
© Walter Scott

Page 187
© Louise Liliefeldt

Page 189
© Johanna Householder

Page 191
© Keith Cole

Page 193
© Lillian Allen

Page 195
© Ame Henderson
and Evan Webber

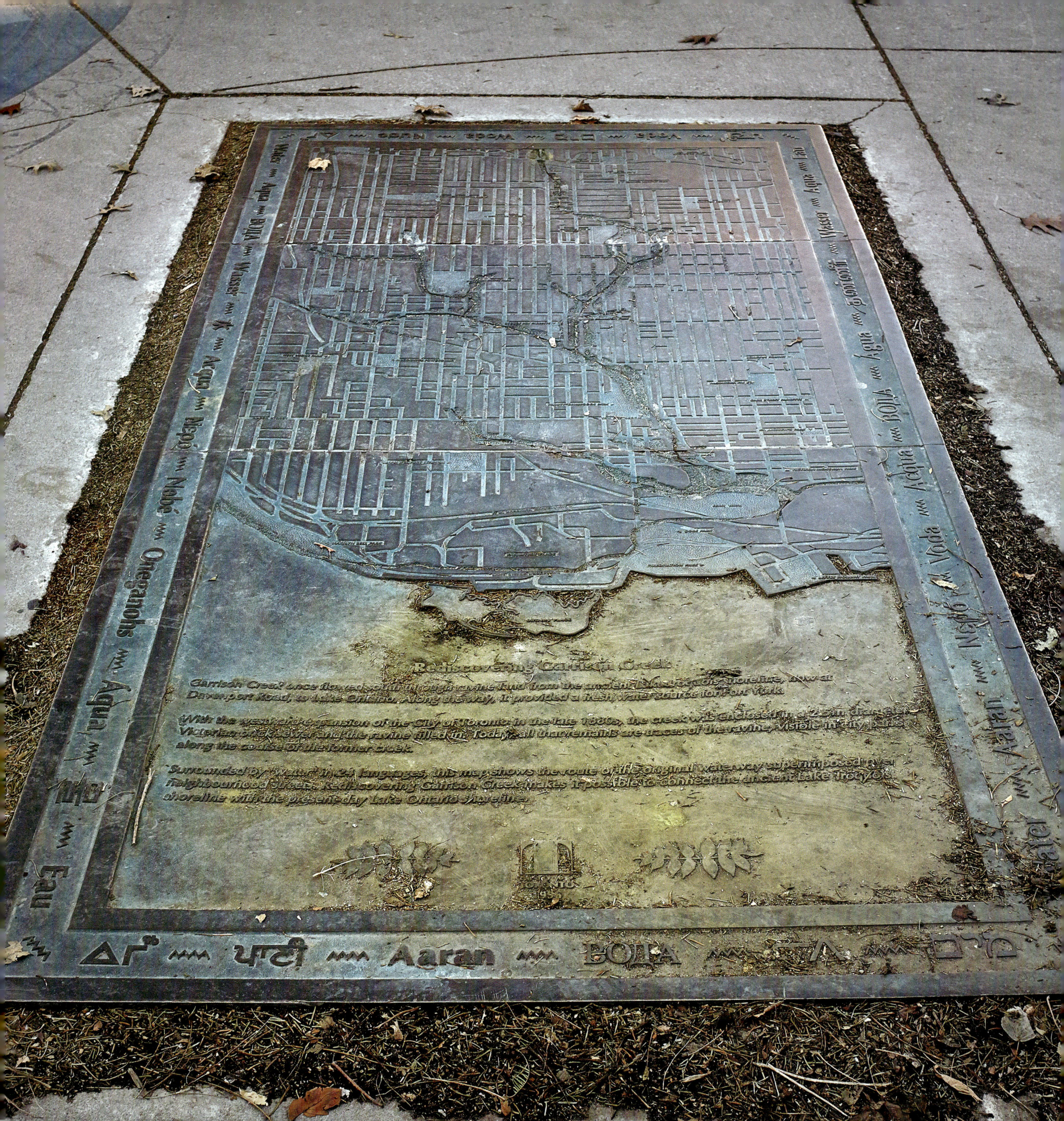

Rediscovering Garrison Creek
Aaran
ВОДА
ਪਾਣੀ
Agua
Eau
Voda
Onegaohs